The MAILBOX®

The Idea Magazine For Teachers®

PRIMARY

1998–1999

YEARBOOK

Diane Badden, Editor
Sharon Murphy, Associate Editor

The Education Center, Inc.
Greensboro, North Carolina

The Mailbox® 1998–1999 Primary Yearbook

Editor In Chief: Margaret Michel
Magazine Director: Karen P. Shelton
Editorial Administrative Director: Stephen Levy
Senior Editor: Diane Badden
Editorial Traffic Manager: Lisa K. Pitts
Associate Editor: Sharon Murphy
Contributing Editors: Amy Erickson, Kimberly Fields, Njeri Jones, Mary Lester,
Susan Hohbach Walker
Copy Editors: Karen Brewer Grossman, Karen L. Huffman, Tracy Johnson, Scott Lyons,
Debbie Shoffner, Gina Sutphin
Staff Artists: Cathy Spangler Bruce, Pam Crane, Teresa R. Davidson, Nick Greenwood, Clevell Harris,
Susan Hodnett, Sheila Krill, Rob Mayworth, Kimberly Richard, Rebecca Saunders, Barry Slate,
Donna K. Teal, Jennifer L. Tipton
Editorial Assistants: Terrie Head, Laura Slaughter, Wendy Svartz, Karen White
Librarian: Elizabeth A. Findley

ISBN 1-56234-295-9
ISSN 1088-5544

Printed in the United States of America.

The Education Center, Inc.
P.O. Box 9753
Greensboro, NC 27429-0753

Look for *The Mailbox*® 1999–2000 Primary Yearbook in the summer of 2000. The Education
Center, Inc., is the publisher of *The Mailbox*®, *Teacher's Helper*®, *The Mailbox*® BOOKBAG®,
Learning®, and *The Mailbox*® *Teacher* magazines, as well as other fine products. Look for these
wherever quality teacher materials are sold, or call 1-800-714-7991.

Contents

BULLETIN BOARDS

Bulletin Boards ....

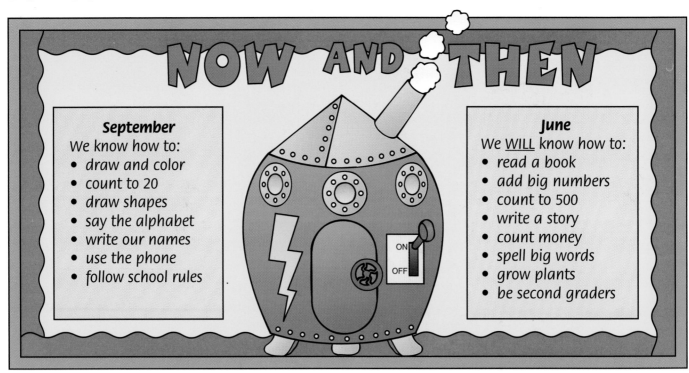

What does the future hold for your students? To find out the answer to that question, go right to the source! Mount the title and a time machine similar to the one shown. Then, under your students' guidance, prepare two lists: one that details what the students know right now and one that details what the students plan to know at the end of the school year. Showcase the completed lists at the display. The future looks bright!

Whitney Sherman—Gr. 1, Seven Pines Elementary School, Sandston, VA

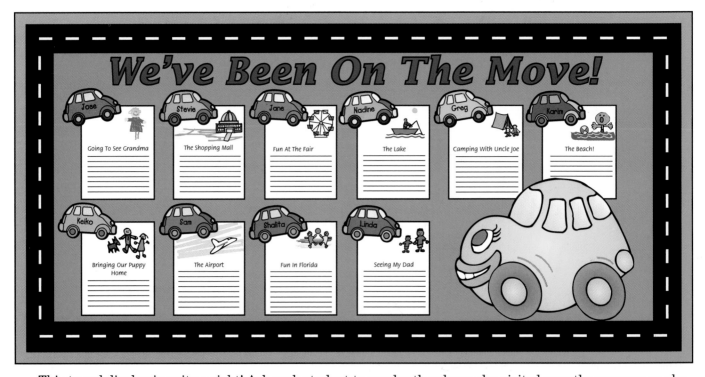

This travel display is quite a sight! Ask each student to ponder the places she visited over the summer as she personalizes, colors, and cuts out a car-shaped paper topper (see pattern on page 19). Then have her write and illustrate a story about one place she visited. Display the students' stories and paper toppers as shown. Invite students to continue their travels by reading about their classmates' trips!

adapted from an idea by Angie Kelley—Gr. 3, Weaver Elementary School, Anniston, AL

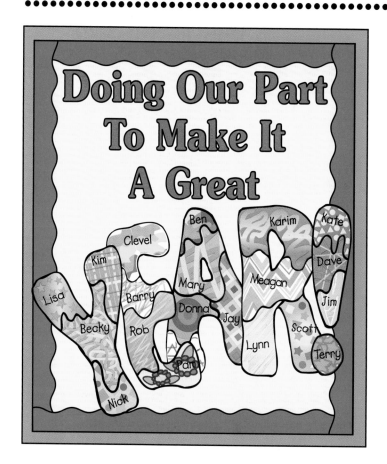

Great things are created with teamwork, and this display is a perfect example! Mount a border and the phrase "Doing Our Part To Make It A Great." From poster board cut large letters to spell "YEAR." Visually divide the letter cutouts into a class supply of puzzle pieces; then label each piece for a different student. Code the back of each letter cutout (for easy reassembly) before cutting it apart. Have each child decorate his puzzle piece. Then, with your youngsters' help, assemble and mount the puzzle pieces as shown. It's going to be a great year!

Mary Jo Kampschnieder—Gr. 2
Howells Community Catholic School
Howells, NE

Create miles of smiles with this back-to-school display. Cover a bulletin board with white paper. A student uses assorted arts-and-crafts supplies to create her self-likeness on a construction-paper oval. Then she mounts her self-likeness and precut letters spelling "ME" on a colorful rectangle. Display the projects in a checkerboard pattern, leaving room for the title near the top. You can count on plenty of students, parents, and staff members checking out this display!

Linda Macke—Gr. 3, John F. Kennedy Elementary, Kettering, OH

Star Author Of The Week

About The Author

Name _Sam G._

Family _mom, dad, sister_

Pets _dog named Minnie_

Hobbies _playing soccer_

Favorite Toy _my bike_

Favorite T.V. Show _Fudge_

Favorite Food _pizza_

The Author's Favorite Books

• _Charlie The Caterpillar_
• _Pigsty_
• _The Napping House_
• _Ferdinand_

Spotlight budding authors at this 3-D display! Use wallpaper, fabric, and other decorative items to fashion a chair, a lamp, and a table. Also create laminated posters for showcasing author information. Each week draw an outline of the featured author on paper and cut it out. The student decorates the cutout to resemble himself and designs a book cover. Display these items and use a wipe-off marker to program the posters with information about the author. Exhibit some of the author's original work nearby. Autographs, anyone?

Sarah Mertz—Grs. 1–2, Owenton, KY

Provide a year's worth of estimation practice at this fetching display! Have each student personalize and cut out a bone pattern (page 19). Mount the cutouts, the title, and a canine character. Each Monday attach a bag of items to be estimated and blank adding-machine tape for student answers. A student writes his estimate next to his personalized cutout. He may adjust his estimate throughout the week. On Friday divide the contents of the bag among your students for an official count.

Maryann D'Amelio—Gr. 2
Roy Gomm Elementary School
Reno, NV

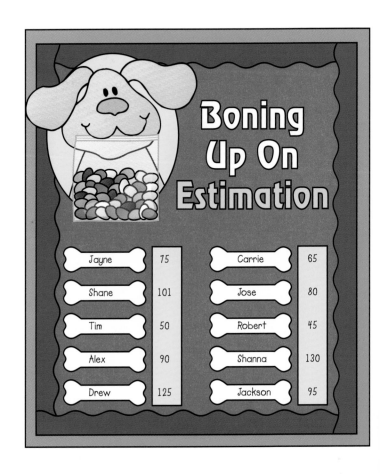

Boning Up On Estimation

Jayne	75	Carrie	65
Shane	101	Jose	80
Tim	50	Robert	45
Alex	90	Shanna	130
Drew	125	Jackson	95

Why not put your youngsters in charge of this monthly bulletin board? Begin each month with background paper and a title. Ask each student or pair of students to create a project for the display. Also enlist your youngsters' help in creating a desired seasonal border. Mount the border cutouts and student projects, and your work is done!

Loretta Frances, Mt. Airy, NC

Make penmanship practice a daily goal at this interactive bulletin board! Post the title and cutouts, a laminated poster with handwriting lines, student directions, a supply of laminated handwriting paper, and a Press-On Pocket containing a cloth and several wipe-off markers. Use one marker to write a cursive letter on the poster. Each day students head to the practice field to fine-tune their cursive writing skills!

Kelly W. Mize, Gr. 2, Heritage Christian School, Huntsville, AL

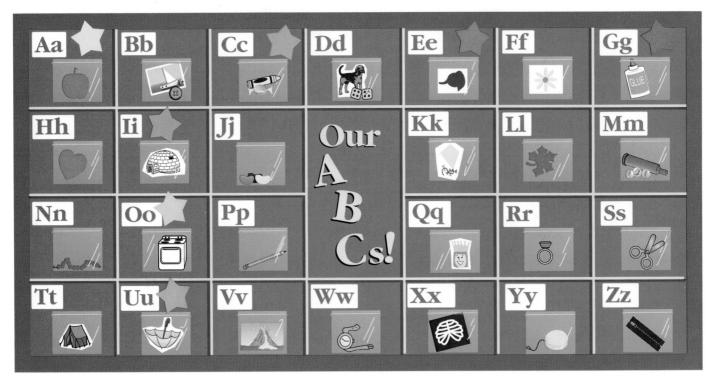

Beginning sounds are in the bag! Use yarn to visually divide a bulletin board; then add the title. In each remaining section secure an alphabet card, a star (if the letter makes more than one initial sound), and an empty resealable plastic bag. Invite students to place paper cutouts and small nonperishable items in the bags to represent the beginning sounds. Now that's a hands-on display with year-round appeal!

Linda Parris—Gr. 1, West Hills Elementary, Knoxville, TN

This Thanksgiving create a feast for the eyes! Mount the title, a grinning gobbler, and a length of bulletin-board paper titled "Look What We've Read!" Then, under your students' guidance, list book titles that you've read to the class and titles that the class has read. Ask the students to vote for their favorite book from the list, and attach a blue ribbon beside the title that earns the most votes. Gobble, gobble!

adapted from an idea by
Robin Kopecky—Grs. 1–3
Lake Louise School
Palatine, IL

WE'RE FEASTING ON BOOKS!

Look What We've Read!
- Clifford's Good Deeds
- Teeny Tiny Woman
- I Went Walking
- Clifford The Firehouse Dog
- Columbus
- Popcorn
- Curious George
- Clifford's First Halloween
- Nate The Great And The Phony Clue
- Who Said Boo?
- Hello Cat, You Need A Hat

Gifts Of The Season, Straight From The Heart

The gifts on this sleigh come straight from the heart! Seat students in a circle and give each child a large sheet of construction paper bearing his name. On your signal, each child passes his paper to the right. Then he signs the paper he is given and writes a positive note about the classmate who is named. Continue in this manner until each child receives his original paper. After each student reads the gifts he's been given, have him fold his paper in half and decorate it to resemble a holiday package. Display the gifts throughout the holiday season.

adapted from ideas by M. J. Owen—Gr. 3, Baty Elementary, Del Valle, TX, and Denise Lapine—Special Education, Rockwell Elementary School, Nedrow, NY

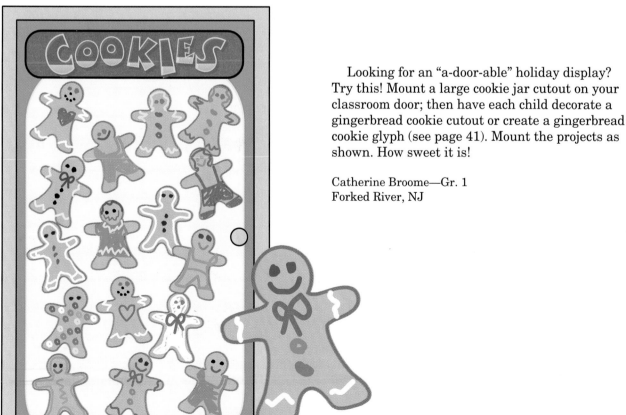

Looking for an "a-door-able" holiday display? Try this! Mount a large cookie jar cutout on your classroom door; then have each child decorate a gingerbread cookie cutout or create a gingerbread cookie glyph (see page 41). Mount the projects as shown. How sweet it is!

Catherine Broome—Gr. 1
Forked River, NJ

Students will have a ball drafting cool resolutions for the New Year! Have each child write one goal for the New Year in the center of a six-inch doily and then tape a four-inch doily atop his writing so that a flap is created. Give each child a second four-inch doily (for a snowpal's head), two twigs (for arms), and access to supplies so he can complete his snowpal. Display the projects on a snowy backdrop like the one shown. Happy New Year!

Kim Castro—Gr. 1, Engelwood Elementary School, Orlando, FL

In remembrance of Martin Luther King, Jr.'s dream of peace and compassion for all, ask students to ponder their dreams for their community. Have each child write his thoughts on white paper and then trim the paper to create one large thought bubble and several small connecting bubbles. Provide the supplies that students need to create self-portraits like the ones shown; then mount each child's project for all to see.

adapted from an idea by Debbie Dalton—Gr. 2, C. M. Bradley Elementary School, Warrenton, VA

Spotlight your readers *and* future leaders at this patriotic display. Have each student illustrate herself on drawing paper as a future leader, glue her artwork on red or blue paper, and add foil stars. Display the personalized projects; then staple a laminated poster-board strip below each one. A student uses a wipe-off marker to keep her strip programmed with the book title she is currently reading. Read on!

Cynthia Adams—Gr. 3, Jefferson Elementary, Hobbs, NM

The value of love escalates at this two-for-one holiday display! Each student traces a provided heart shape onto red, orange, yellow, green, blue, purple, and pink paper squares. Then he cuts out the shapes, and programs the pink cutout with his definition of love. Mount the heart cutouts and two black pot cutouts (pattern on page 20) as pictured. Love is definitely in the air!

Helen Hawkins, Beverly Gardens School, Dayton, OH

Tip your hat to Dr. Seuss in celebration of his birthday—March 2! Give each child a white construction-paper copy of the hat pattern on page 20 to color. Tell students to leave the second and fourth stripes white. Ask each student to write one word of a rhyming word pair on each white stripe, then cut out the hat. Mount the hats along with a title and a likeness of a favorite Dr. Seuss character. Happy birthday, Dr. Seuss!

Betsy Crosson—Gr. 1, Pleasant Elementary, Tulare, CA

Greet the arrival of spring with this picture-perfect vocabulary display! Write a student-generated list of words or phrases that contain the word *spring*. Have each child copy a different word or phrase from the list onto a paper strip; then on desired paper have him write and illustrate a sentence that features this word or phrase. Display the students' work as shown. Spring is everywhere!

Sue Lorey, Arlington Heights, IL

Spill the beans—the jelly beans, that is—about the science process. Mount the title and a large jar cutout that contains a paper jelly bean labeled for each step of the science process. As students experience the different steps, ask volunteers to post their findings. For added appeal, have each volunteer color-code her work with a jelly bean cutout to show the step on which she is reporting.

Lisa Kelly—Gr. 1, Wood Creek Elementary, Farmington, MI

Getting the word out about your students' favorite storybook characters is a foolproof plan for promoting an interest in reading. A child illustrates his favorite character on a white oval and then he names and describes the character on a second white oval of the same size. He glues these cutouts to opposite sides of a slightly larger brown oval. Use a hole punch and ribbon length to display each project. Read on!

Pam Wilson—Gr. 3, Ebenezer School, Statesville, NC

Propel your students' self-esteem to extraordinary heights with this star-studded display. Have each child write his name in the center of a large star cutout and then illustrate one of his special talents, hobbies, or favorite things in each star point. Provide time for each child to explain his star to his classmates; then display the projects as shown. There's no doubt about it—everyone's a star!

Kathie Eckelkamp—Gr. 2, Most Precious Blood School, St. Louis, MO

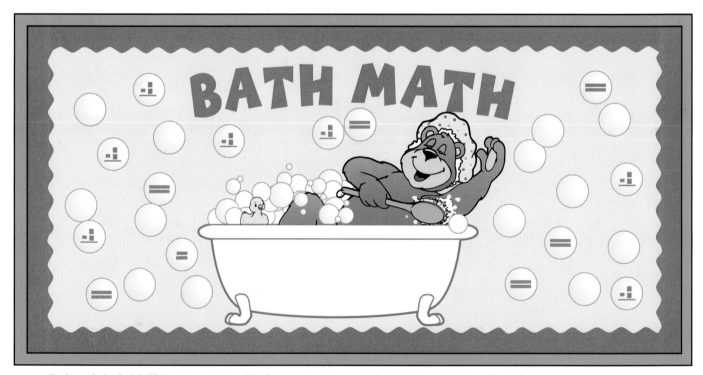

Rub-a-dub-dub! This interactive display may cause student interest in math to bubble over! Program one side of several bubble cutouts with math-related problems. Use pushpins to display the bubbles facedown. When time allows, choose a bubble and challenge students to solve its corresponding problem. When the problem is solved, reattach the bubble to the display faceup. Be sure to plan a bubble-related celebration when all the problems are solved!

Amy Barsanti—Gr. 2, Pines Elementary School, Plymouth, NC

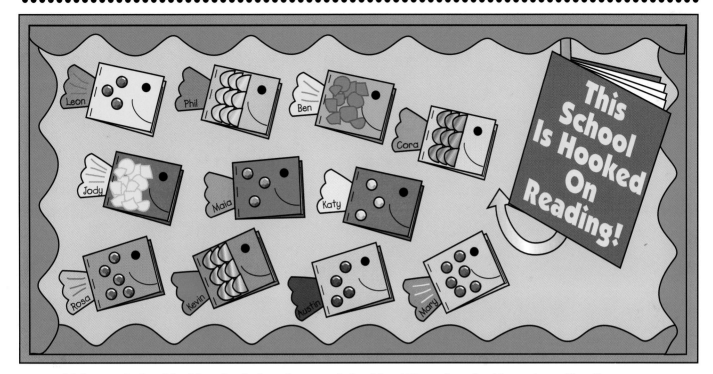

Make a splash with this school of student-made booklets! To make a booklet, trim a 3" x 4" paper rectangle to resemble a fish tail. Next staple one end of the tail and a supply of blank paper between two 4 1/2" x 6" construction-paper covers. Each child personalizes and decorates his booklet cover; then he lists and describes his favorite books inside. Showcase the projects as shown. What a catch!

Sharma Houston—Gr. 2, Pearsontown Elementary, Durham, NC

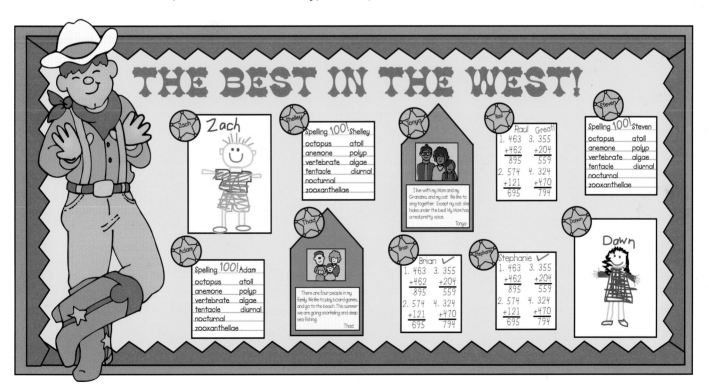

Lasso your wranglers' outstanding work at this star-studded display. Mount the character and title. Have each youngster create a personalized badge cutout as shown and then round up a sample of his finest work. Display each work sample with its corresponding badge. To keep the display current, invite wranglers to replace their work as frequently as desired. Yee-hah!

Kathy Marquar—Gr. 1, J. E. Moss Elementary, Antioch, TN

This display is brimming with student achievements! A student uses assorted arts-and-crafts supplies to create her self-likeness on a paper circle. She also cuts out a desired hat shape from paper and decorates it. She reveals her greatest achievement of the year by copying and completing this sentence on a blank card: "Our hats are off to [student's name] because…" Attach each child's card to her paper hat; then mount the projects and the title as shown.

Lisa Kelly—Gr. 1, Wood Creek Elementary, Farmington, MI

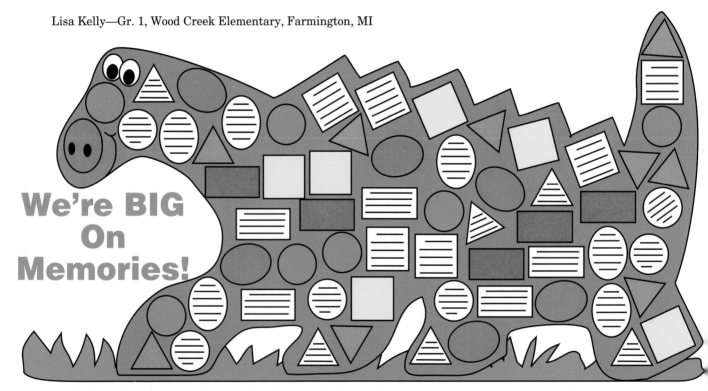

Make a big impression with this colossal collection of memories. A student traces a shape template (oval, square, etc.) onto writing paper and art paper. He cuts out each shape; then, on the lined cutout, he describes a favorite memory from the school year. Assist students in arranging the cutouts on colorful paper to resemble a dinosaur; then have them glue the cutouts in place. Cut out the dinosaur shape and embellish it as desired. Mount the one-of-a-kind lizard for all to enjoy!

adapted from an idea by Sharma Houston—Gr. 2, Pearsontown Elementary, Durham, NC

Use with "Boning Up On Estimation" on page 8 and "Where, Oh Where Has That Big Dog Gone?" on page 204.

Patterns

Use the pot pattern with "A Rainbow Of Love" on page 13 and "Pot O' Gold Sentences" on page 29.

Use the hat pattern with "Hats Off To Dr. Seuss!" on page 14.

LEARNING CENTERS

Learning Centers

Buggy Over Addition!

Since ladybugs gather in groups to hibernate in the fall, this self-checking math center comes just in the nick of time! For each student, program a slip of paper with a different addition fact. Place the slips in a decorated container. Also duplicate a class supply of the patterns on page 52. Place the container, the patterns, scissors, black sticky dots, brads, black construction-paper scraps, glue, and white and black crayons at a center. A student cuts out a ladybug body and a pair of wings; then he uses a brad to attach the wings to the body as shown. Next he draws a math fact from the container. On each wing he writes one addend and attaches a corresponding number of black sticky dots. Using a white crayon, he draws an addition symbol on the bug's head; then he spreads the wings and writes the fact sum on its body. Lastly he closes the wings and attaches two construction-paper antennae.

The following week provide addition-fact practice by featuring the completed ladybugs at the center. For each ladybug, a student reads the math fact and states its sum; then he carefully spreads the ladybug's wings to check his work.

Debra Veronica—Gr. 2, Early Childhood Center #54
Buffalo, NY

All Around

Over, around, across, and through. Inside, outside, and upside down, too! Reinforce positional words at this easy-to-make center. Use colorful markers to program each of several sheets of drawing paper with a positional word. Store the programmed sheets—one per student—in a folder; then place the folder, crayons, and a supply of stickers at a center. A student selects a paper from the folder and illustrates the meaning of the featured word by incorporating a sticker into a desired scene. On the back of her illustration, she writes a descriptive sentence about her work that includes the positional word. Compile the students' completed work in a class book titled "All Around" for further reading enjoyment.

June Newton—Gr. 1, St. Mary, Star Of The Sea School
Indian Head, MD

"Tree-mendous" Writing!

Students won't want to "leaf" this creative-writing center! Display a paper tree trunk at a center. Next number and program each of several fall-colored leaf cutouts with different story starters. Also number a writing journal to correspond with each leaf. Pin the leaves on the tree, and place the journals and several pencils at the center. A student selects a leaf, then copies the story starter and writes his story in the corresponding journal. When he is finished writing, he signs his name, closes the journal, and returns the leaf to the tree. One student may visit the center several times—choosing a different story starter each visit. Keep writing interest high by routinely replacing the story starters and their corresponding journals. Now that's a "tree-mendously" appealing writing center!

Kathleen Lynch—Gr. 3, St. Aloysius School, Jackson, NJ

22

Clip It!

Students will think this initial-consonant center is a snap! Cut out pictures from discarded workbooks or magazines, and glue each one on a colorful card. At the bottom of each card, label the picture—replacing the initial consonant with a blank. Then, for self-checking, write the full word on the back of the card. Laminate the cards for durability and store them in a resealable plastic bag. Next program a spring-type clothespin for each letter of the alphabet. Place the clothespins and the bag of cards at a center. A student removes the cards from the bag. One at a time he reads each card, clips a clothespin onto the card to complete the word, and flips the card to verify that the word he spelled matches the word written on the back. Then he removes the clothespin and completes the next card. Plan to make similar centers to reinforce final consonant sounds, vowel sounds, blends, and more! It's a snap!

Melinda Casida—Gr. 1, Crowley Elementary, Visalia, CA

Month To Month

Reinforce your students' sequencing and problem-solving skills with the help of discarded wall calendars. You will need one calendar picture for each month of the year. If possible, gather pictures that clearly represent the 12 months. Randomly number the pictures and create a word bank of month names. Laminate the pictures and the word bank for durability; then place the laminated items, pencils, and a supply of writing paper at a center. A student arranges the monthly pictures in chronological order beginning with January. On his paper he lists each month (referring as needed to the word bank for correct spelling), the number of the calendar picture that he feels represents the month, and a brief explanation for his choice. Wow! What a year!

Lynn Gilbertson—Grs. 1 & 2
James Sales Elementary
Tacoma, WA

Train Track Math

This colorful locomotive is sure to keep students on track with math facts. Fashion an engine and a caboose from construction paper; then make a series of boxcars by gluing two black construction-paper circles to the bottom of each of several 4" x 8" construction-paper rectangles. Sequentially number the boxcars; then laminate the engine, the boxcars, and the caboose for durability. Using a wipe-off marker, write an unsolved math fact on each boxcar; then showcase the resulting Math Fact Express under your chalkboard ledge or near the bottom of a classroom wall. Nearby place student directions, a supply of paper and pencils, and an answer key. A student copies and solves each math fact on her paper, then uses the answer key to check her work. Each week reprogram the boxcars with different math facts and create a new answer key. All aboard!

Kristin McLaughlin—Gr. 1
Daniel Boone Area School District
Boyertown, PA

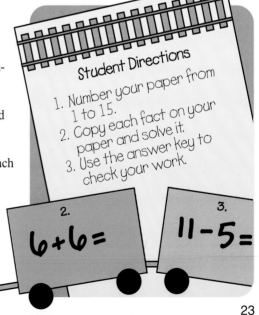

Student Directions
1. Number your paper from 1 to 15.
2. Copy each fact on your paper and solve it.
3. Use the answer key to check your work.

Math Fact Express

1. 10-3=

2. 6+6=

3. 11-5=

Learning Centers

Jolly Jack-O'-Lanterns

These jolly jack-o'-lanterns are just "ripe" for providing number, numeral, and number-word recognition. Make a pumpkin mat like the one shown. To make a jack-o'-lantern face, cut out two yellow triangles for eyes and a yellow jack-o'-lantern mouth. Write a numeral on one triangle and a corresponding dot set on the other. Write the matching number word on the mouth. Program the backs of the facial cutouts for self-checking. Create a desired number of jack-o'-lantern faces; then laminate the cutouts for durability and store them in a resealable plastic bag. Place the pumpkin mat and the bag of cutouts at a center. A student sorts the cutouts into three piles: numerals, dot sets, and number words. To make a jack-o'-lantern face, he places two eyes and a mouth of equal value on the pumpkin mat; then he flips the cutouts to check his work. If his work is correct, he puts the three cutouts in the bag. When all the facial cutouts are returned to the bag, the student's work is finished. For a variation, program the two eye shapes with addends and the mouth shape with their corresponding sum.

Betsy Liebmann—Gr. 1, Gotham Avenue Elementary School, Elmont, NY

Picture This!

Sharpen students' reading skills at this picture-perfect center! Label individual folders with different classifications, such as "Things To Wear," "Things To See," and "Things To Eat." To complete each folder, cut pictures from discarded magazines and catalogs that represent the folder's classification, and then glue the cutouts inside. Number each picture and write the name of the picture on a card. Also write the number of the picture on the back of the card for self-checking. Laminate the folders and the word cards for durability. Place each folder's word cards in a resealable plastic bag and clip the bag to the folder. Store the folders and bags at a center. To complete each folder, a student matches the words to their corresponding pictures; then she flips the cards to check her work.

Joanna Biello—ESL Grs. K–5, Ferderbar Elementary School, North Wales, PA

Trick Or Treat!

Here's a sweet way to shape up your students' geometry skills! Fill a plastic jack-o'-lantern with individually wrapped candies in a variety of geometric shapes (such as cubes, cones, cylinders, spheres, and boxes). Consider choices like caramel candies, Hershey's® Kisses®, miniature Tootsie Roll® candies, Smarties® candies, Starburst® fruit chews, sour balls, and chocolate balls. Place the container of candy, a class supply of paper lunch bags, and crayons at a center. Also post a laminated sign, like the one shown, that can be reprogrammed each day with guidelines for filling a trick-or-treat bag. A student decorates a paper bag, then reads the guidelines and fills her bag accordingly. After a classmate verifies her work, she chooses one piece of her candy to eat; then she takes her remaining candy home.

Shelly Lanier, Reeds Elementary, Lexington, NC

Place these candies in your bag:

- 2 cylinders
- 1 sphere
- 4 cones
- 3 cubes
- 1 box

24

Guide-Word Sandwiches

Celebrate Sandwich Day (annually November 3) and provide guide-word practice with this appetizing center. To create a sandwich project like the one shown, cut two bread slices, a cheese slice, a lettuce leaf, a tomato slice, and one or two lunch-meat shapes from construction paper. Write a guide word on each bread slice. On each sandwich stuffer write an entry word that comes between the two guide words. Program the front of each bread slice and the back of each sandwich stuffer with the same symbol. Create a desired number of sandwich projects, making sure that the guide-word pairs do not alphabetically overlap. Laminate the cutouts for durability; then place the bread slices in one resealable plastic bag and the sandwich stuffers in another. Store the plastic bags in a lunchbox at a center. To assemble each sandwich, a student finds two bread slices with matching symbols; then she uses the guide words to identify the appropriate sandwich stuffings. To check her work, she flips the sandwich stuffers. Now that's a center activity students can really sink their teeth into!

Diane Gonzalez—Gr. 1, Carteret School, Bloomfield, NJ

Thanksgiving Math

Create a cornucopia of story-problem practice! Cut a large cornucopia shape from brown poster board and several fruit and vegetable shapes from colorful construction paper. Number the food cutouts and program them with Thanksgiving-related word problems. Next add desired details to the cutouts and program the back of each food shape for self-checking. Laminate the cutouts for durability; then use Velcro® to attach each food shape to the cornucopia. Place the cornucopia, pencils, and a supply of blank paper at a center. A student removes one food shape from the cornucopia, solves the story problem on his paper, and flips the food shape to check his work. When he has solved all the story problems, he refastens the foods to the cornucopia. Happy Thanksgiving!

1.
For Thanksgiving Grandma made three pumpkin pies. Mom made a chocolate cake. My aunt baked an apple cobbler. How many desserts were there in all?

Surprising Stories

These story bags are packed with writing inspiration! Gather picture cards from a discarded Memory game or make picture cards by attaching stickers to tagboard rectangles. Then, for each picture card, program a corresponding word card. Laminate all the cards. In each of several resealable plastic bags, sort four picture cards and their matching word cards. Store the resulting story bags, pencils, and a supply of paper at a center. A student chooses a story bag and matches each picture card to a word card. Then she writes a story that includes the four pictured items. Just imagine the surprising stories that will result!

Beth Jones—Gr. 2, Stevensville Public School, Stevensville, Ontario, Canada

Learning Centers

Seasonal Nouns

Reinforce plural and possessive nouns with this seasonal flip-book project. Place crayons, scissors, pencils, and a supply of 9" x 12" drawing paper at a center. To make a flip book, a student folds a sheet of drawing paper in half (to 4 1/2" x 12") and makes two equally spaced cuts in the top layer to create three flaps. She chooses a seasonal noun (a person or thing). On the first flap she illustrates the singular form of the noun; then she writes the singular noun under this flap. On the second flap she illustrates a plural form of the noun; then she writes the plural noun under this flap. On the third flap she illustrates the singular noun showing ownership; then, under this flap, she writes the singular possessive form of the noun. As an added challenge, ask each student to write (under each flap) a sentence that includes the featured noun form. Happy holidays!

Tina E. Fox-Henderson—Gr. 2, Christiansburg Primary School, Christiansburg, VA

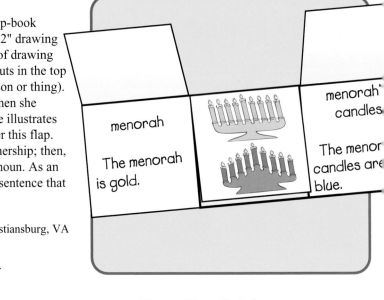

Trees For Sale!

'Tis the season for money-counting skills! Cut out a supply of tree shapes from green construction paper; then glue a yellow construction-paper star to the top of each tree. Use coin stickers, paper coins, or a stamp pad and a set of coin stamps to label each tree with a different coin combination. Also draw desired decorations, such as tinsel or candy canes, on the trees. To make a price tag for each tree, program a blank card with its corresponding money amount. Laminate the resulting price tags and the trees for durability. Use a permanent marker to program the back of each tree for self-checking. Store the cutouts in a holiday gift bag at a center. A student matches each price tag to a tree; then he flips the trees to check his work. What a "cents-ational" sale!

Diane Gonzalez—Gr. 1, Carteret School, Bloomfield, NJ

"Fictionary" Dictionary?

Students dig into the dictionary at this one-of-a-kind center! Place a student dictionary, a hole puncher, a binder, crayons, pencils, and a supply of paper at a center. A student creates a new word by combining words (and/or word parts) found in the dictionary. Then she writes the word and its definition on her paper, and illustrates her work. Next she hole-punches her project and places it in the binder in alphabetical order. This binder will quickly become a unique dictionary with plenty of kid appeal!

Shea Lauria, Port Washington, NY

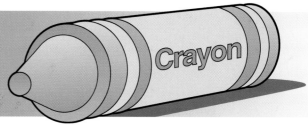

Flavorful Fractions

This math center makes learning about fractions a sweet treat! For each student, place 12 miniature flavored marshmallows in a resealable plastic bag, making certain that each bag contains all four colors and no more than eight of any one color. Store the bags in a decorated container; then place the container, crayons, pencils, and student copies of page 34 at a center. Each student chooses a bag of marshmallows from the container and uses it to complete the reproducible activity. After a student has had a classmate verify his work, he eats his marshmallows in fractional portions! Mmmm, that 5/12 of marshmallows was delicious!

Pam Williams—Gr. 3, Dixieland Elementary, Lakeland, FL

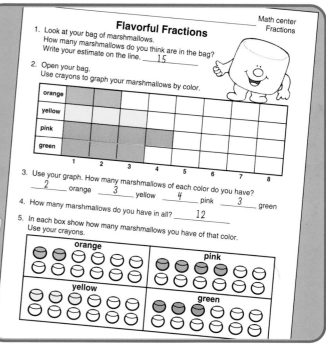

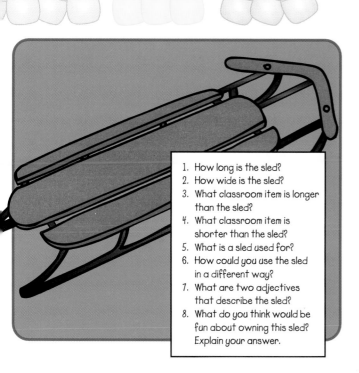

1. How long is the sled?
2. How wide is the sled?
3. What classroom item is longer than the sled?
4. What classroom item is shorter than the sled?
5. What is a sled used for?
6. How could you use the sled in a different way?
7. What are two adjectives that describe the sled?
8. What do you think would be fun about owning this sled? Explain your answer.

Shapely Snow Pals

Even if snow isn't in the forecast, your students will have plenty of frosty fun creating these geometric snow pals! Place glue and a supply of each of the following construction-paper cutouts at a center: 8-inch white circles (faces), 4 1/2" x 5 1/2" black rectangles (hats), 1 1/2" x 9" black rectangles (hat brims), 3" x 9" colorful rectangles (scarves), and an assortment of small circles (eyes) and triangles (noses, mouths, and scarf fringe). Ask each student to use these materials to create a snow pal like the one shown. Then have each child write the number of circles, triangles, and rectangles he used on the back of his project. What a fun way to shape up geometry skills!

Becky Shelley—Gr. 1, Anderson Elementary, Anderson, MO

Winter Wonderland

Beat the wintertime blues with this critical-thinking center! Place a winter item—such as a sled, a scarf, a ski, a snowshoe, or a ski boot—at a center and create a list of questions about the chosen item. Place the questions, a supply of writing paper, pencils, and materials needed to answer the questions at the center. A student answers each question on her sheet of paper; then she asks a classmate to verify her work. Too cool!

Mary Jo Fesenmzier, Lake Geneva, WI

Learning Centers

"Hearts" Of Speech

Students will take this parts-of-speech center to heart! Label each of several heart shapes with a different valentine message. Underline a part of speech on each heart and program the back of the cutout with the corresponding part-of-speech name. Decorate the heart shapes to resemble cookies; then laminate them for durability. Label one cookie tin for each part of speech being reviewed. Place the labeled cookie tins and a cookie sheet at a center. Arrange the heart cutouts on the cookie sheet. A student sorts the cookies into the tins; then he removes the cookies from each tin to check his work. If desired, keep a tin of store-bought valentine cookies at your desk and reward each child who completes the center with the real thing!

Heather Graley—Gr. 3
Eaton, OH

Spending Money

Students go on a buying spree at this money-skills center! From discarded catalogs and store circulars, cut pictures of several kid-pleasing items and their prices. Glue each picture and its corresponding price on a construction-paper card. Laminate the cards for durability. Next number five resealable plastic bags. In the bags place coin sets of varying values that can be used to purchase one or more of the pictured items. Place the bags, the picture cards, a supply of paper, and pencils at a center. A student writes the cash value of each coin set on her paper, followed by the name(s) of the item(s) she can buy with that amount of money. If desired provide an answer key for students to check their work. Now that's a bargain!

Trudy White—Gr. 2
Mayflower Elementary
Mayflower, AR

The Doctor Is In!

Give youngsters a healthy dose of language arts practice at this center. On individual paper strips, write several sentences that include a variety of mistakes. Create a corresponding answer key on a large index card. Place the sentences, the answer key, a class set of colorful bandages, and a stethoscope in a doctor's bag (or something similar). Place the bag, a supply of paper, and pencils at a center. A student removes the *sick* sentences from the bag and slips the stethoscope around her neck; then she makes the sentences *well* by writing them correctly on her paper. Next she uses the answer key to check her work. If each of her sentences is healthy (correct), she attaches a bandage to her paper. Now that's just what the doctor ordered!

Tanya Bomberger—Gr. 1
Lawnton Elementary, Harrisburg, PA

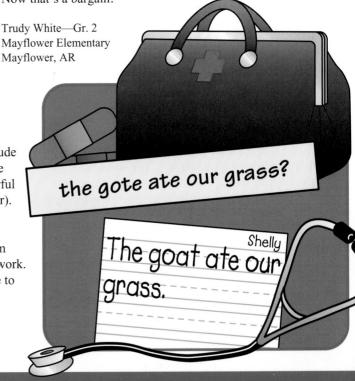

28

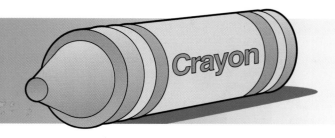

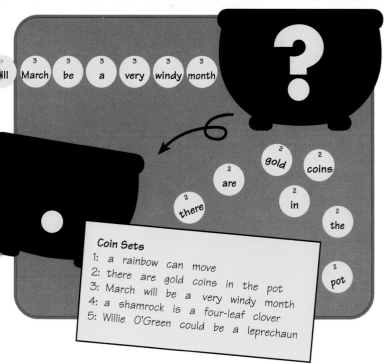

Pot O' Gold Sentences

At this seasonal center, students discover that word order has great value! Glue a question-mark cutout and a period cutout to opposite sides of a black paper pot (pattern on page 20). Next trace 30 circles on yellow paper. To make coin set 1, write "1" near the top of four circles; then write the four words in the set (See "Coin Sets.") on these circles. Make the remaining coin sets in a similar manner. Laminate and cut out the coins and the black punctuation pot. Store each coin set in a resealable plastic bag. Place the coin bags, the pot, a supply of paper, pencils, and an answer key at a center. A student uses each coin set (and the punctuation pot) to make a telling sentence and then an asking sentence. She writes both sentences on her paper (providing capitalization as needed). When all ten sentences are written, she uses the answer key to check her work.

Laura Mihalenko—Gr. 2
Truman Elementary School
Parlin, NJ

Coin Sets
1: a rainbow can move
2: there are gold coins in the pot
3: March will be a very windy month
4: a shamrock is a four-leaf clover
5: Willie O'Green could be a leprechaun

For Good Measure

Students size up their measurement skills at this center. On individual cards write measurement-related questions that can be solved in the classroom. Consider questions like "How many inches wide is the door?" and "Which weighs more—the red marker or the ruler?" Write student directions on a large card, and program the back of this card with an answer key. Laminate all the cards for durability. Place the question cards in a plastic two- or four-cup capacity container. Place the container, the direction card, a supply of paper, pencils, and the materials needed to answer the questions at a center. A student solves each measurement question and writes his answer on his paper. Then he uses the answer key to find out how his measurement skills measure up!

Tori Herrera—Gr. 3
Cook Elementary
Goshen, OH

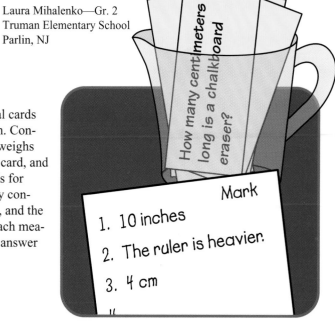

How many centimeters long is a chalkboard eraser?

Mark
1. 10 inches
2. The ruler is heavier.
3. 4 cm

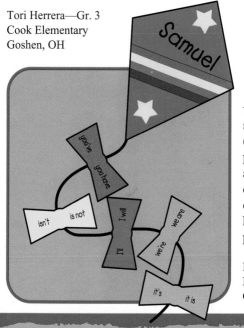

High-Flying Contractions

Contraction practice takes flight at this center! Write several contractions on individual paper slips and store them in a container. Place the container, kite- and bow-shaped templates, colorful construction paper, scissors, crayons, pencils, yarn, and glue (or tape) at a center. A student traces one kite shape and five bow shapes on construction paper, and cuts along the resulting outlines. He personalizes and decorates the kite shape and sets it aside. Next he selects five contractions from the container. He writes each contraction and its corresponding word pair on a bow cutout; then he glues the bow cutouts at equal intervals along a yarn length. To assemble his kite, he glues the top of his resulting kite string to the bottom of his personalized kite cutout. Display the projects on a bulletin board titled "Contractions Are A Breeze!"

Peggy A. Perry—Gr. 2
Pine Tree Elementary School
Center Conway, NH

Learning Centers

"Eggs-traspecial" Art

Students will be eager to have a crack at this open-ended art center! Cut out several egg-shaped tracers from tagboard. Place the egg tracers, a supply of white paper, crayons, glue, drawing paper, and pencils at a center. A student traces an egg shape onto white paper, colors the shape, and cuts it out. She decides how to incorporate her egg cutout into a one-of-a-kind picture, and then she glues the cutout to a sheet of drawing paper and uses crayons to complete the illustration. Now that's "egg-ceptional" artwork!

Karen M. Ruess—Substitute Teacher
Youngstown, OH

Listen And Draw

Reinforce descriptive language and listening skills at this partner center. Place a double-sided easel, a supply of drawing paper, and two identical sets of crayons at a center. Each partner clips his paper to a different side of the easel. While one partner describes and the other partner listens, the students attempt to simultaneously illustrate matching pictures. (Encourage clear and specific, step-by-step directions that indicate color, size, shape, and placement.) When the drawings are complete, the partners compare pictures to see how well they match. Then the students turn their papers over, switch roles, and repeat the activity. For an individual activity, tape-record directions for creating a picture and provide a sample of the illustration for an answer key.

Alyce Pearl Smith—Gr. 1
Butzbach Elementary
APO, AE

Place-Value Egg Baskets

Crack open students' place-value skills at this math center! Collect three baskets, an empty egg carton, and a dozen plastic eggs. Tuck cellophane grass in the baskets and label them as follows: "Hundreds," "Tens," and "Ones." Number the eggs and 12 paper strips from 1 to 12. Write a three-digit numeral on each paper strip and underline one digit per numeral. Create an answer key like the one shown. Place the labeled strips in the corresponding eggs and store the eggs in the egg carton. Place the baskets, the carton of eggs, and the answer key at a center. A student cracks open each egg, reads the numeral inside, and identifies the value of the underlined digit. Then he returns the paper strip to the egg and sorts the egg into the appropriate basket. When all 12 eggs are sorted, he uses the answer key to check his work.

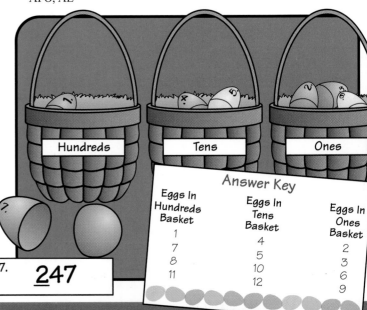

Eggs In Hundreds Basket	Eggs In Tens Basket	Eggs In Ones Basket
1	4	2
7	5	3
8	10	6
11	12	9

7. 247

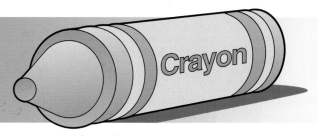

Thank-You Notes

In honor of National Teacher Day (annually Tuesday of the first full week in May), ask students to write thank-you notes to their favorite educators. Place stationery or notecards, envelopes, and assorted writing instruments at a center. Also display a colorful poster that shows the parts of a thank-you note. A student selects a current or former teacher and pens a note of thanks to him or her that includes a memorable learning experience. Next he labels an envelope with the teacher's name and seals his note inside. Have students hand-deliver their notes or assist them in preparing their notes for mailing—whichever is appropriate. These kindhearted messages will generate miles of smiles!

Leslie Bussey—Gr. 1
Millbrook Elementary School
Aiken, SC

Flower Petal Sums

Watch your students' addition skills blossom as they practice the commutative property of addition! Make a math mat like the one shown (without the petal cutouts). Also cut out nine petal shapes from each of two colors of construction paper. Laminate the math mat and the petal cutouts for durability and then store the petals in a resealable plastic bag. Place the mat, the bag of cutouts, addition flash cards, a supply of paper, and pencils at a center. A student selects a math fact and positions petals around the flower center to represent the addends. She records the math fact and its answer on her paper. Next she switches the petals from one flower center to the other to show the inverse of the fact. She records this number sentence on her paper too. She then flips the flash card to check her work. The student continues in this manner until she has solved a predetermined number of math facts.

Kristin McLaughlin—Gr. 1
Amity Elementary Center
Douglassville, PA

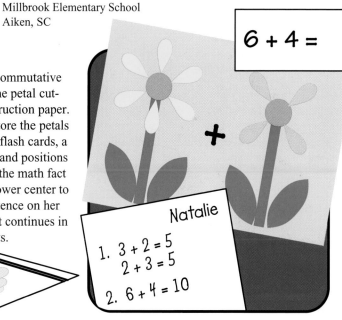

What's The Scoop?

Extra! Extra! Read all about it! At this writing center students write just-for-fun newspaper articles. Use a blue marker to label an envelope "Who?" and to write the names of several different people on individual paper strips. Place the color-coded strips in the envelope. In a similar manner create a color-coded envelope and a set of paper strips for each of the following questions: What?, When?, Where?, Why?, How? Store the envelopes, writing paper, and pencils at a center. A student selects a paper strip from each envelope and incorporates the information into a newsy story. After each student has completed the center, edit the stories and have each youngster write his final draft on a five-inch-wide strip of writing paper. If desired, provide blank paper for illustrations. Glue the students' work onto the pages of a discarded newspaper; then place this hot-off-the-press edition in your classroom library for all to read.

Mary Anne Murphy—Grs. 3–4
Andrew Jackson Language Academy
Chicago, IL

Learning Centers

Picture-Perfect Memories

Students travel down memory lane at this picture-perfect writing center! Gather snapshots of your students engaged in assorted learning experiences from the past year. You need one photo per student. Store the photos at a center along with glue, clear tape, pencils, and a class supply of 7" x 10" white paper and 9" x 12" colorful construction paper. A student chooses a photo and tapes it on a piece of white paper. On the remainder of the paper, she describes the learning experience, providing as many interesting details as possible. Then she glues her work onto a sheet of colorful construction paper. Post the completed projects on a bulletin board titled "Remember When…"

If photos are not available, post a list of memorable learning-related events at the center. Have each student choose an event, illustrate and describe her memory of it on white paper, and then complete the center as described.

Sue Lorey, Arlington Heights, IL

In October our class went to Hill Ridge Farm. We went on a hayride and visited a country store. We also got to pet the animals in the barn. The best part was when we learned about a pumpkin's life cycle and then got to pick pumpkins from the patch.

Annie

Mike

For Sale!

Cash in on money-counting skills with this profitable center! To make an activity that's easy to reprogram, laminate a blank sheet of poster board. Cut out four pictures of kid-pleasing items from discarded catalogs or store circulars, and tape each one to the poster board. Use a wipe-off marker to number and price each item. Display the poster at a center. Also provide a stamp pad and a set of coin stamps, pencils, and a supply of blank paper. To complete the center, a student numbers his paper to 4, leaving plenty of space between the numbers. Then, for each number, he shows three different coin combinations that equal the value of the corresponding item. To keep shopping interest high, routinely reprogram the poster with different sale items and prices. What a bargain!

What's The Location?

Keep your students' critical-thinking skills on the move at this center! On each of ten cards, write three clues that describe a different mystery location such as the beach, the grocery store, or the park. Number the cards and create a corresponding answer key. If desired, laminate the items for durability. Place the cards, the answer key, pencils, and a supply of paper at a center. A student numbers her paper to 10. Next she reads each card and writes on her paper the name of the mystery location. Then she uses the answer key to check her work. Now that's a center that really goes places!

Diana Boykin—Gr. 3, DeZavala Elementary, Midland, TX

1. popcorn ticket big screen

2. ball hoop referee

Maddie

1. movie theater
2. basketball game
3.
4.
5.
6.
7.

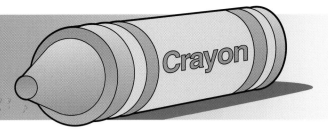

"The School Times"

Time keeps on ticking at this center—elapsed time, that is! Stock the center with 5" x 6" pieces of drawing paper (five per student) and 6" x 10" pieces of newspaper (one per student). Also provide discarded newspapers, scissors, glue, pencils, a black marker, and a stapler. A student cuts out five examples of time spans from the discarded newspapers and glues each example on a piece of drawing paper. On the back of the paper, she writes how much time elapses during the time span. Next she folds a 6" x 10" piece of newspaper in half and uses the marker to write "The [school name] Times" and her byline on the front of the resulting booklet cover. She stacks the five pages she has created, keeping the time spans faceup, and staples the stack inside the cover.

The following week, provide additional practice with elapsed time by featuring these hot-off-the-press booklets at the center. For each booklet a student reads, she calculates the elapsed time in each featured time span and then turns the page to check her work.

Mary Ann Lewis, Tallahassee, FL

Clip And Spell

Stir up an interest in weekly spelling practice at this partner center! Program a spring-type clothespin for each letter of the alphabet. Label extra clothespins for frequently used letters. Store the clothespins and a paint stick in a bucket or a clean and empty paint can; then place the container and a copy of the weekly spelling list at a center. One student becomes the *caller*, and his partner is the *speller*. The caller says the first word on the list and then watches closely as his partner spells the word by clipping clothespins onto the paint stick. If the correct spelling is given, the speller removes the clothespins from the paint stick, and the caller reads aloud the next word on the list. If an incorrect spelling is given, the caller repeats the word, and the partners work together to spell it. After each word on the list is correctly spelled, the partners change roles and repeat the activity. Reprogramming the center is a snap—simply replace the spelling list each week.

Amy Ekmark—Gr. 1, Eastside Elementary, Lancaster, CA

Same And Different

This easy-to-make center provides plenty of practice with comparing and contrasting! Place discarded catalogs, scissors, glue, pencils, and a supply of drawing paper at a center. A student cuts out two pictures of distinctly different items from a catalog. She draws a Venn diagram on her paper and then glues one picture above each circle. Next she studies the pictures and lists the similarities and differences that she observes in the appropriate areas of the diagram. Comparing and contrasting have never been more interesting!

Kimberly Minafo, Tooker Avenue School, West Babylon, NY

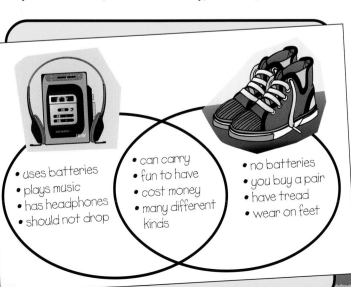

Flavorful Fractions

1. Look at your bag of marshmallows.
   How many marshmallows do you think are in the bag?
   Write your estimate on the line. _____

2. Open your bag.
   Use crayons to graph your marshmallows by color.

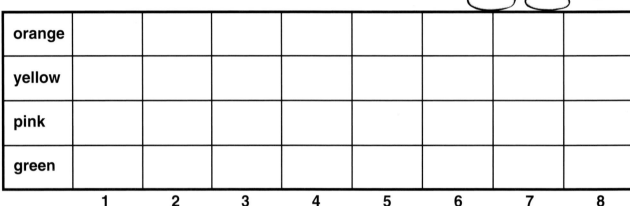

orange								
yellow								
pink								
green								
	1	2	3	4	5	6	7	8

3. Use your graph. How many marshmallows of each color do you have?
   _____ orange   _____ yellow   _____ pink   _____ green

4. How many marshmallows do you have in all? _____

5. In each box show how many marshmallows you have of that color.
   Use your crayons.

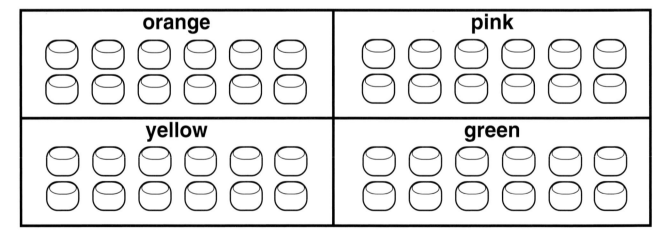

6. Study each box in Number 5. Write a fraction that describes it.

   $\frac{\quad}{\quad}$ = orange $\frac{\quad}{\quad}$ = yellow $\frac{\quad}{\quad}$ = pink $\frac{\quad}{\quad}$ = green

ARTS & CRAFTS

Arts & Crafts

Sunny Delight

If there's a patch of sunflowers your students can visit, make a beeline for it; then march from the patch into this bloomin' art project. In advance, cut several potatoes in half and trim some of the halves to make petal-shaped prints and some to make one-inch-square prints. To create a sunflower, dip a square printer into brown paint; then repeatedly press it onto a large sheet of art paper, creating a circular design. Outside this, use a petal-shaped printer and yellow paint to encircle the brown area. When the paint has dried, cut out the flower. To turn a bulletin board into a patch of sunny sunflowers, staple each student's blossom atop a green-paper strip embellished with some green-paper leaves. That's sunny all right! Now where did I leave my shades?

Teresa Williams—Gr. 1
Coquihalla Elementary
Hope, British Columbia, Canada

Personality Plus

Personality! These projects are packed with it. But not only that; each student's likeness will also reveal something about his family members and pets!

1. Give each child a large T-shirt shape cut from a 9" x 12" sheet of construction paper. Ask that he take the shirt cutout home, decorate it with drawings or pictures of family members and pets, and return the cutout to school.
2. When all the cutouts are returned, have each student paint a 12" x 18" sheet of art paper with a skin-toned paint that approximates his own coloring.
3. When the painted paper has dried, have the student draw two arm outlines and a head-and-neck outline on his paper, then cut them out.
4. Have each student glue the arm and head cutouts onto his T-shirt cutout that was decorated at home.
5. Encourage each student to cut out and decorate a construction-paper hat of his own design, then glue it on the head cutout.
6. Have each student use colorful markers to draw facial features.
7. To complete the effect, have students glue on paper and yarn to represent hair and accessories.

Ellen M. Stern—Gr. 1
Alberta Smith Elementary
Midlothian, VA

Brightening The Breezes

With their dangling legs dancing in the breezes above your students' heads, these leaf people are certain to stir up the feeling of fall. To make a leaf person, trace one large leaf shape and four smaller ones onto construction paper. Cut them out; then use a marker to draw a comical face on the larger leaf. Glue four accordion-folded construction-paper strips to the back of the larger leaf for arms and legs. To finish your leaf person, glue the remaining leaves to the dangling ends of the strips.

Carolyn Williams—Gr. 2
North Augusta Elementary
North Augusta, SC

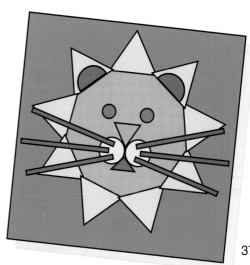

Pretty As A Picture

It's easy for students to try their hand at the art technique called *pointillism.* To begin, cut a tree trunk that has plenty of branches from brown construction paper. Glue the cutout to art paper. Dip a pencil eraser or cotton swab in one color of tempera paint; then press it repeatedly onto the area on and above the tree branches.

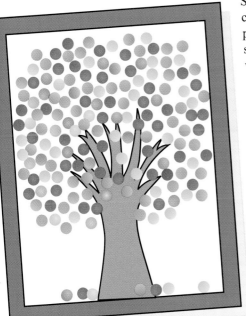

Similarly dip another pencil eraser (or cotton swab) in a second color of paint, and press it repeatedly in the same general area. Continue in this way, using a variety of colors until colorful dots cover the tree branches and the area that surrounds them. Also paint a few stray dots near the base of the tree to represent fallen leaves. When the paint has dried, mount the project on a slightly larger sheet of colorful construction paper. Be sure to have the students admire their paintings from afar; then, as a class, discuss how the dots merge together to create trees that are full of color!

Amy Erickson—Gr. 1
Montello School
Lewiston, ME

Shapely Critters

Encourage students to let their imaginations run WILD as they consider animal subjects for this art project! To begin, share Lois Ehlert's *Color Farm* (HarperCollins Children's Books, 1990) or *Color Zoo* (HarperCollins Children's Books, 1989) with your students. Prompt plenty of discussion about the shapes that Lois Ehlert uses and the effects that she achieves. To make a shapely critter, a student cuts out different-sized paper circles, triangles, and rectangles in a variety of colors. Next she manipulates the cutouts on a paper of a contrasting color. When the student has created an eye-appealing animal likeness, she glues the cutouts in place.

Valerie Smith
Exton, PA

Arts & Crafts

Sail On!

Look what's on the horizon—a seaworthy project just in time for Columbus Day! Cut an eight-inch circle from white construction paper. Using watercolors, paint ocean waters on the bottom half of the circle and a colorful sky on the top half. While this dries, cut out a ship's hull, sails, and masts from construction-paper scraps. Add details to the cutouts with crayons or markers. To assemble the project, glue the painted circle atop a slightly larger, black construction-paper circle; then glue the construction-paper cutouts to the painted surface. Land ahoy!

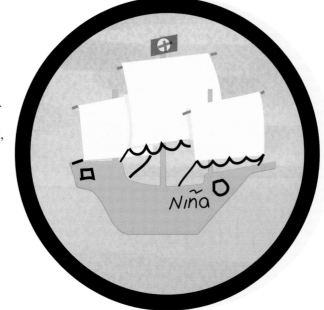

Pumpkins With Personality

Transforming paper lunch bags into pumpkin personalities is easy and fun! Using a ruler and alternating between two different colors of crayons, draw vertical and horizontal lines on the front and back of a white lunch bag. Cut out desired facial features from construction paper and glue them in place (be sure to allow room to fold down the top of the bag). Partially fill the bag with crumpled newspaper; then fold and staple the top closed. Near the fold tape a few lengths of curled ribbon for vines. Lastly fold a 3" x 5" rectangle of green paper in half and cut out a two-sided stem that connects at the fold (see the illustration). Partially unfold the stem and glue it to the top of the bag. Now there's a pumpkin that's packed with personality!

Twinkle, Twinkle, Little Bat…

No doubt "a-bat" it, your youngsters will find these flashy fliers simply irresistible! To make a bat, fold a 6" x 12" strip of black construction paper in half. On the folded paper, trace a wing template like the one shown. Cut on the resulting outline and unfold the paper wings. Trim a three-inch square of black felt into an oval and mount the resulting body in the center of the paper wings. From black construction paper, cut a 1 1/2-inch circle (head), ears, and feet. Glue the paper ears and two wiggle eyes to the head; then add other desired facial features. Next glue the bat's head and feet to the project. Lastly use a glitter pen to indicate an arm, a thumb, and four fingers on each bat wing. Mount the project on a 9" x 12" sheet of construction paper, add a bat fact, and display on a bulletin board titled "Batty About Bats!"

Yolanda Matthews—Gr. 2, Monrovia School, Huntsville, AL

A bat is a mammal.

Lovely Leaves

Be prepared for plenty of "ohhhhs" and "ahhhhs" as these lovely leaf-print projects take shape! To make a leaf, drizzle liquid tempera paints in a variety of fall colors onto a 9" x 12" sheet of white construction paper. Then, using the teeth of a plastic comb, swirl the paint colors together until a desired effect is achieved. When the paint is dry, cut a large leaf shape from the project. Mount the cutout onto a slightly larger piece of fall-colored construction paper; then trim the construction paper to create an eye-catching border. For a spectacular fall display, punch a hole near the top of each leaf cutout and use monofilament line to suspend the shapes from the ceiling. Autumn has definitely arrived!

Tall "Tail" Turkeys

Will the turkey with the tallest tail feathers please step forward? To make one of these gobblers, use red, yellow, brown, and orange fingerpaints to paint an eight-inch square of tagboard. To make the turkey's body and head, use brown paper to cover one and one-half empty toilet-tissue tubes. When the painted tagboard is dry, trim it to create a set of tail feathers. Then glue the paper-covered tubes to the feathers. Cut out two eyes, a beak, and a wattle from construction-paper scraps and glue the cutouts in place. Attach construction-paper feet, and this gobbler is ready to strut its stuff! For a fun follow-up, have each child write a very tall *tale* about his tall-tailed turkey!

Laura LaPerna—Grs. K–2
Tedder Elementary
Pompano Beach, FL

Tissue-Paper Turkeys

Check out the fancy feathers on this gorgeous gobbler! Cut a supply of one-inch squares from brown, yellow, orange, red, green, blue, and purple tissue paper. To make a tissue-paper turkey, sketch a large turkey shape on a 9" x 12" sheet of construction paper. Glue a different color of overlapping tissue-paper squares to cover each tail feather. Next glue brown, overlapping tissue-paper squares to cover the head and body areas. To make eyes, feet, a beak, and a wattle, ball up individual tissue-paper squares in desired colors and glue them to the project in the appropriate places. Now that's one fine fowl!

Jan Minter—Gr. 3
St. Pius V School
Long Beach, CA

Arts & Crafts

Glowing Menorah

The cheerful glow of this menorah project is a warm reminder of the great miracle it represents.

For each menorah you will need:

one 1" x 4" strip of red construction paper
eight 1" x 3" strips of red construction paper
nine 1" x 1 1/2" pieces of yellow tissue paper
one 3" x 11" strip of blue construction paper
one 9" x 12" sheet of black construction paper

scissors
glue
pencil

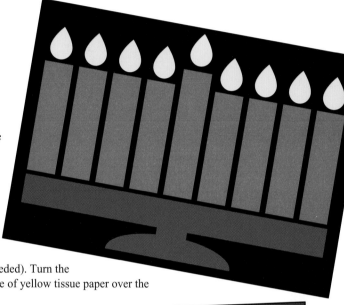

Directions:

1. **For the menorah base,** fold the blue paper in half. Trace a template like the one shown on the folded paper; then cut along the outline. Glue the cutout near the bottom of the black paper.
2. **For the shammash,** glue the longest red rectangle slightly above the center of the base.
3. **For the eight candles,** glue four red rectangles on each side of the shammash, taking care to align the bottoms of the candles with the shammash.
4. **For the flames,** draw a flame atop the shammash and each candle. Carefully cut out each flame (provide assistance with this step as needed). Turn the project over. Drizzle glue around each flame cutout and press a piece of yellow tissue paper over the opening.
5. **Display** the completed project in a window for a glowing effect.

Rebecca Brudwick—Gr. 1
Hoover Elementary School
North Mankato, MN

Step 1

Creative Christmas Tree

The sky is the limit when students take a multimedia approach to decorating poster-board Christmas trees! Give each child a simple tree shape cut from a 9" x 12" rectangle of poster board (or cardboard). Provide a wide assortment of craft supplies that includes construction paper, scissors, glue, tempera paints, paintbrushes, yarn, fabric scraps, foil stars, gift wrap, crayons, and markers. Each student shapes his tree (if desired), then picks and chooses from the provided supplies to decorate a tree that's fit for the season. Happy holidays!

Joan Mary Macey—Art Teacher
Binghamton City School District
Binghamton, NY

A Gingerbread Glyph

Try as you might, you won't find a more unique gingerbread project than this one! Make available the following colors of construction-paper scraps: pink, blue, white, orange, red, green, yellow, purple, and black. Each student also needs a large paper cutout of a gingerbread pal, glue, scissors, crayons or markers, a pencil, and a copy of "Gingerbread Decorations" on page 48. A student completes page 48 by following the provided instructions; then she uses the resulting code to make hair, buttons, stripes, and facial features to glue on her gingerbread cutout. Display the completed projects and an enlarged version of page 48 on a bulletin board titled "A Gingerbread Who's Who."

Bonnie Hansen—Gr. 1
Ashton Elementary
Sarasota, FL

Snazzy Snow Globe

Create a flurry of excitement with these handcrafted snow globes. To make a snow globe, cut an eight-inch circle from light blue construction paper and another from white construction paper. Cut the white circle in half and set aside one half for later use. Trim the straight edge of the remaining half circle to resemble fallen snow; then glue this cutout atop the blue circle. Next use construction-paper scraps, a hole puncher, glue, and crayons or markers to create a snowy scene. When the glue is dry, wrap the project with clear plastic wrap. Use clear tape to secure the plastic wrap to the back of the project. To make the snow globe's base, trace the outline of a protractor (or something similar) onto brown or black paper, and cut along the resulting outline. Glue the plastic-covered project to the base. Let it snow!

Snowflake Snow Pal

You can sum up these snow pals with one word: unique! To make the body, fold a nine-inch white circle in half three times and make a series of desired cuts. Then unfold the paper and glue a four-inch white circle (head) to the top of the body. Add desired facial features. Next cut out a paper scarf and hat for the snow pal. Use markers or crayons to brightly color the clothing cutouts, creating a striped or checkered pattern if desired. Glue the clothing to the project and the snow pal is ready to display. Very cool!

Mary Napoli—Gr. 1
Swiftwater, PA

41

Arts & Crafts

More Than Just A Hat

Who would have thought hats could be used for more than just head coverings? Abraham Lincoln, that's who! Abe had a habit of tucking bills, notes, and other legal papers inside his hat. Just like Abe, your students can use these stovepipe hats for another use—valentine holders.

Materials For One Valentine Holder:

one 9" x 12" sheet of black construction paper	white crayon
one 12" x 18" sheet of black construction paper	scissors
red, pink, and purple construction-paper scraps	glue

Steps:
1. Roll the 12" x 18" sheet of black paper into a cylinder and glue the overlapping edges together. Allow drying time.
2. Cut six 2-inch slits, equally spaced, in one end of the cylinder.
3. Fold the resulting tabs outward; then center the cylinder onto the 9" x 12" sheet of black paper and glue the tabs to the paper.
4. Use the white crayon to personalize the base of the resulting holder.
5. Cut out several different-size heart shapes from the construction-paper scraps. Glue the hearts to the project as desired.

Diane Gonzalez—Gr. 1
Carteret School
Bloomfield, NJ

Cutie-Pie Cowpoke

Saddle up for this rootin'-tootin' art project! You just may lasso some of your buckaroos' geometry skills, too!

Materials For One Cowpoke:

two 6" squares of light blue construction paper (pants)
one 6" square of dark blue construction paper (shirt)
one 3" square of red construction paper (bandana)
one 3" circle of skin-toned construction paper (head)
one brown construction-paper copy of the hat, boot, and glove patterns on page 49

construction-paper scraps
markers or crayons
scissors
glue

Steps:
1. Cut out the hat, boot, and glove patterns. Set them aside.
2. To make the body, fold each of the three 6-inch squares in half to create a triangle. Position the dark blue triangle (shirt) with the fold at the top. Unfold the paper and glue each glove cutout directly below the crease line. Next glue the two light blue triangles in place to create pants; then refold the shirt and glue it closed.
3. Glue each boot cutout to the bottom of a pant leg.
4. To make the bandana, fold the red construction-paper square in half to create a triangle; then slide the top of the shirt inside the resulting bandana and glue the bandana in place.
5. Glue the hat cutout to the top of the skin-toned circle. Use markers or crayons to add facial features to the circle; then glue the resulting head to the top of the bandana.
6. Use the construction-paper scraps and markers to decorate your cowpoke.

Kim Clemente—Gr. 2, Schnieder Grade School, Farmer City, IL

Kite Weaving

Creating this wonderfully woven kite is a breeze! Search through a discarded magazine to find two colorful pictures, each of which is at least six inches square. Trace a six-inch square template onto each magazine picture and cut on the resulting outline. Next cut one picture into 1/2-inch strips. Set the strips aside. Fold the other magazine picture in half. Then use a pencil and a ruler to draw parallel lines from the fold. The lines should be 2 1/2 inches in length and spaced about 3/4 inch apart. Next cut on the lines; then unfold the paper and weave the magazine strips through the resulting slits. When all the strips are woven, glue the ends of each strip in place. Glue the completed weaving to a six-inch construction-paper square. To create a kite tail, hole-punch one corner of the kite and thread a two-foot length of curling ribbon through the hole; then tie the ribbon and curl the ends.

Elizabeth Searls Almy, Greensboro, NC

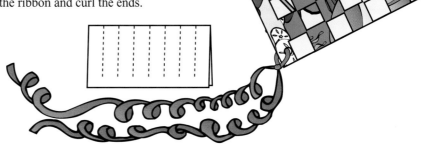

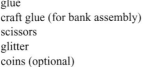

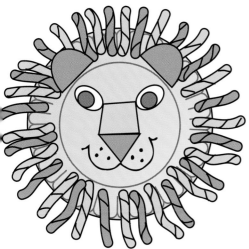

A Lovable Lion

Whether March comes in like a lion or not, you're sure to get a roaring response to this project! To make a lion, color or paint a thin, nine-inch white paper plate yellow or light brown; then add facial features. To make the lion's mane, glue three-inch lengths of brown yarn and yellow yarn (in an alternating fashion) around the entire plate rim. Then cut a pair of lion ears from brown paper and glue them in place. No "lion"! That's a fine-looking animal!

Catherine Strickland—Gr. 2
Myers Elementary School
Gainesville, GA

Pot O' Gold Bank

If you can't catch a leprechaun and his loot, collect your own with this pot o' gold bank!

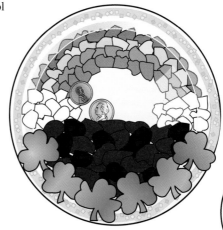

Materials For One Bank:

2 clear plastic dessert plates
1 green construction-paper copy of the shamrock patterns on page 49
red, yellow, green, blue, white, and black construction-paper scraps

glue
craft glue (for bank assembly)
scissors
glitter
coins (optional)

Steps:

1. **To make the back of the bank,** cut a 1 1/2-inch rectangle from the rim of one plate. Position the plate with the opening at the top; then, in collage fashion, tear colorful paper pieces and glue them on the top half of the plate to create a rainbow. Glue torn white paper pieces to each end of the arch to resemble clouds.
2. **To make the front of the bank,** invert the other plate; then tear black paper pieces and glue them onto the lower half of the plate to resemble a pot. Cut out the shamrock shapes; then place a dot of glue in the center of each shamrock and place the shamrocks near the base of the pot. For a 3-D effect, curl the shamrock leaves.
3. **To assemble the bank,** squeeze a trail of craft glue around the rim of the plate from Step 1. Then align the plate from Step 2 atop the glue, making sure the artwork from both plates is correctly positioned.
4. **For a bit of added sparkle,** squeeze a trail of glue around the rim of the top plate and sprinkle it with glitter. When the glue is dry, shake off the excess glitter and, if desired, place a coin or two in the bank for good luck!

Elizabeth Searls Almy

Arts & Crafts

Bunny Bags

Tuck a few treats into these student-made bags to top off your Easter festivities. "Every-bunny" is sure to love them!

Materials For One Bunny Bag:

one white paper lunch bag
two spring-type wooden clothespins
one 3" x 5" piece of white construction paper (outer ears)
one 2" x 4" piece of white construction paper (arms)
one 3" x 5" piece of white construction paper (feet)
one 2" x 4" piece of pink construction paper (inner ears)

construction-paper scraps
black marker
one cotton ball
glue
scissors
wrapped candies (optional)

Steps:

1. **For the bunny's body,** open the paper lunch bag and then fold down the top 2 1/2 inches of the bag. Clip the clothespins to the fold.
2. **For the bunny's ears,** fold in half lengthwise one 3" x 5" piece of white paper and cut out two matching ear shapes. Fold in half lengthwise the 2" x 4" piece of pink paper and cut out two matching inner-ear shapes. Glue one pink cutout inside each white cutout. Glue each resulting ear to a clothespin.
3. **For the bunny's arms,** fold in half lengthwise the 2" x 4" piece of white paper and cut out two matching arm shapes. Fold one end of each arm cutout to create a tab. Glue each tab to the front of the bag as shown.
4. **For the bunny's feet,** fold in half the other 3" x 5" piece of white paper and cut out two matching foot shapes. Glue the feet to the bottom of the bag.
5. **For the bunny's face,** cut out eyes, a nose, and teeth from construction-paper scraps. Glue the cutouts to the folded flap of the bag.
6. **To complete the bag,** use a marker to add desired details to the bunny's face, arms, and feet. Glue a cotton-ball tail to the back of the bag. Then, if desired, remove the bunny ears, carefully open the bag, and tuck a few Easter treats inside!

Mariko Layton
Johnstown, PA

Touchable Tulips

Students will want to reach out and touch these terrific springtime tulips! To make the three-dimensional vase, roll a 4 1/2" x 6" piece of construction paper into a cylinder and glue the overlapping edges together. When the glue dries, secure the seam of the vase near the bottom of an 8" x 11" sheet of colorful construction paper. Next trace a tulip-shaped template (patterns on page 50) onto a colorful party napkin three times. Cut out the shapes. With the napkin design facedown, use a small drop of glue to attach a cotton ball to the center of each tulip cutout. Next squeeze a thin trail of glue around the perimeter of each cutout. Turn over each tulip and secure it above the vase as shown. Cut out green paper stems and leaves and glue them in place. Mount the completed project atop a 9" x 12" sheet of contrasting construction paper.

Elizabeth Searls Almy
Greensboro, NC

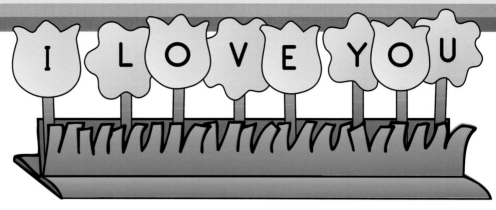

Flowers For Mother's Day

Loved ones will bloom with pride when they receive these colorful Mother's Day mementos.

Materials For One:
green construction paper:
  one 9" x 12" sheet
  eight 1/2" x 2 1/2" strips
colorful construction-paper scraps
scissors
crayons
glue

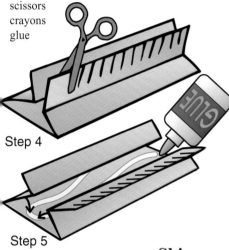

Step 4

Step 5

Steps:

1. Fold the large green paper into thirds lengthwise (prefold if desired). Unfold.
2. Fold the top edge of the paper to the top fold line and then unfold the paper and reverse-fold it.
3. Fold the bottom edge of the paper to the bottom fold line and then unfold the paper and reverse-fold it.
4. Fringe-cut the bottom edge of the paper, being careful to not cut through the closest fold line.
5. Spread glue over the midsection of the paper. Bring the top fold and the bottom fold together in the center of the glued surface as shown. Set aside to dry.
6. Cut out eight flower shapes from colorful construction-paper scraps. Use a crayon to write one letter from the phrase "I love you" on each flower. Glue each flower cutout to a green construction-paper strip.
7. Glue the back of each flower stem to the uncut lip of the green paper. Carefully bend the fringed edges forward for added effect.

Elizabeth Searls Almy, Greensboro, NC

Shimmery Dragonflies

A display of these dazzling dragonflies is sure to attract plenty of attention! To make a dragonfly, fold a 9" x 12" sheet of white construction paper in half (to 4 1/2" x 12"). Place a tagboard template of the pattern on page 50 on the folded paper as shown; then trace around the shape and cut along the resulting outline. Unfold the cutout. Working atop a newspaper-covered surface, use tempera paint to paint the cutout as desired. Sprinkle the wet paint with glitter. Or wait for the paint to dry, brush a thin layer of diluted glue over the project, and sprinkle glitter atop the glue. Mount the dazzling dragonfly on a 9" x 12" sheet of construction paper before putting it on display. Spectacular!

Allison Haynes
Lexington, NC

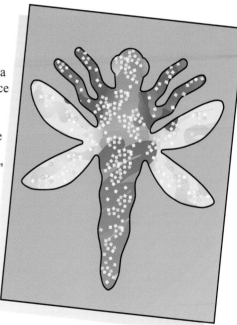

Terrific Turtles

Students will take a shine to these irresistible reptiles! To make the shell, cut one-inch lengths of masking tape and attach them in an overlapping fashion to an inverted seven-inch paper plate. Be sure to cover the entire plate surface, including the rim. Next use the sponge-tip applicator on a bottle of brown shoe polish to paint the tape-covered plate. When the resulting shell is dry, cut out a turtle head, tail, and four legs from construction paper. Add desired details to the cutouts with marker and then glue the cutouts under the rim of the painted shell. Snap to it!

Melanie J. Miller, Nashport, OH

Arts & Crafts

Dazzling Dots

Add an outdoor touch to a simple work of art, and the results are downright dazzling! Render a large sketch of a desired object on white construction paper. Then head outdoors with the drawing and crayons. Place the drawing, sketch side up, on a dry sidewalk. Carefully color the sketch, bearing down hard while coloring. (The object will look as if it were colored with tiny dots.) Then return to the classroom and create a backdrop for the object by coloring the rest of the paper on a smooth surface. Mount the completed project on a slightly larger sheet of brightly colored construction paper. Very impressive!

Elizabeth Searls Almy
Greensboro, NC

Beautiful Butterflies

Students jump into this butterfly project with both feet! To make the butterfly's wings, a youngster stands on a sheet of white construction paper so that his shoe-clad feet are side by side and touching. He asks a classmate to trace around his shoes, then he cuts out the shape and colors the resulting butterfly wings as desired. Next he fashions a butterfly body and head from construction paper. He uses a white crayon to add desired facial features before he glues the cutout(s) near the center of the wings. To finish his fancy flier, he attaches bent pipe-cleaner antennae.

Kara Main
Penn Wood Elementary School
West Chester, PA

Dad, I've "bean" wanting to tell you how much I LOVE YOU!

Magnetic Picture Frame

These handcrafted picture frames will attract plenty of attention from fathers and other chosen recipients. Securely mount a self-photo on colorful poster board. Trim the poster board as needed to leave a 1 1/2- to 2-inch margin on all sides. To decorate the resulting frame, use a fine-tipped marker or a glitter pen to write "[Name], I've 'bean' wanting to tell you how much I love you!" Then use glue and dried beans in a variety of colors to add other desired decorations. Lastly, attach a strip of magnetic tape to the back of the project that is just slightly shorter than the width of the frame. Someone is going to be very excited to exhibit this gift of love!

D. Martinez—Gr. 1
Fredericksburg Christian School
Fredericksburg, VA

Rainbow Swimmers

Make a colorful splash with these fancy fish! Begin the project with a white construction-paper copy of the fish pattern on page 51 and a supply of tissue-paper squares in the following rainbow colors: red, orange, yellow, green, blue, and purple. Cut out the fish pattern and then glue the appropriate color of tissue-paper squares in each section, overlapping the squares as you go, until the cutout is completely covered. (If desired, use diluted glue and a paintbrush to adhere the tissue-paper squares.) After the glue dries, trim excess tissue paper from the edges of the cutout, then use a black marker to draw desired details on the fish. What a catch!

Gina Marinelli—Gr. 2
Bernice Young Elementary School
Burlington, NJ

Star-Spangled Sparklers

These festive sparklers are the perfect addition to a patriotic celebration! Glue two red, two white, and two blue 2" x 6" construction-paper strips to a paper towel tube, alternating the colors as shown. Next tape half-inch silver paper strips (cut from wrapping paper) to the inside rim of one end of the tube. Embellish the tube with star-shaped cutouts or foil stickers. Hip, hip, hooray for the red, white, and blue!

Melissa A. Stanek—Grs. K–6
Better Beginnings
Oneonta, NY

Bug Bungalows

Your youngsters will go buggy over these clever creature carriers!

Materials For One Bungalow:
one cardboard cylinder (precut with a 2" square opening) and its lid
one 3" square of clear plastic
construction-paper scraps
various art supplies such as pom-poms, yarn, felt, and sequins
one 12" length of curling ribbon
masking tape
glue
scissors
pencil, pen, or other fine-tipped tool for punching holes

Steps:
1. Position the plastic over the square opening in the container and securely tape it in place.
2. Use glue and construction-paper scraps to cover the remainder of the container, then attach other desired decorations.
3. Use the fine-tipped tool to poke tiny ventilation holes in the lid. *(Assist students as needed.)*
4. To make a handle, poke two small holes in opposite sides of the lid. *(Assist students as needed.)* Thread the curling ribbon through the holes and securely tie the ends. Pull the handle upward and snap the lid on the container.

To use the bungalow, remove its lid and carefully collect an insect guest to observe. (Assist students in choosing harmless bugs.) If desired, place some grass, twigs, and soil from the insect's environment in the container. Then snap on the lid. After a short while, return your guest to its original habitat.

Elizabeth Searls Almy
Greensboro, NC

Gingerbread Decorations

Circle each answer that describes you.
Then follow the directions to make decorations for your project.

Which Am I?

girl = pink
boy = blue

Cut out two eyes from
the color you circled.

How Old Am I?

6 = orange

7 = red

8 = green

9 = yellow

Cut out a nose (△) from
the color you circled.

How Many Brothers?

0 1 2 3 4 5 more

For each brother, cut
out one white stripe for
each arm.

How Many Sisters?

0 1 2 3 4 5 more

For each sister, cut out
one white stripe for
each leg.

When Is My Birthday?

January	=	white blue
February	=	red pink
March	=	green yellow
April	=	yellow purple
May	=	pink green
June	=	blue green
July	=	red white blue
August	=	yellow red
September	=	blue red
October	=	orange black
November	=	yellow brown
December	=	red green

Cut out hair from the
colors you circle.

What Do I Like To Do?

read = ⊙ blue

watch TV = △ white

play outdoors = ⊙ red

play indoors = ▢ black

use a computer = ⊙ orange

draw pictures = △ purple

write stories = ⊙ green

dance = ▢ yellow

Make one button for
each circled item.

What Pet Do I Like Best?

dog =

cat =

fish =

bird =

other =

Draw the mouth that
matches your answer.

The Education Center, Inc. • THE MAILBOX® • Primary • Dec/Jan 1998–99

48 **Note To Teacher:** Use with "A Gingerbread Glyph" on page 41.

Use the hat, boot, and glove patterns with "Cutie-Pie Cowpoke" on page 42.

Use the shamrock patterns with "Pot O' Gold Bank" on page 43.

Patterns

Use with "Touchable Tulips" on page 44.

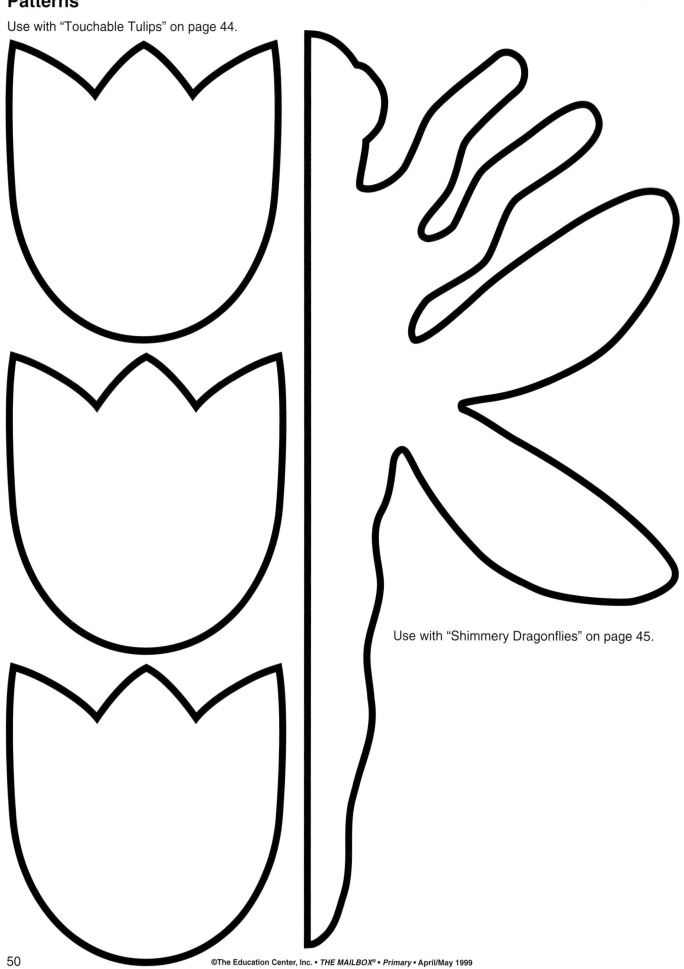

Use with "Shimmery Dragonflies" on page 45.

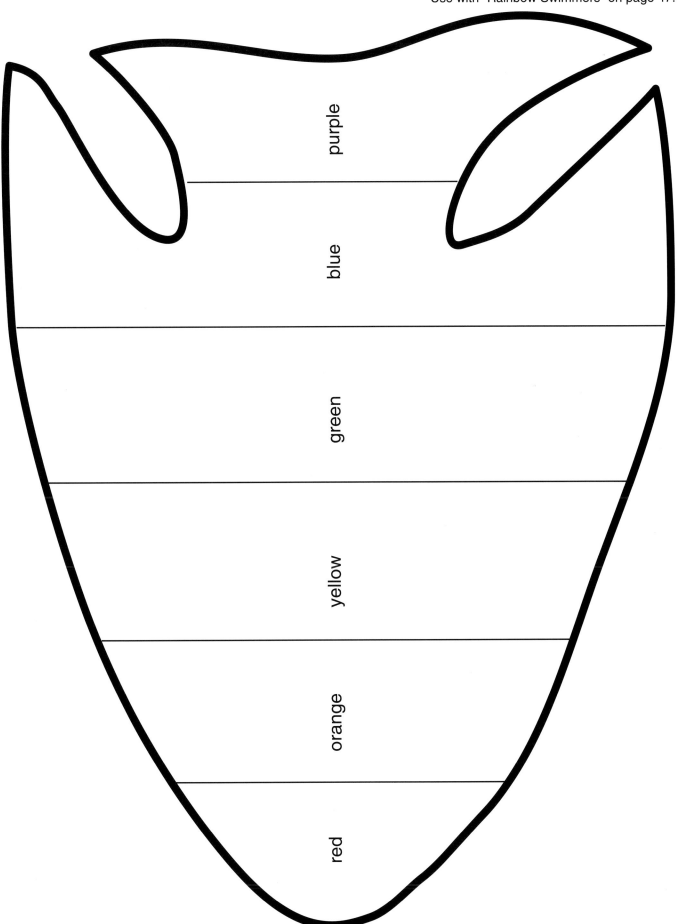

purple

blue

green

yellow

orange

red

Patterns

Use with "Buggy Over Addition!" on page 22.

Ladybug Body
Duplicate one body on black construction
paper for each student.

Ladybug Wings
Duplicate one pair of wings
on red construction paper
for each student.

TEACHER
RESOURCE IDEAS

Hot Off The Press!
Tips For Buddying Up Your Students

Here's the inside scoop: peer teaching makes learning more fun and more meaningful! Whether you pick and choose from this newsworthy collection of tips or you put each suggestion into action, you can count on students giving this learning approach rave reviews.

ideas contributed by Jean Anziano, Angela Lovelett, and Jeannette McCaleb

Buddying Up

Check out this list of ideas for buddying up your youngsters. You may decide to choose one option and carry it out throughout the year. Or if you and your youngsters prefer a bit of variety, try assigning new buddies each grading period.

- Pair each student with a classmate.
- Pair each student with a student from a lower grade.
- Pair each student with a student from an upper grade.
- Pair each student with a child from another classroom on the same grade level.

Getting Acquainted

Before you launch into official activities, plan time for buddies to get to know each other. For a fun icebreaker, distribute student copies of page 55 and have each youngster record his buddy's answers to the questions (or devise a system that works well for your buddying situation). Then have each child illustrate himself and his buddy in the provided boxes. Or, if desired, make two photocopies of each child's school picture and give each child and his buddy a copy to glue in the corresponding box.

Kim Richard

Activities For Buddies

Once buddies get to know each other, they'll be eager to begin peer teaching! The following suggestions will get you started. No doubt you'll have several ideas of your own to add to the list. And there's a good chance that your youngsters will enjoy submitting ideas for buddies' activities, too!

- **Share A Book With Your Buddy:** Ask each student to choose a story to read with or to his buddy.

- **Buddying Up For Spelling:** Set aside time for buddies to complete designated partner activities or have the buddies test each other on their weekly spelling words.

- **Math Counts With Your Buddy:** Math assignments are a cinch when buddies put their heads together! Buddies will also enjoy playing a variety of math-fact games.

- **Lunch Buddies:** Designate one day per week or month for buddies to lunch together. For added variety, arrange for the lunchers to dine in unique locations like the library or principal's office. Or decorate a corner of the lunchroom especially for this purpose. A tablecloth, placemats, a seasonal centerpiece, and a buddy can turn an ordinary lunch into a special occasion!

- **Hey, Buddy! What's Cookin'?:** Periodically provide an easy-to-make, no-cook recipe for buddies to prepare. Two tasty choices are Friendship Fruit Salad and Best Buddy Banana Splits.

- **Buddy Biographies:** Have each student write, illustrate, and publish a biography about his buddy. Vary this idea to best suit your buddying situation.

- **Buddy Book Exchange:** Every now and then, hold a book and magazine swap for buddies. A few days before each exchange, send a letter to parents informing them of the event.

The Classroom Times

Read All About My New Buddy!

This is me.

This is my buddy whom I am interviewing.

1. What is your full name? _____

2. Is this your first year at this school? _____

3. Where were you born? _____

4. When is your birthday? _____

5. How many people and pets are in your family? _____

   _____

6. What is your favorite thing to do? _____

7. What is your favorite food? _____

8. What person do you admire the most? _____

   Why do you admire this person? _____

   _____

9. What is your best subject in school? _____

10. What would you like to learn in school this year? _____

    _____

Note To Teacher: Use with "Getting Acquainted" on page 54.

Hosting A Student Teacher
Can Be As Easy As 1, 2, 3!

Count on a positive experience hosting a student teacher with these teacher-tested tips! From preparing youngsters for the intern's arrival to saying "Farewell," this handy collection of ideas adds up to success!

Meet My Class!

Lights, camera, action! A picture is worth a thousand words, so why not introduce youngsters to your student teacher with a video letter? At least a week before the student teacher begins, videotape each student stating his name and sharing some information about himself and the school. Be sure to take a turn telling about yourself too. View the completed videotape with your young stars; then send it to your student teacher. What a great opportunity for her to become acquainted with the students and get a head start on learning their names!

Betsy Crosson—Gr. 2
Pleasant School, Tulare, CA

"Hand-y" Tote Bag

This welcome gift is sure to be a hands-down favorite! First decorate a plain canvas tote bag. To do this, apply fabric paint to each student's palm and have her carefully make her handprint on the bag. Then have each student use a fabric marker to sign her name near her handprint. Fill the decorated bag with a variety of teaching goodies—such as a lesson-plan book, stickers, decorative notepads, and grading pens—and then present the bag to your student teacher. No doubt she will appreciate the convenience of having these materials on hand!

Kelly A. Lu—Gr. 2, Berlyn School, Ontario, CA

Roll Out The Banner!

Set the stage for the arrival of your student teacher with this decorative class project! On a long, narrow sheet of bulletin-board paper, write a welcome message in large, block letters. Or use a computer to design and print a jumbo banner. Ask youngsters to take turns coloring or painting the letters. Have each youngster personalize the project; then add a note from the class and your signature. Display the completed banner in a prominent classroom location. Now that's a king-sized welcome!

Teresa A. DeMatties—Gr. 2
Walberta Park School
Syracuse, NY

Student Teacher Of The Week

What better way to acquaint youngsters with the student teacher than by featuring him as Student *Teacher* Of The Week? With your students' permission, take a week off from your existing Student-Of-The-Week program to feature your intern. During his first week, ask the newcomer to bring to school a few items, such as family photos and favorite books. Using your established Student-Of-The-Week format or a modified version, have the student teacher share and display these special items. With this ice-breaking activity, youngsters will soon feel at ease with your intern. Plus he will feel honored to have had a turn in the spotlight!

Julie Davenport—Gr. 1
W. A. Wright Elementary
Mt. Juliet, TN

Welcome, Miss Perry!

Dear Miss Perry,
Hi! My name is Tanya. I really like math. I can't wait to meet you!
Sincerely,
Tanya

Welcome Book

First-day introductions will be a snap with this letter-perfect class book! Have each youngster write a letter to the anticipated student teacher, leaving space for an illustration or a photograph of himself. Encourage each student to include information in his letter about his family, friends, interests, and/or favorite subjects. After each child has taped to his letter a photo of himself (or drawn and colored a self-portrait), bind the completed projects and a welcome letter from you between student-decorated covers. Surprise your student teacher with this special keepsake on her first day. The intern will no doubt appreciate (and enjoy!) this directory of student information!

Debbie Fly—Gr. 3
Edgewood School
Homewood, AL

Welcome-Book Variation

For a high-tech variation of the welcome-book project on this page, have each student type his letter using a word-processing program such as ClarisWorks®. Take his picture with a digital camera; then insert the picture into his letter.

LeAnn Knoeck—Grs. K–5 Learning Disabilities
Taft Elementary
Neenah, WI

Everything You Need To Know About...

Put your student teacher in the know with a student-made handbook! Have students brainstorm important information about their school as you record their ideas. Then ask each youngster to select a fact from the list to describe and illustrate on drawing paper. Bind the completed pages and title the resulting handbook "Everything You Need To Know About [school name]." Invite student volunteers to decorate the front and back covers of the book. Present this unique handbook of school-related information to the student teacher on her first day.

Teresa A. DeMatties—Gr. 2
Walberta Park School
Syracuse, NY

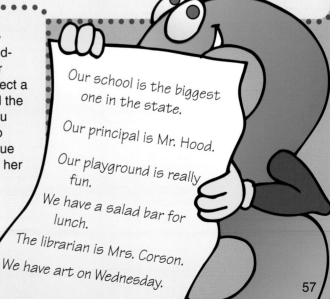

Our school is the biggest one in the state.

Our principal is Mr. Hood.

Our playground is really fun.

We have a salad bar for lunch.

The librarian is Mrs. Corson.

We have art on Wednesday.

Take Note!

These toe-tapping tunes are guaranteed to make your student teacher smile! Have youngsters greet her with the first song shown. Then, at the end of her student-teaching experience, have students sing the second tune. These "class-y" songs are sure to bring rave reviews!

Welcome Song
(Tune: "Jingle Bells" chorus)

[Name],
[Name],
We welcome you today!
We're glad you've come to join our class.
We hope you'll like your stay!

[Name],
[Name],
What fun we'll have with you!
We love to read; we love to write.
We hope you'll like it too!
Hey!

Farewell Song
(Tune: "Jingle Bells" chorus)

[Name],
[Name],
Good luck and good-bye!
Oh, what fun we've had with you—
We think we just might cry!

[Name],
[Name],
Bet you just can't wait
To have a class of your very own.
You will do just great!
Hey!

Kathi Delp—Gr. 2
Paterson Elementary
Orange Park, FL

Home, Sweet Home

Here's a thoughtful idea that will make your student teacher feel right at home! Designate a desk (or table) for his use only and stock it with a decorative teacher's mug; a pencil cup; and a basket full of school supplies, such as scissors, tape, glue, chalk, and pens. Be sure to add a nametag to the desk too. Your student teacher will appreciate having his own space and teaching supplies!

Teresa A. DeMatties—Gr. 2
Walberta Park School
Syracuse, NY

Pack Up For Recess!

It's important to be prepared when duty calls—recess duty, that is! Give your student teacher a helping hand by assembling a recess-supply kit for her. Fill a fanny pack with important items, such as first-aid supplies, office passes, and a pencil. Then use a length of cord or heavy string to attach a whistle to the zipper pull. Your student teacher will be packed up and ready for recess in a jiffy!

Betsy Crosson—Gr. 2
Pleasant School
Tulare, CA

Scheduling Savvy

Looking for a way to communicate the responsibilities your intern can expect? Try this weekly timetable! With your student teacher's input, establish a weekly schedule that outlines her duties during the practicum. Then make a copy of the schedule for the student teacher and file the original for future reference. With this plan, your intern will know what to anticipate and she can prepare accordingly!

Lu Brunnemer—Gr. 1
Eagle Creek Elementary, Indianapolis, IN

Schedule: First Four Weeks

Student Teacher: Jane Brown
Cooperating Teacher: Mrs. Brunnemer

Week 1: Observe, small-group work

Week 2: Lead calendar, transport students to specials, teach math

Week 3: Teach science and social studies lessons

Week 4: Team teach language arts all week

58

Observation

Student Teacher: Joe
Lesson: Place Value
Date: December 7

Strengths	Opportunities To Grow	Plan
met curriculum objectives hands-on student interaction	on-task behavior assessment	1. Circulate among all students. 2. Specify student expectations.

Ms. McGregor
Classroom Teacher

Joe Murray
Student Teacher

Optimal Observations

This tip provides your student teacher with accurate and prompt feedback about his teaching. Create a form like the one shown. Each time you watch your student teacher conduct a lesson, list the strengths and opportunities for growth you observed on a copy of the form. Then review your notes with the student teacher. Together select one or two areas from the second column to address the following day. Brainstorm specific strategies for these areas and record them in the third column. After you have both signed the form, make a copy for your files. Repeat this observation process on a regular basis. When it's time to write an evaluation of your student teacher, the feedback forms will be a handy reference.

Ann McGregor—Gr. 2
Emily Carr Public School
London, Ontario, Canada

Photo Opportunities

Plan to take lots of photos of your student teacher as she works with youngsters. Countless ideas and projects can develop! For example:
- Use the photos to create student-made language-experience books.
- Display the photos with student-written captions on a classroom or hallway bulletin board.
- Feature the photos and other classroom mementos in a scrapbook for the student teacher.
- Make a farewell photo album and present it to the student teacher on her last day.
- Present the student teacher with a set of photos that she can use in a professional portfolio.

Debbie McAuley—Gr. 2
Albany Avenue School
North Massapequa, NY

Valuable Viewpoints

Use a two-step feedback process to establish clear communication with your student teacher. Each day as your student teacher conducts a lesson, record your observation notes in two columns labeled as follows: "What Went Well" and "Suggestions For Future Lessons." After the lesson, have the student teacher reflect upon the teaching experience and note her thoughts in these areas: "What Went Well," "Things I'd Like To Change," and "Goals." At the end of the day, meet with the student teacher and compare your observations with her notes. Focus on positive aspects of the observed lesson; then discuss her goals and possible strategies for reaching them. Lastly, photocopy your observations and her notes so that each of you can file one set for future reference. This ongoing feedback will be a priceless part of the student-teaching experience!

Teresa DeMatties—Gr. 2
Walberta Park School
Syracuse, NY

A Few Extra

Extra reproducibles can add up to a fantastic student-teacher gift! Decorate and label a large box with your student teacher's name. Then place the box in the teachers' workroom near the copier. Post a note asking each teacher to place in the box an extra copy of each item she duplicates. (Also request that the teacher write her name and/or room number on the back of each copy.) Give the student teacher this box of reproducibles during the last week of her practicum. If she has a question about any page, she can ask the teacher who donated it. Now that's a simple and inexpensive way to gather a large assortment of teaching materials!

Maryann Chern Bannwart—Gr. 3
Antietam Elementary
Woodbridge, VA

Weekly Surprise

Keep morale high with small, inspirational gifts! Each week surprise your student teacher with an inexpensive gift, such as a notepad with a humorous preprinted message, a candy bar, or a pack of stickers. Your thoughtful gestures are sure to put a smile on his face!

Lana Stewart—Gr. 2
Wills Point Primary School
Wills Point, TX

Student-Teacher Shower

Surprise your student teacher with a farewell shower! In a note to parents, invite each student to bring a small shower gift to school. Suggest inexpensive items that the student teacher could use in a classroom, such as markers, stickers, and notepads. Next prepare a personalized carpenter's apron for her by writing her name on the front pocket with a fabric marker. Then have students use colorful fabric markers to sign the apron. Lastly, fill the apron pockets with the donated teaching tools. Present the apron and any remaining gifts to the student teacher on her last day in your classroom. Without a doubt, she'll put these tools of the trade to good use!

Margo Stocker—Gr. 3
Tonda Elementary
Canton, MI

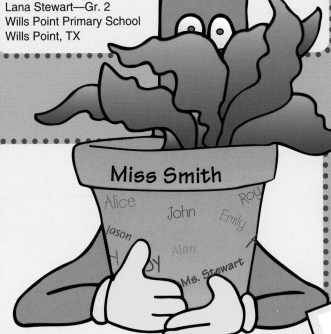

Farewell Flower

Thankful thoughts and good wishes will bloom with this "plant-astic" good-bye gift! On the rim of a clay flowerpot, use a paint pen or permanent marker to write your student teacher's name. Then have each youngster sign his name on the pot with a colorful permanent marker. Be sure to add your signature too. Transplant a small flower or other greenery into the signed pot, and present this unique memento to the student teacher on her last day.

Lana Stewart—Gr. 2

Literary Gift

The end of your intern's practicum marks a new beginning for him. On his last day, honor him with an oral reading of *Oh, The Places You'll Go!* by Dr. Seuss (Random House Books For Young Readers, 1993). This humorous, inspirational book is packed with zany characters and situations, as well as pearls of wisdom about choices and setbacks. As a class, discuss several situations described in the book. Then add an inscription to the book and give it to your student teacher. With this remembrance in hand, you can be certain that he'll be "off to Great Places!"

Kathi Delp—Gr. 2
Paterson Elementary, Orange Park, FL

Keepsake Notebook

Keep this class project top secret—until your student teacher's last day, that is! Without your intern's knowledge, have each student describe and illustrate a special memory of his time with the student teacher. Place each student's completed page in a three-ring view binder and slip a class photo in the binder's cover. Add a title page and a good-bye message that has been autographed by students. Your student teacher will cherish this notebook of memories!

Kathi Delp—Gr. 2

LITERATURE UNITS

Kickin' Up Your Heels With Lilly!

Looking for a fresh way to boost self-esteem and create an understanding of individual differences? Look no further! We've rounded up Lilly, the spunky heroine of *Lilly's Purple Plastic Purse,* to help you out. Her irrepressible and irresistible ways clearly demonstrate the value of understanding and believing in oneself and in others.

ideas by Mackie Rhodes

Read about Lilly in these three books by Kevin Henkes!

Chester's Way
Greenwillow Books, 1988

Julius, The Baby Of The World
Morrow Junior Books, 1995

Lilly's Purple Plastic Purse
Greenwillow Books, 1996

Getting To Know Lilly

Usher youngsters into Lilly's world with a quick character study. Read aloud the three books in which Lily appears (see the list on this page). At the conclusion of each book, write the title of the book and your youngsters' observations about Lilly on a sheet of chart paper. Then, as a class, evaluate the three completed lists and discuss ways in which Lilly is the same (different) in each story.

Next use the completed lists to help students learn more about themselves and their classmates. To do this read aloud selected observations. Beside each one, make a red tally mark for every student who thinks the remark describes himself, a blue tally mark for every student who thinks it does not, and a green tally mark for each student who is unsure. By the end of this activity, students will know a lot about Lilly, themselves, and their classmates!

Lilly's Way

Students will quickly assess that Lilly has her own way of doing things! By the conclusion of *Chester's Way,* Chester and Wilson realize that they should not judge Lilly just because she does things differently than they do. In fact, the two friends discover that learning new things from Lilly is loads of fun. Ask students to recall things that Lilly does her own way. Emphasize that it is not unusual for people to have special ways of doing things; then share a few of your own personal preferences for your students' enjoyment. Next invite youngsters to share their unique habits with this getting-acquainted activity. Begin a rhythmic knee-and-hand clap; then recite the chant shown, naming each child in turn to give a response. If desired, repeat the activity several times so that students can learn more about each other—and themselves!

Hey! Hey!
What do you say?
[Child's name], name something
That you do your own way.

Being Brave

In *Chester's Way,* Lilly doesn't need to advertise her bravery with a barrage of bandages—but that is just her way! Ask students to name ways Lilly shows courage. Ideas might include asking Chester and Wilson to play *(Chester's Way)* and admitting to Mr. Slinger that she had made a big mistake *(Lilly's Purple Plastic Purse).* Also challenge students to think about times they looked, felt, or acted brave. For a fun follow-up activity, have each student illustrate herself engaged in a moment of bravery. Then have her describe this special moment on a colorful copy of the badge pattern from page 66. Finally ask each student to cut out her badge and attach it to her illustration. Invite each child to share her completed work with the class before you display the projects on a bulletin board titled "Lilly's Brave And So Are We!"

Boot-Scootin' Similarities

In this activity students kick up similarities among themselves and their classmates—and do a bit of writing, to boot! Remind students that once Lilly, Chester, and Wilson become acquainted *(Chester's Way),* they learn they have a lot in common. Predict that your youngsters share plenty of similarities too! To find out, pair students and ask each twosome to create a joint list of likes and dislikes. Then give each twosome a pair of red paper boots and two white stars (patterns on page 66). Each pair selects one like and one dislike from its list; then each partner uses the same words to describe these similarities on a boot pattern. Each partner also writes his name on a star pattern. Next each partner cuts out the two patterns that he programmed and glues his star pattern to the blank side of his boot cutout.

Set aside time for the partners to share their projects with the class. Then collect the projects, laminate them for durability, and place them in a center along with directions for playing a Concentration-type game such as Memory.

Thinking Through Comments

Lilly learns firsthand the effects of hurtful actions and comments. Discuss with students how Lilly must have felt in *Chester's Way* when Chester and Wilson try to avoid and ignore her. Then talk about Lilly's reaction in *Julius, The Baby Of The World* when her cousin says mean things about her new baby brother. Help students realize that hurtful actions and comments are unkind, unfair, and unnecessary, and that they reflect poorly on the people who say them. Next ask students to express how they feel when they say or receive positive comments. Lead youngsters to understand the positive benefits of these types of actions and remarks. You can provide each child a chance to share and receive plenty of positive observations with a chair of honor. Position the chair in an open area of your classroom. Then, over several days, invite each child to take a turn sitting in the special chair. While the student is seated there, ask each of her classmates in turn to make a positive observation about her. Now that's a fun and easy way to build your students' self-esteem!

Susan Clark and Michele Kivitt—Gr. 3
Centre City School
Mantua, NJ

A Green-Eyed Lilly

Lilly's experiences in *Julius, The Baby Of The World* are the perfect springboard for a discussion about feelings of jealousy. Help students recall that Lilly becomes increasingly more jealous of the attention and affection bestowed upon her new baby brother. Explain that feeling jealous in this circumstance is natural. Then take a class poll to find out if your youngsters believe Lilly handled her jealous feelings in acceptable ways. Prompt students to offer suggestions for dealing with jealous feelings. Wrap up the discussion by emphasizing that feeling jealous is completely natural. However, to get along well with others, a person must learn to deal with jealous feelings without being hurtful to others.

For a fun hands-on exploration of jealousy, try this! Have each child fashion a handheld pair of spectacles like the ones shown from two green pipe cleaners. As students practice viewing through their green-rimmed glasses, tell them that the term *green-eyed* is used to describe a person who has jealous feelings. Then, in turn, invite each student to view through his spectacles as he tells the class about a time when he felt green-eyed or jealous. Next ask him to lower his glasses and explain how he coped (or would now cope) with these feelings. Suggest that each child take his green-rimmed glasses home as a reminder of the dos and don'ts of feeling jealous.

The Students Of The World

Boost your youngsters' self-esteems with this goal-setting project! Begin the activity by asking students to recall the events of *Julius, The Baby Of The World*. Then ask them to imagine how Lilly might have felt if her parents had recognized her in another special way—perhaps by calling her "the sister of the world." Discuss the positive feelings associated with being recognized for a job well done. Then challenge each child to set a school-related goal that will make him feel good about himself and earn him a bit of recognition too!

Label a length of bulletin-board paper "The Students Of The World," add a decorative border, and display the resulting poster in a prominent location. Then have each student write his goal (like "reading 15 minutes each night for a month" or "learning to count to 100 by twos") and three ways to accomplish his goal on a form like the one shown. Ask each child to take his form home and post it on the family refrigerator. When a student meets his goal, he records the date of his accomplishment on his form and presents the form to you. With great fanfare, initial the form. Then present the student with a colorful star to personalize (enlarge the pattern on page 66 for this purpose). Mount the star on "The Students Of The World" poster. Encourage each student to repeat the procedure several times, setting a new goal each time. Before long there will be a slew of stars on the poster, which can only mean one thing: "The Students Of The World" are living up to their new name!

adapted from an idea by Beverly Sperry Bippes—Gr. 1
Humphrey Public School
Humphrey, NE

Name _Millie_
My goal is _to learn my subtraction facts._

Three ways to meet this goal are:
1. _Practice a lot_
2. _Do my homework_
3. _Eat cheese so I feel good_
Date goal was met: _____
Teacher's initials: _____

From Anger To Apology

In *Lilly's Purple Plastic Purse,* Lilly lets her angry feelings get the best of her, only to later regret what she has done! There's a good chance that every youngster in your classroom has experienced something similar. Encourage students to analyze Lilly's emotions and actions. Also talk with students about why it was necessary for Mr. Slinger to take Lilly's purse. Next have students contemplate Lilly's shift of emotions when her purse is returned and she discovers Mr. Slinger's kind and understanding gestures. Then invite students to comment on the positive actions that Lilly took to correct the situation she created. Finally ask each child to think of a time that he acted out in anger and later felt remorseful for his actions. On the chalkboard, write "Ooh! I felt mad when _____. Then I felt sorry because _____. Now I know _____." Invite interested students to tell about their experiences by orally completing the provided sentences. In conclusion, commend the youngsters for having the insight to learn from their own experiences!

Impressive Folks

Lilly's experience with her purple plastic purse taught her that she can learn even more than she thought from her teacher, Mr. Slinger. Remind students that Lilly was very wowed by Mr. Slinger—so much so that she wanted to follow in his footsteps and become a teacher. Then ask them to cite qualities in Mr. Slinger that they also find impressive. Next ask each youngster to think of a person he admires, then consider why he admires this person and what he hopes to learn from him or her.

Next have each child create a page for a class book titled "Our Role Models." Give each child a sheet of drawing paper that is programmed with the interjection "Wow!" as shown. A student writes the name of his chosen person at the top of the page; then he illustrates this person inside the letter "O." Next he writes a list of this person's special qualities followed by a list of personal goals that will help him learn from this positive role model. Bind the students' completed pages (and a page completed by you) between desired book covers. As students page through this class book, they're sure to be impressed!

I Am Me!

Your youngsters are certain to agree that Lilly is self-confident and comfortable with her uniqueness. And hopefully the time they've spent learning about Lilly will have helped your students feel similarly about themselves. Culminate this collection of self-esteem ideas with a one-of-a-kind poster project. First have each child think about his own unique personality and make a list of his special characteristics. To make a poster, a student creates a self-likeness and mounts it in the center of a large sheet of tagboard (see "Personality Plus" on page 36 for easy-to-follow directions for creating individual self-likenesses). Next he uses colorful markers or crayons to title his project "I Am The Best That I Can Be, Because I'm Me!" and to write—graffiti style—the special characteristics that he listed earlier. After each child has shared his poster with his classmates, display the projects in an "I Am Me!" classroom gallery.

Dr. Miller   Troy

WOW!

Dr. Miller's special qualities:
- He is nice.
- He is smart.
- He helps others.

My goals:
- I will be nice to my classmates.
- I will study very hard.
- I will help my mom and my brother with cho...

I Am The Best That I Can Be,
Because I'm Me!

likes bubble gum

loves to read

has a cute pink nose

can outrun fat kitty cats

helps at home

likes to laugh

is very friendly

Mary Lester

Patterns

Use the badge pattern with "Being Brave" on page 63.

Enlarge the star pattern to use it with "The Students Of The World" on page 64.

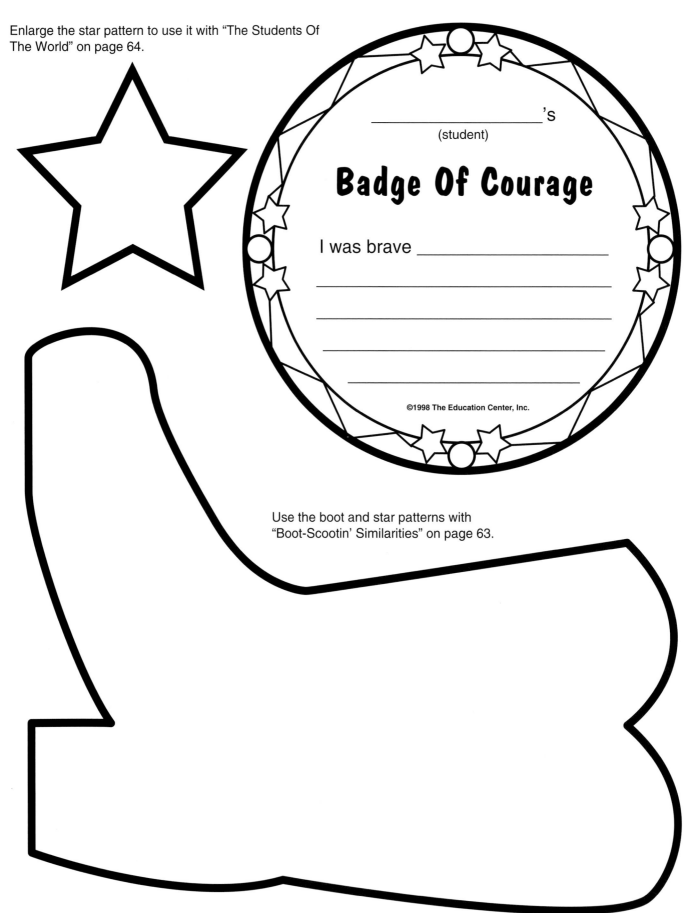

_____'s
(student)

Badge Of Courage

I was brave _____

_____

_____

_____

_____

©1998 The Education Center, Inc.

Use the boot and star patterns with "Boot-Scootin' Similarities" on page 63.

Harry's Mad

Written by Dick King-Smith • Illustrated by Jill Bennett
(Alfred A. Knopf Books For Young Readers, 1997)

Harry Holdsworth's day isn't off to the greatest start. In less than a minute he's stepped on the cat's tail, sent his family's breakfast flying, and had the breath knocked out of him! What could top all that? How about notification that a great-uncle from America has passed away and mentioned Harry in his will? Full of surprises, this lighthearted read-aloud will entertain your youngsters (and you!) until the very last page is read.

ideas by Stacie Stone Davis

About The Author

It makes perfect sense that England is the setting for *Harry's Mad*—after all, that's where the book's author, Dick King-Smith, was born, was raised, and still resides. King-Smith entered the field of children's publishing after spending 20 years farming and six years teaching. Both professions greatly impact his writing. His love of animals is indisputable, as is his success at creating stories that can be enjoyed by both youngsters and adults. King-Smith has earned numerous awards for his writing, and *Harry's Mad* is no exception. Honors for this book include An ALA Notable Children's Book, A *School Library Journal* Best Book of the Year, and the *Parent's Choice* Award for Literature. Perhaps King-Smith's most well-known book to date is *Babe: The Gallant Pig,* which became a major award-winning motion picture.

Some Little Keepsake

Harry's imagination goes wild when he learns that his great-uncle George has passed away and left him something! Could it be a private jet? A custom-built Cadillac? A treasure chest teeming with jewels? Taking care to not reveal the cover of the book, read aloud most of chapter 1—stopping right after Mr. Holdsworth discloses that Harry is to receive his great-uncle's most cherished possession. Then challenge students to guess Harry's inheritance with a game of 20 Questions. If the class has not identified Harry's inheritance after 20 yes/no questions have been answered, reveal that Harry is inheriting a parrot! Before you begin chapter 2, have students ponder what in the world could be so special about Harry's new pet!

Chapter 2
Madison arrives. At first Harry is not very excited. But Madison seems nice, and that makes Harry happy. Harry thinks Madison talks to him!
by Keri and Max

Chapter By Chapter

This easy-to-manage project produces an easy-to-read class version of *Harry's Mad*. At the conclusion of each chapter initiate a discussion about the chapter's main events. Also ask students to suggest illustrations that could accompany the chapter. Then appoint two children to work together to write and illustrate a summary of the chapter. During your oral reading of the story, display the illustrated chapter summaries in sequential order. At the conclusion of the story, bind the sequenced summaries between student-illustrated covers and place the resulting book in your classroom library. Now there's a version of *Harry's Mad* that students can read again and again!

Brenda Gianotti—Gr. 1, Chatterton School, Merrick, NY

What They Learned About Mad

Harry	Mum	Dad

Getting To Know Mad

It doesn't take long for the Holdsworth family to change its opinion about Mad. Help students understand how this change unfolds with the following project. To begin, a student folds a 12" x 18" sheet of drawing paper in half (to 9" x 12"), keeping the fold at the top of the project. Next he visually divides, labels, and illustrates the front of his folded paper so that it resembles the project shown. Each child then creates three flaps by cutting along the two parallel lines. Underneath each flap, the student lists reasons why that character's opinion of Mad changes. In conclusion ask students to talk about times their opinions of someone or something have changed. Lead students to understand that first opinions (or impressions) are based on limited information. As more information is gathered, these opinions often change.

Stolen Bird!

When Mad is stolen from the Holdsworths' home, Mr. Holdsworth makes every possible effort to find him. This includes placing numerous ads in the newspaper and calling every London pet shop. Ask students to brainstorm other ways Mr. Holdsworth might try to find Mad, like going on television or displaying Missing Bird posters around the city. Also discuss as a class why Mr. Holdsworth cannot reveal Mad's very special qualities. Then, working in pairs, have the students prepare speeches or posters that they feel will help find Mad. Set aside time for each pair to share its plea with the class.

Missing Parrot

A very smart parrot named Madison

Loves American brownies

His family misses him.

REWARD! Call 123-4567.

Caring For A Special Pet

Being a pet owner is a major responsibility, especially if the pet is a parrot named Mad! Share the provided pointers for caring for an ordinary pet parrot. Then, on a copy of page 69, have each child write directions for taking care of Harry's Mad. Use the completed pages to assess how well your youngsters are understanding the story.

To extend the activity, have each youngster write and illustrate a story about a time when Mad comes to stay with his family. Suggest that each student title his story "A Visit From Mad."

A pet parrot needs:
- a clean, warm cage that is large enough in which to exercise
- foods such as seeds and fruit
- fresh air
- plenty of water

A Mad Celebration!

At the conclusion of the book, celebrate Mad's homecoming *and* his impending fatherhood with a Mad About Mad party. Plan to serve one of Mad's favorite treats—American brownies. Also provide several of Mad's favorite things to do like crossword puzzles to solve, and board games like Monopoly® to play, and *draughts* (checkers) to play. For added fun, invite students to submit boys' and girls' names for Mad and Fweddy's first offspring. Everyone is sure to have a jolly good time!

Name ______________________________

Taking Care Of Mad

In each category, describe the special needs of Mad.
Remember! Mad is a very special parrot.

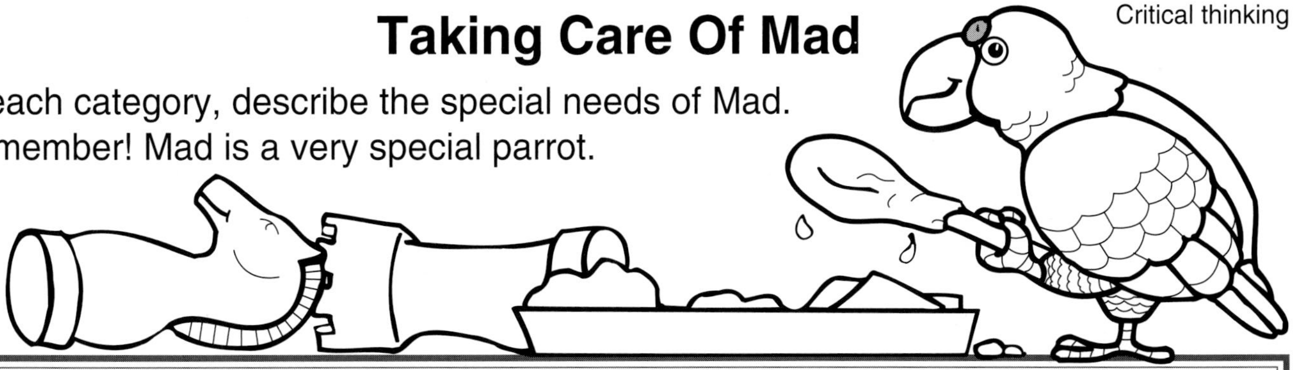

Food: ______________________________

____

____

Living Area: ______________________________

____

____

Entertainment: ______________________________

____

____

____

____

Other: ______________________________

____

____

____

____

Bonus Box: On the back of this paper, draw and color a picture of Mad doing something that an ordinary pet parrot could not do.

Note To Teacher: Use with "Caring For A Special Pet" on page 68.

The Underground Railroad

Former slave Harriet Tubman became the driving force of the Underground Railroad—a network of hiding places and forest trails that led slaves to free northern states and eventually into Canada. There were no rails for the runaways to follow, just the North Star and plenty of tracks and trails. Along the way an occasional lantern or quilt signaled a house where safety, shelter, and food awaited them. The books in this collection tell tales of Harriet Tubman and other brave Americans who traveled and conducted along the Underground Railroad.

by Njeri Jones and Deborah Zink Roffino

Minty: A Story Of Young Harriet Tubman
Written by Alan Schroeder & Illustrated by Jerry Pinkney
Dial Books For Young Readers, 1996

Tender and emotional watercolor illustrations introduce readers to Minty, a spunky and headstrong eight-year-old who holds a special dream tucked inside her heart. For Harriet Tubman's own escape from slavery, and to engineer the freedom of so many others, she needed ingenuity and countless survival skills. This fictional account of her childhood, which is based on extensive research, suggests ways she may have acquired the skills she needed to free herself, and hundreds of others, from slavery.

It took many, many years before Minty's dream came true, but she never gave up! Minty was about 29 years old and known as Harriet Tubman when she finally made her daring escape from the Brodas plantation. Share this information at the conclusion of the book; then draw the outline of a large sunflower on the chalkboard. Remind students how Minty pretended to be a sunflower when no one was looking. Then use the sunflower sketch to show students how Minty kept her dream alive for all those years. To do this, write Minty's wish—"To Escape!"—in the flower center. Next ask students to recall ways that Minty worked toward her dream. Write these ideas on the petals. When each petal is programmed, help students understand that working toward a dream is the best way to make it come true. Then have each child draw an outline of a large sunflower on a 12" x 18" sheet of drawing paper. Ask each child to write his dream in the center of the flower, how he is working toward the dream in the flower petals, and his name inside a leaf outline. Suggest that each student use crayons to outline his drawing and create desired background scenery. Display the projects on a bulletin board titled "Our Field Of Dreams!"

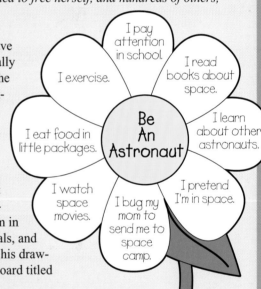

Be An Astronaut
- I pay attention in school.
- I read books about space.
- I learn about other astronauts.
- I pretend I'm in space.
- I bug my mom to send me to space camp.
- I watch space movies.
- I eat food in little packages.
- I exercise.

More Books About Harriet Tubman

A Picture Book Of Harriet Tubman
Written by David A. Adler & Illustrated by Samuel Byrd
Holiday House, Inc.; 1993

Born more than forty years before the Civil War, Harriet Tubman possessed a powerful love for her people and for freedom. This biography touches upon her years as a slave, her perilous escape, her numerous trips as a conductor on the Underground Railroad, and her duties as a nurse during the Civil War. Readers also learn of Harriet's work after the war, which included helping to establish a home in New York State for impoverished Black Americans. Memorable acrylic paintings accent the highlights of Harriet's ninety-plus years.

Harriet Tubman
A Photo-Illustrated Biography
Written by Margo McLoone
Capstone Press, 1997

Divided into 9 one-page chapters, each with an accompanying full-page black-and-white photograph, this beginner's biography is perfect for the primary classroom. After a brief introduction to the brave conductor, readers are presented with an overview of Tubman's life that focuses on key events and accomplishments. The final page of the book features a brief bibliography, useful addresses, Internet sites, and an index.

Aunt Harriet's Underground Railroad In The Sky

Written & Illustrated by Faith Ringgold
Crown Publishers, Inc.; 1995

Ringgold's celebrated folk art takes readers to the skies for an imaginative blend of fact and fantasy. Flying high among the stars, Cassie and her brother Be Be learn about the Underground Railroad and discover why Black American slaves were willing to risk their lives for freedom. The dream sequence, which is conducted by Harriet Tubman herself, is based on Tubman's dream of flying to freedom.

At the conclusion of this story, ask students to recall events from Cassie's trip on the Underground Railroad. Encourage students to tell what they learned about slavery, Harriet Tubman, and the series of trails and hiding places called the Underground Railroad. Then, in celebration of the Underground Railroad and the freedom that it brought to hundreds of slaves, have your students create a class Freedom Train. First ask students to brainstorm symbols of freedom and describe benefits of living in a free country. List the students' ideas on the chalkboard. Then ask each child to choose one idea from the list to illustrate and write a brief caption about on a 9" x 12" sheet of drawing paper. Next have each child trim two 3-inch squares of black construction paper into circles and glue the resulting train wheels near the bottom of his project. Display the train cars, connected by 1" x 4" strips of black paper (hitches), along a classroom wall. Add engine and caboose cutouts, and this freedom train—packed with precious cargo—is ready to spread the word about liberty and justice for all!

Follow The Drinking Gourd: A Story Of The Underground Railroad

Written by Bernardine Connelly
Illustrated by Yvonne Buchanan
Rabbit Ears Books, 1997

This riveting tale recounts one family's treacherous journey along the Underground Railroad. Dependent upon the North Star and other natural landmarks for guidance, the runaways flee through unfamiliar and unfriendly forests. Engaging text and luminous water-color illustrations hold listeners hostage between fear and hope. A compact disc, featuring a resonant retelling of the tale by actor Morgan Freeman, accompanies the book.

Natural landmarks and constellations guide 11-year-old Mary, her brother, and their mother along the Underground Railroad to freedom. Take this opportunity to familiarize students with the Big Dipper, the Little Dipper, and the North Star. Draw a simple sketch of the project (above) on the chalkboard or on an overhead transparency. Begin by having each child use a white crayon to label the perimeter of an eight-inch black construction-paper circle with the name of the four seasons. To check his work, have each child rotate his cutout counterclockwise at one-quarter-turn intervals to be sure the seasons are in correct order. Next give each child 1 large and 13 small self-adhesive foil stars. Have students refer to your diagram to position the stars on their projects; then have them use their white crayons to connect the stars to make the two drinking gourds. By turning their star maps, students can see how the constellations appear in the night sky during each season. Remind students to always look to the north to find the North Star!

Allen Jay And
The Underground Railroad

Written by Marlene Targ Brill
Illustrated by Janice Lee Porter
Carolrhoda Books, Inc.; 1993

When his father is unable to help, young Allen Jay finds the courage to aid a runaway slave. His family's farm is a stop on the Underground Railroad, and the boy's parents, who are Quakers, are secret conductors. It is 11-year-old Allen Jay's first experience as a conductor. The clearly written narrative, seen through the eyes of the heroic young Quaker boy, is based on actual events of the 1840s. Muted pastel illustrations accentuate Allen Jay's gripping story.

Conductors of the Underground Railroad risked their lives to help others whom they felt were being treated unfairly. At the conclusion of this story, have students contemplate the courage that Allen Jay displayed to lend a helping hand to Henry. Also ask students to express feelings Allen Jay may have felt as he shook Henry's hand and wished him a safe trip to Canada. Encourage your youngsters to practice helpful behavior with this follow-up activity. Ask each child to trace the shape of his hand on a sheet of drawing paper, then cut out the resulting shape and label it with his name. Each time a child lends a helping hand throughout the day, he collects the signature of the person whom he helped. At the end of the day he will have a visual reminder of his helpful ways. Before dismissal, invite student volunteers to talk about how it feels knowing that they have helped others that day. If desired, have each child make and label a new cutout to take home and return the following school day. This project is sure to be popular with your youngsters' parents!

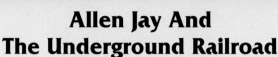

Sweet Clara And
The Freedom Quilt

Written by Deborah Hopkinson
Illustrated by James Ransome
Random House, Inc.; 1995

Based on a true little-known chapter of black history, this powerful picture book tells the story of a young slave girl's plan to map the route of the Underground Railroad. When her last stitch is in place, Sweet Clara has hidden in the squares of her quilt the path that will guide her and many other slaves to freedom. Brightly colored full-page paintings light up the pages of this inspirational tale.

Clara stitches her dreams for the future into a quilt that helps her and others. After reading the story to students and discussing it with them, ask each child to think of a dream that he has for the future that others will benefit from as well. Then have each student illustrate his dream on a six-inch square of white construction paper. Next have each child glue his artwork in the center of an eight-inch square of colorful construction paper that you have punched with a series of equally spaced holes—four per side. To assemble the quilt, divide students into groups of four. Give each group four 1-foot lengths of yarn to use to stitch the group's projects into one large square. Provide assistance as needed. Then have one student from each group volunteer to help stitch the resulting projects into a desired quilt shape. Display the completed quilt for all to see. Later, after students have had time to study the quilt, ask each child to reveal which quilt patch he designed and talk about his dream for the future.

Barefoot: Escape On The Underground Railroad

Written by Pamela Duncan Edwards
Illustrated by Henry Cole
HarperCollins Publishers, Inc.; 1997

Near the floor of the deep, dark woods, the bare feet of a young man creep softly in a desperate move toward freedom. On this stretch of the Underground Railroad, Barefoot trusts only the sounds of woodland creatures to assist his flight. The croak of a frog means water is near; the cry of a heron echoes danger. Dark and powerful illustrations create a shadowy nighttime world that is filled with fear and uncertainty.

After an initial oral reading of the story, have students recall the things that Barefoot hears as he presses forward along the Underground Railroad. List these items on the chalkboard. Then read the story aloud a second time so students can listen carefully for additional sound makers. Make any needed additions to the class list, and with your youngsters' help, assign a sound effect to each listed item. Next, under your direction, have the class practice each sound effect. Before each sound is made, ask students how hearing that sound on the trail might have made Barefoot feel. Then encourage students to incorporate these feelings into their sound renditions. Finally read the story aloud one more time, this time arranging for a different small group of students to make each sound effect on the list. This journey along the Underground Railroad will leave a lasting impression!

Item	Sound Effect
Barefoot's breath	*(three heavy breaths)*
heron	"skreeeeek, skreeeeek"
Heavy Boots	*(stomp feet three times)*
frog	"ribbit, ribbit, ribbit"
mouse	"nibble, nibble, nibble"
mockingbird	"tra la la, tra la la"
squirrel	"scamper, scamper, scamper"
deer	*(crumpling of paper)*
mosquitoes	"buzz, buzz, buzz"
fireflies	"zing, zing, zing"

Jewels

Written by Belinda Rochelle
Illustrated by Cornelius Van Wright and Ying-Hwa Hu
Lodestar Books, 1998

On a sweet summer's night, rocking on the front porch of her great-grandparents' home, young Lea Mae listens to the story of how her ancestors escaped from slavery. The running, the hunger, the sounds of approaching dogs—and then the mysterious appearance of a small woman who leads Lea's ancestors to safety. Lea's great-grandmother is filled with stories about their heritage—each one a jewel to be treasured forever.

This gentle tale is a shining example of the Black American tradition of storytelling. At the conclusion of the story, ask students if they enjoy hearing stories of long ago. Find out why they think the tradition of passing stories from generation to generation began, and how their lives might be different if the tradition had never been started. Next ask each child to think of a *jewel* from her childhood that she thinks future generations might enjoy hearing and can learn from too! Pair students and have each child tell her story to her partner one or more times. Then invite interested students to share their jewels with the class. In closing, read aloud the final paragraph from the book to remind students that stories must be told to be saved. Encourage students to *save* their childhood jewels and to listen to the stories their family members tell so they can begin saving these jewels, too.

The Gadget War

Written by Betsy Duffey
Illustrated by Janet Wilson
Puffin Books, 1994

Kelly Sparks is an inventor of gadgets—43, to be exact! Her ability to invent gadgets has earned her the title of Gadget Wiz, and she loves it! However, her status is quickly questioned when Albert Einstein Jones joins the class and claims that he is the *real* Gadget Wiz of third grade. Thus begins a war of gadgets, as neither of these two masterminds has any intention of being outinvented!

ideas by Stacie Stone Davis

National Inventors Day

What do Kelly Sparks, Albert Einstein Jones, and Thomas Alva Edison have in common? They are all inventors! Edison's birthday, February 11, is now widely observed as National Inventors Day. On this special day, each inventor who has been selected for induction into the National Inventors Hall of Fame is honored. Plan to read aloud *The Gadget War* during the month of February. Then be sure to set aside time on or around February 11 to honor each of your budding inventors!

Kelly's Capers

It won't take your youngsters long to realize that Kelly's love of inventing lands her in some unique situations! Strengthen comprehension and writing skills by having the students chronicle Kelly's capers in individual lightbulb-shaped journals. To make her journal, a student traces a large lightbulb shape onto two 9" x 12" sheets of yellow construction paper and 12 or more sheets of writing paper. Then she cuts out the shapes, staples the writing pages between the construction-paper covers, and personalizes the front cover as desired. At the conclusion of each chapter, have students summarize in their journals what happens in the chapter and write one-sentence predictions about what might happen next!

The Inventor's Guidebook

Inventors invent for a variety of reasons. But many, like Kelly, invent because they want to solve a problem (or satisfy a need). In the third chapter ("Invent It!!!") Kelly identifies her problem—Albert Einstein Jones! Readers then learn about Kelly's *Inventor's Guidebook* and her three-step inventing process. At the conclusion of the chapter, distribute copies of page 77 and challenge each student to use the step-by-step process to plan an invention. Set aside time for the youngsters to share their invention plans with the class; then hole-punch the papers and insert them in a binder labeled "Room [your room number]'s Inventor's Guidebook." Place the project in the class library for further reading enjoyment. Also make extra copies of page 77 available so that your budding inventors can continue inventing!

Inventor **Matthew Proper**

The Gadget War
Planning an invention

A Step-By-Step Process

1. Describe a problem that needs to be solved. My family is gone during the day, and no one is home to pet our dog, Sofie. I think she gets lonely.

2. Describe an invention that can solve the problem. I think a dog scratcher that we plug in when we left would work. Maybe it would have recorded messages, too!

3. List the materials that are needed to make the invention.

motor	cord to plug in
cord	tape recorder
wooden hand	tape
wooden arm	speaker
on/off switch	

4. Draw the invention. Write its name on the line. The Doggie Scratcher

The Doggie Scratcher

Good dog, Sofie. We love you! See you soon.

I couldn't live without a lamp because I wouldn't be able to read in bed.

I wish shampoo had never been invented because then I wouldn't have to wash my hair.

Evaluating Inventions

No doubt your youngsters will agree with Kelly when she decides that some inventions (like cookies, pencils, and toilet paper) make life better and others (like homework, commercials, and bombs) do not. On the chalkboard write a student-generated list of inventions for each category. Next give each child a yellow lightbulb pattern to cut out. Have each youngster illustrate and label an invention that improves his life on one side of his cutout. Then, on the flip side of his cutout, have him illustrate and label an invention he could live without. After the students have shared their work, collect the cutouts and stack them so that the desirable inventions are facing up. On top of the stack, place a lightbulb-shaped cover titled "Great Inventions." Title a second cover "Not-So-Great Inventions" and place it facedown on the bottom of the stack. Then hole-punch the project and thread it onto a metal or plastic ring. You can count on this class book being read from cover to cover—and back again!

I learned that I shouldn't cut hair!

The worst splat I ever got in was when I tried to cut my sister's hair. It didn't look right so I kept cutting. Soon most of her hair was on the floor. I was grounded for a month!

A Grade-A Mishap

By the end of the fifth chapter ("Gadget Grounded"), Kelly has launched ten eggs to test her food-fight catapult. The first nine miss her target, but the tenth egg is a direct hit! Kelly is ecstatic about her success. Her mother, however, is furious about the messy kitchen! Invite students to think about times that they, like Kelly, have ended up in a "splat" because they used poor judgment. Then have each student describe and illustrate one such incident on story paper. Next have her trim a 5 1/2" x 8 1/2" rectangle of white paper to resemble a splattered egg white and glue a large yellow pom-pom (or paper) yolk in the center. On the egg white, ask her to write a lesson she learned from the incident she has described. Then have her mount her story on construction paper and glue her egg cutout to one corner of the project. Display these eye-catching (and educational!) projects on a bulletin board titled "Grade-A Mishaps!"

Gadgets Galore!

The gadget war really escalates in the eighth chapter ("The *Real Real* Gadget Wiz") when both Kelly and Albert list the war gadgets they have made—or are capable of making. For a fun creative-thinking activity, pair students and challenge each twosome to list as many gadget ideas as they can within a two-minute time period. Invite students to list their own gadget ideas and ideas from the story. Next ask each pair to tell the class about two favorite gadgets on its list. Conclude the activity with a hearty round of applause for the budding inventors!

A Slice Of Advice

Disaster strikes in the ninth chapter ("Whoooooosh!! Squooooosh!!") when Kelly uses her food-fight catapult in the cafeteria to launch an orange half. Instead of hitting Albert, the orange lands on the school principal's head! When the chapter concludes, the principal is determined to find out who has thrown that orange! Give each child a half circle of drawing paper; then tell students to color the curved edge orange so that the cutouts resemble orange slices. Ask each child to think about Kelly's predicament and to write what he thinks Kelly should do and why. Then have each child read aloud his slice of advice. Graph the slices on a quickly drawn class graph, if desired. Then distribute real orange slices before reading aloud the next chapter. Students will discover that the situation becomes even *more* complicated!

> I think Kelly should stand up and say she did it. That way, the principal will be proud of her for being truthful.

Everyone Has Potential

Kelly's favorite word is *potential*. She believes that, like other inventors, she sees the possibility in *things*. However, in the next-to-last chapter ("Dum Dum Dee-Dum"), Kelly realizes that she has stopped seeing the potential in *people*. Have students recall how Kelly learns that Mr. Hardeman is more than just a principal. Then ask students to suggest how Kelly's relationship with Albert would have been different from the start if she'd seen his potential as an inventor and as a friend. In conclusion, challenge students to look for potential in others—and in themselves too!

Peace—At Last!

At the conclusion of the book, Albert and Kelly make peace with one another. Survey students to find out if they believe—like Kelly—that it's nicer to make peace than war. Next ask students to share tips for getting along with others. List their ideas on a length of colorful bulletin-board paper titled "Tips For Getting Along With Others." Display the resulting poster in your classroom. For added appeal, ask each child to illustrate himself on a five-inch square of drawing paper. Showcase the students' drawings around the poster.

Learning About Inventors

An investigation of inventors is a natural follow-up to *The Gadget War.* Ask your school librarian to help you locate books that are about inventors and are appropriate for your students. Have each child complete a copy of page 78 about a chosen inventor and then illustrate the inventor on an 8" x 10" sheet of drawing paper. If desired, have each child glue her work onto a 12" x 18" sheet of colorful construction paper. Be sure to set aside time for students to share their reports with the class.

Inventors To Investigate

Inventor	Invention
Ben Franklin	lightning rod
Elias Howe	sewing machine
Samuel F. B. Morse	telegraph
Garrett Morgan	three-color traffic light
Alexander Graham Bell	telephone
Whitcomb L. Judson	zipper
Ruth Wakefied	chocolate chip
Chester Greenwood	earmuffs
James A. Naismith	game of basketball
Levi Strauss	blue jeans
Earl Dickson	ready-made bandage
Ralph Baer	video game

A Step-By-Step Process

1. Describe a problem that needs to be solved. _____
   _____
   _____
   _____
   _____
   _____
   _____
   _____

2. Describe an invention that can solve the problem. _____
   _____
   _____
   _____
   _____
   _____
   _____
   _____

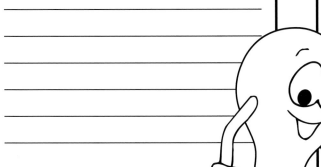

3. List the materials that are needed to make the invention.

   _____   _____   _____

   _____   _____   _____

   _____   _____   _____

   _____   _____   _____

   _____   _____   _____

4. Draw the invention. Write its name on the line.

   _____

Name _____

78

A Famous Inventor

Write about this inventor's work.

_____
_____
_____
_____

Write about this inventor's life.

_____
_____
_____
_____

Inventor's Name

_____

This person is famous for inventing

_____
_____
_____

Write another interesting fact about this inventor.

_____
_____
_____

Describe how this inventor began inventing.

_____
_____
_____

Note To Teacher: Use with "Learning About Inventors" on page 76.

A Slice Of Life

Enjoying Patricia Polacco's Books

Experience one picture book by esteemed author and illustrator Patricia Polacco, and you'll want to experience another and another! Pick and choose from this sampling of Polacco's work and the related classroom activities. In no time at all, you'll feel like a friend of the family!

reviews and ideas contributed by Jan Brennan

Firetalking

Photographs by Lawrence Migdale • Richard C. Owen Publishers, Inc.; 1994

What does Polacco look like? Where does she live? What is a typical day for this author and illustrator extraordinaire? All these questions and plenty more are answered in this 32-page autobiography. Full-color photographs of the author, her family, and her home are especially satisfying. It's a perfect beginning to a study of Patricia Polacco and her books.

There are so many interesting facts presented in this succinct self-portrait, plan to read the book aloud twice. After your initial reading, invite students to recall the things they have learned about the author, her family, and her books. List their ideas on the chalkboard. Then read the book aloud a second time and repeat the exercise. Next have each child choose a different fact from the chalkboard to copy onto a 3" x 12" strip of yellow, red, or orange construction paper. Instruct each child to leave a three-inch margin at the right end of his strip to trim in the shape of a flame. As students are working, remind them of Polacco's fond memories of sitting in front of a warm fire, popping corn, eating apple wedges, and listening to her babushka's wonderful stories. Tell students that you'd like to create warm memories of Patricia Polacco's stories too. To do this, mount a paper fireplace on a class wall where there is ample room for students to sit on the floor near it. Then assist each child in taping his flame inside the fireplace. Mount the title "Firetalking" above the fireplace. When it's time to read aloud a Polacco tale, gather students on the floor in front of the classroom prop, serve a snack of apple wedges or popcorn, and make a memory! After each tale is read, invite students to illustrate their favorite part of the story on provided paper. Display these picture-perfect memories on the fireplace mantel until the next story is shared.

Dream Keeper

Philomel Books, 1996

This engaging video portrait welcomes youngsters into Patricia Polacco's world. Viewers watch her work in her studio; hear her read passages from several of her beloved books, including *Rechenka's Eggs* and *Thunder Cake;* and learn about her childhood, her family, and her sources of inspiration. The 23-minute video is available from the publisher for $39.95 plus tax, shipping, and handling. To order, call toll free, 1-800-526-0275.

Babushka's Doll

Aladdin Paperbacks, 1995

Natasha isn't really a naughty girl; she just doesn't like to wait! And that makes her a very rambunctious gal—just ask Babushka, her grandmother! Then one day Natasha asks to play with Babushka's special doll. Babushka enthusiastically grants the request, for Babushka herself played with this doll just one time, and she knows full well what awaits the youngster!

Natasha learns an important lesson when she spends an afternoon with Babushka's doll—her own behavior stinks! Enlist your students' help in comparing Natasha's behavior at the beginning of the book to the doll's behavior. Then help them understand that once Natasha experiences her own kind of behavior, she realizes how difficult she is to be around. Ask each child to think about her own behavior and the effect that it has on others. Then have her fold a 9" x 12" sheet of drawing paper in half, unfold the paper, and title the resulting halves "Keep" and "Change." Instruct each youngster to describe and illustrate on her paper one behavior she believes she should keep and one behavior she thinks she should change. Encourage students to share their decisions with the people who are most affected by their behavior.

I will keep making my bed each morning.

I think I should stop throwing my clothes on the floor.

Some Birthday!

Aladdin Paperbacks, 1994

Where's the cake, and where's the present? That's what a young Patricia is thinking all day long on her very own birthday. She tries hard to hide her disappointment, especially when her daddy decides it's the perfect evening to head down to the Clay Pit, the so-called haunted home of an elusive monster. Then, as if by magic, a truly disappointing birthday turns into a downright exciting one!

In the end, Patricia has *some* birthday—perhaps the very best ever! Ask students to recall things that make this birthday extra special for Patricia, such as the unexpected trip to the Clay Pit, the monster sighting, and the surprise whipped cream cake. Next challenge students to think about their best birthday celebrations and choose a favorite. For a festive follow-up project, have each child fold a 9" x 12" sheet of white construction paper in half and use scissors to round each corner of the folded paper. Then, keeping the fold at the top, have him unfold the paper and describe his best birthday ever on the lower half, making sure he includes why this birthday was so special. After he illustrates this special occasion on the top half, he refolds the paper. Next he glues a construction-paper candle and flame near the top of the project, and then he personalizes the birthday cake and candle as desired. Display the projects on a bulletin board titled "Our Best Birthdays Ever!" Anyway you slice it, a rousing rendition of a favorite birthday tune is definitely in order!

My Ol' Man

Philomel Books, 1995

Memories are priceless, as Polacco proves in this loving tribute to her father. Each summer since their parents' divorce, Patricia and her brother have spent time in Michigan with Da and Gramma. Da is a traveling salesman who can spin a story as long and wide as a country mile. During this particular summer, Da spins a story about a magic rock. And that story, along with the hope and determination that it fosters, forever changes the lives of this loving family.

At the conclusion of the story, write "magic rock," "memory," and "gift" on the chalkboard. Challenge students to explain how these three things become related in the story. (For example, the *memory* of the *magic rock* becomes a special *gift* that will always be treasured). Next ask each child to close her eyes and recall a memory-related gift that she has—perhaps a special time she shared with a friend or family member. Then provide the supplies needed for each child to paint a picture of her memory, in much the same way that Polacco paints a picture of the magic rock as a child. Next have each child copy and complete the sentence "Remember when…" on a paper strip. When the paintings are dry, help each child staple her pro-grammed paper strip to her painting. Temporarily display the paintings around the classroom for viewing pleasure. Then propose that each child share her painted memory with a person who shares this memory, if possible.

Remember when we took Sophie to the ocean?

My Rotten Redheaded Older Brother

Aladdin Paperbacks, 1998

What could be worse than having an older brother? Patricia knows firsthand. It's having an older brother who constantly reminds you that he's the best at everything! Is she ever able to one-up him? Yes. But more important, she discovers the depth of love that's hidden in all that sibling rivalry.

Create a lively discussion about siblings with the following statement: It doesn't matter whether you are an only child or you have one or more siblings; sometimes you like your sibling situation and sometimes you don't. Follow up this discussion by appointing each child to the writing staff of "The Good News Sibling Gazette." Then have each child write and illustrate a true story that de-scribes something good about his sibling circumstance. Set aside time for students to share their stories with the class; then bind them into a class book. For added ap-peal, fashion a cover from a newspaper page, program the cover as desired, and laminate it for durability. Then fold the cover in half and staple the student-created pages inside.

In Enzo's Splendid Gardens

Philomel Books, 1997

It begins with a boy, a book, and a fuzzy old bee. And it ends with 100 percent pandemonium! This delightful cumulative tale, which describes a riotous (and rhyming) chain of events, introduces readers to Polacco's pasta-making husband, Enzo. Is this wild and wacky Polacco tale a true story? In the wonderful words of Patricia's babushka, "Of course it's true...but it may not have happened."

For a quick dramatization of a chain reaction, arrange several dominoes so that when the first domino in the sequence is set into motion, the action is repeated through the entire domino sequence. Then follow up your dramatization by revisiting the story and helping students pinpoint the events that create a chain reaction. Next divide students into small groups and challenge each group to create a wild and wacky chain-reaction story. To do this, give each group member a blank paper strip to program. Also give each group a paper strip labeled "Who brought us here?" Instruct the group members to work together to create a series of related events (one event per group member) that culminate with the provided question. After each group member writes a different event on his paper strip, have the group practice telling its story. To do this, the individual group members read the events on their paper strips in an established order. Then in unison all group members say, "Who brought us here?" Next the group retells its story in reverse order so that the story ends where it began. When appropriate, ask each group to share its story with the class. This storytelling event is sure to generate plenty of enthusiasm and lots of laughs!

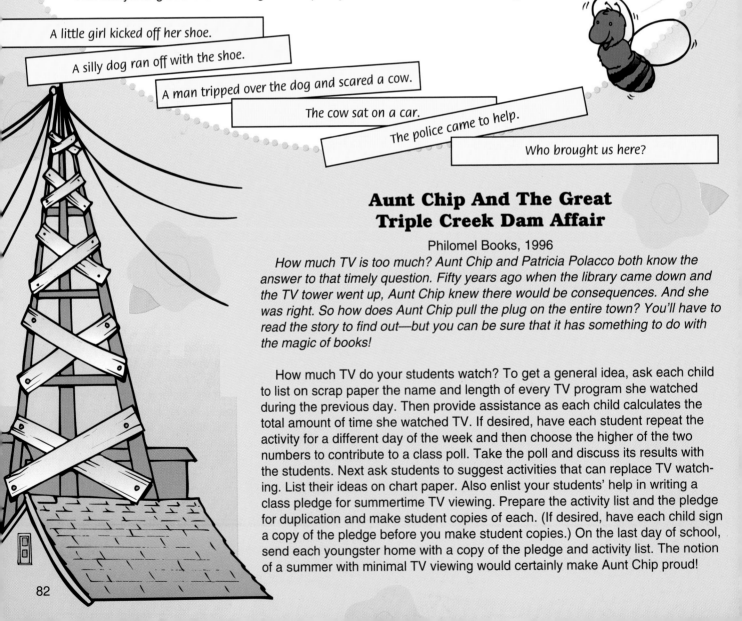

A little girl kicked off her shoe.

A silly dog ran off with the shoe.

A man tripped over the dog and scared a cow.

The cow sat on a car.

The police came to help.

Who brought us here?

Aunt Chip And The Great Triple Creek Dam Affair

Philomel Books, 1996

How much TV is too much? Aunt Chip and Patricia Polacco both know the answer to that timely question. Fifty years ago when the library came down and the TV tower went up, Aunt Chip knew there would be consequences. And she was right. So how does Aunt Chip pull the plug on the entire town? You'll have to read the story to find out—but you can be sure that it has something to do with the magic of books!

How much TV do your students watch? To get a general idea, ask each child to list on scrap paper the name and length of every TV program she watched during the previous day. Then provide assistance as each child calculates the total amount of time she watched TV. If desired, have each student repeat the activity for a different day of the week and then choose the higher of the two numbers to contribute to a class poll. Take the poll and discuss its results with the students. Next ask students to suggest activities that can replace TV watching. List their ideas on chart paper. Also enlist your students' help in writing a class pledge for summertime TV viewing. Prepare the activity list and the pledge for duplication and make student copies of each. (If desired, have each child sign a copy of the pledge before you make student copies.) On the last day of school, send each youngster home with a copy of the pledge and activity list. The notion of a summer with minimal TV viewing would certainly make Aunt Chip proud!

Mrs. Mack

Philomel Books, 1998

Polacco reaches into her childhood and pulls out yet another incredible tale that fortifies the value of friendship, compassion, and determination. A nine-year-old Patricia is pleased as punch that she'll learn to ride a horse this summer! What awaits her at the stables, however, is nothing like what she imagines. Unwilling to give up or give in, Patricia perseveres. The end result is a lifelong lesson about the importance of caring for and respecting both horses and people.

Patricia learns how to ride horses and plenty more during her summer at Dogpatch. Draw and label a chart like the one shown and complete it with student-generated ideas. Help students evaluate the chart to discover important lessons that Patricia learns. To follow up, have each child trace a horseshoe template onto a 9" x 12" sheet of drawing paper. Then, inside the resulting shape, have her complete the sentence "Patricia is lucky to learn…" to describe one or more lessons that Patricia learns that summer. Next ask her to color the horseshoe shape and trim around it. To complete her project, she turns her paper over, draws and colors a second horseshoe, and completes the sentence "I am lucky to have learned…" Encourage each child to take her project home and use it to tell her family about the story.

	First Impression	New Impression
Dogpatch	bad part of town shabby stable	a wonderful place!
Donnie and Nancy	tough looking doesn't like them they ignore her	very nice helpful care about her
Mrs. Mack	snakeskin boots! big smile different, but nice	a wonderful teacher a wonderful person loves horses they are a lot alike
Old Man	not friendly stares a lot	

Patricia is lucky to learn that you need to get to know people before you decide if you like them. People need to get to know you too!

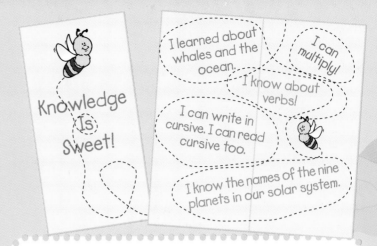

Knowledge Is Sweet!

I learned about whales and the ocean.

I can multiply!

I know about verbs!

I can write in cursive. I can read cursive too.

I know the names of the nine planets in our solar system.

Thank You, Mr. Falker

Philomel Books, 1998

In this heart-wrenching autobiographical tale, Polacco expresses her admiration for all educators as she reveals how her life was forever changed by her fifth-grade teacher. When Trisha enters kindergarten, what she most wants is to learn to read. But year after year, no matter how hard she tries, she can't make sense of the words on a page. And by fifth grade, Trisha is holding a terrible secret deep in her heart—she cannot read! When Mr. Falker realizes Trisha's secret, he dedicates himself to helping her understand and overcome her reading predicament.

Polacco's tale will surely evoke a multitude of emotions from your students. Invite them to talk about the story and describe how it makes them feel. Next sketch a bee on the chalkboard and give each child a bite-size Bit • O • Honey® candy bar to munch on. Remind students how Polacco's grandpa compared knowledge to a bee and its honey. Then use this project to spotlight the knowledge your students have gained this school year. To begin, a child colors and cuts out a bee pattern. Next he folds a 6" x 9" sheet of light blue construction paper in half lengthwise, glues his bee cutout to the resulting front cover, and writes the title "Knowledge Is Sweet!" He then unfolds his paper and writes, graffiti-style, several things he's learned this school year. On the back of his project, he writes his name and the date. Last, he draws dotted lines on the project to indicate the pathway of a very busy bee. Suggest that each child use his project as a bookmark to remind him that knowledge must be chased through the pages of a book. Buzz!

*(**Note from the editor:** At the time of publication, this well-received book was available from our on-line book supplier at www.themailbox.com; however, it was currently out of stock with the publisher. The publisher has assured me that the book will be reprinted. For up-to-date information, call the publisher at 1-800-526-0275.)*

Order books on-line.
www.themailbox.com

Arnold Lobel

Award-Winning Author And Illustrator

Arnold Lobel's endearing characters, insightful story lines, and charming illustrations make his books perfect for classroom use. Step into Lobel's wonderful world of literature with these tried-and-true suggestions.

Meet Arnold Lobel

Arnold Lobel, renowned author and illustrator, was born on May 22, 1933, in Los Angeles, California. Young Lobel often amused his classmates and teachers with his entertaining stories and illustrations. As an adult, Lobel wrote and drew about events in his own life, which he believed to be the key to great storytelling. For Lobel, writing a story required much more patience and perseverance than illustrating one. But he never gave up. When Lobel died in 1987, at the early age of 54, he left a legacy of children's books with lasting and universal appeal.

Mouse Tales
HarperTrophy, 1978

Papa Mouse tells seven entertaining bedtime stories—one for each of his seven mouse boys.

Look high and low, and you won't find a story with more kid appeal than this Lobel favorite! Read aloud "Very Tall Mouse And Very Short Mouse" and then explore each mouse's unique point of view with this categorization activity. Challenge students to recall the items that each mouse greets. List these items on the chalkboard under the appropriate mouse's name. Help students conclude that Very Tall Mouse sees high things and Very Short Mouse sees low things. Next say the provided chant with the class and select a student volunteer to name something that is either high or low. Have the remaining students chorally name the mouse who would be likely to see the item. Confirm the students' response by writing the item on the chalkboard under the appropriate name. Continue the activity in a like manner for as long as desired. "Hello, cloud!"

> Tall mouse, short mouse,
> They went walking.
> Listen to the word
> To see who's talking.

Theresa J. Casey—Gr. 1
Chukker Creek Elementary
Aiken, SC

On Market Street
Illustrated by Anita Lobel
Mulberry Books, 1989

A youngster's incredible shopping spree takes him from A to Z in this Caldecott Honor Book.

Take students on a picture-perfect shopping trip that results in a one-of-a-kind class book! After an initial reading of the book, revisit the illustrations so students realize that each shopkeeper is a creation of his or her wares. Next assign each letter of the alphabet to a student. (If necessary, assign some youngsters more than one letter.) To make his booklet page, a student writes his letter at the top of a sheet of drawing paper and a noun that begins with his letter at the bottom. Then he illustrates a shopkeeper who is composed of his or her wares. Bind the students' pages in alphabetical order between construction-paper covers. Title the resulting class book "On [your school's street address]." You can count on this publication suiting your youngsters' literary interests to a T!

Barbara A. Denlinger—Gr. 1
Akron Elementary School
Akron, PA

C

KISS THE COOK

Cookies

Order books on-line.
www.themailbox.com

Ming Lo Moves The Mountain

Mulberry Books, 1993

Move a mountain? Impossible! Or so it seems until Ming Lo seeks a wise man's advice.

Empower young listeners with this tale's important message. First read aloud the book's title and challenge students to predict how Ming Lo moves the mountain. Then follow up the story by asking students to compare their predictions to the story's outcome. Encourage students to talk about the way Ming Lo feels when he believes he has accomplished the impossible. Next invite students to describe their past achievements and any feelings they associate with them. Lastly have each youngster write about and/or illustrate a dream or an ambition that she has for the future. Display the students' work on a bulletin board decorated with a simple mountain scene and the title "If Ming Lo Can Move A Mountain…"

Whiskers & Rhymes

Mulberry Books, 1988

Lobel puts a new spin on some old favorites with this humorous collection of poems. From Clara, little curlylocks, to Beanbag Jim, Lobel's fanciful felines are sure to delight readers of all ages.

If you're looking for a "cat-alyst" to motivate your young writers, this rhyme activity is a "purr-fect" choice! At the conclusion of the book, discuss with youngsters how Lobel's poems are similar to nursery rhymes. Then challenge each child to write an original version of a familiar rhyme. For added fun, have each student publish his work in a cat-shaped book. To make the pages for his book, a student copies each line of his poem on a 2" x 6" strip of paper, then he stacks the pages in sequential order. To make the book's cover, he folds a 9" x 12" sheet of construction paper in half. He tucks the pages inside the folded paper (flush against the fold) and staples them in place. Next he trims the folded paper as shown to create a cat's body and legs, and then he cuts out a cat's head and tail from construction-paper scraps. After he adds eyes, a nose, and whiskers to the feline's head, he glues the cutouts in place. Meow!

The Rose In My Garden

Illustrated by Anita Lobel
Mulberry Books, 1993

Beginning with one delicate rose, this cumulative tale builds until a tranquil garden is transformed into a flurry of excitement.

Memory skills will blossom with this storytelling activity! As you read the story aloud, encourage students to chime in on familiar phrases. After discussing the story's repetitive nature, engage students in telling a cumulative tale. To do this, gather students in a large circle. Introduce the story with the sentence "This is [name of school]." Then have a student volunteer begin the story by completing the following sentence: "I am [student's name], and I like to [verb or verb phrase] in [teacher's name]'s room." The classmate to this student's right repeats the sentence, and then she completes the sentence herself. The next classmate to the right repeats the previous two sentences before she completes the sentence, and this continues until every child has taken a turn. Conclude the story by having the youngsters repeat the introductory sentence in unison. Telling a story has never been more memorable!

Owl At Home
HarperTrophy, 1982

Owl's innocent nature and unique solutions to daily dilemmas will quickly endear him to readers, young and old alike.

Read aloud the five short whimsical stories about Owl; then put your students' critical-thinking skills to the test with a flip-book project. To make the book, a student folds a sheet of drawing paper in half lengthwise and makes two equally spaced cuts in the top layer to create three flaps. He writes "Owl's Problem" on the first flap; then, under the flap, he describes a problem that Owl confronts in the book. He labels the second flap "Owl's Solution." Under this flap he explains how Owl solves the problem. On the third flap he writes "My Solution," and then he writes how he would solve Owl's problem under the flap. Set aside time for students to illustrate their work; then invite them to share how they solved Owl's predicaments.

Owl had two bumps in the bed. He was scared of them.

Owl's Solution

My Solution

A Treeful Of Pigs
Illustrated by Anita Lobel
Greenwillow Books, 1987

With the help of his wife's ingenuity and some seemingly amazing pigs, a lazy farmer learns a valuable lesson about keeping promises and accepting responsibility.

The farmer will walk the dog on the day that...

I, David Bartlett, will walk the dog...

dogs fly planes.

every day, even when it is raining.

Youngsters will go hog-wild over this investigation into responsibility! As a follow-up to the story, have students compare and contrast how the farmer and his wife handle the duties of pig ownership. (Use a Venn diagram for this step if desired.) Next have students brainstorm responsibilities related to owning pets, and list their ideas on the chalkboard. For a fun follow-up project, have each student visually divide a sheet of drawing paper in half. Ask each youngster to choose a pet responsibility from the class list, then write and illustrate how the farmer would handle this responsibility on the left half of his paper. On the right half of his paper, he writes and illustrates how he would handle the pet-related task. Compile the students' work into a class book titled "A Bookful Of Pets."

Fables
HarperTrophy, 1983

A host of animal characters with surprisingly humanlike qualities is featured in this beautifully illustrated collection of original fables.

What better way to introduce fables to students than with this Caldecott Medal winner? Make a chart similar to the one shown. Explain to youngsters that a fable is a story that teaches a lesson and that most fables have animal characters. Choose one of Lobel's fables to read aloud. Then, under your students' direction, write on the chart the title, characters, and main events of the fable along with a summary of the lesson it teaches. Repeat this procedure for each fable you read aloud until the chart is completed. Then have each student choose a lesson from the chart, and write and illustrate an original fable that reteaches it. Set aside time for each child to read aloud his fable and challenge his classmates to identify its lesson.

Fables

Title	Characters	Main Events	Lesson
The Baboon's Umbrella	Baboon Gibbon	Baboon's umbrella is stuck open. Gibbon tells baboon to cut holes in the umbrella.	Not all advice is good.

Frog And Toad Together
HarperTrophy, 1979

From struggling with the temptation of freshly baked cookies to facing their fears, Frog and Toad do everything together. Their steadfast friendship is portrayed with sensitivity and insight in this timeless Newbery Honor Book.

"A List"

As Toad discovers in this chapter, nothing compares to the satisfaction of completing everything on a to-do list. And there's a good chance your students will agree! To find out, ask each child to list ten things she plans to accomplish during the school day. Then have her tape her resulting to-do list on her desktop. When she completes an item on the list, she draws a line through it. You can count on plenty of smiles at the end of the day when students see how much they've accomplished!

Debbie Erickson—Gr. 2
Sunset Elementary
Whitehall, WI

To-Do List

1. silent read
2. take math fact test
3. go to recess
4. learn about frogs
5. write in my journal
6. eat lunch
7. go to the library
8.
9.

"Cookies"

In this brief tale, Frog and Toad learn that it takes plenty of willpower to stop eating fresh-baked cookies. Review the steps Frog and Toad take to stop eating cookies. Next divide students into small groups and have each group create a plan to help the amphibians resist eating too much of the cake Toad plans to bake. Require that the plan be a series of steps that build upon each other (like in "Cookies") and that each group member participate in presenting the plan to the class. Your students' creativity and memory skills are sure to be enhanced as these willpower plans unfold.

Days With Frog And Toad
HarperTrophy, 1984

Beginning readers will delight in these five tender stories of friendship that feature the lovable amphibian pals, Frog and Toad.

"The Kite"

This adventure finds Frog and Toad trying to fly a kite—only to have it repeatedly crash to the ground. Despite discouraging remarks from some onlooking robins, the two friends persevere until they succeed. At the end of the story, invite students to describe times they had to try again and again to accomplish a goal. Then have each child make a kite to remind himself of the importance of perseverance. To make his kite, a student cuts out a kite shape and four kite bows from construction paper. (Provide tagboard tracers or duplicated patterns for this step.) On each bow he writes something he accomplished by perseverance, and then he illustrates two of these accomplishments—one on each side of his kite cutout. Next he hole-punches the bottom of the kite shape and threads and ties one end of a length of yarn through the hole to make a kite tail. Lastly he glues the bow cutouts back to back along the kite tail, keeping the programming to the outside as shown. If desired, suspend each child's kite above his desk.

adapted from an idea by Diane Afferton
Afton Elementary School
Yardley, PA

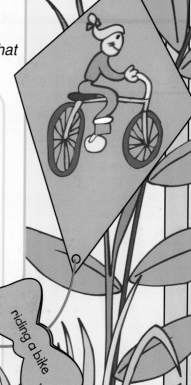

riding a bike

swimming in the deep end

Frog And Toad Are Friends
HarperTrophy, 1979

In this Caldecott Honor Book, Frog and Toad help each other cope with situations that will undoubtedly ring true for readers.

"Spring"

In this funny tale, a fully awake Frog is ready to greet spring, but a very sleepy Toad is not! At the conclusion of the chapter, have students brainstorm words and phrases related to spring. Write their suggestions on the chalkboard; then challenge each child to refer to the resulting word bank as she pens a list poem titled "Spring." For an attractive display, have each student copy her edited poem in the center of an 8" x 11" sheet of white paper and then create a border of colorful springlike art around her writing. Mount each youngster's work on a 9" x 12" sheet of construction paper before showcasing it on a bulletin board titled "Welcome, Spring!"

Janet Gross
Stowe, PA

Spring

Flowers bloom.
Bees buzz.
Ducklings hatch.
Grass grows.
Birds chirp.
Kids play.

Spring

"The Story"

Frog wants to hear a story, and Toad can't think of one to save his soul! Invite students to talk about times they've wanted to tell or write stories and, like Toad, couldn't think of any ideas. Next have students brainstorm remedies for these situations. List the students' ideas on the chalkboard; then, with your youngsters' input, identify the top ten tips for overcoming story block. Use these tips to make a colorful classroom poster for future reference.

Janet Gross

Ten Tips For How To Cure
Writer's Block

1. Talk about the story with a friend.

2. Daydream about the story.

3. Pretend that you are a part of the story.

"The Letter"

Frog leaps into action when he realizes how much better Toad will feel if he receives a letter in the mail. At the conclusion of this story, give each child a copy of page 91 so she too can write a letter to Toad. Instruct each student to cut along the bold lines, turn her paper over, write her letter on the blank side, and then sign her name "Frog [student's last name]." To prepare her letter for delivery, she folds her paper in half along the thin line; then she writes a return and a mailing address on the provided lines. Next she colors the artwork and tapes the envelope closed. Collect the letters. The next day, have students assume the role of Toad and give each child a letter to read that was written by a classmate. Then have each student respond to her new frog pal on another copy of page 91. Invite students to personally deliver these letters. Now that's a "toad-ally" terrific writing activity!

adapted from an idea by Patricia Heilman—Gr. 1
The Bryn Mawr School For Girls
Baltimore, MD

"A Lost Button"

This amusing tale has the two pals frantically searching for Toad's lost button. For a fun follow-up activity, have each child create a personalized version of the story. To do this, a child makes six construction-paper buttons—each of a different size, shape, color, and/or design. Then he incorporates his props into a story that tells how he loses a button, searches for the button in five locations only to find five buttons that are not his, and eventually finds his button. Next pair students and have each child use his props to tell his partner his story. Then have each student take his props home so he can retell his tale for friends and family members.

adapted from an idea by Marilyn Meyerson
Key School
Annapolis, MD

Frog Jones
W. Melrose Ave.
Balto, MD 21207

Toad
1000 Lily Pad Road
Riverdale, MD 00012

Frog And Toad All Year
HarperTrophy, 1984

Follow the beloved amphibious duo throughout the year with this seasonal collection of Frog and Toad adventures. Recognized as an ALA Notable Children's Book, this collection is too good to miss!

"Ice Cream"

After reading about Toad's mishap with melting ice cream, have your youngsters experiment with the melting process. Divide students into small groups and give each group an ice cube in a small plastic container. Have each group document how long it takes for the ice cube to completely melt. Then repeat the experiment with a second and a third ice cube. Each time, challenge the groups to shorten (lengthen) the melting time. After each experiment, ask every group to explain its strategy and share its results. Wrap up the activity by having students identify elements that influence the melting process.

Beth Jones—Gr. 2
Stevensville Public School
Niagara Falls, Ontario, Canada

More With "Ice Cream"

Frog and Toad like chocolate ice cream the best. Use this delicious idea to find out which flavor is tops among your students and their families. Have each student label one paper ice-cream scoop for each family member, herself included. Then have her take the cutouts home, label each one with the named person's favorite ice-cream flavor, and return the cutouts by a designated date. If desired, also invite students to lightly color the cutouts to reflect the flavors they represent. Then use the cutouts to create a class graph of favorite ice-cream flavors. After each youngster has written and/or shared three statements about the completed graph, serve the class a yummy ice-cream treat.

Phyllis Bowling—Gr. 2
Smithville Elementary
Smithville, MS

Erin Strawberry

"The Surprise"

In this humorous chapter, each best friend works selflessly to surprise the other with a kind deed. Lead students to understand that each friend's surprise was a gift from the heart. Discuss the meaning of this phrase with youngsters and then have each student label a colorful heart cutout with another example of a gift from the heart. Mount these hearts on a jumbo paper heart titled "Gifts From The Heart." Display the completed project in a prominent classroom location to remind students of the selfless things that good friends do for each other.

helping with chores

making a get well card

sharing a snack

sharing my jump rope

More About Frog And Toad

Use the activities on this page to follow up any book featuring the two fabulous friends!

Sometimes a friend and I like to play catch.

Forever Friends

Whether Frog and Toad are embarking on an adventure or tackling a problem, they stick together. Ask students to think about the different ways that they spend time with their friends. Then introduce this book-making project. First have each student copy, complete, and illustrate the following sentence on provided paper: "Sometimes a friend and I like to [verb phrase]." Next provide a supply of blank paper and ask each child to make three or more additional booklet pages in the same manner. Explain that the sentences must feature different activities, but that the illustrations may feature the same friend or a variety of friends. To complete the project, have each child make a construction-paper cover for her booklet and then staple her pages inside it. If time allows, invite each child to share her favorite booklet page with the class.

adapted from an idea by Catherine Broome
Melbourne Beach, FL

Friendship Trail Mix

Frog and Toad certainly know the value of teamwork! And since this recipe requires teamwork, it's a perfect follow-up to any Frog and Toad tale. Give each child a resealable plastic bag to take home. Ask him to return the bag on a designated day with one cup of bite-sized snack food (like pretzels, raisins, or toasted oat cereal) sealed inside. As each child pours his snack into a large bowl, have him describe an activity he likes to do with a friend. Then stir the snacks and serve the yummy mix to students as you discuss with them how each person's contribution helped make the treat extra tasty.

adapted from an idea by Tami Bertini—Gr. 1
Gladbrook Elementary
Gladbrook, IA

Now Showing...

Students step into the role of producer when they create visual retellings of their favorite Frog and Toad adventures. For every two or three students, precut a shoebox with a 2" x 5" opening in the bottom and a 2 1/4-inch slit in each end (making sure to align the slits and the opening as shown above). Each group also needs two tissue-paper tubes, a four-foot length of adding machine tape, masking tape, and crayons. Have each group illustrate a favorite Frog and Toad episode, scene by scene, on its length of adding machine tape. (Instruct each group to leave a four-inch margin on each end of its story tape.) When the story tapes are finished, have each group use masking tape to secure the front of its story tape to a tissue-paper tube. To demonstrate how to thread the tape through the box, position a precut box on its side so that the opening faces you. Then, working from left to right, thread the unattached end of the story tape through both slits so that the illustrations can be seen through the opening. Use masking tape to secure the end of the tape to the remaining tube and then roll the story tape onto the tube. To view the tape through the opening, slowly and simultaneously turn the tubes to the left. Now that's impressive!

Jane B. Buggs—Gr. 2
St. Mary School
Janesville, WI

The Boxcar Children®

Mystery Series

Created by Gertrude Chandler Warner

Published by Albert Whitman & Company

Delight your students with the escapades of Henry, Jessie, Violet, and Benny Alden! For a rich appreciation of the Alden family, begin your investigation with the first book in the series, *The Boxcar Children*. It is here that the youngsters, whose parents have died, temporarily set up housekeeping in an abandoned boxcar. Then, in each of the subsequent books, the children find adventure in another unique setting.

Use this trainload of specially engineered activities to enhance *any* book in the Boxcar series.

Meet Gertrude Chandler Warner
1890–1979

Growing up across the street from a railroad station, Gertrude Chandler Warner often dreamed of keeping house in a caboose. Early in her teaching career, Warner wrote *The Boxcar Children* based on this dream. Initially librarians opposed the book because they felt the Alden children were having too much fun without proper parental supervision. And this, of course, was one reason why children loved the story so! In 1942, Warner rewrote the story using less challenging vocabulary. This is the version that children enjoy today. Before her death in 1979, Warner authored 18 additional Boxcar adventures. Today the series continues with the help of new authors who steer the Alden children into a variety of settings and adventures!

To learn more about Miss Warner as a child, an adult, a teacher, and a writer, read *Gertrude Chandler Warner And The Boxcar Children* by Mary Ellen Ellsworth (Albert Whitman & Company, 1997).

Cases To Solve

No matter where the Alden children go, they always find themselves in the midst of a mystery! Since there's little doubt that your young gumshoes will want to help solve each case, have them make magnifying-glass booklets in which to record the clues they gather. To make a booklet, cut out a desired number of eight-inch circles from white paper, two from black construction paper, and one from clear plastic. Center a six-inch template atop one black circle, trace around it, and cut on the resulting outline to create a frame. Also trim a 2" x 8" strip of black construction paper to resemble a handle. To assemble the booklet, stack the white circles. Sandwich this stack between the plastic circle (on top) and the eight-inch black circle. Place the frame atop the stack and staple. Glue the handle to the back cover. Have each child personalize the first white page in his booklet. To store the booklet, fold the handle forward, and keep it flush against the front cover. Paper-clip the handle in place, if desired.

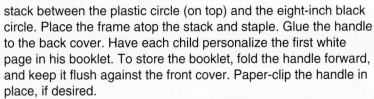

Set aside time at the conclusion of each read-aloud session for students to write any clues they gathered in their booklets. Prior to revealing the ending of the story, invite students to share their ideas of how the mystery will be solved.

adapted from an idea by Katie Robinson—Gr. 3
Limestone Walters School, Peoria, IL

The Mystery Of The Hidden Beach

Chapter 1

Chapter 2

Chapter 3

Chapter 4

Chapter 5

Staying On Track

Keep your students' summarizing skills on the right track with this locomotive display. For each chapter in your upcoming Boxcar mystery, make and label a paper boxcar. (To make a boxcar, glue black construction-paper wheels to the bottom of a 9" x 12" sheet of red construction paper.) Laminate the boxcars and an engine cutout (enlarge pattern on page 285, if desired). Use a wipe-off marker to program the engine cutout with the book's title. Mount this cutout on a classroom wall. Then, at the end of each chapter, use a wipe-off marker to write a student-generated summary of events on the corresponding boxcar. Mount the programmed boxcars behind the engine, in sequential order. Use black paper strips to connect the cars, if desired. Leave the train on display until you're ready to read another Boxcar adventure. Then simply wipe away the programming and repeat the activity.

Jill Hamilton—Gr. 1, Schoeneck Elementary, Stevens, PA

A Mystery From A To Z

An alphabetical review of a Boxcar adventure will suit your youngsters to a T! List the letters of the alphabet on the chalkboard. As students brainstorm story-related words and phrases, write their ideas next to the appropriate letters. Next assign each child one letter and ask him to create a page for an ABC version of the featured mystery. To make his page, a student writes his letter at the top of a sheet of drawing paper and then he writes and illustrates a story-related sentence on the remainder of the paper. If desired, have each child use a crayon to trace over his alphabet letter and to underline the word or phrase associated with it. Bind the completed projects in alphabetical order between construction-paper covers and title the book "The ABCs Of [book title]." Right down to the letter, this book is sure to be a class favorite.

Henry, Jessie, Violet, and Benny spend their summer in a lighthouse.

Kelly A. Lu—Gr. 2, Berlyn School, Ontario, CA

Showing Character

Use the positive character traits that Jessie, Henry, Violet, and Benny display to encourage similar traits in your students. Title a large boxcar shape "Precious Cargo" and display it on a classroom wall. At the conclusion of each read-aloud session, ask the class to recall the children's positive actions and name the character traits that describe them. Write each trait that is discussed on the boxcar (unless it is already listed there). To encourage your students to exhibit these same traits, place pencils and a spiral notebook titled "Boxcar Guests" near the display. Each time a student experiences one of the listed traits, she makes an entry in the guest book. To do this, she writes her name, the name of each person involved, the date, and a brief description of the positive experience. Read aloud several entries each day and praise the spotlighted individuals for demonstrating and recognizing positive traits!

Another Boxcar Series!

The Adventures Of Benny And Watch™ series (Albert Whitman & Company) is written with the beginning reader in mind. Each book in this series stars Benny, the youngest Alden, and his lovable pooch, Watch. Now even the youngest reader can catch Boxcar fever!

Acting It Out

The escapades of the Boxcar youngsters provide excellent opportunities for creative dramatics. As you read aloud the mystery of your choice, keep a list of events that could easily be acted out by small groups of students. At the conclusion of the book, group students and secretly assign each group one event from your list. Allow plenty of time for students to prepare. Then have each group enact its assigned event for the class. At the end of each performance, invite the audience to identify the corresponding part of the story. Then, if desired, have the groups repeat their performances in sequential order as you videotape them. Lights, camera, action!

Jill Hamilton—Gr. 1
Schoeneck Elementary
Stevens, PA

What Memories!

Photographs and mementos capture special events forever, so why not have students make scrapbooks to remember their most recent Alden adventure? Discuss with students the purpose of a scrapbook. Then have each child align two 9" x 12" sheets of construction paper and fold the papers in half. On the cover of the resulting (unbound) scrapbook, write "The Alden Family Scrapbook," followed by the title of the Boxcar mystery. On the chalkboard write a student-generated list of story events. Have each child choose six different events to feature in her scrapbook and illustrate each one on a white 4" x 5" rectangle to resemble a photograph. She glues each picture on a separate scrapbook page and adds a caption. On each page she also illustrates a related souvenir (or she crafts one from scrap paper and glues it to the page). Finally, she punches two holes near the fold of her scrapbook, threads a two-foot length of yarn through the holes, securely ties the yarn ends, and fashions a bow. Be sure to set aside time for youngsters to share the keepsakes they've created!

The Alden Family Scrapbook

The Mystery At Snowflake Inn

Book Report Boxcars

Students will be eager to hop aboard this book report project! Have each child complete a copy of page 95 about a selected Boxcar mystery. Then have him cut around his report on the bold lines and fold back each tab along the thin line. Next demonstrate how to bring the folded edges to the center of the report and then flatten the paper. Have students do the same. Provide assistance as needed.

To make a boxcar cover for his report, a student transforms a 7" x 12" sheet of red construction paper into a boxcar by adding crayon details and attaching construction-paper wheels. He folds his boxcar in half, unfolds it, and cuts along the resulting crease line. Then he aligns and glues each half of his boxcar to the corresponding tab of his folded project. It's full steam ahead for book reports!

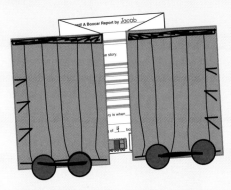

Mystery Writers

The Alden children are not the only ones who visit new places and take part in exciting activities! For this writing activity, students use a school-related event like a field trip or a school assembly as the basis for a Boxcar adventure. Select a recent event and ask students to share their memories of it. List their recollections on the chalkboard. Next have students brainstorm possible mystery plots that could be associated with this occasion. Then challenge each child to write and illustrate a mystery that is based on the school event and that features the Alden family and himself as story characters. No doubt students will be eager to share the adventures they've written, *and* help solve the mysteries their classmates have written, too!

Kari Koebernick—Gr. 3, Enders-Salk School, Schaumburg, IL

A Tasty Addition

If you're looking for a tasty addition to an Alden family adventure, locate a copy of *The Boxcar Children Cookbook* by Diane Blain (Albert Whitman & Company, 1991). From Boxcar Brown Bread to Jessie's Apple Pie, the cookbook contains a collection of recipes based on meals eaten by the family during its mystery escapades.

Glue right half of cover on this tab.

All Aboard! A Boxcar Report by _____

Title: _____

Setting: _____

Here is a summary of the story.

Beginning _____

Middle _____

End _____

The best part of the story is when _____

I give this book a rating of _____ boxcars.

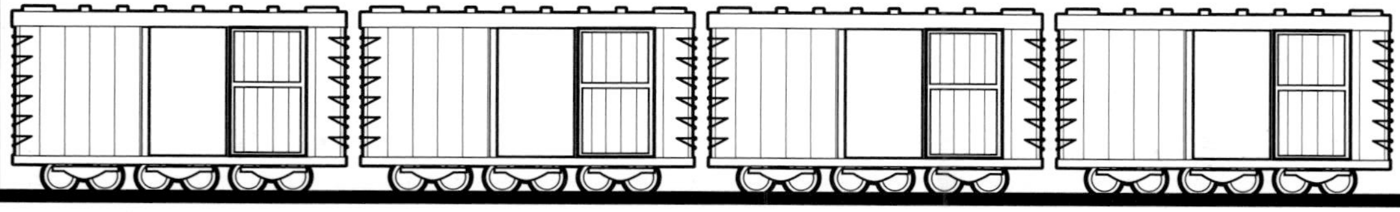

Boxcar Code

1 = OK   3 = very good
2 = good   4 = excellent

Glue left half of cover on this tab.

Note To Teacher: Use with "Book Report Boxcars" on page 94.

Wow, What A Character!

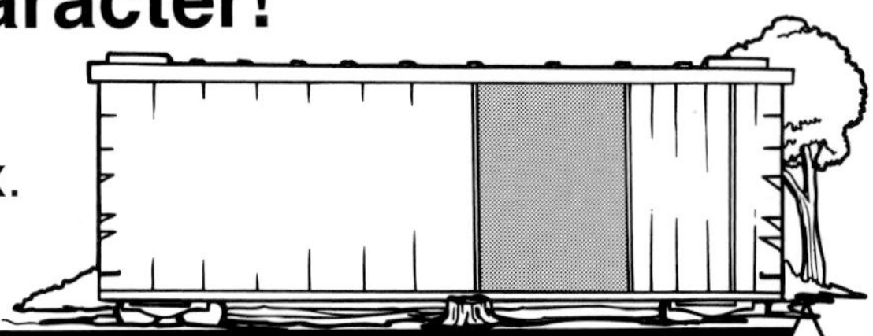

Choose your favorite character from the story.
Draw and color a picture of the character in the box.
Complete the activity from his or her point of view.

My name is _____.

Here is a description of myself:

_____

_____

_____

_____

Here is a picture of me!

My role in the book was _____

_____

_____

_____

I think the most important event in the book was _____

_____

_____

One way I am like you is _____

_____

_____

One way I am not like you is _____

_____

_____

Note To Teacher: Use this activity after completing any book from the series.

Language Arts
Units

Cheep! Cheep! Cheep! Cheep!

More Than A Dozen Opportunities For Speaking Skills Practice

Make way for this "eggs-traordinary" collection of classroom-tested ideas! You'll find tips and activities for nurturing speaking skills, along with suggestions for boosting your youngsters' speaking confidence. We thank our subscribers for their Grade A contributions, and we think you will, too! Cheep, cheep!

Classy Microphone

A teacher-made microphone is the perfect prop for persuading reluctant speakers to participate in class discussions and small-group presentations. Use clear tape to secure a large ball of crumpled foil to one end of a paper-towel tube; then cover the tube with black paper. Embellish the resulting microphone as desired. Plan to use the prop to emcee question-and-answer sessions by speaking into the microphone each time you ask a question. Have students answering the questions do the same. Also encourage students to incorporate the prop into their small-group presentations. The youngsters will have so much fun using the microphone, they'll forget their worries about speaking in front of the class!

Julie Plowman—Gr. 3, Adair-Casey Elementary Adair, IA

Who's Behind That Paper?

Do you have students who hold their papers in front of their faces during oral presentations? Try this! Instruct each child to hold her paper near her waist, about where a belt buckle would be. Explain that keeping her paper here allows her voice to project over the paper and out into the audience. If desired, bring a belt with a large buckle to school and invite each student to wear the belt during her presentation. When a student's paper begins to creep upward, quietly whisper "Belt buckle." The youngster will immediately know to lower her paper. It works like a charm!

Sharon L. Brannan—Gr. 2, Holly Hill Elementary, Holly Hill, FL

Tape-Recorded Presentations

If the thought of speaking in front of the class makes your students weak in the knees, have them record their presentations on audiotape. Then play each recording without revealing the speaker's identity. Ask the audience to share five positive comments about the presentation before inviting them to guess who was speaking on the tape. After the speaker is identified, encourage students to ask their classmate questions about her presentation. In no time at all your recording artists will feel confident enough to present live for their classmates!

Kathleen DiGrigoli—Gr. 1
Osbornville School
Brick, NJ

Bragging Rights

Set the stage for a series of successful speaking engagements with a bragging bag. You need a sturdy piece of discarded handheld luggage. Label the luggage "The Bragging Bag" and decorate it as desired. Inform each student that he will be talking to the class about a very important topic—himself! Suggest that during his speech he brag about his special interests, hobbies, and accomplishments. Post a speech schedule and invite each student to use The Bragging Bag to transport precious props for his presentation between home and school. Since each youngster will be talking about the topic he knows best, a positive speaking experience is in the bag!

Kara M. Carr—Gr. 3
Republic Elementary II
Republic, MO

Show-And-Tell Strategy

Show-and-tell has always been a good speaking skills opportunity. But by guiding your students' selections, you can enrich their learning, too. For students and their parents, list your units of study for the upcoming month and suggest related show-and-tell items. If you'll be studying weather, for example, your list may include different types of weather instruments, weather-related articles and charts, and family photographs taken in unusual weather. When it's time for show-and-tell, ask that each child say three or more sentences about the item he brought to share. Practicing good language habits, like conveying interesting facts in complete sentences, may improve your students' written language skills, too!

Fran Clay—Gr. 2, Meadow View Elementary School
Parsons, KS

Weekly Reading Recommendations

Students quickly learn to anticipate and love this speaking opportunity! The day prior to your class's weekly visit to the library, have students take turns sharing their opinions about the library books they are about to return. Offer each child a chance to name the title of the book she read and give one reason why she did or did not like it. Not only is this event an informal opportunity for students to ad lib before an audience, it can generate volumes of reading enthusiasm!

Andrea Hunter—Gr. 1
Fullington Academy
Pinehurst, GA

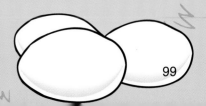

Building Speaking Confidence

Arranging for your students to speak to younger crowds of enthusiastic listeners is a surefire way to build speaking confidence. And it's also a great way to reinforce information that has recently been taught. After a space unit, for example, a small group of students might demonstrate how to build an air-powered rocket and explain how it works. Or a student who has been reading biographies could share a few facts about a famous basketball player and demonstrate some ball-handling tips. To provide your students with ongoing opportunities for speaking skills improvement, make these sharing sessions a monthly event!

Fran Brooks—Gr. 3, St. Anthony Cathedral School
Beaumont, TX

Roving Reporters

Even shy students will step into the limelight when they know their classmates are depending on them to report late-breaking news! Have students watch the evening news to research the role of a news reporter, or show segments of the news that you've prerecorded for their viewing pleasure. Discuss how a news reporter prepares her story, emphasizing that a good reporter keeps an objective point of view and reports only the facts. Post a list that shows which day each child will give a news report to the class. Ask each youngster to prepare a brief script for her presentation. Also clarify that she may report on a variety of newsworthy topics including things she heard or saw on other news reports, family-related news, and topics of personal interest. Provide a clipboard, a trench coat, and a teacher-made microphone as optional reporter props. In addition to having a great time, students experience a real-life application of the importance of speaking skills.

Sharon Earls—Gr. 3, Whittier Elementary School, Camden, NJ

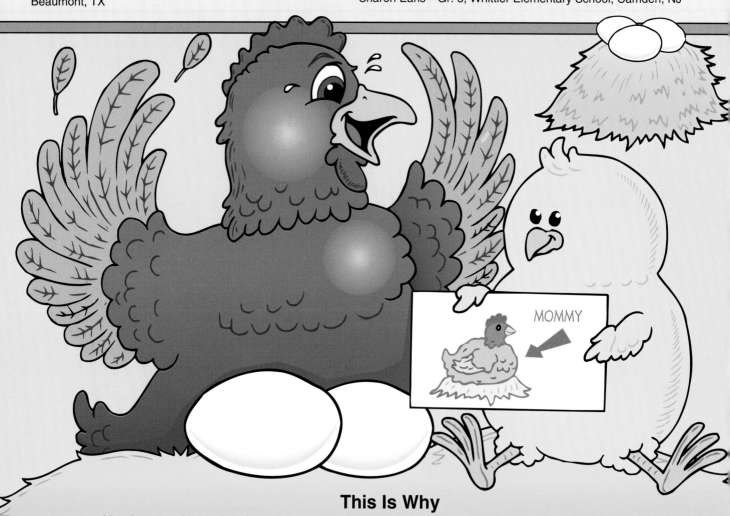

This Is Why

Here's a speaking-related activity that students request to repeat! Give each child three large blank cards and a make-believe scenario like "Tomorrow you will set sail with a group of pirates. You will be at sea for one month. You may take only three things with you. Each item must be something that you feel you simply cannot live without while you are on the pirate ship." Give each student plenty of time to make his choices. Then have him illustrate and label each item he will take on a different card, then write the reason he is taking the item on the back. Set aside time for each student to show his classmates what he's taking on the trip and why. To repeat the activity, simply change the scenario. After all, spending a month on a deserted island would surely require different items than those needed on a pirate ship!

adapted from an idea by Diana Boykin—Gr. 3, DeZavala Elementary, Midland, TX

A Few Minutes At The Improv

Encourage spontaneity, imagination, and dramatics with this speaking activity. Using discarded magazines, cut out several pictures that show pairs of children engaged in a range of activities—from sedentary scenes to extremely active ones. Mount each picture on construction paper; then stack the pictures facedown on a tabletop. Randomly choose pairs of students. Have each pair take the top picture from the stack and then dramatize the scene—making up the dialogue along the way. With shared emphasis on action and oral language, even your reluctant speakers will be eager to participate.

Amy Polcyn—Substitute Teacher
South Lyon Community Schools
South Lyon, MI

What Day Is Today?

Put your students in charge of the daily calendar routine, and they'll clamor to be front and center. Each day (or week) assign a different child to be the calendar person and have him lead his classmates through questions associated with the current day and date. The speaker will get a kick out of calling on other students and posting the correct information on the calendar. Every day is a great day to practice speaking skills!

Holly Rivera—Gr. 2

Weekend Adventures

Most students are eager to share their weekend adventures on Monday mornings. Capitalize on this weekly opportunity to have students exercise their speaking skills. Divide students into groups of four or five. Then ask each person to share with his group something exciting he did during the weekend. Challenge each person in the group to remember the adventures he hears. After everyone has had an opportunity to share, call on one representative from each group to summarize for the class the activities described in his group. Starting the day with a social activity that transitions into a speaking opportunity is a very productive way to ease into the new school week!

Holly Rivera—Gr. 2
Saint John's School
Guaynabo, Puerto Rico

Engaging Experiments

This scientific formula leads to speaking success! Collect an assortment of simple hands-on science experiments from teacher resource books and co-workers that individual students (or student pairs) could safely demonstrate for the class. Distribute the experiments. Provide time for students to practice their experiments and prepare their presentations. Then have each child (or pair) demonstrate his experiment for the class, explain the results, and answer his classmates' questions about the demonstration. Your budding speakers will now be budding scientists, too!

Leigh Anne Newsom, Chittum Elementary, Chesapeake, VA

Clevell Harris

Newsworthy Events

Giving oral summaries of newspaper articles sharpens speaking skills and nurtures interest in current events. Invite students to read the newspaper and select articles that interest them. Or cut out newspaper articles that you feel are most appropriate for classroom use and have each student select one. Then have each youngster prepare an oral summary of his article. Require that each summary include *who* and *what* the article is about and *when, where, why,* and *how* the newsy event took place. If desired, provide copies of the form on page 103 for students to use for this purpose. After each child gives his report to the class, have him address any questions or comments his classmates may have. Now that's a newsworthy speaking experience!

Emily Stoffelen—Gr. 3
Aiken Preparatory School
Aiken, SC

Caught On Tape!

Videotaping your students' presentations has plenty of benefits. The presence of a video camera often spurs students to rise above your greatest expectations. And by allowing students to check out the videos to share with their families, you'll nurture an open line of communication between home and school. The tapes also give each child a chance to evaluate his own performance and elect how he will improve his next presentation. And lastly, the tapes are a wonderful method of showing students how their speaking skills have improved throughout the school year.

Josephine Reale—Gr. 1
Georgian Forest Elementary School
Silver Spring, MD

Featured Guests

Students will be speaking up a storm when it's time for "Write And Revise," a class-created talk show of which you are the host. When a student author has written a first draft of a story he wishes to publish, ask him to appear on the show. To set up for the show, make or obtain a microphone like the one described in "Classy Microphone" on page 98 and position two chairs at the front of the classroom. Begin the show by briefly interviewing the author. Then ask him to read his work for the audience. When he finishes, go to the audience for comments. First the author calls upon three classmates who each have a positive comment to share about his work. As talk show host, move to each selected speaker so that he or she can speak into the microphone. Then the author calls upon three audience members who each have a helpful suggestion for improving his work. After these three students share their comments, wrap up this segment of the show by giving the author a generous round of applause. This talk show format encourages students to do their best work, provides numerous speaking opportunities, and reinforces the writing process. And that's a winning combination!

Cheryl Phillips—Gr. 3, Mount Washington Elementary School, Baltimore, MD

Name ____________________

Newspaper
Identifying important details

Here's The Scoop!

Who
What
When
Where
Why
How

Note To The Teacher: Use with "Newsworthy Events" on page 102 and other newspaper-related activities. Or white-out the programming on each egg and then label or program the eggs as desired.

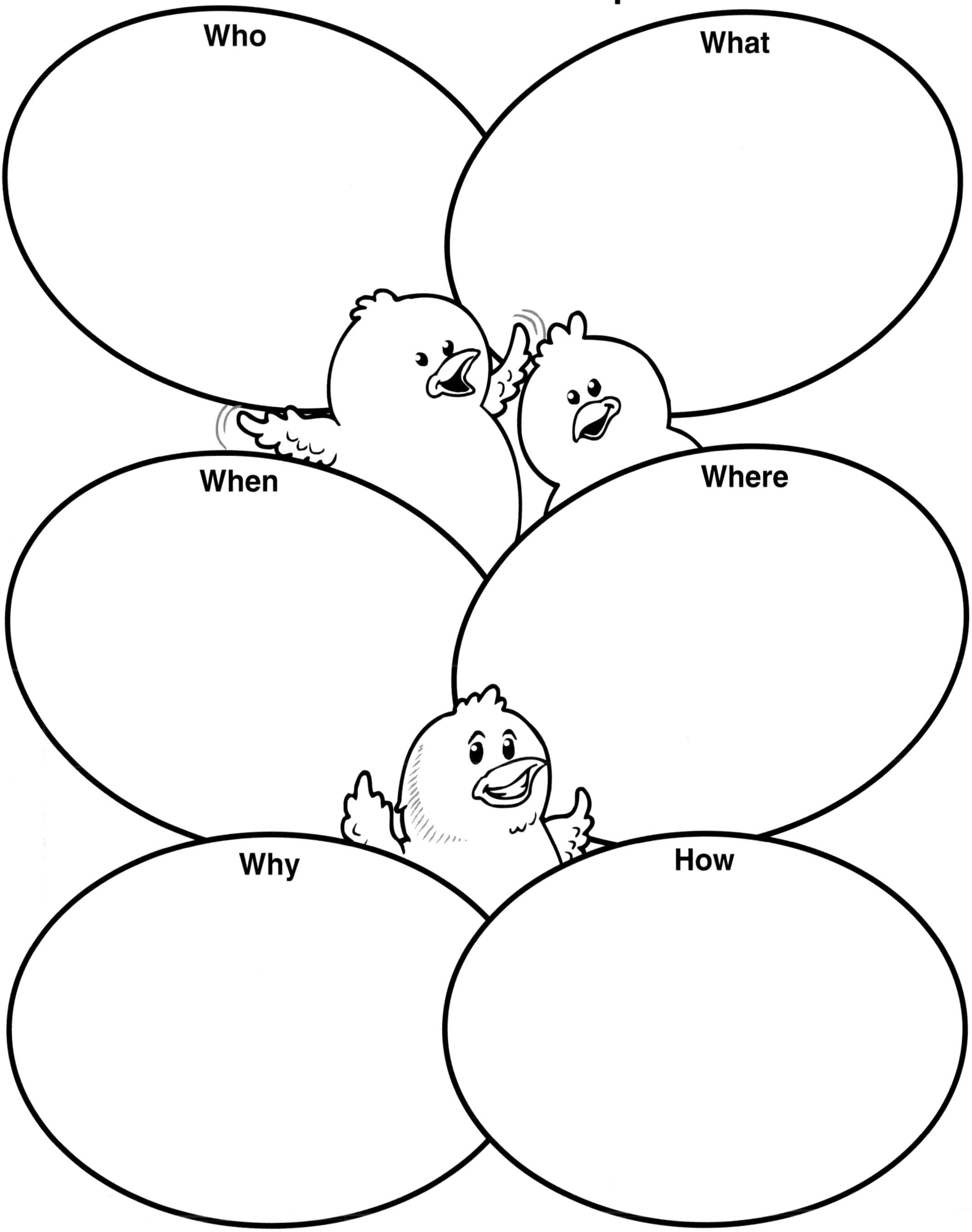

GETTING A JUMP ON PUNCTUATION AND CAPITALIZATION!

If you're constantly looking for ways to improve your students' punctuation and capitalization skills, this collection of teacher-tested ideas will have you jumping for joy!

"BETCHA" CAN'T PUNCTUATE JUST ONE!

Whet your youngsters' appetites for punctuation with this center activity! Gather three disposable bowls and a clean and empty potato chip can. Label the rim of each bowl with a different ending punctuation mark. Then, from yellow construction paper, cut out potato chip shapes that are slightly smaller than the opening of the can. On each chip cutout write a sentence with no ending punctuation; then write the missing punctuation mark on the back of the chip. Laminate the chips for durability and store them in the can. Place the can of chips and the three bowls at a center. A student empties the can of chips and sorts them into the corresponding bowls, checking her work as she goes. Punctuation practice has never been more appetizing!

Lou Murray, Browns Summit, NC

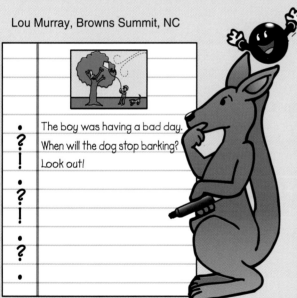

PICTORIAL PUNCTUATION

Here's a picture-perfect way for students to show off their punctuation skills! Mount an interesting photograph or magazine picture near the top of a sheet of chart paper. Draw a vertical line down the left edge of the paper; then, in the resulting column, write an ending punctuation mark on each writing line. Make a second sentence chart in the same manner, making sure that you have one labeled writing line per student. Display the sentence charts in easily accessible locations and place a marker near both of them. Each child takes a turn writing a sentence on one line of a chart. His sentence must relate to the chart's picture and end with the provided punctuation. After all the students have contributed their sentences, post the charts at the front of the room and invite each child to read aloud the sentence that he wrote. Now that's picture-perfect punctuation practice!

MAGNETIC MARKS

This approach to punctuation practice attracts plenty of student interest! Label several individual poster-board rectangles with ending punctuation marks, laminate the rectangles for durability, and attach a self-adhesive magnetic strip to the back of each one. Display the magnetic marks around the border of your chalkboard (or another magnetic writing surface). Write a series of kid-appealing sentences on the chalkboard that do not include ending punctuation. Then have a different student read aloud each sentence and attach the needed magnetic mark. At the end of the lesson, return the magnetic manipulatives to the edge of the writing surface. Plan to repeat the activity periodically, using different sentences each time. In addition, occasionally omit ending punctuation from other chalkboard writing, and let the student who discovers your *error* attach a magnetic mark where it is needed. Who knew punctuation practice could attract so much attention!

Shirley Luetkemeyer—Gr. 1, Null Elementary School, St. Charles, MO

A SENTENCE HUNT

No one wants to be left behind when it's time for a sentence hunt—there's so much ending punctuation to see! Copy the chant shown and post it in a prominent classroom location. To establish a reading rhythm, pat your knees in an alternating fashion (left, right, left, right) and ask students to join in. Next read aloud the first line of the chant, and pause for students to echo the line back to you. Continue in this manner until the entire chant is read and echoed. Then send students on individual sentence hunts. To do this, have each student fold a sheet of drawing paper in half twice, unfold the paper, and label the four resulting boxes "Statements," "Commands," "Questions," and "Exclamations." Then give each child a discarded magazine or newspaper section. Instruct the youngsters to cut out examples of the four kinds of sentences (including their ending punctuation marks) and glue them on their papers in the appropriate sections. Happy hunting!

We're Going On A Sentence Hunt
(chanted to the rhythm of "We're Going On A Bear Hunt")

We're going on a sentence hunt.
We're looking for some sentences
That end with punctuation marks.

First we'll find a statement.
A statement tells something.
It ends with a period.

Then we'll find a command.
A command gives an order.
It ends with a period.

Next we'll find a question.
A question asks something.
It ends with a question mark.

Then we'll find an exclamation.
You say it with feeling!
It ends with an exclamation point.

We're going on a sentence hunt.
We're looking for some sentences.
Ready to go a-hunting?
HERE WE GO!

Kayla Milam—Gr. 2, Robinson Springs School, Millbrook, AL

PUNCTUATION WORKOUT

Use this punctuation review to get your students' punctuation skills in tip-top condition! Write several sentences on a transparency, omitting desired punctuation marks. Next have the class agree upon a specific movement for each punctuation mark being reviewed. For example: exclamation point = hop, question mark = twist, comma = toe-touch, and period = squat. Then have each child stand beside her desk. Using an overhead projector, display the first sentence on the transparency and ask students to read it silently. Then slowly read the sentence aloud as students pantomime the missing punctuation in the appropriate places. Continue in this manner until all the sentences have been pantomimed and punctuated. Now that's a punctuation workout!

IN THE CARDS

For this large-group activity, it takes two cards to create a punctuated sentence. Program half of a class set of cards with individual sentences, omitting one punctuation mark per sentence. Program the remainder of the cards with the missing punctuation marks. Randomly distribute the cards. Instruct each child to read his card, then hold it so that his classmates can read it. Next have each student quietly search for a card that, when added to his card, creates a punctuated sentence. When two students discover that their cards go together, they sit down and raise their hands. After you have approved their teamwork, they lower their hands and wait for the rest of the class to finish. To repeat the activity, simply collect, shuffle, and redistribute the cards. Your young cardholders will give this activity a definite thumbs-up!

Becky Shelley—Gr. 1, Anderson Elementary, Anderson, MO

CAPITALIZATION CLOUDS

Here's a shapely idea for reviewing capitalization rules during the month of March! On each of several desired days, cut out a large cloud shape from white paper and use a colorful marker to label it with a different capitalization rule. Post the cloud in a classroom location that is easily accessible to students. Challenge each child to find an example of the featured rule in a discarded magazine and cut it out. Later that day, ask each child to share the example he found before he glues it to the cloud poster. As additional clouds are posted, encourage students to continue to cut out and add examples of previously reviewed rules to the clouds on display. The forecast is cloudy with a good chance of capitals!

Capitalize all proper nouns.

Sally Smith won the award this year.

The party was at Spaghetti Palace.

The flowers were grown in Holland.

The teacher's name was David Wood.

Call Terry Allen at 1-234-5678.

We saw the Atlanta Braves play.

The dog's name is Sofie.

DRAW THREE

Capital letters and creativity go hand in hand at this center! Place a set of capital-letter cutouts in a gift bag. (Or write the capital letters on individual cards.) Place the gift bag, pencils, and a supply of writing paper at a center. A student draws three letters from the container; then she writes a sentence on her paper that includes these capital letters. She then returns the cutouts to the gift bag and repeats the activity four more times. As an alternative, place story paper at the center. Have each child write one sentence in the manner described, then illustrate her work. Either way, drawing three is the key to this capitalization review!

A SENTENCE A DAY

Provide one-of-a-kind punctuation and capitalization practice by capitalizing on your youngsters' comments and actions. Keep an ongoing list of things your students say and do. Each morning write a student-related sentence on the chalkboard that includes capitalization and punctuation errors. Ask each child to write a corrected version of the sentence in his writing journal or on provided paper. Then invite one student—preferably one who is mentioned in the posted sentence—to correct the teacher-written sentence. A sentence a day is sure to keep skills sharp!

Melissa Gierach—Gr. 2, Ventura Elementary School, Orlando, FL

CAPITALIZATION COUNTDOWN

This kid-pleasing review takes place without pencils and paper! Each child needs his library book and a partner. Assign the students five points each and challenge them to count down to zero in the following manner. To lose a point, each child in turn reads aloud a sentence from his book, shows the sentence he read to his partner, and explains why each word in the sentence is capitalized. When both partners reach zero, the activity is over. After a few 5-point reviews, challenge students to 10-, 15-, or 20-point reviews!

ON THE LOOKOUT

Spark an interest in punctuation and capitalization practice by having students politely point out someone else's mistakes—yours! Have each student program a blank card with the word "Oops!" and store it in her desk. Periodically, as you're writing on the chalkboard or using the overhead projector, omit one or two capital letters and/or punctuation marks. When a student spots a mistake in your writing, she quietly displays her "Oops!" card. Call upon one of your eagle-eyed proofreaders to correct each mistake. Students enjoy and benefit from applying their knowledge of punctuation and capitalization. Plus this approach is a great way to keep students tuned in and motivated!

Sr. Barbara Flynn—Gr. 2
St. Raphael School
Bridgeport, CT

STAYING IN TOUCH

This whole-group activity keeps students in touch with capitalization and punctuation. Give each student a golf ball–sized portion of modeling clay. On the chalkboard write a sentence that is missing a capital letter or a punctuation mark. Challenge each child to identify the missing element, then use his clay to form it. Quickly verify the youngsters' work; then, as the students roll up their clay, erase the sentence and write another one. Repeat the activity as many times as desired. You can bet students will be eager to get their hands on this review activity!

Kristin McLaughlin—Gr. 1
Amity Elementary Center
Douglassville, PA

ZEROING IN

Students zero in on punctuation and capitalization errors with this kid-pleasing activity. Each morning, before the class arrives, write two sentences on the chalkboard that contain punctuation and capitalization errors. As part of your regular morning routine, select a different student to zero in on each sentence. Each child who is chosen uses colorful chalk to draw a large zero around every mistake she sees in the sentence. Then she explains the mistake before she corrects it. This daily grammar review will quickly become a class favorite!

adapted from an idea by Sr. Maribeth Theis—Gr. 2
Mary Of Lourdes Elementary
Little Falls, MN

Check It!

✓ Does each sentence begin with a capital letter?

✗ Does each sentence end with a punctuation mark?

M Did you read each word you wrote? Does your writing make sense?

CHECK IT OUT!

Promote a habit of capitalizing and punctuating with a class poster of self-editing guidelines. Custom-design the poster to match your youngsters' writing needs and preface each guideline with a different symbol, letter, or number. Display the poster in a prominent classroom location. Before a student turns in his work, he refers to the poster. After he follows each guideline and makes any needed corrections to his work, he draws the corresponding symbol in the lower left-hand corner of his paper. This clever approach to the editing process teaches students to be responsible for their work.

Mary Anne Pisano—Grs. K–8 Reading Specialist
Lancaster–Lebanon I. U. #13
Manheim, PA

Awards Use with "Daily Specials For Spelling Success" on pages 109–114. Duplicate and present awards to students as desired.

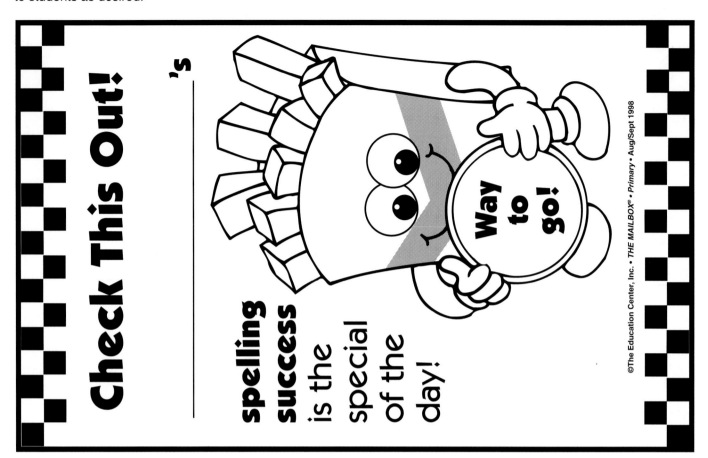

Check This Out!

_____'s

spelling success is the special of the day!

Way to go!

_____ is serving up perfect spelling!

Congratulations!

Daily Specials For
Spelling Success!

Students will quickly develop a taste for spelling when you begin dishing out this delicious spelling cuisine! Each enticing entree is served with a scoopful of spelling reinforcement and a slice of irresistible fun. There's no doubt that these daily specials are made-to-order for spelling success!

Spelling That Scores

Youngsters will have a ball playing this unique spelling game! Write "1" on two tennis balls, "2" on two others, and "3" on two more. Place all six tennis balls in a paper bag. Divide students into four teams and write each team's name on the chalkboard. Then have each team line up single file facing its name. To begin play, the first player in each line steps up to the chalkboard and the remaining students sit in place. In turn ask each player to write a different word on the chalkboard. If a player correctly spells his word, randomly remove a tennis ball from the bag and bounce it to him. He reads the numeral on the ball and records this number of points near his team's name. If a player misspells his word, his turn is over. Then each first-round player moves to the back of his team's line and a new round of play begins. The team with the most points wins. No doubt this team approach will net world-class spelling skills!

Sue Crosby, Camey Elementary, Colony, TX

Weekly Special

Reinforce spelling and proper word usage with wearable words! Every Monday use a wipe-off marker to write the spelling words for the week on a laminated poster titled "This Week's Specials." Review the word list with students and encourage them to use the words in class discussions throughout the week. One day each week, reinforce your students' oral usage of their spelling words with self-stick labels. Each time a student correctly uses a different spelling word in a sentence, give her a label. The student programs the label with the corresponding spelling word and attaches it to her clothing. The spelling of these words is sure to stick!

Jill Hamilton—Gr. 1
Schoeneck Elementary, Stevens, PA

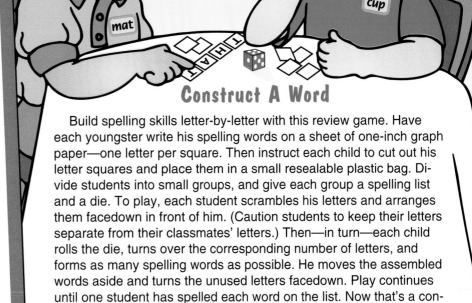

Construct A Word

Build spelling skills letter-by-letter with this review game. Have each youngster write his spelling words on a sheet of one-inch graph paper—one letter per square. Then instruct each child to cut out his letter squares and place them in a small resealable plastic bag. Divide students into small groups, and give each group a spelling list and a die. To play, each student scrambles his letters and arranges them facedown in front of him. (Caution students to keep their letters separate from their classmates' letters.) Then—in turn—each child rolls the die, turns over the corresponding number of letters, and forms as many spelling words as possible. He moves the assembled words aside and turns the unused letters facedown. Play continues until one student has spelled each word on the list. Now that's a constructive approach to spelling!

Kyle Welby—Gr. 1, Epstein Hebrew Academy, St. Louis, MO

Spell And Sort

Strengthen alphabetizing and sorting skills with this hands-on spelling activity. Have each student fold a sheet of blank paper in half three times, then unfold the paper and write a different spelling word in each box. Next have her cut apart the boxes and arrange the eight resulting word cards in alphabetical order. Verify each student's work before inviting her to sort her word cards by self-selected categories, such as vowel sounds or number of syllables. To wrap up the activity, have each student name the spelling words in each of her categories and ask her classmates to identify what sorting rule(s) she used. Students will have all sorts of fun with this engaging activity!

Sue Crosby
Camey Elementary
Colony, TX

Roll 'em!

This small-group game adds up to "die-namite" spelling! Give each group a pair of dice. Each student also needs his spelling list, a sheet of writing paper, and a pencil. To play, each group member takes a turn rolling the dice and adding the two numbers shown. The youngster who rolls the greatest sum wins the round and copies two spelling words on his paper. Play continues in the described manner until one student has listed all of his spelling words and is declared the winner. Count on this high-rolling game to be a race to the finish!

Jennifer Von Pinnon—Gr. 3
Eastwood Elementary
West Fargo, ND

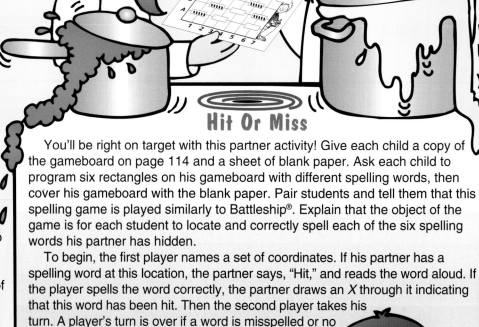

Hit Or Miss

You'll be right on target with this partner activity! Give each child a copy of the gameboard on page 114 and a sheet of blank paper. Ask each child to program six rectangles on his gameboard with different spelling words, then cover his gameboard with the blank paper. Pair students and tell them that this spelling game is played similarly to Battleship®. Explain that the object of the game is for each student to locate and correctly spell each of the six spelling words his partner has hidden.

To begin, the first player names a set of coordinates. If his partner has a spelling word at this location, the partner says, "Hit," and reads the word aloud. If the player spells the word correctly, the partner draws an X through it indicating that this word has been hit. Then the second player takes his turn. A player's turn is over if a word is misspelled or no word is located (a miss). Play continues until one student hits all six of his partner's spelling words. With this strategic game, students' spelling skills will be shipshape in no time at all!

Dianne E. Hammond—Gr. 3, North School
Londonderry, NH

Spell-O

Dish up this appetizing lotto game to strengthen spelling skills! Give each child a blank 16-space lotto board. Or have each child fold a blank sheet of paper in half four times, then unfold his paper to reveal 16 spaces. Then have each student randomly program his gameboard spaces with different spelling words. Also give each youngster a handful of Alpha-Bits® cereal to use as markers. To play, announce a word and spell it aloud with students. If a child has this word on his gameboard, he covers it with a piece of cereal. Continue in this manner until one player covers four spaces in a vertical, diagonal, or horizontal row and announces, "Spell-O!" To win the game, he reads aloud each word in the row for verification. The declared winner of the first game becomes the caller for the second game. After a desired number of games, invite students to munch on their markers!

Sue Crosby, Camey Elementary, Colony, TX

What A Deal!

This classroom version of "Let's Make A Deal®" is a prize-worthy approach to spelling! Collect a supply of small prize items like stickers, homework passes, wrapped candies, and coupons for free time, extra time at the class computer, or lunch with the teacher. For added fun, also gather some humorous prizes like last-person-in-line cards and pencil stubs. Use colorful paper to cover the sides and bottoms of three empty cans. Then invert the cans; number them "1," "2," and "3"; and slide a prize under each one. You will also need a supply of buck coupons like the one shown. In turn ask each student to spell a word aloud. If a student spells the word correctly, he may either collect a buck coupon for later use or choose a container and receive the prize that it conceals. If a student misspells the word he is given, his turn is over. Continue play—replacing prizes as needed—until each student has taken a turn. Plan to play this game once a week or as often as time allows. A student who collects five buck coupons may redeem them for the prize of his choice.

Linda J. Baranowski—Gr. 2, Green Lake Public School, Green Lake, WI

ONE BUCK COUPON
ABC
ONE BUCK COUPON

Hidden Words

This puzzling idea is quite a find! Have each youngster incorporate his spelling words into a word-search puzzle. To do this, he writes the words horizontally, vertically, and diagonally on a sheet of 1/2-inch graph paper—one letter per square. Then he fills in the remaining squares with miscellaneous letters. Next he trades puzzles with a classmate. For added fun have students try these simple variations as they solve the puzzles:

- Use a different color to circle each spelling word.
- Circle nouns in red and verbs in blue.
- Use a marker to highlight smaller words that are hidden within spelling words (Ex.: where).

Sue Crosby

Money Madness

You can bank on this idea to reinforce math *and* spelling skills! Display a poster that shows each alphabet letter with an assigned dollar value. Then challenge students to determine the cash value of each word on their spelling lists. Provide calculators for students' use if desired. Then, for added fun, budget time for the following worthy extension activities:

- Instruct students to write their spelling words in order from least to most expensive or vice versa.
- Pair students. Have each student dictate three spelling words to his partner. Each partner writes these words on his paper and determines their collective sum. The student who dictates the word list of lesser (greater) value wins the round.
- Challenge students to find words (other than spelling words) that are worth more (less) than $25, $50, and so on.
- To give students practice using decimal points, create a new code that features coin values such as "A = $.01" and "B = $.02."

Shirley Freeland—Gr. 3
Jefferson Parkway Elementary
Newnan, GA

Money Madness

A $1	J $10	S $19
B $2	K $11	T $20
C $3	L $12	U $21
D $4	M $13	V $22
E $5	N $14	W $23
F $6	O $15	X $24
G $7	P $16	Y $25
H $8	Q $17	Z $26
I $9	R $18	

Nifty Mnemonics

Create a memorable spelling lesson with this mnemonic activity! Explain to students that *mnemonics* is a strategy for committing tough-to-spell words to memory. To demonstrate the strategy, say the following phrase: "slam any inside door." Repeat the phrase as you write the first letter of each word on the chalkboard. Then ask youngsters to read the resulting word. Next write the phrase below the word and underline the first letter in each word. Repeat the activity, using a variety of hard-to-spell words. Then have each child design a page for a class book of mnemonic phrases. To do this, a child chooses a word that he has difficulty spelling and writes the word in crayon near the top of a sheet of drawing paper. Near the bottom of his paper, he writes a mnemonic phrase for the word in pencil and underlines the first letters in crayon. Then he illustrates his work. Bind the pages into a class book titled "Spelling Memory Boosters." Place this unique spelling resource in a writing center or another easily accessible classroom location.

Sue Crosby, Camey Elementary, Colony, TX

about

a bear opens up trees

Letter By Letter

Here's a hands-on task for letter-perfect spelling review! Have each student use a crayon to write the alphabet letters on one-inch graph paper—one letter per square. Instruct each child to repeat this activity three times, then cut out the resulting letter squares. Give each child a resealable plastic bag in which to store her letters; then have each student store her bag of letters in her desk. For a spontaneous spelling review, have students use the letters from their stored bags to spell words from the weekly list. Or surprise students and ask them to arrange their letters to spell words related to a current topic or theme being studied. This activity is spontaneous and it's fun, which means youngsters could decide this type of spelling is a perfect free-time activity!

Sue Crosby

Buddy Spelling

Double up on spelling practice with a buddy approach. Give each youngster an envelope to personalize. You will also need a colorful supply of paper slips. After a spelling test or writing conference, have each youngster correctly write each word she misspelled on a paper slip, then store the word slip(s) in her envelope. Every few days provide time for students to practice spelling their envelope words with different partners. After a desired number of weeks, have each student choose five to ten words from her envelope. Ask the student to spell these words for you (orally or on paper). Each word that is correctly spelled can be taken home. A misspelled word is returned to the student's envelope. Spelling accuracy will improve on the double!

Pat Urbach—Gr. 1, BA Kennedy, Prairie Du Chien, WI

Speedy Spelling

Students love the chance to outscore their teacher! And this spelling game provides plenty of opportunities! For each round of play, write a different spelling word on the chalkboard. Choose one student to oversee an egg timer and ask the remaining students to copy the word from the chalkboard onto their papers. The object of the game is to continually write the spelling word from the moment the egg timer is inverted until the student watching it calls out, "Time!" Then each student speller awards himself one point for every correct (and legible!) spelling for that round and writes his score near his word list. Identify the student who earns the highest score; then, with your youngsters' help, determine your score for the round by tallying the words you wrote on the chalkboard. If the student wins the round, award the class one point. If you win the round, award the teacher one point. When each spelling word has been speedily spelled, determine whom the speedier speller is: you or your students!

Laine Barresi
Central Academy Nongraded
Middletown, OH

Bonus Words

Motivate your young spellers with individualized bonus words. Label a large index card for each child. Each week date and program the card with a bonus word that is appropriate for the student's spelling skills. A youngster may keep his bonus spelling-word card at his desk, or you may store the cards in a central location. Throughout the week provide special bonus-word activities like "When you finish your math paper, use a crayon to write your bonus spelling word three times near the bottom of the page," or "During recess spell your bonus word out loud for everyone to hear!" When you administer your weekly spelling test, ask each child to write his bonus word in a complete sentence. If a student successfully completes this task, give him a foil star to attach near the word on his bonus spelling card. If he is not successful, encourage him to try again the following week. Each young speller will beam with pride as his galaxy of starred bonus words grows!

Diane Benner—Gr. 2
Dover Elementary
Dover, PA

113

Spelling
Partner game

Hit Or Miss!

	1	2	3	4	5	6	7
E							
D							
C							
B							
A							

Note To Teacher: Use with "Hit Or Miss" on page 110.

MATH UNITS

Monkeying Around With
Math And Literature

There's no monkey business in this unit—just practical, literature-related ideas for making math meaningful...and FUN!

ideas contributed by Judy Johnson, Lisa Kelly, Sharon Murphy, and Sr. M. Francesca Santacroce

The Greedy Triangle

Written by Marilyn Burns & Illustrated by Gordon Silveria
Scholastic Inc., 1995

The greedy triangle loves being busy! Each day it supports bridges, makes music, holds up roofs, and much, much more. For most shapes this lifestyle would be fulfilling. But not for the greedy triangle. Always eager to try new things, the triangle decides it is time to add another line and angle to its shape. Unfortunately this new shape isn't a perfect fit either. Thus begins a succession of new shapes until the greedy triangle no longer knows which side is up!

Use the greedy triangle's shapely experiences to shape up your students' geometry skills! After a just-for-fun oral reading of the story, revisit the book to help students remember what the triangle did as a three-sided shape. List these activities on the chalkboard. Also ask students to suggest other things a triangle could do, and add them to the list. Repeat this activity for each shape that the triangle became. Then, reveal that the students will be making a mural of a geometry kingdom that is similar to the greedy triangle's home. To do this, each student chooses a different shape and activity from the lists on the chalkboard. Then using provided supplies—such as a shape template, construction paper, glue, and markers—the student creates the shape he chose engaged in the activity he chose. Showcase the students' projects on a paper-covered bulletin board titled "Welcome to Shapesville!" Now that's a king-size way to size up shapes!

12 Ways To Get To 11

Written by Eve Merriam & Illustrated by Bernie Karlin
Aladdin Paperbacks, 1996

When this innovative picture book begins, all the numerals from 1 through 12 are present and accounted for—except 11. Where did it go? Is it hiding? Could it be wearing a disguise? The search for the elusive 11 takes the reader to 12 scenes that each feature a different combination of items. And guess what? The items in each scene add up to 11!

So what are the 12 ways to get to 11? To find out have each student number his paper from 1 to 12; then read the story aloud a second time. Stop after each number combination is presented and have the students write the corresponding addition sentence on their papers. Before you proceed have the class read in unison the sentence that they wrote. After all 12 combinations have been written and read, challenge the class to create other addition sentences that equal 11. Write each combination on the board, and ask each student to number and copy the sentence on his paper. Continue in this manner until the total number of addition sentences on each student's paper equals the class enrollment. Then have every student copy a different sentence from his list onto a large sheet of drawing paper and illustrate it. Challenge older students to write descriptive sentences about their illustrations, too. Invite each student to share his work with the class; then bind the projects between two construction-paper covers. Accurately title the book (for example, "23 Ways To Get To 11"); then place it in your classroom library for further reading enjoyment.

In the jungle are 10 bananas and 1 very happy monkey.

Pigs Will Be Pigs

Written by Amy Axelrod & Illustrated by Sharon McGinley-Nally
Simon & Schuster Children's Books, 1994

The Pig family has a problem. There's no food in the house, the family is temporarily out of cash, and everyone is hungry! Mrs. Pig knows just what to do! It's time to search the house—from top to bottom—for loose change and forgotten bills. Luckily for the pigs, there's plenty of money to be found, and before long the family is pigging out in a favorite restaurant.

Students will go hog-wild adding up the cash the Pig family finds! For this large-group activity, place a shoebox of transparent coin and dollar-bill cutouts near your overhead projector. You will need a cutout for each of the following coins and bills: penny, nickel, dime, quarter, half-dollar, $1, $2, $5, $10, $20. Then, during a second oral reading of the story, stop after Mr. Pig finds his lucky two-dollar bill. Ask a student volunteer to display the appropriate money cutout on the overhead projector; then write the amount near the top of the screen and return the cutout to the box. Continue your oral reading. Every time money is found, stop and ask a different volunteer to display on the overhead each type of coin or bill that was collected. Then, with input from your students, determine how much money was discovered and add the amount(s) to what has been collected so far. Students will discover that the Pigs have a whopping $34.67 when they leave for the restaurant!

To continue the fun, give each child a copy of the order ticket on page 121 and a copy of a menu from a local restaurant or a menu that you created. Challenge each student to use the menu and his estimation skills to write a dinner order for the pig family that costs no more than $34.67. Next have each child use a calculator to tally his ticket. Then take a class count to find out how many students stayed within the spending budget. Repeat the activity as many times as desired, providing student copies of the order ticket each time. Order up!

Pigs On A Blanket

Written by Amy Axelrod & Illustrated by Sharon McGinley-Nally
Simon & Schuster Children's Books, 1996

The Pig family is back again and this time it's looking for a change of pace. At 11:30 the pigs decide a day at the beach is the perfect remedy. After all, the beach is only an hour away, and they can be ready to hit the road in a manner of minutes—or so they think! Delays at home, delays on the road, and delays at the beach impede the pigs. And when the family is finally ready to swim, it's 5:30 and the beach is closing. My, how time flies!

Oink! Oink! Provide loads of hands-on time-telling practice with these precious piggy timepieces! To make a clock like the one shown, a student paints a flattened paper plate pink. After the plate dries, she uses colorful paper, markers or crayons, a brad, precut hour and minute hands, glue, and scissors to create an animated clock face that resembles a pig. To use the clocks, read the story aloud a second time and have each youngster manipulate the hands on her clock to coincide with the piggies' activities. For even more fun, invite each student to tell a story about a real or an imaginary family trip that includes several time-related references. As each student tells her story, have her classmates manipulate the hands on their clocks to coincide with the story events. Time sure flies when you're having fun!

117

Each Orange Had 8 Slices: A Counting Book

Written by Paul Giganti, Jr. & Illustrated by Donald Crews
Greenwillow Books, 1992

From ducks to oranges, this brightly illustrated counting book features a series of number-related scenarios that are each accompanied by three related questions.

This story provides the perfect opportunity for students to practice their counting and problem-solving skills. As you read the book aloud, stop after each set of three questions so students can study the picture. Next reread each question and enlist your students' help in answering it. After the final problem has been solved, have students make a class version of the book.

To begin, a child chooses a place that he likes to visit and imagines several things that he might see on his way there. Then he writes a description of what he sees on a 12" x 18" sheet of drawing paper. Ask each child to begin his writing with the phrase "On my way to…" Next the youngster carefully illustrates his description and writes three questions about it. Lastly he turns his paper over and on the back answers each question. Bind the students' work into a classroom volume titled "On My Way To…." Then display the book and challenge students to solve the problems!

A Fair Bear Share

Written by Stuart J. Murphy & Illustrated by John Speirs
HarperCollins Publishers, Inc.; 1998

Mama Bear promises to make her special blueberry pie if her four cubs gather the nuts, berries, and seeds that she needs. The cubs gather one ingredient at a time and bring it home to count. Mama Bear teaches the cubs to count quickly by putting each ingredient into piles of tens and ones, and she shows them how to regroup a ones pile into a ten. One little cub has another lesson to learn, too—there'll be no pie unless each cub does its "fair bear share" of gathering ingredients.

You can count on your students doing their fair share of work in this small-group activity! For every group of four students, program a card with three numbers that have a sum of less than 100. (Do not write the sum on the card.) Appoint a recorder in each group, and give this student the programmed card, a pencil, and paper. Give a paper plate to each remaining group member. In the center of each group, place a container of 99 unshelled peanuts or sunflower seeds, or purple jelly-bean berries.

To begin the activity, the recorder assigns each group member one number from the card. Then, using the cubs' counting strategy, these students count out their assigned number of ingredients onto their paper plates. To find the total number of ingredients collected, two group members combine their ingredients, regrouping if necessary. The recorder draws a picture or writes a number sentence on her paper to document this step. Then the third student adds her ingredients to the collection. The recorder documents this step as well, arriving at the total number of ingredients the group gathered. Check each group's work; then collect the cards and redistribute them to different groups and new group recorders. Then repeat the activity. Continue in this manner until each student has been a recorder. Conclude the activity by serving each youngster a "fair share" of a blueberry treat!

Right this way, please.

Dinner At The Panda Palace

Written by Stephanie Calmenson & Illustrated by Nadine Bernard Westcott
HarperCollins Children's Books, 1995

It's a very busy night at Panda Palace restaurant and Mr. Panda, the owner, must find seating for several hungry animals. Whether it's one hungry elephant, two carsick lions, or three pigs running from a wolf, Mr. Panda finds room for them all!

To set the stage for a place-value activity, make an minor adjustment during your first oral reading of the story. Rather than revealing the total number of patrons Mr. Panda seats and serves, replace the story line "Feeding fifty-five diners was no easy task" with the line "Feeding this many diners was no easy task." Then, at the conclusion of the story, ask students how many animals Mr. Panda fed. After a bit of discussion, tell students that you have an idea. Explain that if Mr. Panda seats his patrons at tables for ten, he could easily count his customers. Draw six large circles on the chalkboard and read the story aloud a second time. Stop reading after the first patron, the elephant, enters the restaurant. Ask a student volunteer to mark an X beside one circle to indicate that the elephant has been seated. Continue in this manner until all of Mr. Panda's customers are seated. Then have the students tally the tens and ones to determine the total number of animals Mr. Panda served. Older students can complete a similar seating arrangement on paper.

Give Me Half!

Written by Stuart J. Murphy & Illustrated by G. Brian Karas
HarperCollins Children's Books, 1996

There's a typical sibling situation unfolding in this simple rhyming story. A brother and a sister have different ideas about how to split a pizza for lunch. They can't agree on dessert portions either. Or on how much beverage each should get. For a third party, who most likely is a parent, the picture is clear—split everything in half!

Here's a fraction activity with plenty of taste appeal! At the conclusion of the book, give each student three 8-inch circles that you have visually divided as follows: one into halves, one into thirds, and one into fourths. A student decorates all three circles to resemble her favorite kind of pizza. Then, one at a time, she cuts each pizza apart and labels the backs of the pieces with the appropriate fraction. Next have students use their pizza slices to answer questions, such as "What is the smallest piece of pizza that you have?", "Which is more: one-half or one-third of a pizza?", or "How many fourths equal a half?"

Provide additional fraction practice with this appetizing activity. Give each youngster 12 candy pieces in a variety of colors. First ask the students how many candy pieces they would get to keep if they shared their candy with one friend (or two, three, or four friends). Then have each child determine what fractional part of his candy each color represents. (For example, if 5 candies are red, then 5/12 of the candy is red.) Finally have students eat a portion of their candies and repeat the activities using their new sets. Now that's an idea students will be glad to sink their teeth into!

Twelve Snails To One Lizard: A Tale Of Mischief And Measurement

Written by Susan Hightower & Illustrated by Matt Novak
Simon & Schuster Books For Young Readers, 1997

Milo the beaver needs a branch to patch a hole in his dam. The problem is he can't figure out exactly how long the branch needs to be. His buddy Bubba Bullfrog is full of measurement ideas—from one-inch snails to foot-long lizards to a boa that measures exactly one yard. These pond-side residents might (or might not!) be the perfect measurement tools for getting the job done.

Students will inch their way to better measurement skills with this partner activity! For each student pair, duplicate 12 snail patterns onto brown construction paper and 3 lizard head and body patterns onto green construction paper (see the patterns on page 121). Have the partners cut out their patterns and glue each lizard head to a lizard body. Also have each twosome decorate a one-yard length of adding-machine tape to resemble a boa.

To begin the activity, write the titles "Snail," "Lizard," and "Snake" on the chalkboard. Then, under your students' direction, list classroom items under each title that could be measured using the corresponding nonstandard unit. Next have each student pair write one or two items from each list on a sheet of paper, measure each item, and write its measurement beside its name. To conclude the activity, invite students to share the measurements they gathered for the items listed on the chalkboard. Students will quickly see how well they measure up!

How long?		
Student	all day	half day
Milo	X	
Percy	X	
Sally		X
Jack		X

The Best Vacation Ever

Written by Stuart J. Murphy & Illustrated by Nadine Bernard Westcott
HarperCollins Children's Books; 1997

It's time for a family vacation and this busy family can't even find the time to decide where to go. Should the place be warm or cool? Near or far? Exciting or relaxing? It's the youngest family member who decides to collect a little data and determine the perfect vacation spot for her active family!

It will probably take only one oral reading of this delightful picture book and your youngsters will be ready to plan their own family vacations! Instead suggest that the students use the method described to plan a special classroom event. To begin, ask students to brainstorm a variety of questions that will help them determine what type of special event to plan. Questions might include "Should the event be inside or outside?", "Should the event be related to math, reading, social studies, or science?", and "Should students dress up for the event?" Next design a simple chart that can be used to collect data for each question. Rather than listing every child's name on each chart, make it each child's responsibility to sign and indicate his answer on every chart. Then post the charts in an area that is easily accessible and make available a variety of colorful markers for students to use to record their answers. When each child has had an opportunity to contribute to each chart, enlist your students' help in calculating and recording the total number of responses for each answer. Then help the students use the information they've gathered to plan a special classroom event. Let the fun begin!

Use the lizard patterns with *Twelve Snails To One Lizard* on page 120.

Use the order ticket with *Pigs Will Be Pigs* on page 117.

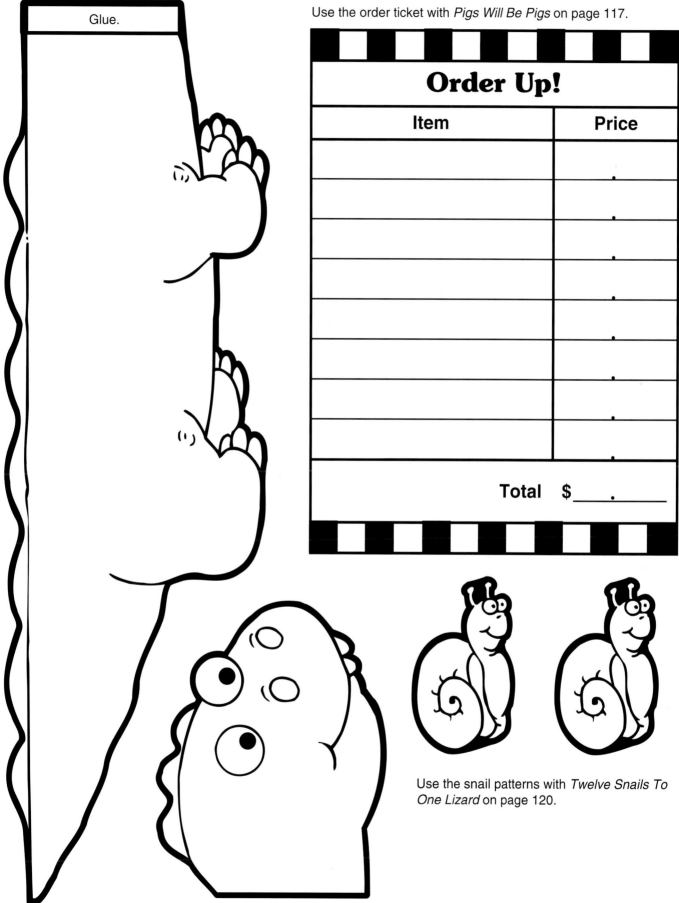

Glue.

Order Up!

Item	Price
	.
	.
	.
	.
	.
	.
	.
	.
	.
Total	$ ___ .

Use the snail patterns with *Twelve Snails To One Lizard* on page 120.

Keep your youngsters' multiplication skills on course with these teacher-tested maneuvers!

Need Ideas For Reinforcing Addition And Subtraction Facts?
Look for this symbol (✳) at the end of an activity. These ideas can easily be adapted for this purpose.

Stamping Sets

Steer students to a picture-perfect understanding of multiplication with Crayola® Washable MiniStampers! Give each child a ministamp marker to keep as her own, or keep a class supply on hand. For a large-group activity, announce individual multiplication facts. A student writes the fact on her paper. Then she uses a marker and her pencil to create the corresponding set or sets before she writes the fact answer. Encourage students to use this technique when working independently, too. Vroom!

Anne Fuchs—Grs. K–2 Title I, Rosemount Elementary
Rosemount, MN

Colorful Beadwork

Need to refuel your youngsters' understanding of multiplication sets? Try this colorful hands-on approach! Every student needs a pipe cleaner and access to a supply of colorful craft beads. First have each child knot one end of his pipe cleaner. Then have each student thread beads onto his pipe cleaner to show the set(s) associated with a specified fact. For example, to show "2 x 3," a student might thread three red beads onto his pipe cleaner, followed by three blue beads. Then have the students announce the product of the fact before they remove the beads from their pipe cleaners and await the next fact. Continue in this manner for as long as desired. Confusion over multiplication sets will be a thing of the past—and that's a fact!

Vicki Kulp—Gr. 3
Bushkill Elementary School
Nazareth, PA

A Matter Of Multiples

Try this crowd-pleasing plan for reinforcing multiples! Each day for math warm-up, play a game of Secret Number. To play, draw a line on the chalkboard. Write a number to the left of the line; then write a greater number to the right of the line. Explain that the secret number is between these two numbers. Also tell what the secret number is a multiple of. Then have students ask questions about the number's identity. Require that each question include a multiple of the provided multiple. For example, if the secret number is a multiple of four, a student might ask, "Is the number between 12 and 24?" or "Is the number greater than 28?" When the secret number is identified, the game is over. Mastering multiples will make memorizing multiplication facts a breeze!

Trisha Owen—Gr. 3
Libbey Elementary School
Wheatland, WY

Communicating Commutative Property

Take the illusion out of commutative property at this pit stop! Tell students that the product of a multiplication fact stays the same when the factors are reversed. To prove your point, have each child trim a 9" x 12" sheet of black construction paper into the shape of a magician's hat. Then give each child 12 animal crackers. Write "3 x 4" on the chalkboard and instruct students to arrange their manipulatives into three groups of four crackers each on their hats. Then write "4 x 3" on the chalkboard and have the students use the same manipulatives to form four groups of three crackers each. Presto—it's the same product! Repeat the exercise using other facts having products of 12 or less. Then, for the ultimate vanishing act, invite each student to eat his math manipulatives. Hey, that's zero times zero!

Rebecca Brudwick—Gr. 1
Hoover Elementary School
North Mankato, MN

In The Cards

Spark additional interest in fact practice with this partner game. Remove the face cards and aces from a deck of playing cards; then store the remaining cards at a center. To play, one partner shuffles the cards and places them facedown on the playing surface. Then, in turn, each partner draws two cards from the stack and places them faceup. Next, each partner announces the product of his two cards. The student with the highest (lowest) product wins the round and keeps all four cards. If the players' products are equal, each partner draws one more card. Then he multiplies the numerals from two of his cards to create the highest (lowest) possible product. The player who wins the round keeps all six cards. The game is over when one player holds all the cards! ✽

Jolene DuBose—Gr. 2
A.T. Mahan Elementary School
Keflavik, Iceland

Pass It Along!

This fact review is a ball of fun and speedy, too! In advance, use a permanent marker to randomly label an inflated beach ball with numerals from 0 to 10. To play, have students quickly line up single file. Toss the ball to the first person in line. When this student catches the ball, he reads aloud the factor that is closest to each thumb in the form of a multiplication problem, then answers the problem out loud. As soon as his answer is approved by you, he quickly passes the ball between his legs (or over his head) to the student behind him. This student repeats the procedure. When the last person in line answers his problem, he tosses the ball to you. Store the ball for later use. Plan to play this fast, fun, and factual review one or more times a week! ✽

Dawna Salldin—Gr. 3
Wadsworth Elementary School
Palm Coast, FL

Barry
Slate

Daily Lotto

A daily practice lap of lotto is a surefire way to reinforce multiplication facts! Have each child store in her desk a zippered bag that contains paper markers and a laminated lotto card of fact answers. Each day, begin math by announcing the lotto game of the day (like Black Out, Four Corners, Four In A Row, etc.). When the students are ready to play, write individual fact problems on the overhead or chalkboard. If the problem's product is on a student's lotto board, she covers it with a paper marker. The first student to cover the lotto spaces needed to win the game announces "Lotto!" Reward the winner of each day's game with a seasonal sticker. This daily practice is sure to help students memorize their facts! ✽

Nicole Weber—Grs. 2–3, Waterloo Elementary School
Waterloo, WI

Multiplication Basketball

Speed and accuracy count when it comes to this fast-paced fact game! All you need to play is a set of multiplication flash cards, an empty wastepaper basket, and a small rubber ball. Divide students into two teams. After asking one member from each team to stand, display a flash card. The student who is first to provide the correct answer earns one point for his team and a shot at the basket. If the player shoots the rubber ball into the wastepaper basket, he earns two more points for his team. Choose two different players for the next round of play. Continue playing until every child has participated at least once. The team with the most points at the end of game time wins! *

Sonya Huss—Gr. 1
Windsor Woods Elementary
Virginia Beach, VA

A Piece Of Cake!

Your young drivers will be eager to prove that multiplication is a piece of cake—especially when their efforts are rewarded with cake! As soon as each child masters a predetermined number of multiplication factors (for example, factors through five), ask a parent volunteer to bake and frost a large sheet cake for the students. For added fun, suggest that the parent volunteer cut the cake into serving-size portions, then use decorating gel to program each portion with a multiplication fact. When the cake is served to the class, you can count on each student to answer his fact *and* eat his cake, too! *

adapted from an idea by Debbie Lerner—Grs. 1–3 Multiage
Red Bridge Elementary
Kansas City, MO

WINNER'S CIRCLE

Tasty Motivation

Entice students to memorize multiplication facts with the promise of a taco party. How does this plan work? The students, working at their own pace, earn party refreshments by mastering their multiplication tables! Program a copy of "Taco Party!" on page 125 with a party date; then duplicate a class supply of the form. Have each child personalize his form and keep it in his math folder or another designated location. Each time a child shows mastery of a times table, date and sign his form. On the day of the party, each child enjoys the refreshments he has earned. Now that's a "taco-rific" plan! *

Shannon Jones—Gr. 3, John Redd Smith Elementary
Collinsville, VA

Ready, Set, Multiply!

Use the handy form on page 125 to create an individualized speed-drill program. First program a copy of the form for each factor, zero through ten (or 12). Do this by writing the factor in the star on the car. Then duplicate a supply of each programmed form and file it in an individual folder labeled with the corresponding factor. Each child begins the program with factor zero. Each time a student shows mastery of a factor, he progresses to the next higher factor. To take a speed drill, a student revs up his engine by first writing the car's number in each circle. Then he waits patiently for a starting signal from you. When the signal is given, he answers as many facts as he can in the time allotted. Ready, set, multiply!

Name _____

Taco Party!

Memorize your facts!
Earn a taco and more!

The party will be ___

Fact	Date Mastered	Signature	Party Item
x 0			cup
x 1			drink
x 2			paper plate
x 3			taco shell
x 4			meat
x 5			napkin
x 6			lettuce
x 7			tomatoes
x 8			cheese
x 9			ingredient of your choice
x 10			chips and salsa

©The Education Center, Inc. • *THE MAILBOX®* • *Primary* • Feb/Mar 1999

Name _____

Ready, Set, Multiply!

Answer each fact.

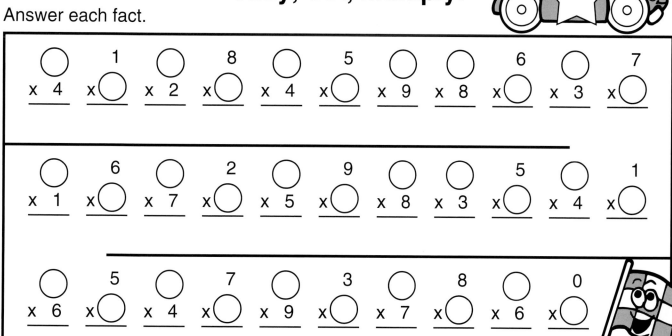

○ x 4	1 x ○	8 x 2	○ x 4	5 x ○	○ x 9	○ x 8	6 x 3	○ x ○	7
○ x 1	6 x ○	2 x 7	○ x 5	9 x ○	○ x 8	○ x 3	5 x 4	○ x ○	1
○ x 6	5 x ○	7 x 4	○ x 9	3 x ○	○ x 7	○ x 6	8 x ○	○ x ○	0

©The Education Center, Inc. • *THE MAILBOX®* • *Primary* • Feb/Mar 1999

Note To Teacher: Use the taco incentive plan with "Tasty Motivation" on page 124. Use the speed-drill form with "Ready, Set, Multiply!" on page 124.

125

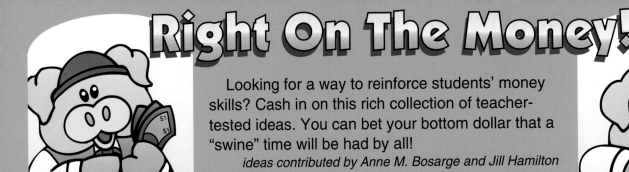

Right On The Money!

Looking for a way to reinforce students' money skills? Cash in on this rich collection of teacher-tested ideas. You can bet your bottom dollar that a "swine" time will be had by all!

ideas contributed by Anne M. Bosarge and Jill Hamilton

Coin Collections

To complete the activities in this unit, each student needs a collection of coins. For easy management give each child a personalized envelope (or resealable plastic bag) to serve as a wallet, and a set of imitation coins to store inside. If you prefer real coins, request in a note to parents that each child bring a specific set of coins to school for this purpose.

Money, Dough, Or Moolah?

Get your money unit off to a profitable start with this intriguing activity. Show students a dollar bill and a handful of coins. Ask students what these items are called and write their responses on the chalkboard. Broaden your youngsters' vocabularies by adding to the list some less familiar names for money, like *sawbacks, moolah, greenbacks, bread, bucks, oof, gelt, bits, skins,* and *cabbage.* Then, for added fun, share several money expressions from the provided list and challenge students to determine the meaning of each one.

Money Expressions

"A dime a dozen"
"Your bottom dollar"
"Two cents' worth"
"A penny for your thoughts"
"Time is money."
"Money talks."
"Money doesn't grow on trees."
"Show me the money!"
"A fool and his money are soon parted."
"The love of money is the root of all evil."
"Money can't buy happiness."
"Penny-pincher"
"You look like a million bucks!"
"A penny saved is a penny earned."
"Nickel-and-diming"

Kimberly Richard

Profitable Patterns

If your students need practice identifying coins, this patterning activity is a wise investment! Pair students and give each partner an identical set of coins. In turn each student uses his coin set to create a pattern; then his partner uses his set of coins to continue the pattern. Next the two students work together to state the name and value of each coin in the pattern they created. To increase the difficulty of the task, have each student pair determine the total value of each completed pattern. Wow! Who would have thought coin patterns could be so profitable!

The Banker Says...

Reinforce coin-recognition and listening skills with this variation of the popular game Simon Says. Give each small group a penny, nickel, dime, and quarter for every group member except one. (For example, a group of six students will receive five of each coin.) Ask each group to randomly arrange its coins on a playing surface. Also select one member in each group to be the banker. To play, a banker tells his group to pick up a specific coin. The group members should respond only if the banker's request is prefaced by "The banker says." After the banker has verified the coins that were selected, the coins are returned to the playing surface. A student who chooses an incorrect coin or who responds without the banker's okay sits out for one round of play. After a designated amount of game time, appoint a different banker for each group and resume play. Continue in this manner until each group member has been the banker. Now that's a game plan you can take to the bank!

Pick up a quarter.

Days Of The Week	Number Of Pockets	1¢ Pocket Value	5¢ Pocket Value
Monday	48	48¢	$2.40
Tuesday	60	60¢	$3.00

Pocket Change

Cash in with this daily small-group activity! Give each group a supply of pennies and ask each child to put one penny in each pocket she is wearing. Next have the students remove the pennies from their pockets and determine the cash value of each group member's pockets and the cash value of the entire group's pockets. Then assist the class in finding the total cash value of all the students' pockets. For older students, extend the activity by challenging the small groups to determine similar totals based on a pocket value of five or ten cents. If desired, record this information on a chart like the one shown. Plan to repeat the activity every few days during your study of money. No doubt your youngsters' money skills will grow right along with the number of pockets they are wearing!

Breaking The Bank!

Oink! Oink! This small-group game provides plenty of practice with coin identification. On pink construction paper, duplicate a class supply of the piggy-bank pattern on page 131. Laminate and cut out the piggy banks. Also make a spinner wheel (like the one shown) for each group. Divide the class into small groups. Give each group a spinner wheel, a sharpened pencil, and a large paper clip to use as a spinner. Then give each group member a piggy-bank cutout and a predetermined number of coins to place on her bank. (The total value of the coins may vary, but the *number* of coins must be the same.)

To play, each player in turn spins the spinner and removes from her bank the coin that matches the value she has spun. She places this coin in a personal discard pile. If a student spins the pig, she acts like a little pig and puts the coins from her discard pile back in her bank. The first player to empty her bank wins the game!

Dollar Details

Because the dollar bill is used more frequently than any other paper money, it has the shortest life span—only 18 months. During that time, a dollar bill changes hands an average of 400 times! Use "The Dollar Song" and "Dollar Booklet" on this page to reinforce the value of this very popular greenback.

The Dollar Song

(sung to the tune of "Ten Little Indians")

10 little, 20 little, 30 little pennies.
40 little, 50 little, 60 little pennies.
70 little, 80 little, 90 little pennies.
100 pennies make a dollar!

2 small, 4 small, 6 small nickels.
8 small, 10 small, 12 small nickels.
14 small, 16 small, 18 small nickels.
20 nickels make a dollar!

1 tiny, 2 tiny, 3 tiny dimes.
4 tiny, 5 tiny, 6 tiny dimes.
7 tiny, 8 tiny, 9 tiny dimes.
10 dimes make a dollar!

1 big, 2 big, 3 big quarters.
4 big, 4 big, 4 big quarters.
1 big, 2 big, 3 big quarters.
4 quarters make a dollar!

Rebecca Brudwick—Gr. 1
Hoover Elementary School
North Mankato, MN

Dollar Booklet

Here's a great way for students to make some bucks and brush up on their money skills, too! To make a dollar booklet, a student stacks three 8 1/2" x 11" sheets of white paper and holds the pages vertically. He slides the top sheet upward approximately one inch and the bottom sheet downward approximately one inch. Next the student folds his papers forward to create six graduated layers or pages; then he staples the resulting booklet close to the fold. The student writes the title "[Student's name]'s Dollar Booklet" on the cover and labels the bottoms of the booklet pages as shown. To complete his booklet, he illustrates the dollar bill and stamps the appropriate coin impressions on the corresponding booklet pages.

Shari Sullivan Marshall, Crested Butte, CO

21¢

dollar bill
quarters
dimes
nickels
pennies

Money March

Students march toward better money-counting skills with this game plan! To make a trail of coins like the one shown, enlarge the coin patterns on page 131 and duplicate a supply of each coin on an appropriate color of paper. Laminate and cut out the coins; then tape a path of cutouts on the floor. (Store the extra coins for later use.) Post the cash value of the coin path in a designated location. A student orally adds the coin values as he marches alongside the path. Then he verifies his cash total with the one that you've posted. Modify the coin path every few days, remembering to post its corresponding cash value each time. You can count on improved money-counting skills in no time!

Money Necklaces

You can count on this large-group activity creating quite an interest in money and fashion! To make a money necklace for each child, fold a blank card in half and hole-punch the card near the fold. Thread a length of yarn through the resulting holes and tie the yarn ends. Next stamp a set of coin impressions on the front flap of the card (a different set for each child); then lift the flap and write the value of the coins.

Divide students into two equal-size groups (A and B). In an open area, have the members of Group A stand in a circle and face outward. Then have Group B form an outer circle that faces inward. Align the students so that each member of Group B is facing a partner from Group A. Allow time for each student to count the money shown on his partner's necklace and check his sum. Then, on a predetermined signal, have the students in Group B rotate clockwise one student, and repeat the activity. Continue in this manner until the students are rejoined with their original partners. Counting money has never been so stylish!

Money Spin-Off

Take students' money-counting skills for a spin! For this large-group activity, use your overhead projector to display a transparent spinner for class viewing. To make the spinner, visually divide a transparent circle into four sections and program each section with a different coin value. Then, using a fastener, snap a loose spinner in the center of the wheel. Each student will need a supply of coins and a sheet of paper to use as a workmat. To begin the activity, spin the spinner. Announce the designated value and have each student place the corresponding coin on his workmat. Then spin again and have each student place this coin on his workmat. In between spins ask the students to tell you how much money they have collected. For easy counting, encourage students to reduce the number of coins on their workmats by continually exchanging coins of lesser value for those of higher value. Continue play until $1.00 or another predetermined amount is collected.

Once students are familiar with the activity, divide the class into two teams. Enlist one player from each team to be the team spinner. The team spinners alternately spin for cash amounts. The first team to collect a predetermined amount of cash wins the game.

Cups O' Coins

Cups of coins are great investments in your youngsters' money skills. Sequentially number one Styrofoam® cup for every two students; then place coin sets of varying values in the cups. Pair students and give each twosome a cup of coins, a pencil, and a sheet of paper. One student in each pair sequentially numbers the paper to match the total number of coin cups created. Then each twosome gently spills its coins onto a work area, determines the cash value of the coins, and writes this amount on the paper beside the cup's number. On a signal from you, each pair passes its cup of coins to the next twosome along a designated route. The activity continues in this manner until each pair has counted and recorded a cash amount for each cup. What a "cent-sational" way to improve your youngsters' money-counting skills!

Bags Of Money!

Shake up an interest in counting money with this partner activity. For every two students, place ten or more coins of various values in a paper lunch bag and fold down the top of the resulting money bag. Then pair students and give each twosome a money bag, and scrap paper and a pencil for keeping score. In turn, each partner shakes the money bag, then reaches inside it without looking and removes three coins. Next each partner determines the total value of the coins he is holding. The student who has the higher money value earns one point for the round of play. Then both partners return their coins to the money bag, and another round of play begins. The player with the most points at the end of game time wins! As students perfect their money-counting skills, increase the number of coins they remove from the bag.

The Coin Exchange

Your young tycoons will jump at the chance to try their luck at the Coin Exchange. Pair students and give each twosome a die. Also give each student a duplicated gameboard similar to the one shown and the following coins: five pennies, two nickels, two dimes, and one quarter. To play, each partner in turn rolls the die. If a student rolls a five or less, she places an equivalent number of pennies atop the penny spaces on her gameboard. If she rolls a six, her turn is over. When a player fills all five penny spaces, she exchanges the pennies for a nickel. When she earns two nickels, she exchanges them for a dime, and so on. The first player who exchanges her coins for a quarter strikes it rich as the winner of the game!

The Piggy General Store

Reinforce students' money skills at a specialty store that only accepts piggy currency! Label a classroom area "The Piggy General Store." Stock this area with low-cost or donated items, such as paperback books, erasers, small toys, wrapped candies, posters, and pencils. Price each item—making sure to vary the prices so that some items will be easily affordable and others will require students to save their earnings. You will also need a toy cash register (or something similar) that you've stocked with duplicated piggy coins and dollars (see the patterns on page 132). Finally post a sign that tells the days and times that the store will be open for business.

Next have students suggest ways that they can earn spending money. Encourage ideas that reinforce positive behaviors, such as helping others, wearing school colors, sharing materials, and keeping a clean desk. Then list the students' ideas on poster board and beside each item, indicate its cash reward. Display the resulting chart in a prominent classroom location.

Throughout your money unit, use piggy currency to reward your students' positive actions as outlined on the posted chart. If desired, have each student save his earnings in a resealable plastic bag. Students make desired purchases from The Piggy General Store during business hours. No doubt students will give this shopping experience three oinks!

Michelle McClanahan–Gr. 3, Christa McAuliffe Elementary, Lewisville, TX

Use the coin patterns with "Money March" on page 128.

Use the pig pattern with "Breaking The Bank!" on page 127.

Piggy Currency Patterns

Use with "The Piggy General Store" on page 130.

A JUNGLE OF GEOMETRY

If you'd like to know how other teachers across the country reinforce geometry concepts, take a trek through this jungle. Nestled among the foliage you'll find ideas for strengthening a menagerie of skills, from recognizing flat shapes to understanding symmetry. It's just what you need to get your youngsters into the swing of geometry!

BACKGROUND FOR THE TEACHER

In this collection of ideas, the term *flat shape* will describe a two-dimensional shape (also called a *plane figure*), such as a circle or a square. The term *solid shape* will describe any three-dimensional shape (also called a *space figure*), such as a sphere, cone, or cube.

SHAPELY JUNGLE

Do you wish your students were WILD about geometry? Try this! Create a simple jungle backdrop for a large bulletin board and add the title "Shapely Jungle." To introduce the activity, share with your students Lois Ehlert's *Color Farm* or *Color Zoo* (both published by HarperCollins Publishers, Inc.; 1997). In each book, assorted flat shapes are used to create nine animals living in the named habitat. Have students recall the flat shapes used in the book and name additional ones. Then write a student-generated list of jungle animals. Next challenge each child to create a jungle animal for the display by cutting out and gluing together assorted construction-paper shapes. For best results, provide shape templates in a variety of sizes. Showcase the completed projects at the display.

Vickie Carter
Keller, TX

SHAPE DETECTIVES

Put your youngsters hot on the trail of flat shapes! Ask students to pretend that they are detectives who have been assigned to a very important case—tracking down missing flat shapes. Provide a list of shapes that are hiding throughout the classroom, such as circles, squares, triangles, and rectangles. Then have each supersleuth choose a shape from the list and write its name on a copy of page 139. To complete the activity, the student illustrates an animated likeness of the flat shape, then he carefully describes the shape, lists three or more places where it has been seen, and signs his name. Set aside time for students to share their completed work with their classmates. Now that's a fun way to track down shapes!

Debbie Murphy, Goodnoe Elementary
Holland, PA

Barry Slate

MISSING SHAPE

Name of shape: Sneaky Square
Description of shape: It has four lines that are all the same length. It has four corners. It is a closed shape.

This shape has been seen posing as: the cover of a book, a yellow sticky note, a section of the calendar, and a space on a gameboard.

Information provided by Detective: Gregory Cap

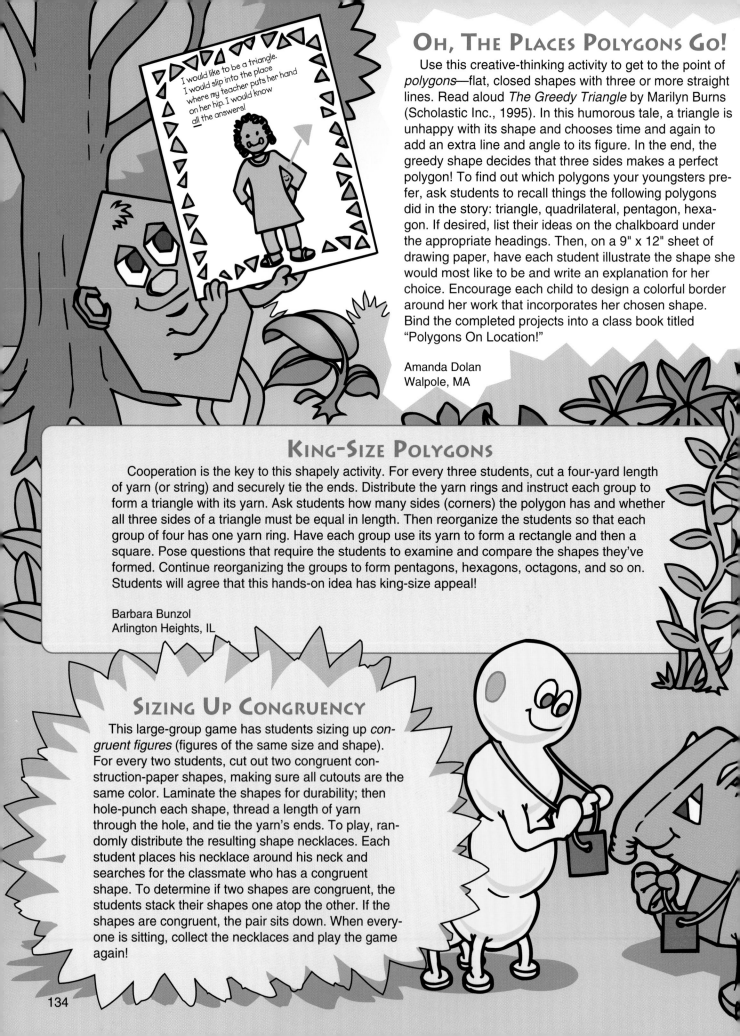

OH, THE PLACES POLYGONS GO!

Use this creative-thinking activity to get to the point of *polygons*—flat, closed shapes with three or more straight lines. Read aloud *The Greedy Triangle* by Marilyn Burns (Scholastic Inc., 1995). In this humorous tale, a triangle is unhappy with its shape and chooses time and again to add an extra line and angle to its figure. In the end, the greedy shape decides that three sides makes a perfect polygon! To find out which polygons your youngsters prefer, ask students to recall things the following polygons did in the story: triangle, quadrilateral, pentagon, hexagon. If desired, list their ideas on the chalkboard under the appropriate headings. Then, on a 9" x 12" sheet of drawing paper, have each student illustrate the shape she would most like to be and write an explanation for her choice. Encourage each child to design a colorful border around her work that incorporates her chosen shape. Bind the completed projects into a class book titled "Polygons On Location!"

Amanda Dolan
Walpole, MA

KING-SIZE POLYGONS

Cooperation is the key to this shapely activity. For every three students, cut a four-yard length of yarn (or string) and securely tie the ends. Distribute the yarn rings and instruct each group to form a triangle with its yarn. Ask students how many sides (corners) the polygon has and whether all three sides of a triangle must be equal in length. Then reorganize the students so that each group of four has one yarn ring. Have each group use its yarn to form a rectangle and then a square. Pose questions that require the students to examine and compare the shapes they've formed. Continue reorganizing the groups to form pentagons, hexagons, octagons, and so on. Students will agree that this hands-on idea has king-size appeal!

Barbara Bunzol
Arlington Heights, IL

SIZING UP CONGRUENCY

This large-group game has students sizing up *congruent figures* (figures of the same size and shape). For every two students, cut out two congruent construction-paper shapes, making sure all cutouts are the same color. Laminate the shapes for durability; then hole-punch each shape, thread a length of yarn through the hole, and tie the yarn's ends. To play, randomly distribute the resulting shape necklaces. Each student places his necklace around his neck and searches for the classmate who has a congruent shape. To determine if two shapes are congruent, the students stack their shapes one atop the other. If the shapes are congruent, the pair sits down. When everyone is sitting, collect the necklaces and play the game again!

SHAPE IT!

Get students in touch with solid shapes! Give each child a golf ball–size portion of modeling clay. Announce a solid shape—such as a sphere, cube, cone, box, or cylinder—and challenge students to form the shape with their clay. Verify each child's work; then repeat the activity for each solid shape being studied. This kinesthetic learning process is sure to give students a good feel for solid shapes.

Ruth Heller—Gr. 3
Public School 156
Laurelton, NY

THE GREAT SHAPE HUNT

Head outdoors for this solid shape hunt! You need a camera and film with enough exposures for every two students to take one photograph. Pair students and lead them around the school grounds. Ask each twosome to locate an object that represents a solid shape the class is studying. Assist each pair in photographing the object it identifies and make a note of what the pair photographs. When the pictures are developed, have each twosome make a page for a class book. To do this, a pair glues its photograph on a 6" x 9" sheet of construction paper. Then it describes the photographed shape on a large index card. In its description, the pair includes the name of the photographed object, where it is located, and the solid shape it represents. Then the pair glues its index card to the back of its mounted photograph. Compile these pages into a class book titled "Name That Shape." Place the book at a math center. To complete the center, a student studies each photograph, determines the solid shape it represents, and turns the page to check his answer.

Carrie Hursh—Gr. 1
Harrison Elementary
Harrison, OH

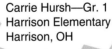

This picture shows the flagpole at the front of our school. The flagpole is a cylinder.

SNACKTIME SHAPE-UP

This solid shape review is a tasty experience! Give each student a resealable plastic bag containing snack items that are cubes, boxes, cylinders, spheres, and cones. Consider items like cheese cubes, caramel candies, stick pretzels, marshmallows, malted milk balls, Bugles® corn snacks, and candy kisses. Then announce a solid shape and ask students to remove the corresponding snack items from their bags. Have the students examine the snack items to determine how many sides, corners, and edges (if any) the solid shape has; then invite the students to eat those snacks. Repeat the activity for each snack shape. Delicious!

Cindy Boger—Gr. 2, Balls Creek Elementary School, Newton, NC
Dianne Neumann—Gr. 2, Frank C. Whiteley School, Hoffman Estates, IL

IMPORTANT SHAPES

What's so important about solid shapes? Plenty! To prepare for this writing activity, write the name of each solid shape your students are studying on an individual length of bulletin-board paper. Also display a sample of each shape. To review each shape, have the students pass around the sample and name the shape's unique qualities. List their ideas on the appropriate poster. Next read aloud Margaret Wise Brown's *The Important Book* (HarperTrophy, 1990). Discuss the repetitive nature of the book's text and talk about how this pattern can be used to create pages for a class book titled "The Important Book Of Solid Shapes." To make her page for the book, a student chooses a solid shape and describes important things about it. If desired, specify that each student page tell how many *faces, corners,* and *edges* the shape has and name three or more objects of that shape. After reading this class publication, students are sure to agree that solid shapes are very important!

Katherine Ritchie Dent—Gr. 2
Miami Country Day School
Miami, FL

The important thing about a **CUBE** is that all of its faces are the same size.

A cube looks like an ice cube or an alphabet block. A game die is a cube too.
A cube has 8 corners.
A cube has 6 faces.
A cube has 12 edges.
But
the important thing about a cube is that all of its faces are the same size.

GROCERY BAG GEOMETRY

Recognizing solid shapes is in the bag—the grocery bag that is! For this small group activity, you need one large paper grocery bag per group. For easy management, program each bag with a different number or letter; then, in each bag, place ten nonbreakable, everyday items that represent the solid shapes your students are studying. Be sure to vary the contents of each bag. To begin, have each group remove and study each item in its bag. Then, on your signal, have each group return the ten items to the bag. Next challenge each group to recall each item it studied and write the name and shape of the item on a sheet of paper. When appropriate, have each group check its resulting list against the items in its bag. Then rotate the bags among the groups and repeat the activity. Continue in this manner until each group has completed the activity with every bag.

adapted from an idea by Shelly Lanier
Reeds Elementary
Lexington, NC

WELCOME TO SHAPESVILLE

Find out how well your youngsters' knowledge of shapes is shaping up with this hands-on activity. A week or two in advance, invite students to bring to school clean and empty boxes (cereal, gift, shoe), cardboard tubes, and other such items that represent solid shapes. Also provide an assortment of construction paper and shape templates. When there is an ample supply of materials, inform students that their next geometry assignment is to create a community called Shapesville from shapes! Ask students to brainstorm structures and locations to include in the community, and list their ideas on the chalkboard. Next have each child select one or more items from the list to create. On a designated date, have each child present his completed project(s) to the class and identify several of the shapes he used. Then enlist your students' help in organizing the projects on a paper-covered table. For a fun follow-up, each day post the name of a solid or flat shape and challenge students to find as many examples of the shape as they can in Shapesville!

Sherra Sterling—Grs. 2–3
Colonial Hills Elementary
Houston, TX

SCENES OF SYMMETRY

Students' symmetry skills take shape right before your eyes with this picture-perfect project! First demonstrate how to cut an object (like a heart) from folded paper. Show students the unfolded cutout and explain that when objects are cut out in this way, the fold line is a line of symmetry. Then have students cut out a variety of shapes from folded paper scraps, unfold the shapes, and use their pencils to trace the lines of symmetry. As a finale, have each child design a scene of symmetry. To do this, a student cuts out colorful symmetrical shapes that relate to a specific setting; then he glues the cutouts on a sheet of construction paper, creating a desired scene. Display the projects with the title "Scenes Of Symmetry."

Amanda Dolan
Walpole, MA

ANSWER KEY

Symmetrical	Not Symmetrical
A B C D E H I K M O Q T U V W X Y	F G J L N P R S Z

ALPHABET SYMMETRY

Symmetry in the alphabet? You bet! Use this math center to convince students of this fascinating fact. Store a set of vinyl or felt uppercase letter cutouts in a resealable plastic bag. Place the bag of letters, a supply of paper, an answer key, and pencils at the center. A student draws a line of symmetry on his paper and labels the two resulting columns "Symmetrical" and "Not Symmetrical." Next he removes the letters from the bag. He bends each letter cutout in several directions to determine if it is symmetrical; then he writes the letter on his paper in the appropriate column. When all the letters have been examined, he uses the answer key to check his work. Don't be surprised if students request to inspect a set of lowercase letters, too!

Diane Fortunato—Gr. 2
Carteret School
Bloomfield, NJ

SYMMETRICAL DESIGNS

Reinforce symmetry with this partner activity! To begin, each student draws a line of symmetry on a sheet of one-inch graph paper. Then he uses crayons to color a desired design on one side of the symmetry line. Next each student trades places with a classmate—leaving his design and his crayons at his desk. Each child now carefully colors his partner's paper so that a symmetrical design results. Allow time at the end of the activity for each twosome to evaluate its designs for accuracy. Keep a supply of graph paper on hand! You can count on students being eager to repeat this partner activity again and again.

adapted from an idea by Donna Urbach
Muscoda, WI

INVESTIGATING ANGLES

Angles are everywhere, and that's exactly what this activity teaches youngsters! Tell students you are sending them on an angle investigation. To prepare, have every student label a sheet of drawing paper for each angle he is investigating. Then give each child a discarded magazine, and ask him to cut out examples of each angle and glue them on the appropriate paper. Compile the student's completed projects into a class book titled "Getting The Angle On Angles." To extend the learning, invite students to investigate their surroundings for examples of angles, and set aside time for the students to describe the angles they've seen.

Carol Perks
Miami, FL

ANGLE WORKOUT

Create additional interest in angles with this movement activity. On the chalkboard draw and label a *right angle* (90°), an *acute angle* (less than 90°) and an *obtuse angle* (more than 90° and less than 180°). Then challenge each child to sit on the floor and form a right angle. To do this, she extends her legs out in front of her, keeps her back straight, and extends her arms straight above her head. Next direct the students to adjust their angle formations according to your oral directions. To form an acute angle, a students leans forward. To form an obtuse angle, she leans back. "Obtuse! Right! Obtuse! Acute! " Who knew a lesson on angles could be such great exercise?

Debbie Murphy
Goodnoe Elementary
Holland, PA

GEOMETRY BOOK CORNER

Get a whole new angle on geometry with these kid-pleasing literature connections!

When A Line Bends...A Shape Begins
Written by Rhonda Gowler Greene
Illustrated by James Kaczman
Houghton Mifflin Company, 1997

Three Pigs, One Wolf, And Seven Magic Shapes
Written by Grace Maccarone
Illustrated by David Neuhaus
Math Activities by Marilyn Burns
Scholastic Inc., 1997

Shape Up!:
Fun With Triangles And Other Polygons
Written by David A. Adler
Illustrated by Nancy Tobin
Holiday House, Inc.; 1998

Sir Cumference And The First Round Table
Written by Cindy Neuschwander
Illustrated by Wayne Geehan
Charlesbridge Publishing, Inc.; 1997

Not Enough Room!
Written by Joanne Rocklin
Illustrated by Cristina Ong
Math Activities by Marilyn Burns
Scholastic Inc., 1998

So Many Circles, So Many Squares
Written & Photographed by Tana Hoban
Greenwillow Books, 1998

Shapes, Shapes, Shapes
Written & Photographed by Tana Hoban
Mulberry Books, 1996

Order books on-line.
www.themailbox.com

MISSING SHAPE

Name of shape: _____

Description of shape: _____

_____

_____

_____

This shape has been seen posing as _____

_____

_____

_____

_____

Information provided by Detective _____

Note To Teacher: Use with "Shape Detectives" on page 133.

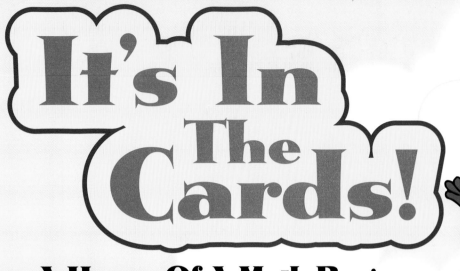

It's In The Cards!

A Honey Of A Math Review

What's all the buzz about? Math! You'll have a happy hive when you introduce these math review games.

ideas contributed by Sr. Helen Teresa and Marla Hawthorne

Busy Bee Cards

Each of the following games requires playing cards. The busy bee cards on page 144 are provided for your convenience. Simply duplicate the cards on construction paper or tagboard, laminate them for durability, and then cut them out. Make one set for each child or make several sets and store them at a center. Regular playing cards may also be used to play these games. Remind students to use pencil and paper for scorekeeping.

Spill A Sum

Skill: Column addition

Players: Two to four
Materials: Scrap paper and pencil for each player, busy bee cards 1 to 10, paper lunch bag
Directions: In turn, each player puts the cards in the bag; then he closes the bag and gently shakes it. Next he spills the cards onto the playing surface and adds the values of the cards that land faceup. The player with the highest sum wins the round and scores one game point. If there's a tie, each player scores a point. Continue play in this manner. The first player to score five game points wins.

What's The Difference?

Skill: Subtraction facts to 10

Players: Two to four
Materials: Scrap paper and pencil for each player, busy bee cards 1 to 10
Directions: Shuffle the cards and stack them facedown in the center of the playing area. Each player draws one card from the stack; then each player draws a second card from the stack. In turn, each player shows her two cards, states the values on the cards as a subtraction fact, and answers the fact. The player with the lowest difference wins the round and scores one game point. If there's a tie, each player scores a point. Continue play in this manner. Reshuffle and stack discarded cards as needed. The first player to score five game points wins.

Build A Number

Skill: Place value

Players: Two to four
Materials: Scrap paper and pencil for each player, busy bee cards 1 to queen
Directions: Shuffle the cards and stack them facedown in the center of the playing area. Face cards are wild. Each player draws one card from the stack; then each player draws a second card from the stack. A player uses her two cards to create the largest number possible. The player with the largest number wins the round and scores one game point. If there's a tie, each player scores a point. Continue play in this manner. Reshuffle and stack discarded cards as needed. The first player to score five game points wins.

Right On The Money

Skill: Odd and even numbers, addition of money

Players: Two to four
Materials: Scrap paper and pencil for each player, busy bee cards 1 to queen
Directions: Shuffle the cards. Even cards = 5¢, odd cards = 10¢, and face cards = 25¢. Dealer deals three cards to each player. Each player totals the value of her cards. The player with the largest value wins the round and scores one game point. If there's a tie, each player scores a game point. Continue play in this manner. Reshuffle and redeal discarded cards as needed. The first player to score five game points wins.

Make Ten

Skill: Addition

Players: Two
Materials: One set of busy bee cards (1 to queen) for each player
Directions: Dealer shuffles the combined cards and then he deals each player five cards. He stacks the rest of the cards facedown in a chance pile. The object of the game is to make sums of ten from pairs of cards. Face cards equal zero or ten. In turn, each player checks his hand for a card pair that equals ten. If he has one or more pairs, he lays each pair faceup on the playing surface in front of him and his turn is over. If a player does not have a pair that equals ten, he draws the top card from the chance pile. Play continues in this manner with each player laying a pair down or drawing one card during his turn. When all the cards in the chance pile are drawn, a player draws from his opponents hand. When no more pairs can be made, the player with the most pairs of ten wins the game.

141

Sum It Up

Skill: Addition

Players: Two

Materials: One set of busy bee cards (1 to queen) per player

Directions: Dealer shuffles all 24 cards and lays them facedown between himself and his opponent. Each player selects two cards and announces their sum. Face cards equal zero. The player who has the larger sum puts all four cards in his hive (or win pile). If the sums are equal, each player puts his own cards in his hive. Play continues in this manner until all cards have been selected. The player with the most cards in his hive wins.

Subtract, Then Add

Skill: Addition and Subtraction

Players: Two

Materials: Paper, pencil, and one set of busy bee cards (1 to queen) for each player

Directions: Dealer shuffles all 24 cards and deals them out. Each player stacks his 12 cards facedown in front of him. Each player turns over the top card in his stack. Face cards equal zero. The player with the higher card scores the difference between the two cards and records his score. (For example, if a five and three are showing, the player with the five scores two points.) These cards are placed in a discard pile. Play continues in the manner described until all cards have been played. Then each player tallies his score. The player with the higher score wins.

Count Down

Skill: Subtraction

Players: Two

Materials: Paper, pencil, and one set of busy bee cards (1 to queen) for each player

Directions: Combine the cards, shuffle them, and stack them facedown. Each player writes the number 25 at the top of her paper. In turn, each player draws a card from the stack. She subtracts the value of the card from 25 to determine her score. Face cards equal zero. Play continues in this manner. Reshuffle and stack discarded cards as needed. The first player to lose all her points wins.

High Or Low

Skill: Multiplication facts

Players: Two to four

Materials: Scrap paper and pencil for each player, busy bee cards 1 to 10

Directions: Dealer shuffles the cards, announces "high game" or "low game," and deals each player one card. Then he stacks the remaining cards in the center of the playing area and turns the top card on the stack faceup. This is the game card. Each player multiplies the number on his card with the number on the game card. If the dealer has called "high game," the player with the largest product wins the round and scores a point. (For "low game," the players with the lowest product wins the round.) If there's a tie, each player scores a game point. Continue play in this manner. Reshuffle and stack discarded cards as needed. The first player to score five game points wins.

Make A Number Sentence

Skill: Problem solving

Players: Two to four

Materials: Scrap paper, pencil, and one set of busy bee cards (1 to queen) per player

Directions: Dealer collects and shuffles cards, then deals each player five cards. Face cards are wild. Each player tries to make a math equation using the cards he has been dealt. Addition, subtraction, or multiplication can be used. (For example, a player with the cards 7, 3, and 4 could make the equation 7 − 3 = 4. A player with two 7s and a wild card [or a 4 and a 9] could make the equation 7 x 7 = 49.) In turn, each player shows his equation or he passes. A correct equation earns one point. All cards are then passed to a new dealer who reshuffles and redeals them. The first player to score five points wins the game.

Buzzing Into Summer

Keep your busy bees buzzing with math enthusiasm all summer long! To do this, send each child home for the summer with two sets of busy bee cards (the maximum number of cards required to play any two-person game), a copy of the games in this collection, and a letter to the parent in which you suggest that each child teach his family members and friends how to play the math games included. Now that's a honey of an idea that's sure to please the whole hive!

Busy Bee Cards

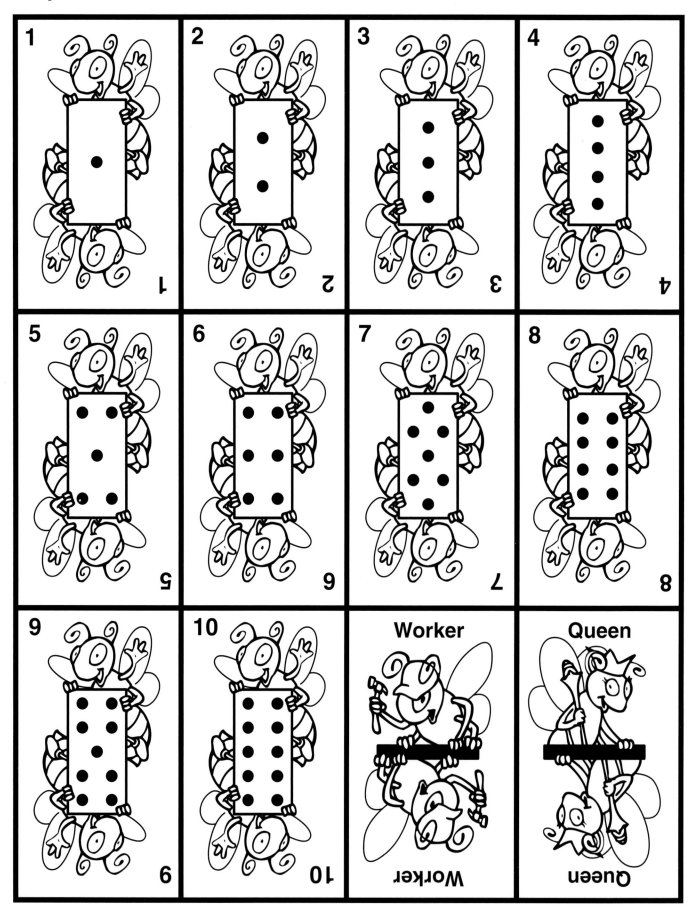

Note To Teacher: Use with "It's In The Cards!" on pages 140–143.

Review your youngsters' addition and subtraction skills with this high-interest math activity where each student manages a just-for-fun checking account!

idea by Denise Zonder and Joanne Kokoszka—Gr. 3, Isbister Elementary, Plymouth, MI

Getting Started

Mention making checkbook covers and your young tycoons will be all ears! To make a checkbook cover, fold up the bottom two inches of a 9" x 12" sheet of tagboard and staple each end of the folded flap to make a pocket. Cut out a copy of the checkbook register (on page 146) and staple it to the top of the tagboard as shown. Next fold the tagboard just below the register, keeping the pocket to the inside, and then fold down the top of the project. Allow time for each child to personalize and decorate his checkbook cover as desired.

Checks For The Checkbook

For a one-week checkbook project, give each child five blank checks (pattern on page 146). Have each child cut out his checks, number them from 1 to 5, and store them in sequential order in the pocket of his checkbook.

Getting Started

Talk with students about how a checking account works, including the definitions of *deposit* and *balance.* Then have each student enter the same deposit in his check register. For example, suggest a $500.00 deposit if students are regrouping over zeros or a $99.99 deposit if students are not yet regrouping. To add to the fun, tell students that the money is a gift from your great-aunt Moneybags.

Next announce that the electric bill is due on the spot! Have each child remove check number 1 from his checkbook and write his name in the top left-hand corner. Demonstrate how to write this check and have each child write his check in the same manner. Next show how to enter the check amount in the check register and how to calculate the account balance. Have students do the same. Verify that everyone's account balance matches. Quickly evaluate the written checks; then have each child store his written check at the back of his checkbook pocket.

Daily Transactions

Each morning write directions on the chalkboard for paying a bill or making a purchase (see "Sample Transactions" for ideas). Occasionally notify the class that Great-Aunt Moneybags has sent money and a deposit is in order. Before the end of each day, evaluate the checks the students have written and help them agree on a current account balance.

Check Number	Date	Description	Amount of Check	Amount of Deposit	Balance
	6/7	Money from Great Aunt Moneybags		99.99	$ 99.99
1	6/7	Purple Power Company	$35.10		35.10
					$ 64.89
					$.
					$.
					$.
					$.
					$.
					$.
					$.
					$.
					$.

Check 1

Name Anne Salisbury

Pay to the order of Purple Power Company $ 35.10

Thirty-five dollars and ten cents

Busy Bee Bank

Anne Salisbury
signature

Check 2

Closing The Account

When the final check is written and the account is balanced, inform students that it's time to close the account. For a fun writing extension, have each child write and illustrate a paragraph describing how he plans to spend his account balance (be sure it's generous). Post these projects on a bulletin board titled "Show Me The Money!" Then send your budding bankers home with their completed checks and balanced checkbooks. Won't their parents be impressed?

Sample Transactions
- Pay the phone bill so Great-Aunt Moneybags can continue to call!
- Buy a computer game at Computers Are Cool.
- Buy pizza and soft drinks for your family.
- Pay the doctor bill. Someone ate too much pizza!
- Donate money to the local animal shelter.

Patterns

Use with "Take It To The Bank!" on page 145.

Check Number	Date	Description	Amount of Check	Amount of Deposit	Balance
					$.
					.
					$.
					.
					$.
					.
					$.
					.
					$.
					.
					$.
					.
					$.
					.
					$.
					.
					$.

Check _____

Name _____

Pay to the
order of _____ $_____ . _____

_____

**Busy
Bee
Bank**

_____
signature

SCIENCE & HEALTH
UNITS

The Fascinating World Of Owls

From the tops of their feathery heads to the tips of their needle-sharp talons, owls are full of fascinating surprises! Use this integrated study to investigate these remarkable raptors. There's no doubt that you and your youngsters will have a hootin' good time!

ideas contributed by Carrie Geiger, Kathleen Kopp, and Sharon Strickland

An Ancient Bird

Owls have been around for a very long time—over 50 million years! For this reason the owl is an integral part of many cultures. To some the owl is a symbol of life and good health. To others it is a symbol of bad luck, even death. Before introducing your owl study, investigate your youngsters' owl-related knowledge and beliefs. Then plan your activities so that knowledge is enhanced and beliefs are respected.

Fine-Feathered Facts

"Whooo" has the facts about owls? Your students will when you carry out this fact-sharing idea! Mount a large owl cutout in a prominent classroom location and copy the ten owl facts provided in "Have You Heard?" onto individual sentence strips. Each day post one owl fact and read it aloud. Discuss the fact as a class and, if desired, have each student copy the fact in an owl-shaped journal like the one described in "An 'Owl-some' Journal" on page 149. When all ten facts are posted, invite students to submit additional owl facts for the display. By the conclusion of your owl study, your youngsters will be all the wiser—and that's a fact!

Have You Heard?

- An owl can hear a mouse 60 feet away.
- All owl eggs are white.
- An owl has three sets of eyelids.
- Owls cannot move their eyeballs.
- An owl can turn its face upside down.
- An owl can swing its head around and look behind its back.
- Owls live on every continent except Antarctica.
- An owl can open and close its ears.
- An owl's coat is made of thousands of feathers.
- Owls use many different sounds to communicate.

Mary Lester

An "Owl-some" Journal

These student-made journals are a hoot to make and a wise place for students to record their owl-related knowledge! Give each student a white construction-paper copy of page 153. To make her journal, a student colors the owl on the page; then she carefully cuts along the dotted line that outlines the beak—stopping at the black dots. (Provide assistance with this step as needed, or you may wish to complete this step before distributing student copies.) Next the student staples a stack of 3 1/2" x 8 1/2" writing paper to the bottom of the page where indicated, folds the project forward on the thin line, and tucks the folded portion of the project under the beak flap. Lastly she adds a title and her name to the front of the project. Write on!

All About Owls
By Sharon

Tip To Tip

From head to talon and wing tip to wing tip—no two kinds of owls are exactly the same! During this small-group measurement activity, students size up their arm spans and the wingspans of several owls. Post the wingspan information that is provided; then divide students into small groups. Give each group yarn, a ruler or yardstick, scissors, masking tape, and pencils.

To begin, have each student (with the help of another group member) cut a length of yarn that equals his arm span. Then have each child fold a piece of masking tape over his yarn length and label the tape with his name. Before the group members cut and label a yarn length to equal each posted wingspan, ask them to predict which wingspans will be longer or shorter than their arm spans. When the lengths are cut and labeled, have each group order its yarn lengths—wingspans and arm spans combined—from shortest to longest. Set aside time for the groups to compare their results; then, as a class, discuss the accuracy of the groups' predictions. Now that's a measurement activity that's beyond compare!

Wingspans
Barn Owl—44 inches
Great Horned Owl—60 inches
Screech Owl—22 inches
Hawk Owl—34 inches
Pygmy Owl—15 inches
Long-Eared Owl—40 inches

Night Owls

Most owls—but not all—are creatures of the night. They sleep during the day and hunt from dusk to dawn. Have students consider the advantages and disadvantages of sleeping during the day. (For a great literature connection, read aloud *The Owl And The Woodpecker* by Brian Wildsmith [Oxford University Press, 1996]. It's a delightful tale about a woodpecker and an owl who share the same forest, but not the same sleeping schedules.) Then give each child a sticky note. If a student thinks he'd rather sleep during the day, he illustrates an owl on his note. If a student likes sleeping at night, he illustrates a woodpecker or another diurnal bird. Then have each child in turn attach his illustrated note to a graph like the one shown. Summarize the graph as a class; then have students refer to the graph to answer a series of questions, like "If each night owl hoots twice when it awakes, how many hoots are heard?" and "If only seven early birds were awake when the sun rose, how many early birds overslept?"

Kind	Number											
Night Owl												
Early Bird												

Homes Around The World

Where do owls live? Just about everywhere! Owls live on every continent except Antarctica, in places like forests, deserts, fields, mountains, swamps, caves, and even cities. Their homes vary greatly, but most have one thing in common—they are not built by owls. Use the booklet project on page 154 to introduce students to six owls and their homes. To begin, give each child a white construction-paper copy of the page. Read each description aloud; then ask the students to color the habitat that is described—without coloring the owl. Next tell students that even though owls can look quite different from each other, they are usually a combination of the following colors: brown, gray, black, and white. Explain that the unique markings of each kind of owl help it blend into its natural habitat. Then challenge your students to color the owls using their newfound knowledge.

To make the booklet, each child cuts along the bold lines, pairs each scene with its matching description, and glues each pair of cutouts on a 4 1/2" x 6" rectangle of construction paper. While the glue is drying, the student folds a 6" x 9" sheet of construction paper in half to make a booklet cover. He writes "Owl Homes" and his name on the front cover; then he decorates the cover. Lastly he stacks the booklet pages, slips them inside the cover, and staples near the fold. Now that's a handy habitat reference!

Barn Owl
I might live in a barn, a cave, a tree, or an old building. I might even live in the city!

A Peek At Pellets

Scientists find looking at owl pellets a very eye-opening experience, and so will your youngsters! Remind students that owls are bird of prey which means that they hunt and eat other animals. Also explain that owls do not have teeth, which means that they swallow their food whole or in large pieces. Because much of what an owl eats cannot be digested, several hours after eating, an owl coughs up a pellet of undigestible matter.

Tell students that scientists study pellets to learn about what owls eat; then ask your students to do the same. Give each small group of students a pellet, paper towels, plastic knives or toothpicks, and a magnifying glass. (Pellets are available from Carolina Biological Supply Company. Call 1-800-334-5551 or fax 1-800-222-7112 for ordering information). Challenge each group to carefully pick apart its pellet to find out what kinds of items were eaten by the owl. Set aside time for each group to tell what it found, and if possible for each group to see what the other groups found in their pellets. Very interesting!

Hoot! Hoot!

Believe it or not, there are as many different owl calls as there are species of owls! This small-group activity is a fun way for youngsters to learn that owls do more than hoot! Give each small group a construction-paper strip that you have labeled with a different owl call—however, do not tell students that *all* the calls are made by owls. Allow some practice time; then have each group perform its call two or three times for the class. After each performance, tape the group's paper strip to the chalkboard and take a class vote to find out how many students believe the call is authentic (made by a real owl) or fake. Write the result of the class vote beside the paper strip. When all the calls have been made and voted on, reveal that each call is real; then, beside each call, write the name of the owl that makes it. Won't your youngsters be amazed?

Owl	Call
Screech Owl	kyew…kyew…kyew…
Pygmy Owl	whee…whee…whee…
Barn Owl	cirrrrrrrrrrr…cirrrrrrrrrrrr…
Long-Eared Owl	oo-oo-oo…oo-oo-oo…
Short-Eared Owl	boo-boo-boo…boo-boo-boo…
Eagle Owl	ooo-hu…ooo-hu…ooo-hu…
Tengmalm's Owl	poo-poo-poo…poo-poo-poo…
Little Owl	hoo…hoo…hoo…hoo…hoo…

An Owlish Snack

Your owl enthusiasts are sure to enjoy making and eating these barn owl look-alikes. And it's the perfect opportunity to share a few additional facts about this unique-looking owl!

Barn Owl Look-Alikes

Ingredients:
1 slice of brown bread
1 slice of white bread
2 black olives
1 cheese triangle
peanut butter

Directions:
1. Use cookie cutters to cut a heart from the white bread and a slightly larger circle from the brown bread.
2. Use peanut butter to attach the heart shape to the center of the circle.
3. Use dabs of peanut butter to attach olive eyes and a cheese beak.

From Egg To Barn Owl

Look what just hatched—an "egg-citing" life-cycle project! Share information about the barn owl's life cycle. (In addition to the information provided, *Barn Owls* [A Carolrhoda Nature Watch Book, 1992] and See How They Grow: *Owl* [Dorling Kindersley Publishing, Inc.; 1992] are both excellent resources with outstanding photography.) Then have each student make a booklet that features a barn owl's life cycle.

To begin, a student folds a 4" x 16" strip of white construction paper in half twice; then he unfolds the paper and refolds it accordion style. Keeping the project folded, he carefully trims off each corner to create an egg-shaped booklet that resembles the white, almost-round egg of the owl. Next the student unfolds the booklet, and on the bottom half of each page describes—in sequential order—a different stage of a barn owl's life cycle. Then he illustrates each stage on the top half of its page. Lastly he refolds the booklet, writes "The Life Cycle Of The Barn Owl by [his name]" on the front cover, and draws a line to represent a crack in the egg. Students will be proud to share these adorable booklets with their families and friends!

The Life Cycle Of The Barn Owl By Russ

The owlet starts growing feathers. It starts to move around. Then it starts practicing to fly.

The owl is fully grown. It flies. And it hunts its own food.

Believe it or not, the barn owl...

- is the most common of all owls
- does not always live in a barn
- does not hoot like most owls
- often lives near humans, though humans rarely see it
- is also called the *monkey owl* because of its looks and actions
- has smaller eyes than most other owls

Life Cycle Of The Barn Owl

Stage 1: A mother owl lays one white egg every two to three days. Some barn owls lay up to 10 or 11 eggs in all.

Stage 2: After about 28 days, the eggs begin to hatch in the order they were laid. When it is first born, an owl chick has a thin coat of down and its eyes are closed. After two weeks its eyes are open and it is covered with thick, fluffy down.

Stage 3: As an owlet grows, its down is replaced by adult feathers. After about one month, an owlet becomes very active and it begins investigating outside the nest. When its wings are strong enough, it begins to practice flying. After two months the owlet can fly, but it hasn't yet developed hunting skills.

Stage 4: At 12 weeks old, a barn owl is fully feathered and able to hunt on its own.

Legendary Owls

Throughout history, people have been fascinated by owls. Many ancient legends about the owl were inspired by its unique appearance and behaviors. For example, in the legend *Why Owl Comes Out At Night* (Troll Communications L.L.C., 1996), the owl's nocturnal habits are explained. A legend explaining why the owl has such big eyes is included in *Owl: American Indian Legends* (Scholastic Inc., 1995). Read aloud a legend or two about the owl. Then challenge each youngster to write and illustrate a legendlike story that explains an interesting fact about the bird, like why the owl can see in the dark, why the owl can turn its head upside down, or why the owl can fly so silently. After each child has shared his work, bind the tales into a class book titled "New Legends About A Very Old Bird."

"Whooo" Cares?

Who cares about the livelihood of owls? Your students will after this important real-life lesson! Explain that at one time, farmers killed owls because some owls occasionally prey on chickens. However, farmers soon realized how important owls are in controlling rodent and insect populations. Today it is against the law to kill or capture an owl. Yet the future of many types of owls is still threatened by habitat destruction (such as the clearing of forests) and the use of insecticides.

After discussing this issue with students, inform them that there are things they can do to protect owls, such as build nest boxes for them, never use insecticides that might kill owls, and spread the word about the importance of owls. Conclude the activity by having each child decorate a construction-paper circle to create a "Give A Hoot" badge like the own shown. Then hole-punch the badges and use a safety pin to attach each child's badge to his clothing.

Never use insecticides that can kill owls. Cut down trees only if you have to. Spread the word that owls eat rodents. Build a nest box for an owl.

Give A Hoot!

Fine-Feathered Assessment

Choose this fine-feathered (and fun!) approach to assessing your youngsters' knowledge about owls. First help each child make and label an owl-shaped flap book like the one shown (see the directions below). Then have each child write what he knows about each topic on the corresponding booklet page. "Whooooo" knew assessment could be so much fun!

All About Owls
by Carrie

Kinds Of Owls

What Owls Eat

Where Owls Live

More Facts About Owls

Step 1

Step 2

Making An Owl Booklet

Step 1: Fold a 9" x 12" sheet of brown construction paper in half lengthwise and trace a template like the one shown on the folded paper. Cut on the resulting outline; then unfold the paper and set it aside.

Step 2: Stack and align the lower edges of a 9" x 12" sheet of orange paper, a 9" x 12" sheet of brown paper, and a 9" x 6" piece of yellow paper. Holding the pages vertically, slide the top sheet (yellow) upward approximately one inch and the bottom sheet (orange) downward approximately one inch. Next fold the tops of the brown and the orange sheets forward to create five graduated layers.

Step 3: Place the folded project atop the owl cutout and align the lower edges. Staple near the fold. Flip the resulting booklet over and trim the folded papers to match the shape of the cutout.

Step 4: Turn the booklet faceup. Glue beak and eye cutouts in place. Scallop the bottom of each booklet page; then label each page with a desired owl-related topic.

Fold here.

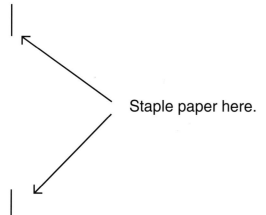

Staple paper here.

Note To Teacher: Use with "An 'Owl-some' Journal " on page 149.

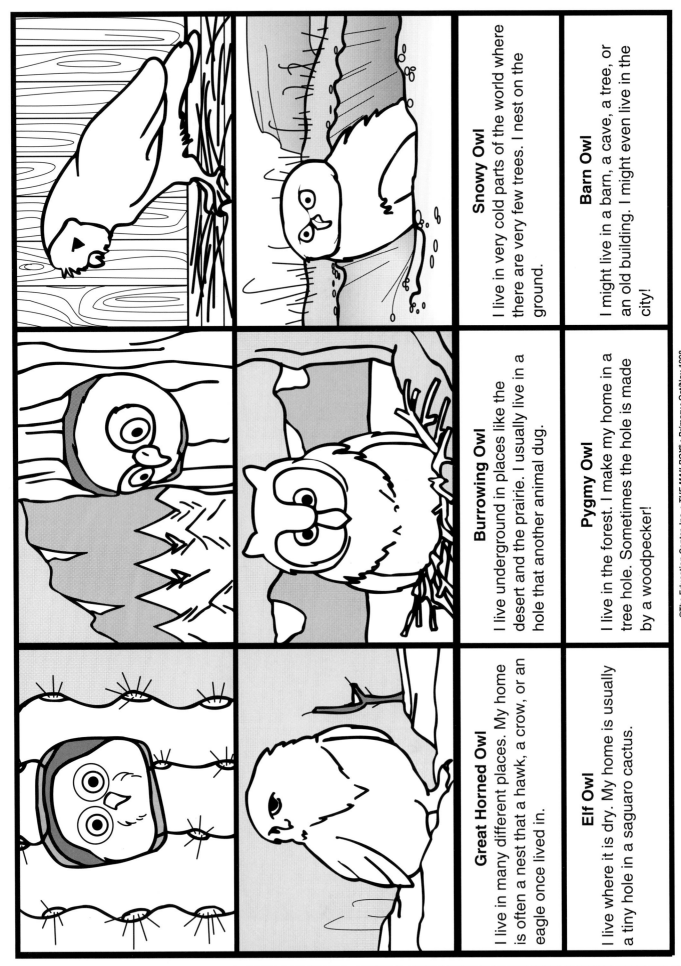

Snowy Owl
I live in very cold parts of the world where there are very few trees. I nest on the ground.

Barn Owl
I might live in a barn, a cave, a tree, or an old building. I might even live in the city!

Burrowing Owl
I live underground in places like the desert and the prairie. I usually live in a hole that another animal dug.

Pygmy Owl
I live in the forest. I make my home in a tree hole. Sometimes the hole is made by a woodpecker!

Great Horned Owl
I live in many different places. My home is often a nest that a hawk, a crow, or an eagle once lived in.

Elf Owl
I live where it is dry. My home is usually a tiny hole in a saguaro cactus.

Something To Hoot About!

Read each sentence.
If the sentence is a **fact,** color the box
   in the fact column.
If the sentence is an **opinion,** color
   the box in the opinion column.

Remember…
A **fact** can be proven.
An **opinion** is what someone thinks.

	Fact	Opinion
1. Most owls fly almost silently.	R	O
2. Owls are very strange birds.	W	L
3. Most owls hunt at night.	A	L
4. An owl has three sets of eyelids.	P	S
5. Owls are the most sneaky hunters.	A	S
6. Owls make several different sounds.	T	R
7. Owls are the wisest of all birds.	E	L
8. Owls have four toes on each foot.	O	A
9. An owl cannot turn its eyes.	R	H
10. Owls are really boring during the day.	O	C
11. Owls cannot smell.	S	O
12. Owls are more unique than all other birds.	T	F

Write the letters you did not color in order on the lines below.

__ __ __ __ __ __ __ __ __ __ __ __ __ __ !

Bonus Box: Read the sentence you wrote. Do you agree with this
opinion? Write and explain your answer on the back of this paper.

Dandelions!

Spring has sprung, and so have the dandelions! Use these activities to explore this one-of-a-kind wildflower.

ideas contributed by Ann Flagg

Getting Started: Introducing Dandelions

Begin your study by reading aloud a dandelion-related picture book. Two outstanding titles—both of which are beautifully illustrated—are *The Dandelion Seed* by Joseph Anthony (Dawn Publications, 1997) and *Dandelion Adventures* by L. Patricia Kite (The Millbrook Press, Inc.; 1998). Ask youngsters to be on the lookout for dandelions. For the next several days, list the places students report seeing dandelions on a large dandelion cutout. Your youngsters will quickly realize that dandelions grow just about anywhere!

Activity 1: Taking A Close Look

What each small group needs:
blooming dandelion plant, harvested   paper towel   hand lens

What to do:
Have each small group lay its plant on the paper towel. Allow time for each group member to view the plant through the hand lens. Encourage each child to touch and smell the plant.

Questions to ask:
1. How is a dandelion like other plants? How is it different?
2. What plant parts do you see?

This is why:

A dandelion has leaves, flowers, and a root like other plants. Unlike other plants, it has a very short stem that only grows about a half inch above the ground. The notched leaves of the dandelion look a bit like teeth and could be how the dandelion got its name. (The word dandelion *comes from three French words,* dent de lion, *which mean "lion's tooth."*) The leaves are arranged in a circle at the base of the plant. Each bloom—which is really a cluster of small flowers—sits atop a hollow flower stalk that rises from the circle of leaves. The dandelion root is a tap-root (like the carrot plant) and can grow up to three feet in length!

Activity 2: Learning The Life Cycle

In advance:
Have each child sponge-paint a white paper plate yellow and a paper-towel tube green.

What each student needs:
copy of the dandelion wheel on page 158   scissors
yellow sponge-painted paper plate   brad
green sponge-painted paper-towel tube   tape
eight 3" x 6" rectangles of green paper   glue
crayons

What to do:
Ask students why they think some dandelions have colorful flowers and others have puffy, white heads. Then investigate the dandelion's life cycle by first having each child color and cut out his copy of the dandelion wheel. Next have him use his brad to attach the wheel to the center of his sponge-painted paper plate. Ask each student to find the picture of the seed in the ground. Then use the wheel and the information in "This is why" to explain the plant's life cycle. Invite and answer questions from students. To complete the project, help each child tape one end of his green painted tube (hollow flower stalk) to the back of his paper plate. Then have each child cut a notched dandelion leaf from each of his green paper rectangles and glue (or tape) the cutouts around the base of his project.

This is why:

Tiny hooks help a dandelion seed work its way into the ground. A thick root begins to grow, green leaves appear, and tiny flower buds form. If the days are warm and sunny, colorful flowers soon burst from the buds. Each dandelion flower is a cluster of tiny flowers called florets. At the end of each floret a seed forms. Within several weeks the dried-up flower parts on the dandelion stalk fall off, but the seeds remain. Small green leaves called bracts close over the seeds to protect them. The protected seeds grow and develop. The flower stalk continues to grow. As soon as the seeds are ripe, the bracts bend back and a fluffy, white head is exposed. Attached to the seeds are fine white hairs that act as parachutes when the seeds are launched by the wind. Each time a seed falls to the ground, the life cycle of the dandelion can begin again.

Order books on-line.
www.themailbox.com

Activity 3:
Observing Changes

(This activity requires students to observe growing dandelions. If dandelions are not growing on the school grounds, consider having students complete the activity for homework.)

What each student needs:
personalized craft stick
crayons
construction-paper copy of the diary cover on page 158
3" x 3 1/2" blank paper
access to a stapler
pencil
growing dandelion to observe

What to do:
Have each student personalize and color his diary cover. Then have him cut out the cover, fold it in half along the thin line, and staple his blank paper inside. Next take the class to an area where dandelions are growing. Each youngster needs his craft stick, his diary, and a pencil. Direct each child to poke his craft stick into the ground near a blooming dandelion. Next have him study the dandelion and write and date an observation in his diary. Set aside time each day for students to observe the plants and describe in their diaries the changes they see. Every other day randomly group the students. Have the members of each group compare and contrast their observations. Continue the project until at least one bloom on each child's plant is transformed into a fluffy seed head.

Activity 4:
Why So Many?

In advance:
Harvest one fluffy seed head for every three students. To harvest a seed head, carefully slip a resealable plastic bag over it, snip the flower stalk, and seal the seed head inside the plastic bag.

What each trio needs:
resealable plastic bag with a dandelion seed head inside
9" x 12" sheet of black construction paper
clear tape
white self-adhesive label
pencil

What to do:
Ask students why there are so many dandelions. After students have shared their ideas, tell them that this activity reveals one reason. Remind students that each colorful dandelion bloom is really a cluster of tiny flowers and that each tiny flower produces a dandelion seed. Ask students to predict how many seeds one bloom might produce. Write their predictions on the chalkboard. Then instruct each trio to carefully count the seeds in its bag by grouping the seeds into clusters of five and taping each cluster to the black paper. Next have each trio write its total number of seeds on the self-adhesive label and attach the label to the bottom right corner of the paper. Allow time for the groups to share their results and compare them to the posted predictions.

Questions to ask:
1. What surprised you most about this activity?
2. Why do you think some groups had more seeds than others?
3. How many seeds do you think one dandelion *plant* makes?
4. How does this information help you understand why dandelions are so plentiful?

This is why:

Dandelions are plentiful for many reasons. In addition to producing a tremendous number of seeds, the dandelion plant is extremely resilient and adaptable. It can live for years, in spite of severe weather conditions. Dandelion leaves are not easily destroyed by frost. And the unique arrangement of the leaves (in a circle at the base of the plant) helps to protect the dandelion's root, where a large amount of food is stored. The root system itself is also strong and deep. If only a piece of the main taproot remains in the ground, a dandelion plant can grow again.

Patterns

Use the dandelion wheel with
"Activity 2: Learning The Life Cycle"
on page 156.

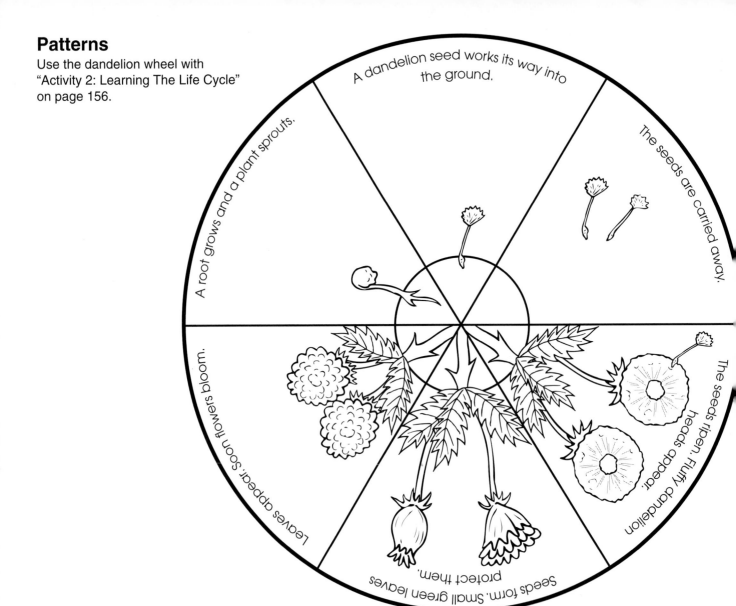

A dandelion seed works its way into the ground.

The seeds are carried away.

A root grows and a plant sprouts.

The seeds ripen. Fluffy dandelion heads appear.

Leaves appear. Soon flowers bloom.

Seeds form. Small green leaves protect them.

Use the journal cover with "Activity 3: Observing Changes" on page 157.

Dandelion Diary

_____'s

©1999 The Education Center, Inc.

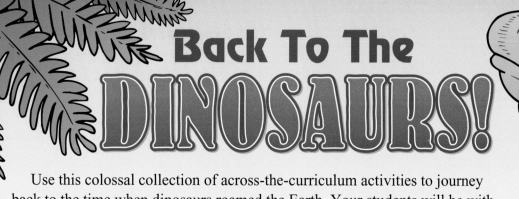

Back To The DINOSAURS!

Use this colossal collection of across-the-curriculum activities to journey back to the time when dinosaurs roamed the Earth. Your students will be with you every step of the way!

ideas contributed by Amy Erickson and Kim Taylor

Tracking Facts

Put youngsters hot on the trail of dinosaurs with the fact organizer on page 163. It's a perfect tool for budding paleontologists to use when researching dinosaurs. Once the forms are completed, youngsters can incorporate the facts they've gathered into interesting and informative reports. Or gather the forms and bind them into a class anthology of dinosaur facts. Who knows? You may even have an aspiring paleontologist who is interested in authoring a personal collection of dinosaur discoveries!

Dinosaur Web Site

If you're looking for a student-friendly dinosaur Web stop, here's one that really delivers. "All About Dinosaurs" at *http:/www.enchantedlearning.com/ subjects/dinosaurs/* is a comprehensive site designed for budding paleontologists of all ages and levels of comprehension. It has an easy-to-use structure that allows a reader to start with basic information on an array of dinosaur-related topics, then progress to more advanced details as desired. Superb graphics, which are often animated, are sure to please your dinosaur enthusiasts.

Debbie Erickson—Gr. 2, Sunset Elementary, Whitehall, WI

A Prehistoric Timeline

A student-created timeline of "terrible lizards" makes a wonderful visual aid for your dinosaur study. Tie together three 1-yard lengths of different-colored yarn; then display the resulting timeline in an easily accessible classroom location. Label a card for each of the following prehistoric periods: *Triassic, Jurassic, Cretaceous.* Display these cards above the timeline in the order presented—one card per colorful timeline section. Also ask each child to deposit a paper strip labeled with his name in a designated container. When a dinosaur is introduced, write the dinosaur's name on a three-inch square of paper. Then draw a student's name from the container and ask him to illustrate the dinosaur on the labeled paper. Next assist the child in taping his project to the timeline in the appropriate prehistoric period. Continue in this manner until each child has added a dinosaur card to the timeline. Students will agree—there's nothing "terrible" about this timeline!

Triassic

Jurassic

Cretaceous

Coelphysis

Allosaurus

Stegosaurus

Triceratops

159

Dinosaur Defenses

Dinosaurs had many ways of protecting themselves. Some lived in herds and found safety in numbers. A few were just too big or too fast to be attacked. Others used razor-sharp claws, spiked tails, pointy horns, and thick, leathery skin to defend themselves. Bring dinosaur defenses into the spotlight with this rap-writing activity. Each child uses a rhyming format like the one shown to write a rap that tells how a specific dinosaur defended itself. Then each child draws a simple outline of the dinosaur she described on black paper, cuts out the resulting silhouette, and glues it in the center of a sheet of white paper. On brightly colored paper she draws the dinosaur's defense(s), such as spikes, claws, sharp teeth, and/or a club tail; then she cuts out each shape and glues it to the silhouette as shown. Display each student's rap and illustration as one project on a colorful bulletin board titled "Beware! Dinosaurs On The Defense!"

My name is [dinosaur's name] and I'm here to [rhyming word]
_____ [rhyming word].

My name is Triceratops and I'm here to tell
If you mess with my horns, you won't feel well.

My name is Stegosaurus and I'm here to say
I have spikes on my tail, so stay away.

The Spotted Egg
I found the egg in my closet.
I was looking for my basketball.
The egg was warm and it
wobbled. Then it exploded
and a bumpy green
dinosaur popped out!

"Eggs-tra" Tall Tales

Dinosaurs laid eggs of different shapes and sizes. And since paleontologists can't tell from fossils what color the eggs were—well, they could be any color, right? To prepare for a fun-filled creative-writing activity, have each child make a booklet that resembles a dinosaur egg. To make the booklet a student trims a 9" x 12" sheet of drawing paper into a desired shape; then he traces this shape onto a second sheet of drawing paper and several sheets of story paper. Next he cuts out each shape and staples the writing paper between the drawing paper. Finally he decorates the covers of his resulting booklet to show how he thinks a dinosaur egg looked. Have each student write and illustrate a story in his booklet that describes when and where he finds this egg, and the spectacular pet he acquires when the egg hatches! You can count on plenty of cracking up when students read aloud their creative tales!

Horn In On Math

Horns, spikes, and domes decorated the heads of some dinosaurs. Challenge your youngsters to use their heads to solve this math challenge that focuses on horn-headed dinosaurs. Explain that some horn-headed dinosaurs had just one horn on the nose, others had two horns over the eyes, and a few had all three horns. Some had horns all over their heads! Next ask students to imagine that a group of paleontologists has been digging in an area that was once roamed by three different horn-headed dinosaurs: the Montanoceratops (one horn), the Triceratops (three horns), and the Pentaceratops (five horns). So far these paleontologists have unearthed 15 different horn fossils. Tell students that the paleontologists are trying to determine what combination of dinosaur horns they might have found. For example, they could have found the horns of five different Triceratops or the horns of 15 Montanoceratops. You can count on plenty of participation as students brainstorm possible horn combinations. Now that's a "dino-mite" math lesson!

Practicing Paleontology

The science of paleontology becomes deliciously clear with this hands-on activity. Using the provided recipe, prepare a batch of Paleontologists' Delight; then serve each youngster a portion of the dessert on a large paper plate. Also give each child two toothpicks (or frill picks), a napkin or towelette, a pencil, and a rectangle of blank paper the approximate size of his dessert portion. Challenge each student to carefully dig through the layers of his dessert in search of fossils. On his paper he draws the exact location and position of each fossil he finds; then the student carefully removes and places the fossil near the edge of his plate. Cleanup is easy—simply distribute plastic spoons! As the students eat, invite them to talk about what they've learned from this experience.

Paleontologists' Delight
(makes 25–30 servings)

Ingredients:
3-oz. box of lime Jell-O®
3-oz. box of raspberry, strawberry, or cherry Jell-O®
2 bananas, sliced
1/4 cup raisins
one 16-oz. container nondairy whipped topping
2 cups crumbled graham crackers or Oreos® cookies

Directions:
1. Prepare the lime gelatin according to the package directions and pour into a 9" x 12" glass baking dish. Chill until set.
2. Evenly distribute the raisins and sliced bananas over the chilled lime gelatin.
3. Prepare the remaining gelatin according to the package directions. Chill until slightly thickened; then pour over the raisin and banana layer. Chill until set.
4. Sprinkle the crumbled crackers or cookies over the gelatin layer.
5. Top with a layer of whipped topping.

Tracy Haupt—Grs. 3–4 Learning Support, Stevens Elementary School, Williamsport, PA

Teeth That Tell

Scientists study a dinosaur's teeth to find out what it ate. Strong, razor-sharp teeth suggest a meat-eating dinosaur, while dull teeth indicate a plant-eating dinosaur. A dinosaur that ate both plants and animals might have coarse teeth that could slice and grind. Put your youngsters' dental sleuthing skills to the test with this activity. On the chalkboard draw and number ten different tooth shapes that could have belonged to dinosaurs. Ask each child to number her paper from 1 through 10, study each tooth shape, and write on her paper what she thinks its dinosaur owner ate and why. Next serve each student a snack of "tree-rific" pretzel sticks to munch on while student volunteers share how they solved the tooth-related mysteries.

Fancy Fossil Prints

Make a lasting impression with this dinosaur-related art experience. To make a fossil print like the one shown, use a pencil to etch a dinosaur shape into the bottom of a Styrofoam® meat tray (or something similar). Press heavily. Next paint the tray with a desired color of tempera paint; then invert the tray and press it near the center of a sheet of drawing paper. Carefully lift the tray from the paper. Discard the tray and set your artwork aside to dry. To create the border, trim a piece of a sponge into the shape of a dinosaur footprint or a prehistoric leaf. Use the sponge shape and a contrasting color of tempera paint to create a border around your artwork.

Erin O'Brien—Gr. 3, John Foster Dulles Elementary School Chicago, IL

A Dinosaur Debate

A dinosaur debate will have students sharpening their critical-thinking skills and sharing their two cents worth about what happened to the dinosaurs. Divide students into five groups and assign each group a different theory about why the dinosaurs disappeared. Challenge each group to research its theory and develop a strategy for convincing the rest of the class that its theory is the most credible. On the day of the debate, each group presents its case. Also invite any student who has an original theory to share his point of view. Then have each child vote for the theory he thinks is the most believable. Remind students that scientists are not sure why dinosaurs became extinct and it is unlikely that they will ever know for sure. However, that doesn't keep scientists from pondering different possibilities!

Erin O'Brien—Gr. 3, John Foster Dulles Elementary School
Chicago, IL

Extinction Theories

- small mammals ate all the dinosaur eggs
- a huge meteorite crashed into the Earth
- a change in climate
- volcanoes erupted everywhere
- several bad diseases

Digging Into Dinosaur Names

How do scientists name dinosaurs? Most dinosaur names describe the dinosaurs themselves. Some names reflect where the dinosaurs were discovered. And a few dinosaurs are named for people (see "Understanding Dinosaur Names" for examples). Use the reproducible on page 164 to pique your youngsters' interest in dinosaur names. As a follow-up, distribute student copies of page 163 and have each child complete the form about her new dinosaur discovery. Suggest that students keep the details of their discoveries under wraps until the Prehistoric Press Conference (described on this page). Or videotape each student announcing his discovery and show the resulting class video during the gathering.

Younger students will enjoy combining familiar words with endings like *-saurus* or *-atops* to create dinosaur names like "Bananasaurus Rex," "Bucketasaurus," and "Bookatops." Have each child write the name of her newfound dinosaur on a 12" x 18" sheet of drawing paper, then illustrate the dinosaur and write a brief caption about it.

Ann Nason—Gr. 3
Harold Martin School
Hopkinton, NH

Understanding Dinosaur Names

Dinosaur Name	Meaning
Stegosaurus	roofed reptile
Tyrannosaurus Rex	tyrannical reptile king
Albertosaurus	discovered in Alberta, Canada
Zigongosaurus	discovered in Zigong, China
Lambeosaurus	named for paleontologist Lawrence Lambe

Clevell Harris

Prehistoric Press Conference

Culminate your dinosaur study with a Prehistoric Press Conference! Encourage students to invite family members to this special event. Plan time for the guests to stroll through the classroom and view the class-created prehistoric timeline (page 159), the students' fancy fossil prints (page 161), and the "Beware! Dinosaurs On The Defense!" display (page 160). You can count on the students' "eggs-tra" tall tales (page 160) being a big hit, too. Then gather the group for an unveiling of new dinosaur discoveries ("Digging Into Dinosaur Names" on this page). Conclude the press conference by thanking the guests for their attendance and inviting them to linger for a few minutes longer to snap photographs of the budding paleontologists.

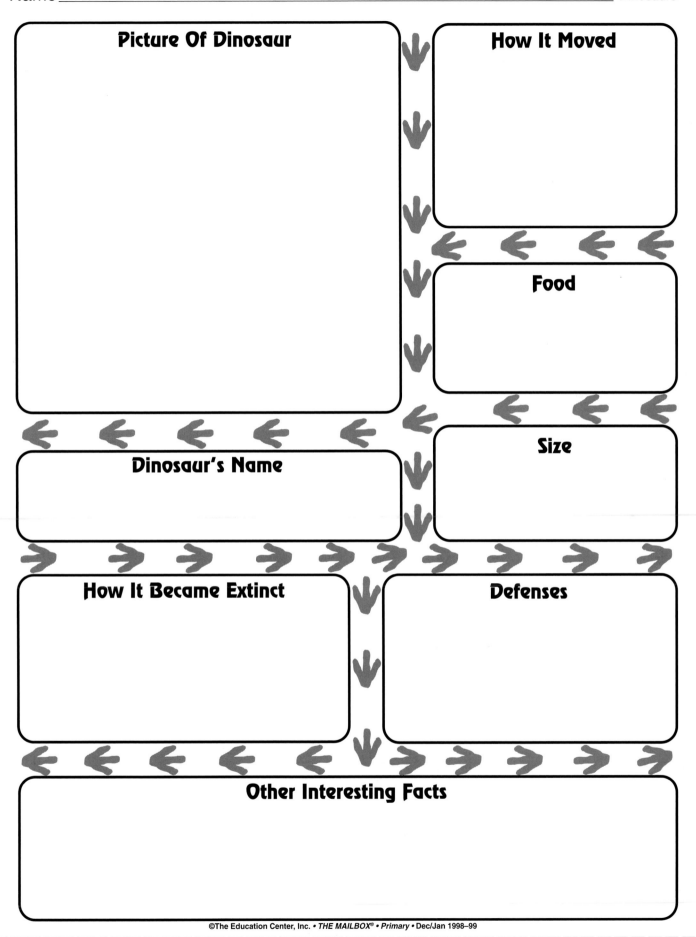

Picture Of Dinosaur

How It Moved

Food

Dinosaur's Name

Size

How It Became Extinct

Defenses

Other Interesting Facts

Name _____

Dinosaurs Discovered!

Each new dinosaur has been given a name that describes it.
Use the Name Box.
Connect each dinosaur name to its matching description.

New Dinosaur Names	Dinosaur Descriptions
Ankylobrachiodromeus	• two foot runner
Tetrastegosaurus	• four foot runner
Megatyrannosaurus	• crooked arm runner
Allocerattops	• giant speedy lizard
Bipoddromeus	• four roofed lizard
Tridontosaurus	• two arm ruler
Segnobarysaurus	• giant ruler lizard
Tetrapoddromeus	• slow heavy lizard
Bibrachiotyranno	• three tooth lizard
Megavelocisaurus	• different horn face

Name Box

word part	meaning	word part	meaning
allo	different	pod	foot
ankylo	crooked	saurus	lizard
bary	heavy	segno	slow
bi	two	stego	roofed
brachio	arm	tetra	four
cerat	horn	tops	face
donto	tooth	tri	three
dromeus	runner	tyranno	ruler
mega	giant	veloci	speedy

Pretend that you have discovered another new dinosaur!
Name your dinosaur and write its name in the box below.
Draw and color a picture of your dinosaur on the back of this paper.

Healthy Teeth = Healthy Smiles!

Smile! February is National Children's Dental Health Month. And that means it's the perfect time for students to brush up on their dental-health habits. This fresh collection of tooth-related activities and literature suggestions is just what you need to promote pearly whites and long-lasting smiles.

ideas by Heather Godwin and Jill Hamilton

Sparkling Smiles Brush Through Here!

Set the stage for your dental-health study with a giant toothbrush door decoration. To make the bristles, cut white plastic garbage bags into strips and tape them to the top of your classroom door frame. Cut a large toothbrush handle from bulletin-board paper and program it with a dental-health motto. Then tape the handle to the bristles to complete the giant toothbrush. No doubt students will be all grins as they *brush* through the doorway each morning!

Smile Maintenance

Promote positive dental-health habits right from the start! Have each student write her name and the date on a copy of "Dental Data" (on page 172). Review the record-keeping activity; then ask each child to post her data sheet on her family's refrigerator. Suggest that the students record their dental data before they go to bed each night. One week later reward each student who returns a completed data sheet with a piece of sugarless gum or a tooth-shaped sticker. Repeat the activity as often as desired, each time challenging students to earn five or more smiling teeth on their data sheets. Reward each student who meets the class goal with a special privilege or treat.

Two Sets!

Here's a fun way to find out what your youngsters know about baby and permanent teeth. Cut out a large baby-tooth shape and a large permanent-tooth shape from white paper; then label and display each one. To introduce the activity, read aloud the poem "Baby Teeth" on this page. Next invite students to tell what they know about each set of teeth as you write their responses on the appropriate cutout. Then increase the students' knowledge by sharing a few more tooth-related facts from the provided lists. Lead students to realize that even though baby teeth are temporary, they have a profound impact on permanent teeth.

Baby Teeth

When I was born, I had no teeth,
And that was fine with me.
Then as I grew, my teeth grew too.
20 baby teeth for me!

Now I'll lose them one by one,
And I know that it's OK.
Because my permanent teeth will come,
And replace them all some day!

Poem by Joanne Robbins
and Robin Hunt—Gr. 1
Pioneer Elementary School
Hanford, CA

Baby Teeth

- Other names for baby teeth are *deciduous teeth, milk teeth,* and *primary teeth.*
- There are ten baby teeth per jaw, 20 in all.
- They begin to form about seven months before a baby is born.
- It is called *eruption* or *teething* when baby teeth push through the gums.
- Most children have their baby teeth at two years old.
- Before a baby tooth falls out, its roots begin to dissolve.
- Each baby tooth is replaced by a permanent tooth.

Permanent Teeth

- Permanent teeth have usually finished forming by age four.
- They push out baby teeth.
- Permanent teeth may begin to appear at age six or seven.
- There are 16 permanent teeth per jaw, 32 in all.
- The last permanent teeth do not appear until ages 17 to 21.

Incisor
- used for biting food
- has sharp edges
- four incisors in each jaw

Canine
- used for biting and tearing food
- also called cuspids or dogteeth
- has a sharp, pointed edge
- two canines in each jaw

Premolar
- used to crush and grind food
- has a broad top surface with lumps, called cusps
- also called bicuspids (two cusps) four premolars in each jaw

Molar
- used to grind food
- larger than premolars
- has three to five cusps
- six molars in each jaw

Tooth Tasks

Students compare four kinds of teeth—incisors, canines, premolars, and molars—with this toothy activity. Under your students' guidance, list information about each tooth type. Then have each student use a handheld mirror to find an incisor, a canine, and a molar in his mouth. (Remind students that premolars are permanent teeth.) For a fun follow-up, have each youngster make an informative 3-D tooth to dangle from his desk!

Give each child four identical (and symmetrical) tooth patterns. (Use the tooth pattern on page 172 as a template if desired.) A student labels each pattern for a different type of tooth; then on the pattern he describes the tooth and what it can do. Next he cuts out each pattern and folds the resulting cutouts in half, keeping the text to the inside. To assemble his project, the student places one folded tooth in front of him. He spreads glue on the top surface; then aligns a second folded tooth atop the glue. In the same manner, he glues the third and the fourth tooth in place. Next he picks up his project, and glues the top and bottom surfaces together. To prepare the project for hanging, he punches a hole near the top; then he threads one end of a length of curling ribbon through the hole and securely ties the ribbon end. Use tape to suspend the projects from each student's desk.

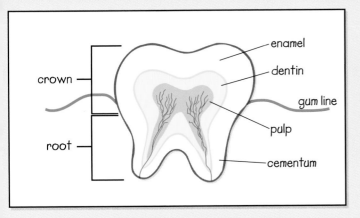

Students will know that cavities are bad, but will they know how cavities form? Probably not! Explain that saliva produces an invisible film on teeth. When bacteria and food particles stick to this film, *plaque* is formed. Foods containing sugars or starches are especially harmful because when bacteria eat these foods, acid is formed. Then the acid makes holes in the enamel, which lead to cavities. Give students an opportunity to see firsthand the need to brush with the easy egg-related experiments that are outlined. After conducting the experiments, ask students to recount the importance of brushing. Without a doubt the experiments will make a lasting impression on your youngsters!

A Closer Look

This hands-on activity gives students a detailed look at a tooth. Give each student a golf ball–sized portion of Crayola® Model Magic® (nontoxic, air-drying modeling compound) to flatten and form into a tooth shape. Set the projects aside to dry overnight. The following day have each student glue his project onto a 9" x 12" sheet of poster board. While the glue dries, review the parts of a tooth. Then have each student use fine-tipped markers to draw a gum line and label the crown and root of his model. Next have each student color and label his tooth's pulp, dentin, enamel, and cementum. Also have each child draw nerves and blood vessels in the pulp section of his tooth project. There you have it! A tooth model, up close and personal!

Easy Experiments

- To show students how plaque can eat through enamel, have students carefully feel the shell of a raw (or hard-boiled) egg and compare it to the feel of a tooth. Then soak the egg overnight in vinegar. The following day compare the action of the vinegar on the eggshell to plaque on a tooth.

- To demonstrate how easily teeth can be stained, place one egg in a jar of water and one egg in a jar of cola. The following day remove the eggs and compare them. Then use a toothbrush and toothpaste to brush away the stain from the cola-tinted egg.

Tooth Facts

- The **crown** is the visible part of a tooth.
- The **root** holds the tooth in the jaw.
- **Pulp** is the innermost layer of a tooth. It consists of nerves that feel pain and blood vessels that nourish the tooth.
- **Dentin** is the yellow substance that surrounds the pulp. It is harder than bone and makes up most of the tooth.
- **Enamel** covers the dentin in the crown of the tooth. It is the hardest tissue in the body, and protects a tooth during chewing.
- **Cementum**, which is about as hard as bone, surrounds the dentin in the root of the tooth. The cementum and enamel usually meet where the root and the crown join.

Practice Makes Perfect

One of the best ways for youngsters to become fantastic flossers is to practice! In advance enlist students' help in collecting a cardboard egg carton (to be painted white) or a white Styrofoam® egg carton for every two students. Cut the lid off each carton; then cut the bottom of the carton in half lengthwise to create two rows of six egg-carton teeth. Give each student a row of teeth, an 18-inch length of dental floss (or yarn), and two pieces of tape to secure each end of his prop to his desktop. Demonstrate how to hold the dental floss by wrapping one end of the floss around each middle finger. Next show students the proper flossing method by using your index fingers and thumbs to gently guide the floss between two egg-carton teeth. Pull the floss up, down, and around to clean the sides of both teeth and the gum area. Provide plenty of time for students to practice this flossing technique on their models. Then send the models home for continued flossing practice. Challenge students to try out their flossing expertise on the real thing, too!

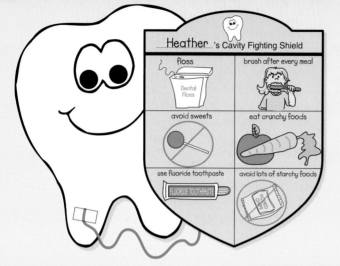

Shield Away Cavities

After a review of how plaque can cause dental decay, make these cavity-fighting shields with your youngsters. Duplicate the shield on page 171 onto gray construction paper—one copy per student. A student writes and illustrates one way to avoid getting cavities in each section of her shield; then she cuts out the pattern. Next she trims a 9" x 12" sheet of white construction paper into a large tooth shape, and draws a face on the cutout. Finally she tapes one end of a 12-inch length of yarn to the front of the tooth and the other yarn end to the back of the shield. Mount the completed projects in the hallway to spread the word about ways to protect teeth from their worst enemy!

Gleaming Graphs

Turn your young cavity fighters into conscientious consumers with this graphing activity! To create a bulletin-board graph like the one shown, mount five 1-foot-wide lengths of colorful paper, five laminated toothpaste-cap cutouts, and a title. Next have each student cut out a white construction-paper copy of "Toothpaste Trivia" (page 172). Ask each child to complete the activity at home and return it the following school day.

Students can use their completed cutouts to create a variety of graphs. To graph toothpaste brands, use a wipe-off marker to label four toothpaste caps with different brand names. Label the fifth cap "Other." Have each child use a pushpin to attach his tooth cutout to the display; then have the students interpret and answer questions about the resulting graph. To find out how many students use a fluoride toothpaste, have students remove their cutouts from the graph. Wipe the toothpaste caps clean, label one cap "Fluoride" and one "No Fluoride," and repeat the activity. You'll find plenty of opportunities to polish your youngsters' graphing skills and their toothpaste trivia!

Dental Care Collages

These king-size collages are a perfect way to review tooth-friendly foods. Cut two large tooth shapes from white bulletin-board paper. Draw a smiley face on one cutout. On the other cutout, draw a sad face and attach a piece of aluminum foil to resemble a cavity. Mount the teeth in an easily accessible classroom location. Remind students that sugary, starchy, and sticky foods are a high cavity risk. Then, from discarded magazines, have each child cut out foods that are good for teeth and foods that are harmful to teeth. Ask each student to present her food pictures to the class before she glues them on the appropriate tooth cutout. The resulting collages are sure to be the topic of numerous dental-related conversations.

Mouthful Of Math

Add a taste of math to your dental-health activities with this hands-on partner activity. On the chalkboard write number-related tooth facts like those shown. Then give each student pair a mouth-shaped math mat cut from red paper and 32 small white manipulatives (navy beans or miniature marshmallows) for teeth. Announce a word problem related to teeth like, "A child starts first grade with all of his baby teeth. By the end of the school year, he only has 17 baby teeth left. How many baby teeth did he lose in all?" Each student pair uses its teeth manipulatives to solve the problem. Present several word problems in the manner described. Then invite students to create dental-health problems for their classmates to solve.

Brushing Up!

These nifty toothbrushes are the perfect place for students to show off their newfound dental-health knowledge. To make the toothbrush bristles, a student writes a rule for maintaining healthy teeth on each of five 1 1/2" x 9" white construction-paper strips. (Alert students to leave a two-inch left margin on each strip.) For the toothbrush handle, she personalizes a colorful sentence strip. Then she glues the bristles to the handle as shown. Encourage students to display their projects at home for a lasting reminder of positive dental-health practices. (For easy transport, have each student fold the handle and bristles of her project in half until she gets home.)

Tooth Tales

Give your youngsters' creativity a tug with these tooth-related writing ideas! If desired, bind the students' stories between two construction-paper covers; then add a personalized tooth cutout and the title "Behind Every Tooth There's A Great Story!" to the front cover.

Just-For-Fun Toothy Writing Prompts
- You have been asked to pull the tooth of a prince or princess. Describe the event!
- So who exactly is the tooth fairy? Reveal what the tooth fairy looks like, where she or he lives, and what she or he does with all those teeth!
- Pretend you are a tooth. Write your autobiography.
- Create a superhero tooth fairy! Write and illustrate an adventure about a tooth fairy who has superhero powers.
- Writing from a tooth's point of view, tell the best way to pull a tooth.

Tracy Welsch, Gr. 2, Camp Avenue Elementary School
North Merrick, NY

Clevell Harris

Natural Tooth Cleaners

Students can sink their teeth into this culminating activity! With the help of a parent volunteer or two, secretly arrange to serve your youngsters a healthful snack of crunchy, uncooked vegetables and fruits on the last day of your dental-health study. Then on the culminating day, tell students that in celebration of their learning, you've planned for them to brush their teeth! When the gasps and groans have subsided, serve them the natural tooth cleaners that the parent volunteer(s) prepared. As students munch on the teeth-friendly snacks, explain that as these foods are eaten they help scrape away bacteria and plaque—making them a perfect snack, especially when it's impossible to brush your teeth after eating. Students will be all smiles!

Toothfully Yours

Have you been using the same tooth-related literature year after year? Then it's time to book a literature checkup! Review this collection of entertaining and informative tooth tales; then extract your favorites and incorporate them into your dental-health unit. It won't hurt a bit, we promise!

by Deborah Zink Roffino

Trevor's Wiggly-Wobbly Tooth

Written by Lester L. Laminack
Illustrated by Kathi Garry McCord
Peachtree Publishers, Ltd.; 1998

Trevor never dreamed he would be the last of the first graders to join the Missing Tooth Club. And now he's learning just how long it can take for a loose tooth to disconnect! His classmates have oodles of suggestions for prying the baby tooth free—from fingers to string to pliers—but it's Trevor's granny who pulls the smartest move of the week. Whimsical illustrations show students the lighter side of losing that first tooth.

Grandpa's Teeth

Written & Illustrated by Rod Clement
HarperCollins Publishers, Inc.; 1997

Sound the alarm! Someone has snuck into Grandpa's bedroom and stolen his precious Swiss teeth! It's a tooth-related tale that will have your students erupting with laughter and realizing that there's more than one way to lose teeth. Zany watercolor illustrations add to the hilarity. The crime is never solved, but a bit of neighborly cooperation saves the day. And a crafty canine gets the very last laugh!

The Crocodile And The Dentist

Written & Illustrated by Taro Gomi
The Millbrook Press, Inc.; 1994

It's a face-off between a big-eyed reptile and a mustachioed dentist. The question is who is the most terrifying: a crocodile with a king-size toothache or a dentist with a dreadful-looking drill? While the two characters' thoughts humorously mirror each other, it's their exaggerated expressions that get most of the laughs.

Andrew's Loose Tooth

Written by Robert Munsch
Illustrated by Michael Martchenko
Scholastic Inc., 1998

Welcome to the wacky world of Munsch and Martchenko, where a loose tooth creates absolute pandemonium! When young Andrew insists that something be done about his loose tooth, his mom and dad do their best to oblige. After each parent gives the tooth a yank, the family dentist is called in, followed by a motorcycle-riding tooth fairy. However, it takes a best friend to solve Andrew's loose-tooth problem. A kaleidoscope of colors and engaging characters spice up this very silly story.

Dr. Kanner, Dentist With A Smile

Written by Alice K. Flanagan
Photographed by Christine Osinski
Children's Press®, 1997

Engaging photographs and easy-to-read text escort readers through a visit to the family dentist. The ins and outs of Dr. Kanner's job are highlighted, and brief introductions to common dentistry equipment and practices are provided. This title is one in a series of books called Our Neighborhood, which explores jobs within the community.

SPARKLE FRESH

SUPER

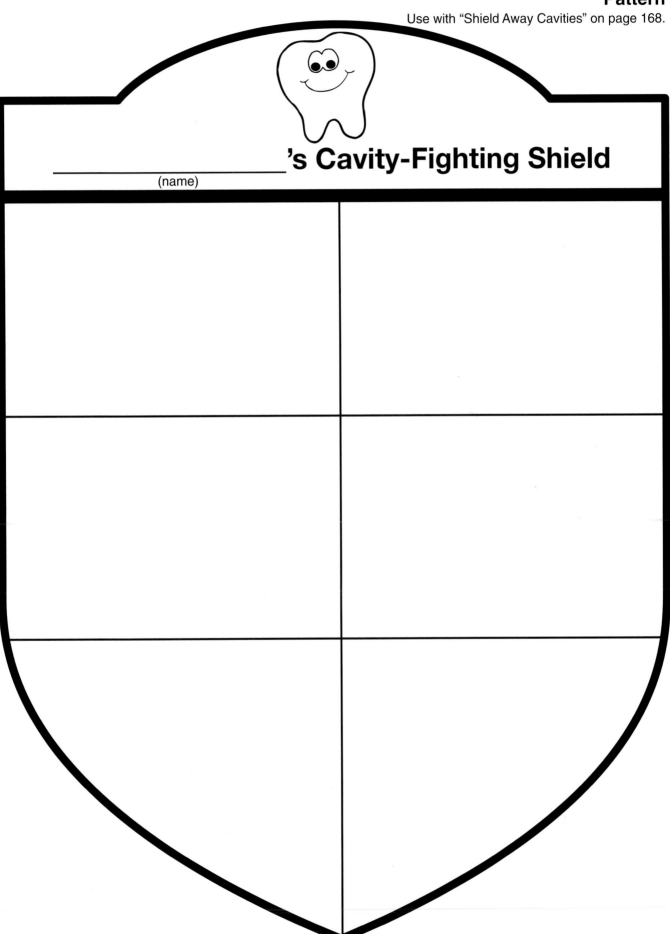

_____'s Cavity-Fighting Shield

(name)

Dental Data

Name _____

Week _____

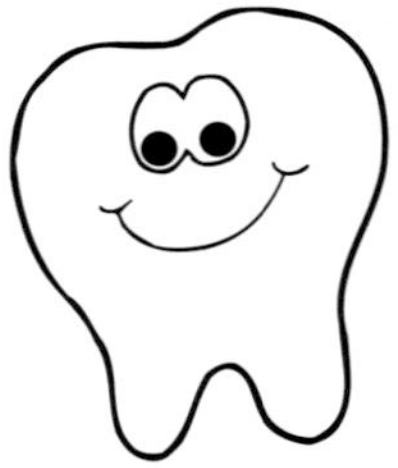

Each Day:
Make a ✓ by each dental practice that you follow.
Count the checks. Use the Code Box.
Draw a face on the tooth.

	Mon.	Tues.	Wed.	Thurs.	Fri.	Sat.	Sun.
brushed at least two times							
used toothpaste with fluoride							
flossed between teeth							
ate crunchy foods							
ate foods containing calcium							
ate two or fewer sugary foods							
ate a balanced diet							
didn't chew on hard or sharp objects							
Daily Total							
Weekly Total							

Code Box: ⌣ = 7–8   — = 5–6   ⌢ = 0–4

©The Education Center, Inc. • *THE MAILBOX*® • *Primary* • Feb/Mar 1999

Name _____

Toothpaste Trivia

The brand of toothpaste I use most often is _____.

Check each benefit of your toothpaste.

☐ fights cavities with fluoride

☐ controls tartar

☐ promotes healthy gums

☐ helps teeth feel less sensitive

Other: _____

©The Education Center, Inc. • *THE MAILBOX*® • *Primary* • Feb/Mar 1999

172

Note To Teacher: Use the data sheet with "Smile Maintenance" on page 165. Use the tooth with "Gleaming Graphs" on page 168. The tooth shape may also be used with other activities throughout the unit.

A Very Busy Place!

Exploring The Pond

At first glance, a pond appears to be a quiet body of water. But don't be fooled! This rich habitat is a happening place! Use this collection of activities and reproducibles to take a peek at ponds.

ideas contributed by Darcy Brown and Jessica A. Feraco

Presenting The Pond

Capture students' interest in ponds, fact by fact! Four days before you plan to dive into a study of ponds, post one fact from "Five Facts to Ponder." On each of the following days, post an additional fact. Explain to students that the facts are clues about an upcoming topic of study. Reveal the final fact on the day your pond investigation is to begin, and ask students to tell *you* what they think they'll be studying! When the topic of ponds is identified, invite students to talk about the ponds they have seen and/or visited.

Five Facts To Ponder
• It can be made by nature or by man.
• It varies in size and shape.
• Most are shallow.
• Lots of plants and animals live there.
• It is an area of fresh, still water.

A Pond Is A Pond

How does a pond compare to an ocean or another body of water? Use a Venn diagram to find out! Draw and label a diagram that compares a pond to an ocean (or another body of water). Then, under your students' direction, list each fact from "Five Facts To Ponder" on the diagram. Each time a new fact about ponds is discovered, repeat the procedure.

Challenge students to continually evaluate the diagram and make suggestions for updating it. By the conclusion of your study, students will have a clear picture of the unique qualities of ponds.

A Lively Habitat

No two ponds are exactly the same! But one thing *is* for certain. If a pond is sunny, sheltered, and pollution-free, it will be teeming with life! Use the following song to introduce students to pond life. Encourage students to create additional song verses as they learn more about this bustling biome.

About The Pond
(sung to the tune of "The Muffin Man")
Do you know about a pond,
About a pond, about a pond?
Do you know about a pond
Where things go plip, plot, plat?

Ponds are homes for animals,
For animals, for animals.
Ponds are homes for animals.
Can you imagine that?

Tadpoles, fish, and dragonflies,
And dragonflies, and dragonflies.
Tadpoles, fish, and dragonflies
Live in this habitat.

Ponds are homes for lots of plants,
Lots of plants, lots of plants.
Ponds are homes for lots of plants.
What do you think of that?

Algae, reeds, and cattails too,
And cattails too, and cattails too.
Algae, reeds, and cattails too,
Grow in this habitat.

What Critters Live Where?

So where do all those pond critters live? Just about everywhere! Amazingly enough, every part of a pond is a home or *habitat*. Invite students to name pond dwellers and tell where these animals live. Students will quickly realize that many pond animals live both in *and* around a pond. The turtle even spends part of its year under the pond! Next give each child a copy of page 177 and challenge him to find a home for each pond critter. To do this, the student colors the pond scene and the animal illustrations. Next he cuts out each critter and matches it to its name. Then he puts a dab of glue on each black dot and glues the pictures in place. Hey, this pond is a popular place!

Dazzling Dragonflies

What pond critter has wings that whirl, flies forward and backward, hovers like a helicopter, and snaps up its prey in midair? It is the far-from-ordinary dragonfly! Students will delight in creating the dragonfly project described on page 45. Plan to showcase these dapper pond dwellers in a prominent location. Passersby are sure to be dazzled! (Be sure to check out the turtle project featured on the same page. Students will surely take a shine to it as well!)

Plenty Of Plants

It's a fact! Plants are *very* important to a pond community. Not only does a pond need plants to stay healthy, all pond critters depend on plants in some way. Use the reproducible activity on page 178 to sprout interest in pond plants. If desired, read each sentence aloud, pausing for students to color each lily pad. (All sentences featured on the page are true.) Invite students to color the artwork. Next have each child glue his paper onto a 9" x 12" sheet of light blue construction paper, cut along the gray dotted line near the bottom of his paper, align the cut edge with the gray water line near the top, and then flatten the paper. Provide time for each child to render an underwater pond scene on the front of his project and, if desired, glue construction-paper reeds inside the project so they poke above the pond's surface as shown. Plants are "pond-errific"!

Linked For Life

Each plant and animal in a pond community is a link on a *food chain*. To help students better understand how a pond food chain works, give each child a copy of the picture cards on page 179 to color and cut out. Then have her mount each of the six cutouts near the center of a 2" x 9" construction-paper strip. Challenge students to arrange their paper strips in food-chain order, reminding them that the top position of a food chain is held by the animal that cannot be eaten by any other chain members. When appropriate, reveal that at the bottom link of this food chain are tiny plants called *algae*. The algae are eaten by the tadpole, which is eaten by the baby turtle. The baby turtle is eaten by the frog, which is eaten by the fish. And the fish is eaten by the heron—one of the largest meat eaters to visit a pond. Then have each student use her strips and glue to create a corresponding paper chain. If desired, have each child add a loop to the top of her chain and label it "Pond Food Chain." Ask each child to take her project home and explain what she has learned to her family.

174

The Changing Seasons

Things are always changing in and around a pond. Use this poster-making project to spotlight some of the seasonal changes that occur each year. Give each child four copies of the pond illustration on page 179 and ask him to write the name of a different season at the top of each one. Use the information below to describe each pond season. After each description, have every student program the thermometer on his corresponding paper with a seasonal temperature and then illustrate the season using a variety of arts-and-crafts supplies. Next have each child cut out four arrow shapes from colorful paper. To assemble his project, he sequences his papers and mounts them clockwise on a 12" x 18" sheet of colored construction paper. Then he glues his directional arrows to his poster and adds a desired title and his name. Display the eye-catching projects on a bulletin board titled "A Year At The Pond."

Cindy Barber—Gr. 1, St. Cecilia Elementary School, Thiensville, WI

Much To See!

Your pond enthusiasts will have a grand time reviewing the pond life they've studied with this upbeat song! Copy each stanza on chart paper. Engage the entire class in singing the first stanza. Then have each student or student pair take a turn singing a version of the second stanza. Challenge students to not repeat plants or animals that have already been named. Conclude the sing-along with a rousing rendition of the first stanza. Wow! There really is plenty to see!

Walking To The Pond
(sung to the tune of "Found A Peanut")

I am walking
To the pond.
Won't you please
Come walk with me?
I will tell you,
I will tell you,
All the things
There are to see!

Found a _____,
Found a _____,
Found a _____ just now.
Just now I found a _____.
Found a _____ just now.

Mary Gardner—Gr. 1
Rahn Elementary
Mount Morris, IL

Reporting From The Pond

As you prepare to wrap up your pond study, have each child write a brief report about her favorite pond plant or animal and publish her work in a pond-shaped booklet! First give each child a copy of page 180 to complete about her chosen topic. To make her booklet, a student cuts apart the four pages, stacks them in order, and staples the stack near the top of a 5" x 7" rectangle of light blue construction paper. Then she trims the blue paper to resemble a pond and traces this shape onto a second rectangle of light blue paper. To make the front booklet cover, she cuts out the shape and adds an illustration that incorporates the topic of her report, if possible. Then she staples the completed cover to her project. Set aside time for interested students to share their reports with their classmates.

A Report From The Pond
by Beth Saunders

Fall
The days get shorter and the nights get cooler. Plants begin to die. Lily pads sink. There are fewer algae in the water, which makes the pond water more clear. Leaves from other plants blow into the pond. Birds fly to warmer winter habitats. Beavers stock their dens with food. Frogs, turtles, and other smaller animals disappear into the mud. Winter is almost here!

Winter
Snow is on the ground and a layer of ice covers the pond. The pond is very quiet. Most animals are hibernating or resting.

Summer
The days are long and warm. The pond is bursting with life! The spring babies are growing up. Young birds learn to fly. Young animals learn to hunt. Plants are thriving. Cattails grow tall. Water lilies bloom.

Spring
The weather warms and the pond begins to awaken. Plants begin to grow and spring flowers bloom. Turtles and frogs crawl out of the mud. Birds return to the pond. Many baby animals are born in the spring.

A Year At The Pond

by Cindy

Snacks With Facts!

Satisfy your youngsters' hunger for the pond with these delicious snacks. Several facts accompany the recipes, making them perfect nourishment for your pond lovers! Or, if you prefer, wrap up your pond investigation with a pond party, complete with pond-related refreshments!

Turtle Talk

Shell out these facts about the turtle as students render edible versions of the unique reptile.

- The turtle is the only reptile with a shell.
- Turtles are toothless. They use their sharp beaks to cut and tear food.
- During the winter, many turtles hibernate in mud at the bottom of a pond.

Tummy-Tickling Turtle

For one:

1 large chocolate chip cookie (shell)
1 mini chocolate chip cookie (head)
2 vanilla wafers (legs)

2 raisins (eyes)
1 cashew (tail)
green-tinted icing

Directions:

1. Break each vanilla wafer in half to make two legs. Use icing to attach the legs to the underside of the large cookie.
2. Use icing to attach the small cookie to the large cookie.
3. Embellish the critter with green icing as desired.
4. Use dabs of icing to attach the raisin eyes and cashew tail.

Donna M. Post
Ressie Jeffries Elementary
Front Royal, VA

Crunchy Cattail

For one:

1/2 peeled banana
Cocoa Krispies® cereal
peanut butter
wooden skewer (tip cut off)

Directions:

1. Carefully push the cut end of the skewer into the cut edge of the banana.
2. Spread peanut butter over the entire banana.
3. Roll the banana in cereal, gently pressing the cereal to the banana as needed.

Researching Reeds

You can bank on this information to interest your pond enthusiasts!

- Cattails, also known as *reed mace,* grow on the banks of ponds.
- Some cattails grow to a height of 13 feet!
- A muskrat builds its lodge from cattails.
- Cattails are useful to humans. Their roots are edible, their pollen can be used like flour, and their leaves can be woven into mats and chairs.

Pondering Lily Pads

"Be-leaf" it or not, lily pads do more than float! Use these fascinating facts to ponder this unique pond plant.

- A lily pad is the leaf of an underwater plant that is rooted in the bottom of a pond.
- The top of a lily pad has breathing holes and a thin waxy coating that repels water.
- The underside of a lily pad has no breathing holes, and it isn't waxy. This side of the lily pad hugs the water to keep from being turned over.
- A variety of pond critters live under lily pad leaves!

Lily Pad Punch

(makes 25 five-ounce servings)

Ingredients:

1 package sugar-free lime Kool-Aid®
2-liter bottle ginger ale
1/2 gallon lime sherbet
water

Directions:

1. Prepare Kool-Aid® according to package directions.
2. Add ginger ale. Stir well.
3. Pour into serving cups. Add a spoonful of sherbet (lily pad) to each.

Name

Critters At The Pond

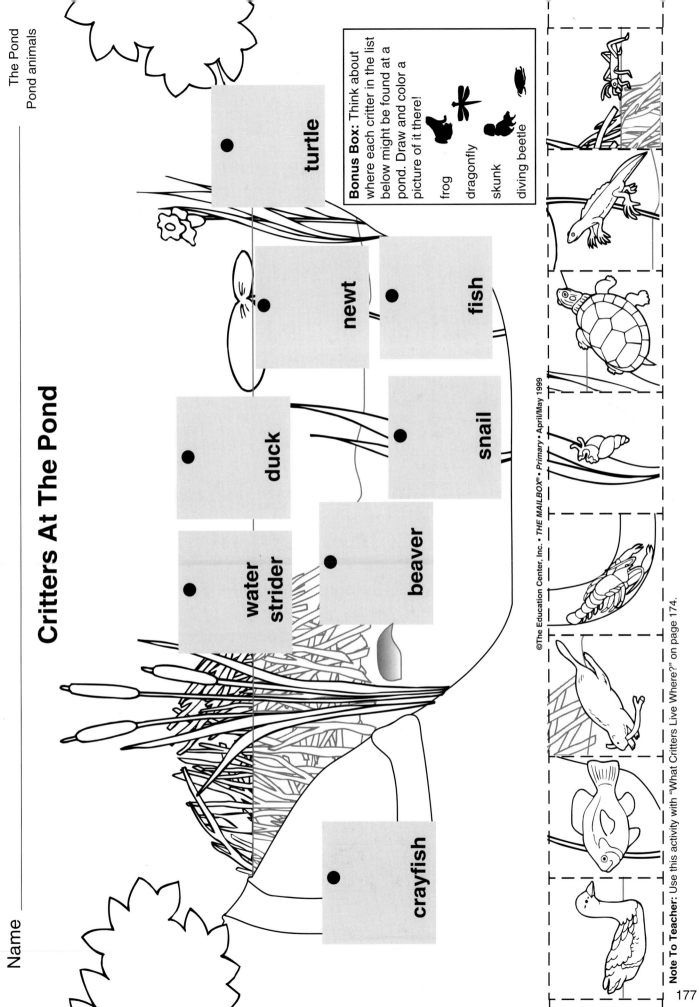

Bonus Box: Think about where each critter in the list below might be found at a pond. Draw and color a picture of it there!

frog
dragonfly
skunk
diving beetle

turtle

newt

fish

duck

snail

beaver

water strider

crayfish

©The Education Center, Inc. • *THE MAILBOX®* • *Primary* • April/May 1999

Note To Teacher: Use this activity with "What Critters Live Where?" on page 174.

177

Plants At The Pond

Read each sentence.
If it is true, color the lily pad green.
If it is not true, do not color the lily pad.

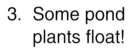

1. Plants grow in every part of a pond. 	2. Pond plants need sunlight to grow. 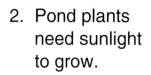	3. Some pond plants float! 
4. Pond plants make good hiding places for pond critters. 	5. Many pond critters lay their eggs on pond plants. 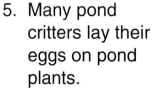	6. There are pond plants so tiny that they cannot be seen. 
7. Some pond plants only grow underwater. 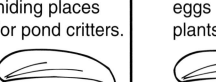	8. There are many plants that grow at the edge of a pond. 	9. Some pond plants have pretty flowers. 
10. Algae is a kind of pond plant. 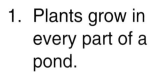	11. Every pond animal depends on pond plants in some way. 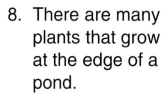	12. Pond plants help keep a pond healthy. 

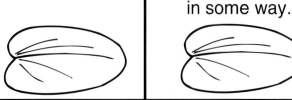

©The Education Center, Inc. • *THE MAILBOX®* • *Primary* • April/May 1999

Note To Teacher: Use this activity with "Plenty Of Plants" on page 174.

Picture Cards And Pond Illustration

Use the picture cards with "Linked For Life" on page 174.

fish

algae

heron

frog

baby turtle

tadpole

Use the pond illustration with "The Changing Seasons" on page 175.

Panel 2

My favorite pond _____
_____ (plant/animal)
is the _____
It can be found _____
_____ .
I like it because _____
_____ .

2

Panel 4

When winter comes, the _____
_____
_____ .
The _____
_____ is
important to the pond because _____
_____ .

4

Panel 1

A Report From
The Pond

by _____

1

©The Education Center, Inc. • THE MAILBOX® • Primary • April/May 1999

Panel 3

Three interesting facts about the _____
_____ are:

1. _____

2. _____

3. _____

3

©The Education Center, Inc. • THE MAILBOX® • Primary • April/May 1999

180   **Note To Teacher:** Use this activity with "Reporting From The Pond" on page 175.

Social Studies Units

NATIVE AMERICANS
OF THE PACIFIC NORTHWEST

Towering totem poles, jumbo canoes, and elaborate celebrations are all part of the rich culture of the Native Americans who made their home in the Pacific Northwest. Use the following activities to supplement an investigation of truly remarkable people.

ideas contributed by Stacie Stone Davis

TEACHING TIPS

As you prepare to teach about Native American people and their cultures, remember that good information, common sense, thoughtfulness, and sensitivity are your best guides. Always differentiate between the past and the present. Avoid activities that perpetuate stereotypes, such as role-playing or the choosing of "Indian" names. Constantly ask yourself how you are increasing your students' knowledge of these rich cultures and ways of life. And always respect the sacred nature of objects and practices associated with Native American cultures. If you are unsure if an activity is appropriate, the best thing you can do is consult a Native American for advice.

PICTURING THE PACIFIC NORTHWEST

The Native Americans of the Pacific Northwest lived in the narrow band of coastal land that stretches from the southern tip of Alaska to northern California. The mild, moist climate made the region one of dense mists, lush evergreen forests, abundant vegetation, and numerous game animals. Rich freshwater fishing and a variety of sea animals provided most of the food supplies, while huge trees furnished the people with materials for tools, clothing, transportation, and shelter. Enlist your youngsters' help in locating the Pacific Northwest region on a U.S. map. Describe the climate and natural resources of the area, and ask students to contemplate how these elements may have affected the day-to-day lives of the Native Americans who lived there. Follow up the class discussion by having students complete the reproducible activity on page 186. The picture is clear: the environment of the Pacific Northwest greatly influenced the lifestyles of the Native Americans who lived there.

"TREE-MENDOUS" TRANSPORTATION

Canoes, carved from large cedar trees, were the basic method of transportation in the Pacific Northwest. An ocean-going canoe might measure more than 60 feet in length and hold more than a dozen men! To give students an idea of the size of these king-size canoes, take them into the hallway and have them sit in a straight line—one behind each other. Invite youngsters to estimate if the line they have formed is longer than, shorter than, or equal to 60 feet. Then place a length of masking tape near the front of the line, and use a tape measure to measure the length of the students' line and a distance of 60 feet. Place a second piece of masking tape at the latter location. Next discuss possible seafaring scenarios with your students: from riding out a rough storm in a 60-foot canoe to paddling it for hundreds of miles to keeping the canoe upright during the capture of a 200-pound halibut! Then take a class vote to find out how many students are eager to set sail in a huge hollowed-out log!

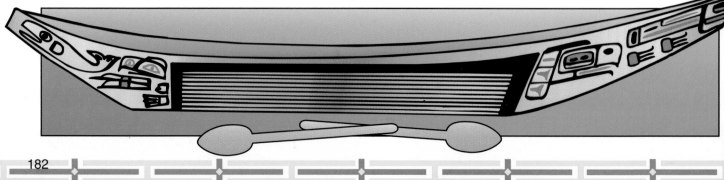

COLOSSAL CANOES

In addition to transportation, the canoe was used for fishing, whaling, trading, *potlatches,* and war. It was not uncommon for native groups to make different kinds of canoes for different purposes. The most impressive canoes were the ceremonial ones that were used for war or potlatches. Have each student make and decorate a colossal canoe for a specific purpose.

To make a canoe, cut away each side panel of a large, brown paper grocery bag; then fold the resulting length of paper lengthwise and trim each end of the paper to create a desired canoe shape. Next flatten the cutout, and use colorful paints to decorate the cutout with symbols or illustrations that tell a story. When the cutout is dry, refold it, and either staple or glue the ends to form the canoe. Cut crossbars from the remaining paper scraps and glue them inside the canoe. Set aside time for each child to present her colossal canoe and tell its story. Then display these vessels around your classroom or in the school library.

VERY BIG HOUSES

The peoples of the Pacific Northwest built massive wooden houses that were even more impressive than their canoes! Each permanent multifamily home measured at least 40 feet by 30 feet. There were no windows and only two small openings: one in the roof for smoke to escape and one at the front of the home. The front entrance may have been part of an elaborately carved and decorated doorway post. To give students a feel for the largeness of these homes, arrange two 30-foot and two 40-foot yarn lengths to form a large rectangle. Ask your entire class to sit inside this rectangle and imagine living in a structure this size with 40 or more family members. Explain that inside the home, woven mats partitioned off each family's living quarters. Each living space opened into the center of the home where fires for heat, light, and cooking were kept burning. Ask students to discuss what they think the advantages and disadvantages of this lifestyle might be. Then see "Under Construction" for a home-building project.

UNDER CONSTRUCTION

Building a wooden house was often an elaborate process marked by ceremonies and feasts. Have your students enlist the help of their family members in getting started on this home-building project. In a letter to parents, ask that each child bring to school a box with a removable lid, such as a shoebox. For easy management, request that the box and its lid each be wrapped with brown paper and that a small hole (about one-inch square) be poked in the center of the wrapped lid. When you have a wrapped box and lid for every student, celebrate with a few extra minutes of recess or free time.

For the next stage of construction, have students complete the interiors of their homes. Provide tissue paper for making flames and brown paper for making partitions. Plan another celebration when this stage of construction is complete.

Finally have each child complete the exterior of his home. To do this, he draws planks on the outside walls and the roof. Next he designs, colors, and cuts out a poster-board doorway post and attaches it to the front of his house. To complete the roof, he glues overlapping paper strips (planks) and small rocks to the lid. Encourage each child to share a fact or two about the home he constructed before putting these projects on display.

WOODEN WONDERS

Nearly everything in the village was made from wood. That included houses, totem poles, canoes, dishes, ceremonial masks—*and* clothing! How was clothing woven from wood? First a section of outer bark was carefully removed from a cedar tree; then the soft inner bark was cut into long strips. Back in the village, this bark was soaked, beaten into soft shreds, and prepared for weaving. A popular hat of the region, called a *spruce root hat,* was woven using the roots of a spruce tree that were heated and then prepared in a similar way.

Students will enjoy making these mock spruce root hats. To make a hat, cut away the center portion of a nine-inch paper plate, leaving only the plate's rim. Place the rim over an inverted 16-ounce Chinet® bowl; then staple the rim to the bowl as shown. Use crayons or markers to decorate the hat.

A TASTE OF THE PACIFIC NORTHWEST

For the Native Americans, salmon was by far the most important fish of this region. To show their respect and appreciation for the bountiful fish, the bones of the first salmon of the year were returned to the river where the fish was caught. This first salmon, called *Chief Salmon,* was honored in prayer and song in hopes that the salmon would return to the same river the following year. Add some flavor to your study of the Pacific Northwest by giving each student a portion of cooked salmon atop a cracker. Since berries were also an important part of their diet, consider serving a few fresh berries too. Or, if you're a bit more adventuresome, bake a berry cobbler for your students to sample. Yum!

TOWERING TOTEM POLES

More than any other item, the *totem pole* is the symbol of the Pacific Northwest. Unfortunately many totem poles were destroyed when missionaries who moved into the area believed that the Native Americans worshipped the poles. This was not the case. The poles—which portray some animals, birds, fish, heavenly bodies, and prominent landmarks—symbolize the highlights of a family's ancestral history. Help students learn more about these awe-inspiring art forms by reading aloud the photo-illustrated book *Totem Pole* by Diane Hoyt-Goldsmith (Holiday House, Inc.; 1994). Then, as a follow-up to the book, have each child bring to school an empty (and clean) 16-ounce can for a totem-pole project.

To begin, divide your students into groups of four and assist each group in taping its four cans together so that the closed ends are exposed. Next have each group wrap a 12" x 18" sheet of tan construction paper around its project, securely tape the paper in place, and lay the project down so that the paper seam is at the back.

Explain that each child in the group will decorate one-fourth of the project to symbolize an important event of his life. Then give each child a four-inch square of blank paper on which to draw his idea. Remind the class that actual totem-pole carvers draw their ideas on paper first too. When the group has agreed on the placement of each child's contribution, each member of the group uses construction paper and/or markers to decorate his portion of the pole.

Plan to raise these poles at a class potlatch (see page 185). Or have each group in turn raise its totem pole for the class; then ask each child in the group to say a few words about his contribution.

FUN AND GAMES

One of the greatest advantages of living in the Pacific Northwest was the availability of food. Because the Native Americans living there could gather a year's food supply between May and September, they had more time during the rest of the year for fun and games. Your students will enjoy playing these two games that have been passed down from Native Americans of the Pacific Northwest.

Just For Laughs: Played by both adults and children, the object of this large-group game is to make the opponent laugh! Divide the class into two equal teams: A and B. Ask one student from each team to come to the front of the classroom. On your signal, the player from Team A has 15 seconds to make the player from Team B laugh. There may be no physical contact. If she succeeds, she earns one point for her team. If she does not, the opposing team earns one point. Then the roles are reversed. When this round is over, select two more opponents. Continue play in this manner until each player has taken at least one turn. The team with the most points wins the game!

How Many Groups?: This guessing game is great for small groups. One player is It and is given 20 or more small sticks (or dried beans or pasta). The remaining players close their eyes tightly while It arranges the sticks in a series of groups on the ground. When It calls "Ready!", the other players—keeping their eyes closed—guess how many groups of sticks were formed. The first player to guess correctly becomes the next It.

PAM CRANE

SHARING THEIR CULTURE

Native American culture is an important part of our country's past and its future. Explain to students that *traditions* in every culture must be passed along from generation to generation to avoid being forgotten. Ask students to describe traditions that their families practice; then help them realize that one day they will pass these traditions on to a younger generation. An excellent example of this transfer of information is described (and photographed) in *A Story To Tell: Traditions Of A Tlingit Community* written by Richard Nichols (Lerner Publications Company, 1998). In this story, a modern-day Tlingit grandmother shares the history and traditions of her people with her 11-year-old granddaughter. By the conclusion of the book, your youngsters—like her granddaughter—will be more knowledgeable about Tlingit culture and traditions, and they will have a much better understanding of the importance of sharing knowledge with others.

A PACIFIC NORTHWEST POTLATCH

A *potlatch*—a Chinook word meaning "to give"—was an enormous feast held by a family group or *clan* to honor another clan. Most potlatches were held during the winter when there was very little other work to be done. The purpose of the potlatch was to confirm a clan's social status and show their wealth. To accomplish this, the host clan showered their guests with food. They also gave each visitor (often totaling several hundred) a gift ranging from a cedar-bark blanket to a canoe! It often took years to prepare for a potlatch, partly because so many gifts needed to be made.

As a culmination to your study of peoples of the Pacific Northwest, hold a variation of the traditional potlatch. For this classroom celebration, have your students share their *wealth of knowledge* about the Native Americans of the Pacific Northwest with their family members. Plan for students to share the projects they've completed during their study, along with additional facts they've learned about the native peoples of this region. Then—after a snack of berry cobbler, crackers and salmon dip, and springwater—read aloud related literature. Now that's impressive!

Name_____

PICTURE THIS!

Color and cut out the five pictures.
Read each clue below.
Put a drop of glue on each •.
Glue the matching picture in place.

The ocean was a source of sea otters, whales, and seals.

There were lots of wild berries for eating.

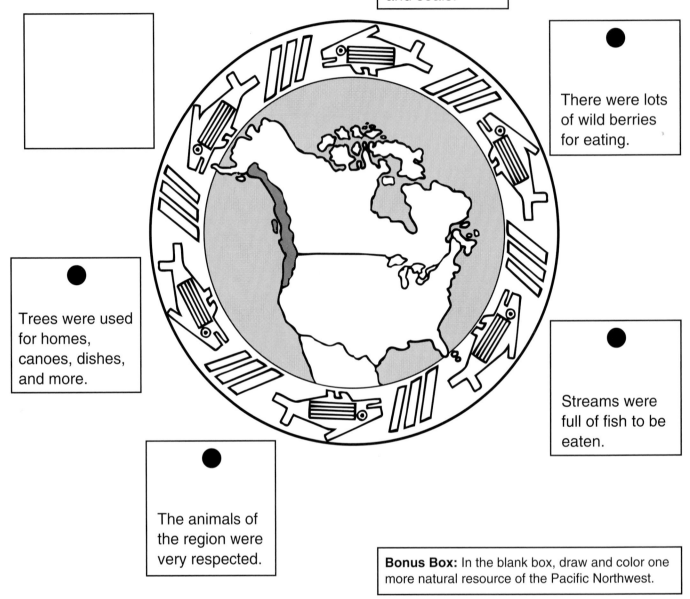

Trees were used for homes, canoes, dishes, and more.

Streams were full of fish to be eaten.

The animals of the region were very respected.

Bonus Box: In the blank box, draw and color one more natural resource of the Pacific Northwest.

©The Education Center, Inc. • *THE MAILBOX®* • *Primary* • Oct/Nov 1998

Note To Teacher: Use this page with "Picturing The Pacific Northwest" on page 182.

Is *Is* England your cup of tea?

For a first-class study of England, incorporate these easy-to-use activities into your itinerary. You can count on students having a merry olde time and plenty of jolly-good learning experiences, too!

ideas contributed by Stacie Stone Davis

Getting To Know England

Gather students around a large world map for an up close look at England. Students may be surprised to discover that England is located on a large island with two other countries: Wales to the west and Scotland to the north. Reveal that no part of England is more than 75 miles from the ocean water; then ask students to suggest advantages and disadvantages of living this close to the sea. Next have students complete the mapping activity on page 190. By jove! England's quite a country!

What About That Weather?

It has been said that the first topic of conversation between two English people is the weather. Find out what all the talk is about with this graphing activity! First have students use a world map to compare the location of their state to that of London, England. Encourage students to talk about elements that might affect the weather in these two locations. Next take a class poll to find out if your students believe the temperatures in London, England, are cooler, warmer, or about the same as the temperatures where they live. Then, over the next several weeks, enlist your students' help in graphing the daily high and/or low temperature in each location. Graph the rainfall too, if you wish. Prompt students to continually evaluate the data by asking them to explain how their day-to-day activities might vary if they lived in London. Look who's talking about the weather now!

English Authors

Enrich your youngsters' England experience by reading aloud books authored by English writers. Label a length of bulletin-board paper "Awesome Authors From England" and display the resulting poster in an accessible classroom location. When you introduce a book by an English author, write the title and author of the book on the poster. At the conclusion of the book, ask a student volunteer to illustrate a character or characters from the story on a four-inch square of paper. Glue the child's illustration to the poster near your programming. You will quickly have an eye-catching and motivational reference of several English authors and their works.

adapted from an idea by
Catherine Broome—Gr. 1
Forked River, NJ

Blossom Comes Home by James Herriot

The Tale Of Peter Rabbit by Beatrix Potter

Awesome Authors From ENGLAND

James And The Giant Peach by Roald Dahl

A Bear Called Paddington by Michael Bond

More About English Authors

Harry's Mad, a beginning chapter book by Dick King-Smith, is featured on pages 67–69. You'll also find ideas to celebrate Pooh Day—the birthday of English author A. A. Milne—on pages 232–234.

Who's In Charge?

Long ago in England a king or a queen made all of the decisions for the country. That is not the case today. The government in England is called a *constitutional monarchy.* This means that Queen Elizabeth II—the present queen of England—has lots of help running the country! Invite students to imagine what it might be like to be a prince or a princess, or even a king or a queen. Then give each child a large sheet of drawing paper on which to illustrate herself as a member of the royal family. Next have her copy and complete the following sentences on her paper: "I think the best thing about being a [royal role] would be…" and "I think the worst thing about being a [royal role] would be…." Bind the projects into a class book titled "Royal Thoughts."

A Look Around London

London—the capital of England and its largest city—is a mixture of new and old. It has been described as "ever changing and ever the same." Show students five popular London sights with this booklet activity. Give each child a white construction-paper copy of page 191. Instruct each child to color the double-decker bus red (just like those in London!), color the bus driver, and illustrate himself and some friends and family members in the windows. Ask each student to cut out his booklet cover; then give each child a 5" x 9" rectangle of construction paper (back cover) and five blank booklet pages. Assist each student in stapling his booklet pages between his booklet covers.

To begin the tour, announce one of the five sights listed on this page and read aloud the provided information. Then have each child color the corresponding picture, cut it out, glue it on a blank booklet page, and write a sentence or two about it (or write class-created sentences on the chalkboard for students to copy). The tour is complete when all five sights have been visited. Cheerio!

Tour Stops

Buckingham Palace: This is the primary home of the reigning monarch (currently the Queen of England). A popular tourist attraction at the palace is an impressive ceremony of marching men in red tunics and black bearskin helmets. It is called the Changing of the Guard.

Trafalgar Square: Many locations in London are on *squares*—open blocks of land that include trees and grass. Trafalgar Square is a popular meeting place in London. It is famous for its fountains and statues.

Tower Bridge: The Tower Bridge is the most famous of all the bridges that cross the Thames River. It leads to the Tower of London, another popular tourist attraction. Several times a week Tower Bridge is raised so tall ships can pass through.

Big Ben: This much-loved London landmark (officially called the Clock Tower) is part of the House of Parliament. The clock has four faces. Each clock face is 23 feet wide and displays Roman numerals that are two feet high! The clock, which is wound by hand, has been ticking since 1859 and it still keeps nearly perfect time!

The British Museum: This incredible museum was founded in 1753. Today it houses the richest and most varied collection of treasures in the entire world! It is open daily for visitors.

Book Links To London

- *Percy To The Rescue*
  Written by Steven J. Simmons
  Illustrated by Kim Howard
  Charlesbridge Publishing, 1998

- *The Inside-Outside Book Of London*
  Written & Illustrated by Roxie Munro
  Penguin Group, 1989

- *You Can't Eat Your Chicken Pox, Amber Brown*
  Written by Paula Danziger
  Illustrated by Tony Ross
  Scholastic Inc., 1996

Hey! That's A Hedgehog!

England has a wide variety of animals. Perhaps one of the most unique ones is the *European hedgehog.* Measuring in at about ten inches long, this quill-covered critter sports short legs and ears, a short tail, and a long nose. It is often compared to a porcupine; however, a European hedgehog actually looks and feels more like a large pinecone. This is especially true when danger is near and it rolls itself up into a spiny ball! Hedgehogs are found in many places around England—including the bushes of a bustling city like London. And because they are easily tamed, some English folks have them for pets! Head to your school library to investigate these interesting creatures with your students.

Jolly-Good Games

Children around the world love to play games and English children are no exception. Find out how many of your students have played games that originated in England, like Ring Around The Rosy, London Bridge, and the hide-and-seek game of Fox And Hounds. Then introduce them to a popular children's party game from England called Ha! Ha! To play this game, seat students in a circle. Ask one player to start the game by saying, "Ha!" The player to his right says, "Ha! Ha!", and the player to his right says, "Ha! Ha! Ha!", and so on around the circle. What's the hardest part of the game? Keeping a straight face! A student who laughs or forgets how many "Ha's" to say is out. For a fast-paced classroom version of the game, simply restart the game when a blunder occurs, allowing all students to continue playing. A jolly-good time is sure to be had by all!

Time For Tea!

Looking for an entertaining way to culminate your study of England? Try hosting an English tea party for famous English folks! Ask each child to come to the tea party dressed as a famous person from England or a famous literary character created by an English author. To avoid duplications have each child sign a class guest list as soon as she determines what role she'll play. Inform students that during the tea party each guest will be asked to introduce herself and tell one or two facts about herself. With the help of parent volunteers, arrange to serve teatime refreshments that include tiny sandwiches, sponge cake, and a kid-pleasing beverage that can be served from a teapot. Now that's a party fit for royalty!

Mary Birch—Gr. 3, St. Theresa School, West Roxbury, MA

The Royal Mail

The British Postal Service, also known as the Royal Mail, was the first postal service in the world to issue postage stamps. As your study of England draws to a close, challenge each student to design a 9" x 12" postage stamp for the Royal Mail. Under your students' direction, write a list of the people, places, events, foods, animals, and so on that they have learned about. Then have each child choose a different item from the list to illustrate and label on a 9" x 12" sheet of drawing paper. For added appeal have each youngster trim the edges of his completed project with pinking shears. Then display the collection of postage stamps on a bulletin board titled "We Give England Our Stamp Of Approval!"

MOST POPULAR

SPORT

Pam Crane

Tea-Party Guest List

Queen Elizabeth II
Princess Diana
John Lennon
Winnie-The-Pooh
Peter Pan
Alice In Wonderland
James Bond
Elton John
Sherlock Holmes
Scrooge
Prince Harry
William Shakespeare

189

Name _____

Exploring England

Color and cut out the small pictures below.
Read each clue.
Put a drop of glue on each •.
Glue the matching picture in place.

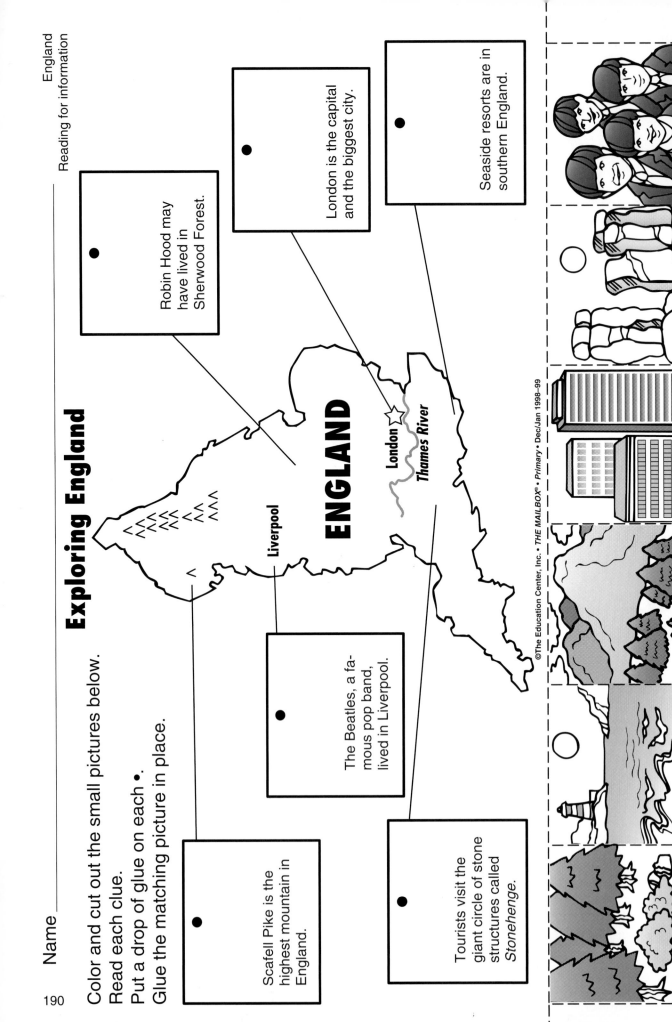

Robin Hood may have lived in Sherwood Forest.

London is the capital and the biggest city.

Seaside resorts are in southern England.

Scafell Pike is the highest mountain in England.

The Beatles, a famous pop band, lived in Liverpool.

Tourists visit the giant circle of stone structures called *Stonehenge*.

ENGLAND

Liverpool

London

Thames River

©The Education Center, Inc. • *THE MAILBOX®* • Primary • Dec/Jan 1998–99

Note To Teacher: Use with "Getting To Know England" on page 187.

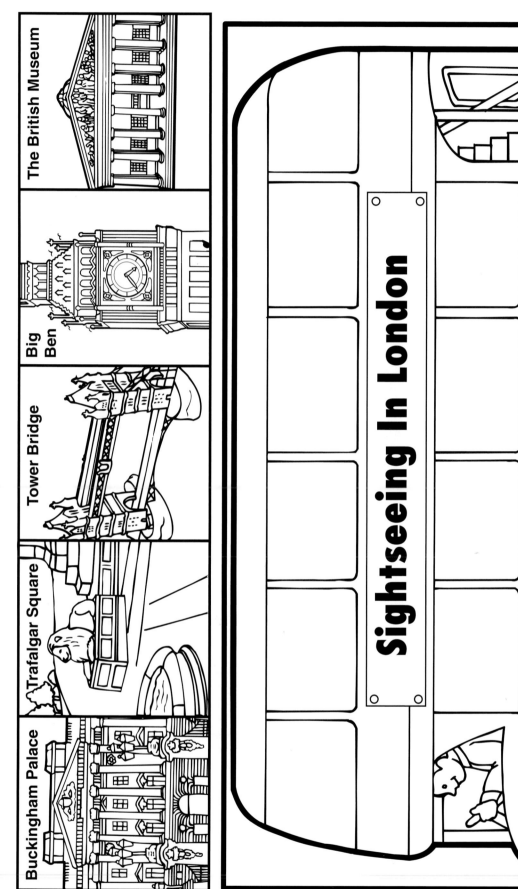

The British Museum

Big Ben

Tower Bridge

Trafalgar Square

Buckingham Palace

Sightseeing In London

Name

©1998 The Education Center, Inc.

Xin Chào, Vietnam!

Anytime is a perfect time to say "hello" to Vietnam! However, we're *hoping* you'll find a few days during February to make a quick visit. Why? Because Tet, the country's most important festival of the year, will be celebrated then. So why wait? Pack your bags with these first-class activities and literature connections. There's a captivating country and a joyful celebration awaiting you and your youngsters!

ideas contributed by
Stacie Stone Davis
books reviewed by
Deborah Zink Roffino

Learning About The Country

Vietnam lies in the southeastern corner of Asia. It is a country with magnificent mountains, lush rain forests, fertile farmlands, and beautiful beaches. Help students locate this *s*-shaped stretch of land on a world map or globe. Then share the following fascinating facts:

- Vietnam is only slightly larger than the state of New Mexico.
- It is home to more than 75 million people. (New Mexico has less than two million people!)
- The Vietnamese say their country is shaped like a bent bamboo pole carrying a rice basket at each end. Most people live in the "rice basket" areas.
- Much of the country is covered by mountains and hills called *highlands*.
- There is lots of water! Over 200 rivers flow from the highlands into the sea.
- Wild animals such as tigers and elephants roam through Vietnam's remote jungles.

Mouthwatering Maps

This mapping project makes learning about Vietnam simply delicious! Pair students and give each twosome a copy of the map on page 196 and a one-foot-wide length of waxed paper. Have each pair center its map beneath its waxed paper. Then, if desired, use tape to secure the project to the work surface. Also ask each child to wash and dry his hands. Next give each pair one-fourth cup of prepared sugar-cookie dough and a spoonful of sugar (in a muffin-tin liner). Working atop the waxed paper, the partners press their dough into the shape of Vietnam, dipping their fingers into the sugar when the dough gets sticky. Then help each pair transfer its shape onto a cookie sheet. While a parent volunteer bakes the cookies, have each child complete a copy of the mapping activity.

To decorate the projects, each pair spreads a layer of green-tinted icing over its cooled cookie to represent the lush forests and rice paddies of Vietnam; then it adds chocolate-chip mountains and blue decorating-gel rivers in the appropriate places. (Have students refer to their completed copies of page 196 for accuracy.) Then, if desired, photograph each pair with its project before inviting the students to munch on their maps.

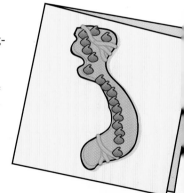

192

Going To School

Students will be eager to learn how schools in Vietnam are similar to and different from their school. Write "teacher," "students," "uniforms," "tests," "September," and "Saturday" on the chalkboard and invite students to make assumptions about Vietnamese schools based on these words. Write their ideas on the board. Next read aloud (and supplement, as desired) the information from "Schools In Vietnam" on this page, making sure students understand that schools in Vietnam vary just as they do in the United States. Then, under your students' guidance, erase any incorrect assumptions from the class list, circle assumptions that have not been confirmed, and add information that is missing. For a fun wrap-up, have each child trace a schoolhouse-shaped template onto drawing paper, label it like the one shown, and list what he knows about schools in each location. Encourage students to add information to their projects as they uncover additional facts.

News About Names

While your class is investigating Vietnam, ask students to adopt the Vietnamese custom of writing names. Explain that Vietnamese people write their family names first, followed by their middle names and first names—opposite of the standard practice in the United States. Be sure to join in on the fun yourself! It is also customary in Vietnam that titles such as Mr. and Mrs. be applied to the first name, not the last. Students are sure to enjoy adopting that custom as well!

Schools In Vietnam

- The school week is Monday through Saturday.
- On Saturday, students recite what they learned during the week.
- The school year is September through May.
- Students respect their teachers.
- Most school days begin with a test.
- Students are not graded. Instead they are ranked from first to last in their class.
- Each month parents are notified of how their children rank in their class.
- Students take turns cleaning their school.
- Games are seldom played during school hours.
- Many students must wear uniforms to school.

School Days

In Vietnam
- The day begins with a test!
- Students wear uniforms.
- It sounds like it is strict!
- There is no time for games.
- There is school on Saturday.

In United States
- Teacher is very nice.
- There are not so many tests.
- There is time for games.
- No school on Saturday!
- Only some students wear uniforms.

Speaking The Language

Even though more than 55 languages are spoken in Vietnam, most people speak some form of Vietnamese. To introduce this language-related lesson, have students describe how the sound of a person's voice can affect the meaning of a sentence like "Go to bed." Help students conclude that in the English language, voice tone conveys emotion. Then reveal that voice tone in Vietnamese conveys meaning. For a quick demonstration, write "ma" on the chalkboard and ask students to say the Vietnamese word using each of the following voice tones—each time telling the meaning of the word: high voice (mother), low voice (rice plant), rising voice (clever), flat voice (ghost). For a fun conclusion, have students consider the comical mistakes that could result if voice tone is incorrect or misheard! "Does your ghost (mother) drink tea?"

Encourage students to learn a bit of Vietnamese as they study Vietnam. The words and pronunciations given in the table below are from North Vietnam.

Vietnamese	Pronunciation	Meaning
Vang	(vahng)	yes
Không	(khom)	no
Xin chào	(sin chow)	hello
Tạm biệt	(tom BEE-it)	good-bye
Tên là gì?	(ten la zi)	What is your name?
Tên tôi là	(ten toy la)	My name is _____.

Pronunciation Key: Marks placed over or under words indicate tones: ´ = rising tone; ` = falling tone; ̣ = low tone that falls and ends suddenly. Words with no markings are spoken in an even tone using a normal voice.

193

A Taste Of Vietnam

Vietnamese food is known around the world for its many spices and flavors, but as in most countries, the food changes from region to region. In all areas, rice and fresh fruits and vegetables are common. If you're interested in preparing an authentic dish from Vietnam, *Cooking The Vietnamese Way* (Lerner Publications Company, 1985) is the perfect resource. In addition to recipes, you'll find interesting information about the country and its cuisine. If this approach is a bit ambitious, see "A Family Affair" on this page for a tasty alternative.

A Family Affair

Eating in Vietnam is a family affair! The members of a family or group gather around a table where individual bowls of cooked rice are filled. Then each person uses chopsticks to select pieces of vegetables, fish, and meat from bowls on the table to put on his rice. When it's time to eat, each person raises his bowl to his mouth and digs in with his chopsticks!

For a tasty experience, divide students into small groups and seat each group around a table. Give each child a small serving of cooked rice. On each table, place bowls of coconut, roasted peanut pieces, sesame seeds, banana slices, diced cucumbers, diced carrots, and other desired ingredients found in Vietnamese recipes. Invite each child to top his rice with the ingredients of his choice. Students may use spoons to eat—or if you're feeling brave, chopsticks!

Stories That Teach

Vietnamese folktales have been passed down from generation to generation. Many of these stories teach important lessons. Two tales your students will enjoy hearing are *The Crystal Heart: A Vietnamese Legend* retold by Aaron Shepard (Atheneum Books For Young Readers, 1998) and *Tam's Slipper: A Story From Vietnam* retold by Janet Palazzo-Craig (Troll Communications L.L.C., 1996). Follow up each story by having students write one- or two-sentence descriptions of the lesson the story taught them. Then group students and have the members of each small group discuss what they wrote.

Facts And Photos

Enrich your study of Vietnam with the information and photographs featured in these recently published nonfiction children's books.

Vietnam: Still Struggling, Still Spirited
Written by Olivia Skelton
Benchmark Books, 1998

Five chapters, neatly divided into subsections for easier understanding, offer an insightful overview of Vietnam. Plenty of pictures, large and small, illustrate the text. A glossary, an index, and a list of facts about the country add value to this resource for upper-level readers.

Children Of Vietnam
Written by Marybeth Lorbiecki
Carolrhoda Books, Inc.; 1997

An appealing blend of panoramic and close-up photographs take readers on a tour of Vietnam. Carefully crafted words that accompany the collage of modern photographs clearly communicate what it's like to grow up in Vietnam.

Postcards From Vietnam
Written by Denise Allard
Stech-Vaughn Company, 1997

Captivating postcard-like photos deliver an inside look at Vietnam and its people. The easy-to-read greetings that accompany the photos are written from the perspectives of youngsters visiting Vietnam. A glossary and an index make this a first-class resource for youngsters.

Vietnam: The Lands, Peoples, And Cultures Series
Created by Bobbie Kalman
Crabtree Publishing Company, 1996

This trio of books offers page after page of full-color photographs and informative, well-organized text for a comprehensive study of Vietnam. From lush rain forests to spectacular beaches, thatched-roof homes to elaborate temples, and cone-shaped hats to business suits, readers visit the past, experience the present, and contemplate the future of a country in the midst of change.

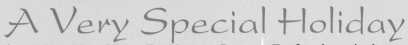

A Very Special Holiday

The Vietnamese New Year, *Tet Nguyen Dan,* or *Tet* for short, is the most important festival in Vietnam. The celebration—which ushers in a new year and the start of spring—begins on the first new moon between January 19 and February 20. The festival is officially celebrated for three days, but the festivities often last up to a week! Use the activities on this page and the reproducible on page 197 to introduce your youngsters to Tet.

Chúc Mùng Năm Mói!
(CHOOK MOUNG num MOOEE)

That's "Happy New Year!" in Vietnamese! To learn more about Tet, read aloud excerpts from *Tet: Vietnamese New Year* by Dianne M. MacMillan (Enslow Publishers, Inc.; 1994). This informative 48-page volume details the history of the holiday, and highlights symbols, preparations, and celebrations associated with it. Numerous photographs, a glossary, and an index add more value to an already great book.

The First Visitor

One standing tradition of Tet is the belief that a family's first visitor of the New Year affects its good fortune for the entire year. A well-respected and successful person is a welcomed first visitor. A person who has recently experienced tragedy is not. For this reason, families invite special guests to their homes on this day. Share this information with your youngsters. For a fun follow-up, ask each child to illustrate on story paper the person he would invite to visit his family. Then have the student write who the person is and why he thinks the person will bring good fortune to his family. Be sure to set aside time for students to share their work!

The Envelope, Please

On the first day of Tet, children who were well-behaved during the past year receive monetary gifts. These gifts are often wrapped in red rice paper or enclosed in red envelopes. Surprise your students with this festive money-counting review. For each child, fold and staple a 4" x 9" strip of red paper into a simple envelope like the one shown. Tuck an assortment of coin cutouts inside each envelope. Then pair the students and give each child an envelope. Have each child remove his coins and write the sum on the outside of his envelope. Next have each student check his partner's work. To extend the activity, ask each pair to write a number sentence on the chalkboard that compares its sums (like "32¢ > 16¢"). Then give each child a sweet treat—red of course. A Twizzlers® strawberry or cherry snack-size bar would be perfect!

Good-Luck Dragons

There is a Vietnamese legend which states that dragons roam the earth each year during Tet. And if a person sees a dragon during Tet, he or she will have good luck all year long. No wonder a dragon dance is part of the Tet celebration! For part of your Tet celebration, have students make good-luck dragon booklets. Duplicate a class supply of page 197 on yellow construction paper. Have each child write his name on the provided line, then write a good-luck wish for his family, his community, and himself on the appropriate pages. Next have each child color the details of his dragon. Suggest that students use plenty of red, explaining that red symbolizes good fortune and happiness. To assemble his dragon booklet, a child cuts out the shapes along the bold lines; then he folds along the thin lines (between the pages and adjacent to the tabs). Next he unfolds the project and glues it together as indicated. Finally he refolds his project along the existing crease lines to create an accordion-folded booklet. Happy New Year!

Investigating Vietnam

Read and follow each direction.
Use the map key.
When you finish, write an X in the box.

Map Key

∧ = mountains

◠ = river

★ = capital

+ = highest mountain peak

●● = coastline begins

■■ = coastline ends

△ = delta

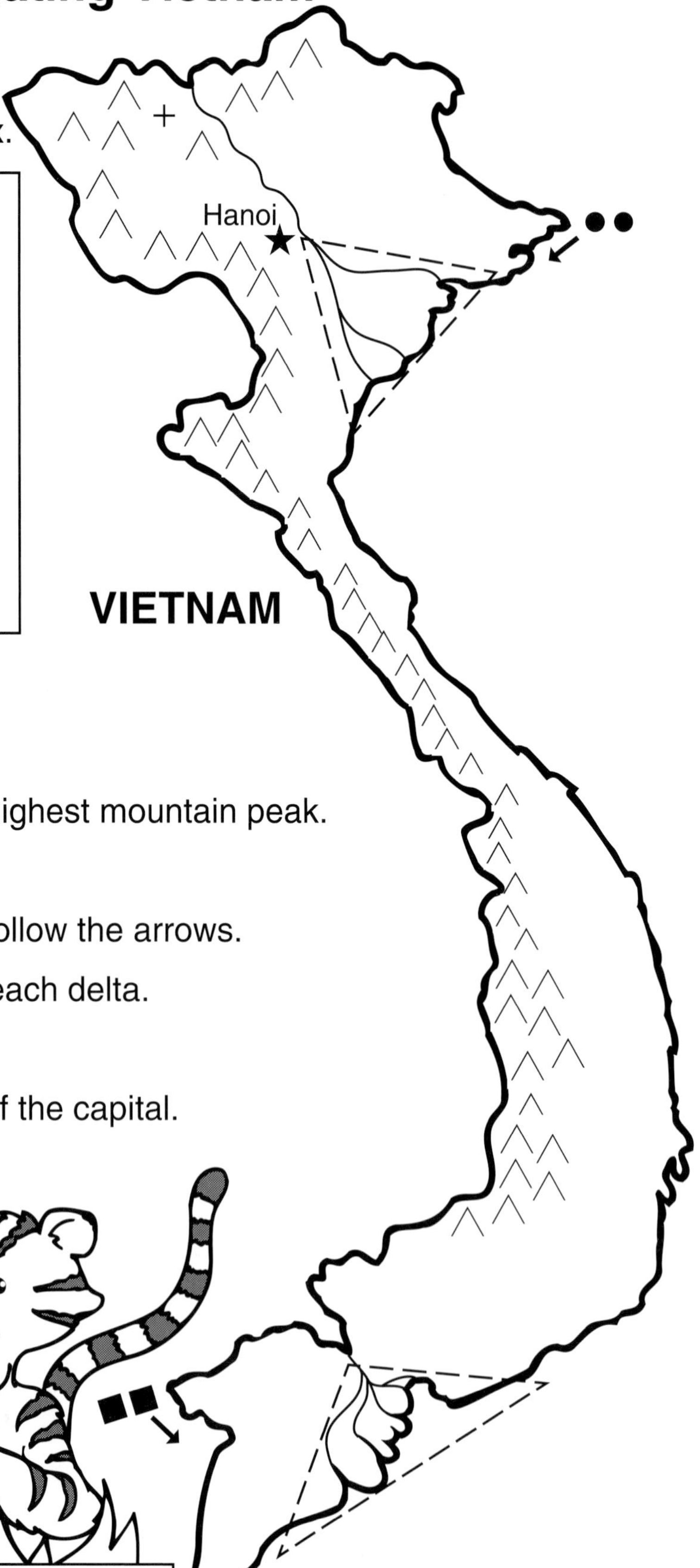

VIETNAM

Directions

☐ Color the mountains brown.

☐ Draw an orange box around the highest mountain peak.

☐ Use blue to trace the rivers.

☐ Use blue to trace the coastline. Follow the arrows.

☐ Connect the dotted lines around each delta.

☐ Color each delta yellow.

☐ Draw a red line under the name of the capital.

Hanoi

What is a delta?

A delta is an area of land at the mouth of a river that is shaped like a triangle.

Bonus Box: Vietnam's flag has a large gold star in the center of a red background. Draw and color the flag on the back of this paper.

©The Education Center, Inc. • THE MAILBOX® • Primary • Feb/Mar 1999

My good-luck wish for
myself is_____
_____
_____
_____
_____

Happy
Tet!

4

Glue page 3 here.

3

My good-luck wish for my
community is_____
_____
_____

2

My good-luck wish for my
family is_____
_____
_____

Glue page 1 here.

Good-Luck Dragon
_____'s

Seeing a dragon during Tet
brings good luck.

1

HATS OFF TO YOUR STATE!

Dorothy was right—there's no place like home! Tip your hat to the state that you and your students call home with these star-spangled ideas.

Stately Gameboards

You'll double the fun and learning when you have student pairs create (and later play) board games that feature their state. Have each twosome trace a large state-shaped template near the center of a sheet of white poster board. Then instruct each pair to create a simple map that shows some of the state's rivers, mountains, and lakes; the name and location of the state capital; and a few other familiar landmarks. Give each pair 15 self-adhesive dots to make a game trail. Also invite each pair to embellish its project with additional state-related illustrations as shown. To make the game cards, each pair labels 20 or more blank cards with multiple-choice questions about the state, programming the back of each card for self-checking. Next have each pair label five more cards with map-related phrases like "Go to the state capital" or "Cross a river." Have each pair shuffle its game cards and store them in a resealable bag. Establish a set of playing rules that apply to all state gameboards. Then set aside time on each of several days for the student pairs to play their games and the games that their classmates have made.

Beth Laible, Atkinson Elementary School, Atkinson, NE

Taking A Closer Look

This center activity prompts students to take a closer look at home sweet home! Display a large state map at a center along with student copies of page 200. Each student uses the map to complete the activity. Collect the students' completed work. When each child has finished the activity, return the students' papers to the center. Then ask each student to revisit the center with a partner. Have each child use the map to verify his partner's answers. Since most questions have more than one correct answer, the students will extend their learning. Plus it won't be necessary for you to check the youngsters' work!

Valerie Birch, Ambler, PA

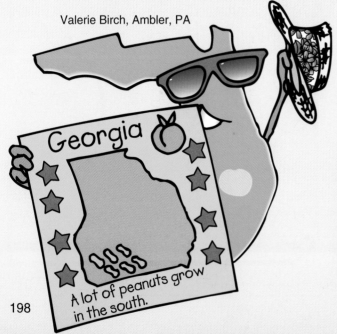

A Really Great State

Reinforce the uniqueness of your state with this fact-based project! Post an ongoing list of the state-related facts your students have learned. When the list includes at least one fact per child, have each youngster trace a state-shaped template near the center of a half-sheet of tagboard. Ask each student to write the state name above his outline. Next have each child choose a different fact from the posted list and copy it beneath his outline. Instruct each student to illustrate his state shape so that the fact he described is reinforced. He may decorate the rest of the project to his liking. (If desired, have each student illustrate his assignment at home.) Designate a day for students to share their work with the class. Then bind the projects into a stately big book titled "[state name] Is A Really Great State!"

Karen Cook, McDonough Primary School, McDonough, GA

198

Postcards Aplenty

Get the picture on different sites around your state with this postcard project! Ask each child to bring to school an unused postcard that pictures a local landmark. (Be sure to have a few extras on hand for those who are unable to donate cards.) Then help each child mail his postcard to a different school within your state, requesting that a postcard from that area be mailed to him. Be sure each child includes your school's mailing address. Display the postcards your youngsters receive on a bulletin board along with a large cutout of your state. Use yarn lengths to show the approximate locations of the pictured sites.

Or have each student choose a different location around the state that he's visited and draw and color a picture of the site on a blank card. Display these student-made postcards in the manner described.

Know Your State

With this Jeopardy®-style game, reviewing your state has never been easier—or more fun! Label five construction-paper squares for each of the following dollar amounts: $5, $10, $15, $20, $25. Laminate the squares for durability and tape them to the chalkboard as shown. Write a different state-related category above each column. Divide students into three or more teams and name a spokesperson for each group. To play, each team in turn picks a category and a dollar amount. Ask the team a question related to its category, making sure that the questions become more difficult as the dollar amounts increase. After the team agrees on an answer, the spokesperson calls it out. If the answer is correct, remove the corresponding square from the chalkboard and pass it to the team. If the answer is incorrect, present the question to the other teams. The first team to supply the correct answer earns the paper square. At the end of the game, each team totals the dollar amounts on the squares it earned. The highest-scoring team wins the game. Collect the laminated squares and reuse them for future reviews!

Sue Majors—Gr. 2, Palmer Lake Elementary, Monument, CO

Internet Site

Stately Knowledge at www.ipl.org/youth/stateknow provides a wealth of facts about each state in the Union. A quick click on a state name reveals a graphic showing the state's location within the United States, followed by a list of facts about the state. A picture of the state flag is included too. The site also features stately knowledge charts and offers other state-related resources to investigate. Be sure to incorporate this cyberstop into your state study!

Riding Round The State

If your students are fans of The Magic School Bus® book series, then climb aboard for a trip around your state! To begin, review the unique format of the books in this series, pointing out that information is presented in a variety of ways including paragraphs, student-written reports, speech bubbles, and illustrations. Then assist your students in planning an imaginary adventure around their state aboard a magic bus driven by you. To begin, ask students to name different locations around the state that they would like to feature in the book. List their ideas on the chalkboard. Also plan a beginning and an ending to the adventure. Then divide the class into small groups. Have each group research a different tour stop and design a two-page spread about it. Recruit student volunteers to write and illustrate the beginning and ending of the story, and fashion a cover. Assemble and share the completed project with the class. Then arrange for each group to present the publication to another class in your school.

Challenge students who have caught the traveling bug to create additional magic bus books that chronicle trips around other states or the world's seven continents!

Nicole Weber—Grs. 2 & 3, Waterloo Elementary School, Waterloo, WI

Hats Off To A Great State!

How much do you know about your state?
Look for each item below on a map of your state.
Write the answer in the box.

Name of a river	Name of a lake	Name of a mountain
City or town with a one-syllable name	City or town with a two-syllable name	City or town with a three-syllable name
Name of a state park	Name of a county	Name of the capital
City or town with two words in its name	Even-numbered road or highway	Odd-numbered road or highway

Bonus Box: On the back of this paper write one more thing you learned about your state by looking at the map.

©The Education Center, Inc. • THE MAILBOX® • Primary • June/July 1999

Note To Teacher: Use with "Taking A Closer Look" on page 198. To adjust the activity to best suit your needs, photocopy the page.
Then mask out unwanted text and reprogram the page as desired.

SEASONAL UNITS

The Back-To-School Express
A Trainload Of First-Day Activities

Here's just what you need to start off the school year right on track—a trainload of first-day ideas from our subscribers! With this precious cargo, it's full steam ahead for a fabulous school year. All aboard!

Teacher Tales

Sharing information about yourself is a great way to help students feel at home in their new surroundings. Gather several photos that span your life. Mount each snapshot on an 8 1/2" x 11" sheet of paper, and write a concise and easy-to-read caption on the page. Slide each completed page into a plastic protector. Arrange the pages in chronological order before placing them in a three-ring binder. Add a title and desired decorations to the cover of the binder; then use the resulting autobiography to introduce yourself on the first day of school. Your students' interest will be piqued and there's a good chance they'll be eager to share something about themselves, too!

This is my cat, K.C. He is soft and cuddly.

Laura Mihalenko—Gr. 2
Truman Elementary School
Parlin, NJ

Colorful Introductions

Brighten up first-day introductions with this colorful activity. Choose a different color of crayon for each child in your class and place one crayon of this color in each of two containers. Gather the class in a large circle and distribute the crayons in one container. To begin the introductions, remove a crayon from the second container. Announce the color of the crayon and ask the student who is holding the same crayon color to tell the class her name and something about herself. Continue in this manner until each child has introduced herself. In no time at all, your students will have a colorful spectrum of new friends!

Sandy Wiele—Gr. 2
Peoria Christian School
Peoria, IL

100 Days

Set the stage for a 100th school-day celebration with a journal-writing activity that really counts! To make a journal for each student, bind 50 pages of story paper between construction-paper covers. On the first day of school, have each student personalize the covers of his journal and glue a copy of a hundreds chart inside the front cover. Near the end of the day, have each student open his journal to the first blank page. Instruct him to write the day's date in the top left corner of the page and the number of days school has been in session (1) in the top right corner. Then, on the same page, have each student write and illustrate a story about his school day. Finally have the student color the corresponding day (1) on the hundreds chart.

Each school day have the students make an entry in their 100-day journals. Then, as part of your 100th-day celebration, invite students to read aloud their favorite journal entries. You can count on this idea to reinforce number concepts as well as reading and writing skills!

Stefanie Wilde—Gr. 1
Plymouth Elementary School
Plymouth Meeting, PA

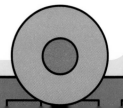

Mary Lester

Hear Ye! Hear Ye!

Usher in a banner year with these noble student introductions! Enlarge the coat-of-arms pattern on page 208 to a desired size; then duplicate student copies on white construction paper. Have each student write his name on the provided line, then complete each section of the pattern by providing the requested information and a related illustration. Next have each child cut out his pattern, mount it on colorful construction paper, and trim the colored paper to create an eye-catching border. Display each student's coat of arms on a bulletin board titled "Hear Ye! Hear Ye! Read All About Our Class!"

Kelly A. Lu—Gr. 2
Berlyn School
Ontario, CA

First-Day Jitters

Your students' first-day jitters will quickly disappear with this hands-on activity! Use the recipe shown to make a class supply of play dough; then divide the dough into equal-size student portions. To prepare each portion, poke a deep hole in the dough, squeeze two to four drops of food coloring inside, and carefully reshape the dough—sealing the food coloring inside. Distribute the dough on the first day of school and ask each student to knead his portion. As the students are working, ask them if they have ever seen play dough change color. Then tell them that you think when this happens it means that a great school year lies ahead. Your classroom will echo with cries of delight when students see their play-dough portions change color right before their eyes!

To extend the activity, ask each child to create a shape from his play dough that reveals one of his interests or hobbies. Invite students to take turns telling their classmates about the shapes they made; then have each student store his portion of dough inside a resealable plastic bag. The dough can then be taken home or stored at school for future uses.

Melinda Phillips—Gr. 2
Donehoo Advanced Technology School
Glencoe, AL

First-Class Summer Memories

Memories of summer arrive special delivery with this postcard project! To prepare for the first-day project, illustrate one side of a large, white index card (unlined) to show a fond summer memory. Program the opposite side of the card to resemble a real postcard by writing a note to the class about your memory, addressing the card, drawing a stamp in the top right corner, and adding a desired postmark. On the first day of school, share the postcard you created; then ask each student to create a postcard about her favorite summer memory. For best results draw a divider line and address lines on one side of a large, blank index card for each student. Also write on the chalkboard the address that you'd like each student to copy on her card.

To display the cards, hole-punch the center top of each card. Thread a length of yarn through the hole and tie the yarn ends. Then suspend the card from a pushpin inserted into a bulletin board titled "First-Class Summer Memories!"

Patti Hirsh—Gr. 3
Casis Elementary School
Austin, TX

Play-Dough Recipe
(Makes about 24 student portions.)

Ingredients:
6 cups flour
3 cups salt
6 Tbsp. cooking oil
6 cups water
4 Tbsp. cream of tartar

Directions:
Mix the dry ingredients in a large cooking pan. Add the oil and water. Cook and stir the mixture over medium heat until it pulls away from the sides of the pan. Knead the dough; then store it in an airtight container.

W is for warthog relatives who come to visit.

I can read!

The ABCs Of Summer

Make a splash with this big-book project! Ask students to brainstorm words that bring to mind their summertime activities. Write their ideas on the chalkboard, grouping together words that have the same beginning letters. Have each child choose a different alphabet letter and complete the following sentence near the top of a 12" x 18" sheet of drawing paper: [Alphabet letter] is for [a corresponding word or phrase from the class list]. Then have each student illustrate his page using crayons or markers.

To assemble the big book, enlist your youngsters' help in alphabetizing the pages. Then hole-punch the students' work and two slightly larger pieces of poster board. Use metal rings to bind the pages between the poster-board covers. Title the class big book "The ABCs Of Summer" and place it in your classroom library for further reading enjoyment. Invite interested students to create additional pages for the book (perhaps for any alphabet letters that were not represented) during free time.

Whitney Sherman—Gr. 1
Seven Pines Elementary School
Sandston, VA

Already Reading!

What could be more satisfying to a non-reader than to become a reader on the first day of school? To prepare for this activity, cut out a variety of familiar names, words, and phrases from discarded newspapers, magazines, and product wrappers. Display the cutouts for your students' perusal. Then ask each child to choose three cutouts that she recognizes and glue them onto a sheet of construction paper labeled "I Can Read These Words!" Invite each child to read aloud her word collection; then use a safety pin to attach a colorful copy of the reader's ribbon on page 208 to her clothing. Each young reader will surely burst with pride when she shares her first-day achievement with her family members!

Julie Bulver—Gr. 1
Rice Elementary
Des Moines, IA

Class,
I am sorry that I missed you in the office. I am on my way to the library. Maybe I will see you there!
Love,
Clifford®

Where, Oh Where Has That Big Dog Gone?

Searching for a big red pooch is a perfect way to acquaint students with the school and staff members. Create a series of messages from Clifford® The Big Red Dog®. Each message should be written from a different school location. Explain that Clifford® is searching for the wonderful students in your class, and end with a clue about the school location he will visit next. Write the first message as if the pooch had come by the classroom while you and your students were out. The next-to-last message should state that the canine is headed back to your classroom, and the final message should express regret for once again missing the youngsters. Copy each message on a paper bone (see the pattern on page 19). Hide the first clue in the classroom; then deliver the remaining bone cutouts to the appropriate school locations. Ask a neighboring colleague to deliver the final message to your classroom—along with a plate of bone-shaped sugar cookies, and a Clifford® puppet or stuffed animal—after the search has begun.

To begin the escapade, discover the first clue from Clifford® shortly after you and your students return to the classroom after lunch, recess, or another outing. As you and your youngsters travel through the school, introduce the staff members you see along the way. No doubt students will have a "paws-itively" grand time tracking down Clifford®!

Tina Bassett—Gr. 1
J. R. Watson Elementary School
Auburn, IN

Classroom Treasure Hunt

Yo ho ho! Welcome your new crew on board with a treasure hunt! Draw a simple classroom map; then on the map "X" and label a variety of classroom locations. Duplicate the map on manila paper. To achieve a look of authenticity, either carefully tear the edges of each map or use a lighter to sear them. Then roll each map into a tube, and tie a length of string or yarn around it. Next decorate a large box to resemble a treasure chest and deposit the rolled maps inside. Also place a supply of adhesive stars at each classroom location marked on the map.

A student removes a map from the treasure chest and uses it to find the classroom locations marked. At each classroom location, he affixes a star to the corresponding point on his map. Your youngsters are certain to have a swashbuckling time exploring the classroom! And they'll each have a star-studded classroom map to share with family members.

Mary Grace Ramos—Gr. 2
Pinewood Acres School
Miami, FL

Name-O

Classroom introductions are a snap with this get-acquainted game. Give each child a 5 x 5 grid, a list of student names, and 25 game markers—beans, buttons, paper squares, etc. If you have fewer than 25 students, add your name and the names of other staff members to the list until it equals or exceeds 25. Then have each student create a playing card by copying a different name from the list in each blank space on his grid.

To play, randomly call out the names from your list. If the name called is on a student's playing card, he covers the space with a game marker. After students have marked their boards, ask the youngster whose name was called to stand and tell his classmates something about himself. (You will need to provide information about any staff member whose name is called.) The first student to cover five squares in a vertical, horizontal, or diagonal row declares, "Name-O" and reads each name in his completed row. For an added challenge, ask the game winner to repeat one thing he learned about each person he names. Continue playing the game until you have called each name on the list one or more times. No doubt your youngsters will think this name game is a real winner!

Pamela Reifsneider—Associate Teacher
Newtown Friends School
Newtown, PA

History In The Making

Students will be thrilled to complete this time-capsule project! To make her time capsule, a student personalizes and decorates a medium-size brown paper bag. Then she puts the following items in the bag: a length of string that equals her height, a self-portrait, a short poem that she copied in her best handwriting, and an interest inventory that she completed about herself. Staple each bag closed; then ask each child to deposit her resulting time capsule in a large box that you have provided for this purpose. Then, with great fanfare, securely seal the box. Later store the box out of sight. At the end of the year, reintroduce the box, open it, and return the time capsules to the students. Your youngsters will enjoy traveling back in time and they'll be proud of the progress that they've made during the school year.

Debbie Fly
Birmingham, AL

Something Special

This first-day strategy eases the transition between home and school. Before the start of school, send a letter to your students' parents. In the letter request that on the first day of school each child bring a special item—small in size—from home. Explain that each child will be asked to tell his classmates something about the item he brings.

Soon after the students arrive, gather them on the floor in a large circle. In turn have each child show his classmates the item he brought from home and tell them about it. A student without a special item may talk about his favorite interests or pastimes. At the conclusion of the activity, ask students to display the items they brought from home in a special classroom location for the remainder of the day. The comfort and anticipation associated with the special items may actually reduce first-day anxieties!

Stefanie Wilde—Gr. 1
Plymouth Elementary School
Plymouth Meeting, PA

Check out this specially engineered collection of school-related literature! It's just the ticket for keeping your first-class passengers on track with reading!

Miss Nelson Is Missing!

Written by Harry Allard & Illustrated by James Marshall
Houghton Mifflin Company, 1985

Miss Nelson's unruly students are eager to have a substitute teacher so that they can goof off all day long and do as little schoolwork as possible. Or so they think! Even in her own "absence," Miss Nelson skillfully teaches her students the value of respect and hard work.

This thought-provoking story about a teacher's creative approach to keeping her unruly class in line may teach your youngsters a thing or two! Prior to reading the story aloud, ask students to brainstorm qualities of a great teacher. List their ideas on the chalkboard under the heading "Great Teacher." At the conclusion of the story, ask students to recall the qualities that Miss Nelson believes great students should have. List these ideas on the chalkboard under the heading "Great Students." Then, under your students' direction, write the best of both these lists in a third list titled "World's Best Class." Guide students to understand how an entire class (including the teacher) can work together to exemplify the qualities that are listed. Reviewing classroom expectations and setting goals in this manner will surely make the grade!

Debbie Erickson—Grs. 2–3 Multi-age
Waterloo Elementary School
Waterloo, WI

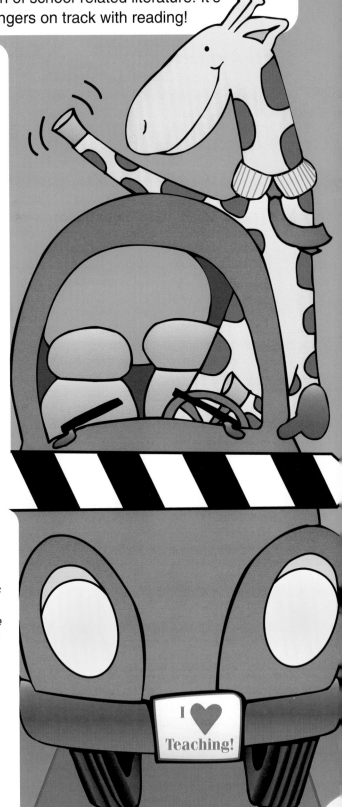

I Don't Want To Go Back To School

Written & Illustrated by Marisabina Russo
Greenwillow Books, 1994

It's a child's worst back-to-school nightmare—a mean teacher, a class full of strangers, a wrong answer, a missed bus stop. Young Ben, about to begin the second grade, has his personal fears fed by his thorn-in-the-side big sister. But in spite of all of Ben's worrying, he has a perfectly wonderful first day at school!

Because the happy outcome of this delightful story will help put your youngsters at ease, make plans to read it early in the day. At the conclusion of the story, encourage students to reveal their worries about the first day of school. List their ideas on the chalkboard, and provide comfort and reassurance as needed. Then near the end of the day, write a second student-generated list on the chalkboard that features first-day highlights. Next have each child visually divide a sheet of drawing paper in half. On the left half of his paper, ask the student to copy, complete, and illustrate this following sentence: "Before school started I was worried _____." On the right half of his paper, have the student copy, complete, and illustrate this sentence: "Now that school has started, _____." Have students take their papers home and use them to tell family members about their first day at school.

Lilly's Purple Plastic Purse

Written & Illustrated by Kevin Henkes
Greenwillow Books, 1996

Lilly absolutely loves school—that is, until her teacher, Mr. Slinger, confiscates her brand-new purple plastic purse! Lilly is so upset at Mr. Slinger that she overreacts in a manner that she later regrets. Lilly hopes that a heartfelt apology and some cheesy snacks will convince her favorite teacher to forgive her.

Mr. Slinger couldn't resist Lilly's father's cheesy snacks. And there's a good chance your youngsters won't be able to resist Lip-Smackin' Cheese Cookies. Prepare the provided recipe, enlisting your students' help if desired. Then, as students enjoy the cheesy snack, engage them in a discussion about times they have regretted their actions. Help students understand that it is wise to think through feelings before acting upon them. However, if a person finds himself in a situation similar to Lilly's, Lilly has set a fine example of how to make amends.

• • • • • Lip-Smackin' Cheese Cookies • • • • • •
(Makes about 30 cookies.)

Ingredients:
3/4 cup softened margarine or butter
1/2 tsp. salt
3 cups shredded Swiss cheese
1 1/2 cups flour
1 egg, slightly beaten

Directions:
In a large bowl, stir together the butter, the salt, 2 1/2 cups of the shredded cheese, and the flour until well blended. Shape the dough into one-inch balls. Place the balls about two inches apart on an ungreased baking sheet. Flatten each ball into a circle that is about 1/4-inch thick. Lightly brush the tops of the cookies with the beaten egg; then sprinkle the remaining cheese on top. Bake at 425° for 10 to 12 minutes or until lightly browned.

Miss Malarkey Doesn't Live In Room 10

Written by Judy Finchler & Illustrated by Kevin O'Malley
Walker Publishing Company, Inc.; 1995

The first-grade youngster who narrates this comical story is convinced that his teacher, Miss Malarkey, lives at school. He imagines her eating dinner in the cafeteria, working out in the gym, and sleeping in the teachers' room. But when Miss Malarkey moves into the youngster's apartment building, he must readjust his thinking!

Miss Malarkey may not spend her nights in Room 10, but her first graders know they can find her there during the school day! This project helps youngsters learn (or review) the names and daytime homes of other staff members. Use the patterns on page 209 to duplicate a colorful construction-paper house and a white construction-paper picket fence for each staff member. Glue a staff photo to the top of each house and complete the information provided about the person pictured. Distribute the projects to your students and ask them to complete the following tasks: draw and color a row of flowers near the bottom of the house, cut out the fence and glue it along the bottom of the house, and cut out the house. Then lead the class on a tour of the school, stopping to tape each project outside the door of the appropriate daytime home. Be sure to share some interesting facts about each staff member and, if possible, introduce the staff member to your class.

To create a cozy display in the hallway outside your classroom, have each student complete a house project. If student pictures are not yet available, have each child illustrate himself on a 2 1/4-inch square of white construction paper, then glue this picture to his house pattern. Display the students' projects with the title "Our Happy Home." Now that's a home away from home!

During the school day, Mrs. Brockman lives in the office

More First-Day Favorites

Here are several more school-related titles for you to pick and "choo-choo-choose" from!

Never Spit On Your Shoes
Written & Illustrated by Denys Cazet
Orchard Books, 1993

Never Ride Your Elephant To School
Written by Doug Johnson
Illustrated by Abby Carter
Scholastic Inc., 1996

The Principal's New Clothes
Written by Stephanie Calmenson
Illustrated by Denise Brunkus
Scholastic Inc., 1989

Sparky And Eddie
Written by Tony Johnston
Illustrated by Susannah Ryan
Scholastic Inc., 1977

Teach Us, Amelia Bedelia
Written by Peggy Parish
Illustrated by Lynn Sweat
Scholastic Inc., 1977

The Teacher From The Black Lagoon
Written by Mike Thaler
Illustrated by Jared Lee
Scholastic Inc., 1989

Patterns

Use the coat-of-arms pattern with "Hear Ye! Hear Ye!" on page 203.

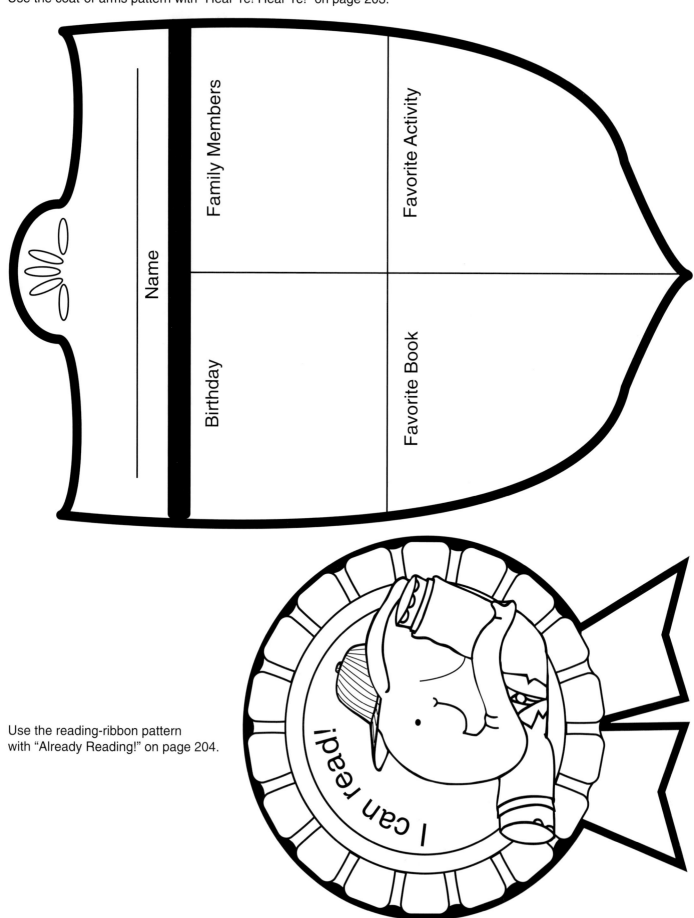

Use the reading-ribbon pattern
with "Already Reading!" on page 204.

Patterns

Use with *Miss Malarkey Doesn't Live In Room 10*
on page 207.

During the school day, _____

lives in _____.

©The Education Center, Inc. • THE MAILBOX® • Primary • Aug/Sept 1998

It's A New World,

What better way to teach students about Christopher Columbus than to transport them back in time to 1492? And this fact-filled class play will do just that! On the following pages you'll find background information, suggestions for easy-to-make props and invitations, and an instructional raplike script with plenty of kid appeal—just what you need to create a showstopping social-studies production.

idea contributed by Michele Morin

Background Information

Early Years

Christopher Columbus was born in Italy. Being the oldest of five children, it was expected that he would grow up to be a wool weaver like his father. But Christopher dreamed of sailing to faraway places. Christopher's first documented voyage was in the mid-1470s aboard a trading ship. By 1476 he had settled in Portugal with his brother who drew and sold maps for a living. According to legend, Columbus's move to Portugal was propelled by a pirate attack at sea. He supposedly swam ashore in Portugal and decided to stay!

The Plan

In the early 1480s, the Portuguese were anxious to discover a quick route to the Indies (now India, China, Japan, and the East Indies) where gold, silk, gems, and spices had been discovered. Columbus thought that he knew such a route. He presented his plan to the king of Portugal, but the plan was rejected because it was believed the length of the journey had been underestimated. About three years later Columbus presented his plan to King Ferdinand and Queen Isabella of Spain, who were at that time unable to finance such an expedition. Over the next several years Columbus's plan was considered and rejected in Spain, England, and France. Then, in 1492, after almost ten years of waiting, Columbus's plan suddenly received royal approval in Spain.

A Famous Voyage

On August 3, 1492, Columbus set sail for the Indies with about 90 crew members and three ships—the *Niña, Pinta,* and *Santa María* (which he captained). Columbus's few navigational tools included a quadrant for determining the ship's position, a compass for plotting the ship's course, and a half-hour glass for measuring time. After about a month at sea, the crew grew anxious and began doubting Columbus's plan. Then, on October 12—more than ten weeks since they set sail—the ships landed on a Caribbean island that Columbus named *San Salvador*. Columbus named the islanders *Indians* because he thought he'd reached the Indies. Columbus and his crew traded bells and beads for the islanders' parrots and cotton.

Homecoming

After a difficult voyage home, Columbus was greeted in Spain with a hero's welcome. He was named the Admiral of the Ocean Sea. It was not until years later that people realized Columbus did not reach the Indies.

Seaworthy Literature

A Picture Book Of Christopher Columbus
Written by David A. Adler
Illustrated by
John and Alexandra Wallner
Holiday House, Inc.; 1992

Christopher Columbus
Written by Stephen Krensky
Illustrated by Norman Green
Random House Books
For Young Readers, 1991

In 1492
Written by Jean Marzollo
Illustrated by Steve Björkman
Scholastic Inc., 1994

Columbus!

Play Preparations

Before introducing the play, tell students about Christopher Columbus and his most famous voyage. The information and literature suggestions on page 210 will be helpful. Next distribute student copies of pages 212 and 213. Assign each child a part in the play and enlist your youngsters' help with the props and invitations described below. To further enhance your production, have each youngster memorize a different fact about Christopher Columbus. Then, at the conclusion of the play, ask each child to step forward and share his fact with the audience. Conclude the festivities by serving your choice of seaworthy refreshments!

Characters

Christopher Columbus *a strong reader and an understudy (if desired)*
Kings and queens *four or more*
Ship's crew *unlimited number*
Islanders *unlimited number*
Cue-card holder *one—perhaps a parent or an uppergrade volunteer*

Props

Ask each student to be responsible for the prop(s) needed for his role.

Columbus
- **Hat** Duplicate the hat pattern on page 214 onto brown construction paper. Cut out the shape. Tape or staple a brown paper hatband to the cutout; then tape a white feather near the front of the hat. (See the illustration on page 212.)
- **Scroll** *(optional)* Mount the script on gray paper. Roll the paper, keeping the script inside, and tie it with ribbon. Columbus unrolls the scroll at the beginning of the play and reads his lines.

King Or Queen
- **Crown** Trace a template like the one shown on a 4" x 18" strip of yellow construction paper. Cut out the shape; then size the resulting crown and trim off extra length. Use glue and glitter to decorate the crown as desired; then staple or tape the ends.

Crew Member
- **Cap** A knit or woolen cap.
- **Beads** Craft or paper beads for trading.

Islander
- **Parrot** Use markers, crayons, and/or paints to decorate a white construction-paper copy of the parrot pattern on page 215. Cut out and tape the parrot to a craft stick.

Cue-Card Holder
- **Sign** A poster-board sign that reads "EVERYONE."

Invitations

Complete a copy of the invitation on page 214; then duplicate student copies and a few extras on white paper. A student colors the border of an invitation; then he cuts out the invitation and mounts it on a 4" x 9" rectangle of gray construction paper. When the glue is dry, he rolls the project (keeping the invitation to the inside) and ties it with a length of ribbon. If desired, prepare and use the extra invitations to invite neighboring classes to a rehearsal or an additional showing of the play.

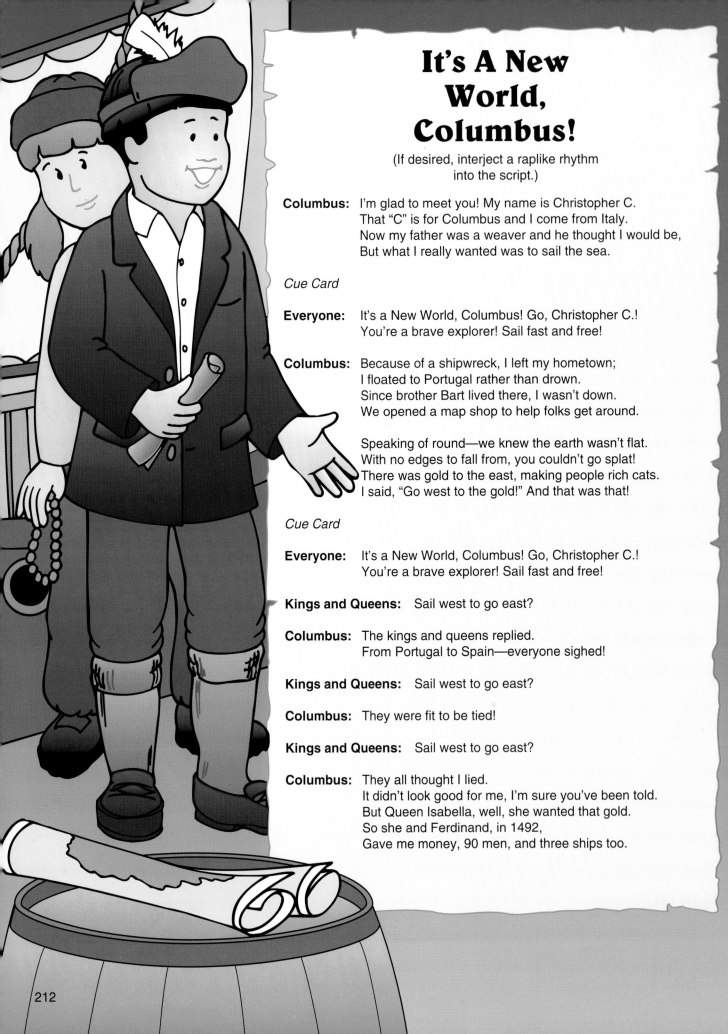

It's A New World, Columbus!

(If desired, interject a raplike rhythm
into the script.)

Columbus: I'm glad to meet you! My name is Christopher C.
That "C" is for Columbus and I come from Italy.
Now my father was a weaver and he thought I would be,
But what I really wanted was to sail the sea.

Cue Card

Everyone: It's a New World, Columbus! Go, Christopher C.!
You're a brave explorer! Sail fast and free!

Columbus: Because of a shipwreck, I left my hometown;
I floated to Portugal rather than drown.
Since brother Bart lived there, I wasn't down.
We opened a map shop to help folks get around.

Speaking of round—we knew the earth wasn't flat.
With no edges to fall from, you couldn't go splat!
There was gold to the east, making people rich cats.
I said, "Go west to the gold!" And that was that!

Cue Card

Everyone: It's a New World, Columbus! Go, Christopher C.!
You're a brave explorer! Sail fast and free!

Kings and Queens: Sail west to go east?

Columbus: The kings and queens replied.
From Portugal to Spain—everyone sighed!

Kings and Queens: Sail west to go east?

Columbus: They were fit to be tied!

Kings and Queens: Sail west to go east?

Columbus: They all thought I lied.
It didn't look good for me, I'm sure you've been told.
But Queen Isabella, well, she wanted that gold.
So she and Ferdinand, in 1492,
Gave me money, 90 men, and three ships too.

Cue Card

Everyone: It's a New World, Columbus! Go, Christopher C.!
You're a brave explorer! Sail fast and free!

Columbus: The *Niña,* the *Pinta,* and the *Santa María* sailed.

Crew: We sailed, and we sailed, and we sailed, and we sailed!

Columbus: I thought my crew was going to have me jailed…

Crew: Because we sailed, and we sailed, and we sailed, and we sailed!

Columbus: After 71 days on the high lonesome seas,
We thought we saw land; then we <u>knew</u> we saw trees!
On October 12 we were all really pleased.
We were sure we had landed in the East Indies!

Cue Card

Everyone: It's a New World, Columbus! Go, Christopher C.!
You're a brave explorer! Sail fast and free!

Islanders: Some beads for our parrots?

Columbus: Man, what a great deal!
My crew and the Islanders traded with zeal!

Islanders: Some beads for our parrots?

Columbus: But where was all the gold
That we'd find in the Indies? (Or so we'd been told!)

Well, the people of Spain thought the parrots were swell.
They liked all the stuff and said I'd done well.
But…
Looking at the maps YOUR stores now sell,
I was really south of Florida. WHOOPS! Don't tell!

Cue Card

Everyone: It's a New World, Columbus! Go, Christopher C.!
You're a brave explorer! Sail fast and free!

Patterns

Columbus Hat
Use with "Props: Columbus" on page 211.

Invitation
Use with "Invitations" on page 211.

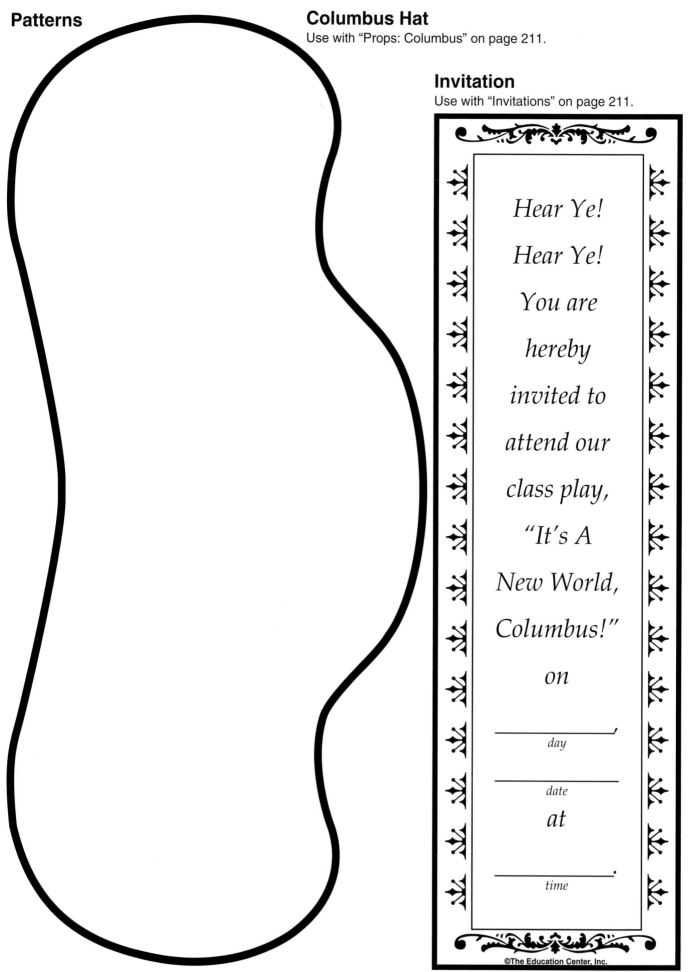

Hear Ye! Hear Ye! You are hereby invited to attend our class play, "It's A New World, Columbus!" on

_____,
day

_____
date

at

_____.
time

Parrot
Use with "Props: Islander" on page 211.

'Tis The Season For...
PUMPKINS

Perk up your pumpkin patch with this sampling of integrated activities.
ideas contributed by Darcy Brown

MUSIC

From Seed To Jack-O'-Lantern

Introduce your youngsters to the life cycle of a pumpkin with this delightful adaption of "The Farmer In The Dell." If desired, challenge students to brainstorm movements to perform for each stanza. Or have each youngster illustrate the stanzas on drawing paper.

The Pumpkin In The Patch

I had a little seed.
I put it in the ground.
Covered it and watered it,
It didn't make a sound.

First there was a sprout
That popped out of the seed.
It started growing through the soil,
At an amazing speed.

Next there was a plant.
It grew and grew each day.
It needed sun and water
To help it on its way.

Then vines began to twist,
Around and round and round.
Thick and strong, they helped the plant
Stay firmly in the ground.

Soon there was a flower.
It started very small.
In a while it would change,
And grow a little ball.

From green to very orange,
The ball, it grew in size.
A big, huge pumpkin is there now,
Right before my eyes.

I picked it off the vine,
And scooped its insides out.
I carved a face right on the front.
Why don't you check it out!

adapted from an idea by
Beth Taylor—Gr. 1
Rahn Elementary
Mt. Morris, IL

WRITING

Just 30 Pounds...

Did you know that during a growth spurt a large pumpkin can gain 30 pounds in a single day? Share this interesting fact with your youngsters. Ask students how their lives might change if they gained 30 pounds of *muscle* in one day. Then have each student write and illustrate a story about the day that it really happened! Bind the stories into a classroom book titled "It Was Only 30 Pounds!"

Missy

The day I grew 30 pounds of muscle I scared my mom. I moved the refrigerator! I leaped over our house and I even carved a pumpkin with my bare hands.

SCIENCE

Pumpkin Circle

Why not invite your students to spend the afternoon in a pumpkin patch! *Pumpkin Circle* —a delightful 20-minute video narrated in verse by Danny Glover with toe-tappin' music by George Winston (Informed Democracy, 1997)—focuses on the changes that occur across the seasons in a backyard pumpkin patch. Contact Informed Democracy at 1-800-827-0949 for more information about purchasing this outstanding video for your school's library. You'll never look at pumpkins the same way again!

COMPUTER

A Site To See!

If you're looking for a fun and informative Web site about pumpkins, visit The Pumpkin Circle at *http://garden@pumpkincircle.com/*. This site features classroom activities, an offer for free pumpkin seeds, and a cropful of information for growing pumpkins. The site also includes details on growing pumpkins, a pumpkin recipe, and links to other pumpkin sites. (Please be sure to preview all Web sites before sharing them with your students.) What a great way to incorporate the computer into your pumpkin unit!

About 350 years ago the Pilgrims were eating pumpkins!

Champion Seeds

Growing a champion pumpkin takes lots of time *and* care. Pumpkin growers will pay top dollar for the seeds from a champion pumpkin—sometimes as much as $10 per seed! For a fun math lesson, have students work in small groups to determine the costs of handfuls of "champion" seeds! Reach into a container of seeds and give each small group a handful. Have each group determine the cost of its seeds (at $10 each) and share its results with the other groups. Then collect the pumpkin seeds and repeat the activity as many times as desired. To extend the lesson, give each group a calculator. Reveal that a champion pumpkin can contain as many as 700 seeds! Then have the groups determine how much money they would need to buy large numbers of champion seeds—all the way up to 700!

SOCIAL STUDIES

A Pumpkin Patch Of Facts

Another fun way to visit a pumpkin patch is by using children's literature. Read aloud a favorite children's book about real pumpkins. (One excellent choice is *The Pumpkin Patch* by Elizabeth King [Dutton Children's Books, 1990]. The book's simple text and colorful photographs take students on a journey from seed to pumpkin.) Ask youngsters to listen for facts mentioned in the book. Then pass around a bag of pumpkin seeds and instruct each child to grab a small handful of seeds from the bag. Next have each student share one pumpkin fact for each seed he has. Or have him glue his seeds to a sheet of paper and write a different pumpkin fact beside each one.

Anne Bustard, Austin, TX

READING

Pick Of The Patch

These books are just what you need in your pumpkin patch!

The Great Pumpkin Switch
Written by Megan McDonald
Illustrated by Ted Lewin
Orchard Books, 1992

Pumpkins: A Story For A Field
Written by Mary Lyn Ray
Illustrated by Barry Root
Harcourt Brace Jovanovich, Publishers; 1992

The Vanishing Pumpkin
Written by Tony Johnston
Illustrated by Tomie dePaola
The Putnam & Grosset Group, 1996

Grandma's Smile
Written by Elaine Moore
Illustrated by Dan Andreasen
Lothrop, Lee & Shepard Books; 1995

Too Many Pumpkins
Written by Linda White
Illustrated by Megan Lloyd
Holiday House, Inc.; 1996

COOKING

Pumpkin Fluff

From pumpkin pie to toasted pumpkin seeds, serving pumpkin is a tradition that has been carried on for many years. Continue this tradition by having your young-sters help make and eat a tasty serving of pumpkin fluff.

Pumpkin Fluff
(makes 25–30 servings)

Ingredients:
two 16 oz. containers of nondairy whipped topping
30-oz. can of pumpkin pie filling
crumbled graham crackers
cinnamon
3-oz. plastic cups

Directions:
1. Mix together the whipped topping and the pie filling in a large bowl.
2. Spoon the mixture into the cups.
3. Top each cup with graham-cracker crumbs and a sprinkle of cinnamon.

A Very Big Pumpkin

A Literary Feast

Are your youngsters craving Thanksgiving literature? This feast of fiction and nonfiction books will surely please their palates! With servings of comical adventures, heartwarming experiences, and true-life tales, your students will be eager to gobble up the delicious offerings. So go ahead and take a gander! Gobble! Gobble!

ideas by Lisa Leonardi

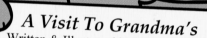

Thanksgiving At The Tappletons'

Written by Eileen Spinelli
Illustrated by Maryann Cocca-Leffler
HarperCollins Children's Books, 1992

Thanksgiving has always been a special day at the Tappletons' and this Thanksgiving is no exception—even though the day is decidedly different from past celebrations! Unbeknownst to each other, catastrophe strikes every family member who is making preparations for the Thanksgiving meal. Fortunately for the family, Grandmother Tappleton sees beyond the dinner disaster and helps everyone at the table realize that there's more to Thanksgiving than turkey and all the trimmings.

After hearing this enjoyable story, students will be hungry to talk about the Thanksgiving foods they prefer! First ask each child to make a prop showing his favorite Thanksgiving dinner. To do this, a student cuts the shapes of his favorite foods from colorful construction paper, then uses markers or crayons to decorate the shapes. Next he glues the shapes onto a nine-inch paper plate. While this project is drying, the student decorates a 12" x 18" sheet of construction paper to resemble a holiday placemat. He also cuts from construction paper (and decorates as desired) a dinner napkin, a drinking glass, and eating utensils. To assemble his project, he glues the bottom of his dinner plate near the center of his placemat, then glues the remaining cutouts in place. Provide time for each child to share his project with his classmates and talk about his favorite Thanksgiving foods.

A Visit To Grandma's

Written & Illustrated by Nancy Carlson
Puffin Books, 1993

Thanksgiving offers an unexpected twist when Tina and her parents visit Grandma, who has just relocated to Florida. Tina expects to find turkey, home-baked pies, and the same ole Grandma. But when Grandma picks up the family at the airport in a flashy red sports car, serves them store-bought pies, and attends aerobics classes, Tina longs for the way things used to be. That is until she discovers change can be quite refreshing!

Talking about Thanksgiving traditions is a natural lead-in to this amusing story. Invite students to share their favorite Thanksgiving memories with the class before you read the book aloud. Then, after your oral reading of the story, ask students to explain why Tina didn't immediately like her grandma's new Thanksgiving traditions and what led her to eventually change her mind. Then have each student write and illustrate a story in which her family celebrates an out-of-the-ordinary Thanksgiving—the sillier the better! Ask students to include in their stories the locations of the get-togethers, the games and activities in which their family members participate, and descriptions of the foods eaten. Encourage students to share their stories with their families on Thanksgiving. Then, after the holiday, ask each student if any of her story events were included in her family's Thanksgiving festivities.

This Thanksgiving my family decided to celebrate in a different way. Instead of going to Grandma's for lunch, everyone

'Twas The Night Before Thanksgiving

Written & Illustrated by Dav Pilkey
Orchard Books, 1990

On Thanksgiving Eve, eight school children take a field trip to Farmer Mack Nuggett's farm. During their visit the students are introduced to eight lovable turkeys that are destined to become holiday fare. The youngsters decide THAT just won't do. So they put a plan into action that enables their new fine-feathered friends to feast on Thanksgiving—rather than being feasted upon!

An oral reading of this hilarious Thanksgiving twist on " 'Twas The Night Before Christmas" will have your youngsters ready to save the turkeys! Ask students to brainstorm foods that could replace turkey on a Thanksgiving menu. List the students' ideas on the chalkboard. Then, working in pairs, have each twosome create an eye-catching poster that encourages others to forgo eating turkey this Thanksgiving. Request that each poster suggest alternate Thanksgiving foods. Encourage students to refer to the student-generated list of foods as needed. Display the completed posters around the school for everyone to see. The posters just might save a turkey or two!

DON'T BE A TURKEY!

Say "NO" To Eating Turkey.
Eat A Peanut Butter
And Jelly Sandwich
Instead!

Extend the fun of Dav Pilkey's Thanksgiving tale with this harmonious retelling!

Dear Mr. & Mrs. Chatterjee,
Thank you for saving me lettuce and cabbage to eat. They were very tasty. I will always be grateful for your kindness. I hope you had a nice Thanksgiving. I sure did!

Your friend,
Gracias

Gracias The Thanksgiving Turkey

Written by Joy Cowley & Illustrated by Joe Cepeda
Scholastic Inc., 1996

In this heartwarming story, a young Puerto Rican boy receives a turkey from his father with instructions to fatten it up for Thanksgiving. But when the youngster discovers that he and the turkey fit together like birds of a feather, he knows the turkey cannot be eaten. Now he must get Papa and the rest of the family to agree. A short glossary defines the Spanish words that are interspersed throughout this touching story.

As his name suggests, Gracias the turkey had many reasons to give thanks on Thanksgiving. Since the day he arrived in New York City, many people showed the turkey the true meaning of family and community. After an oral reading of the story, challenge students to recall the name and actions of each person who helped Gracias. List this information on the chalkboard. Then ask each student to choose a person from the list and write a thank-you note to him or her from Gracias's point of view. Post the completed notes and a colorful turkey cutout on a bulletin board titled "Many Thanks From Gracias."

To The Turkey Farm
(adapted to the tune of "Over The River And Through The Woods")

Over the roads and through the leaves
To Mack Nuggett's turkey farm.
The bus led the way
With eight children one day,
On a field trip that caused quite alarm.

Over the roads and through the night
Fleeing from Mack Nuggett's farm.
The bus sped away
With eight turkeys who prayed
The children would keep them from harm.

Ready to eat on Thanksgiving Day,
Eight turkeys were thankful to be
Happy and able—
And not on the table!
Thanks to the children—they're free!

How Many Days To America?
A Thanksgiving Story
Written by Eve Bunting & Illustrated by Beth Peck
Houghton Mifflin Company, 1990

In this dramatic and touching story about present-day refugees, a family from a Caribbean island embarks on a dangerous boat trip to America. After experiencing severe hardships along the way, the family is welcomed to America with open arms on what turns out to be a very special day—Thanksgiving.

This poignant story provides the perfect prelude to a discussion on refugees. Tell students that a *refugee* is a person who flees his or her country and seeks safety elsewhere. Explain that refugees typically leave their countries to escape war, persecution, or life-threatening disasters such as hunger and disease. Ask students what kinds of challenges a refugee might face moving to a new country. Responses might include difficulty communicating, longing for acceptance, and missing friends and relatives from back home. Next inform students that the United States receives more refugees (and immigrants) than any other country in the world. Ask students why they think people are eager to move to America. Lead students to understand that in the United States, religious freedom, opportunities, and the people are equally protected by the law. And that is something for which we can all be thankful!

Molly's Pilgrim
Written by Barbara Cohen
Illustrated by Michael J. Deraney
Lothrop, Lee & Shepard Books; 1983

Molly, a young Jewish Russian-American, is the target of her classmates' taunts. She longs to be more like the other third graders so that the teasing will stop. When Molly and her classmates are each asked to create a Pilgrim doll, Molly is embarrassed by the uniqueness of her completed project. But in the end, it is her doll that helps Molly discover that she shares an important part of America's Thanksgiving tradition with her classmates. Students will learn, like Molly and her classmates, that when differences are explored, similarities are often revealed.

This follow-up project helps students understand that the rich cultural diversity of America is a result of our country's past and present-day pilgrims (immigrants, refugees). To begin, ask students to name things that people moving to America might bring with them, such as clothing, recipes, toys, traditions, and experiences. Then, as a class, discuss how these things might be shared with other Americans. Next ask each child to interview an older person (this may or may not be a family member) to learn about his or her heritage. If desired, give each child a page of interview questions like those shown below. After the interviews are given, have each student use the information she gathered to create a pilgrim doll in honor of the person's heritage. To do this, each child uses art supplies—such as fabric scraps, construction paper, yarn, felt, and markers—to dress a tagboard clothespin cutout. Set aside time for interested students to share their dolls and the information they gathered. Then display the projects (and interviews) on a bulletin board titled "Thank You, Pilgrims!" Without a doubt, students will agree—our country is a better place because of everyone's contributions!

Learning About The Past

Name Of Person Being Interviewed: _____

1. What country did most of your ancestors come from?
   _____

2. Why did your ancestors come to America?
   _____

3. What language did your ancestors speak when they first came to America? _____

4. What traditions do we have today that we learned from your ancestors? _____
   _____

5. What foods do we eat today that originated in your ancestors' homeland?_____
   _____

6. What kinds of clothes did your ancestors wear?
   _____
   _____

Interview completed by _____

220

BARRY SLATE

On The Mayflower: Voyage Of The Ship's Apprentice And A Passenger Girl
Written by Kate Waters & Photographed by Russ Kendall
Scholastic Inc., 1996

It's an exciting ride for readers as they experience the 1620 voyage of the Mayflower through the eyes of William Small, a 12-year-old ship's apprentice. The young lad describes his day-to-day duties, the ups and downs of being at sea, and his friendship with Ellen Moore, an eight-year-old passenger. Full-color photographs taken on board the Mayflower II, a reproduction of the original Mayflower, add authenticity to this captivating chronicle. Included at the end of the book are several pages of factual information, a diagram of the Mayflower, and a glossary of seaworthy terms.

William and Ellen both endure a difficult journey on the *Mayflower;* however, their experiences are distinctly different. Have each student capture what the journey was like for these two youngsters inside a shipshape booklet like the one shown below. To make her booklet cover, a student folds a copy of page 222 in half, keeping the ships to the outside. Next she folds in half two or three sheets of blank paper. Then she slides the folded paper inside the booklet cover and staples the resulting booklet near the fold. To write about Will's apprenticeship aboard the *Mayflower,* the student first colors and personalizes the cover that is appropriately labeled; then she illustrates Will on board the ship. Next she lifts the cover and writes about Will's journey on the front of each booklet page. To write about Ellen's voyage as a passenger, the student colors and personalizes the remaining cover and illustrates Ellen on board the ship before she lifts this cover and writes about Ellen's journey. Encourage students to use their completed projects to show their families what they have learned about the 1620 voyage of the *Mayflower.*

Sarah Morton's Day: A Day In The Life Of A Pilgrim Girl
Written by Kate Waters & Photographed by Russ Kendall
Scholastic Inc., 1989

Samuel Eaton's Day: A Day In The Life Of A Pilgrim Boy
Written by Kate Waters & Photographed by Russ Kendall
Scholastic Inc., 1993

From sunup to sundown, a day in the life of a Pilgrim youngster is examined in each of these delightful books. The phenomenal color photographs in both books were shot on location in Plimoth Plantation—an outdoor living-history museum in Plimoth, Massachusetts. Each portrayal is based on a real Pilgrim child who lived in 17th century New England. At the conclusion of each book are notes about Plimoth Plantation, the real Pilgrim child and the child who portrays him or her, and a student-friendly glossary.

A single reading of either story quickly reveals how different life was growing up as a Pilgrim. For a fun follow-up, have each student make a two-flap booklet in which to compare and contrast his daily life to that of a Pilgrim child. To make the booklet, a student folds a 9" x 12" sheet of drawing paper in half (to 4 1/2" x 12") and makes one cut through the center of the top layer. On one flap the student illustrates and labels a Pilgrim child and on the remaining flap he illustrates and labels himself. Under each flap he notes information about a day in the life of the illustrated person. Ask students to include facts about clothing, school, chores, food, and family life. Once the students have completed the projects, have them share their work in small groups.

If you are able to share both stories with your students, have each child make a three-flap booklet so that he can compare and contrast his daily life to the lives of both Pilgrim children. To make a three-flap booklet, a child folds in half a 12" x 18" sheet of drawing paper (to 6" x 18") and makes two equally spaced cuts through the top layer.

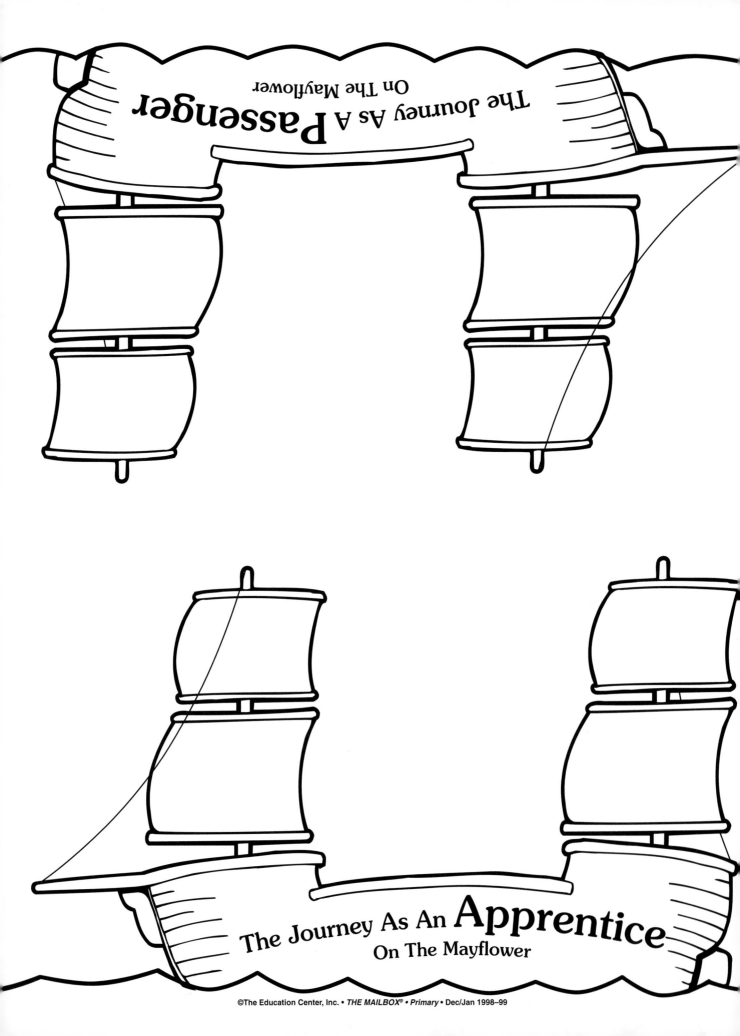

The Journey As A **Passenger**
On The Mayflower

The Journey As An **Apprentice**
On The Mayflower

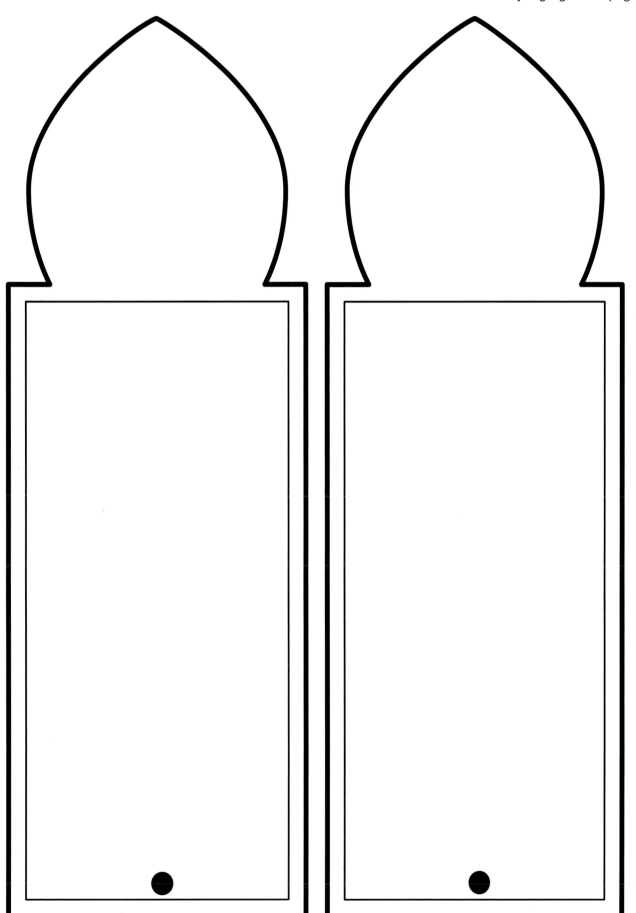

Just "Write" For The Season!

Pick and choose from this sampler of quick-as-a-wink writing projects!
ideas contributed by Jill Hamilton—Gr. 1, Ephrata, PA

Holiday Highlights

This writing project is aglow with versatility! Each student needs three (or more) copies of page 223. She titles one candle "[Holiday] Is A Time To..."; then—on each of her remaining candles—she completes the sentence in a different way, illustrating her work if desired. Next she colors and cuts out each candle shape. Lastly the student stacks her cutouts (placing the titled candle on top) and joins them by poking a brad through each black dot. Happy holidays!

Peekaboo Presents

Students will agree that getting wrapped up in this writing activity is as easy as can be! Each student looks through discarded magazines and newspaper circulars to find one item he would like to receive as a holiday gift. He cuts out that item and glues it onto a half-sheet of construction paper. To make a gift tag, he cuts away two corners of a 4" x 6" card (see the illustration). On the tag he writes three hints about the gift he has chosen. Next he covers another half-sheet of construction paper with a slightly larger piece of holiday gift wrap. He glues the tag and a recycled bow to the gift-wrapped rectangle; then he positions this rectangle atop the rectangle that shows his holiday gift. Finally he uses clear tape to join the top edges of the project. Showcase these gifts on a bulletin board titled "Predict Before You Peek!" You can count on this display being highly interactive!

Peppermint Poems

Penning poetry for a peppermint display can be a tasty experience! Armed with a peppermint candy, a pencil, and paper, each youngster writes a poem of any kind; then she copies her edited poem onto a seven-inch paper circle. Next she makes a paper peppermint on which to glue her poem. For a sweet display, hole-punch the top of each project and suspend the peppermints from your classroom ceiling on lengths of curling ribbon or monofilament line.

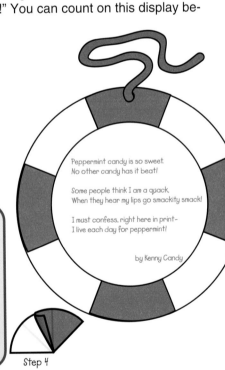

How To Make A Paper Peppermint

1. Fold a nine-inch red construction-paper circle in half twice; then unfold and cut on the crease lines.
2. Fold each of the four equal-sized sections in half; then unfold the sections and set them aside.
3. Repeat Steps 1 and 2 with a nine-inch white construction-paper circle.
4. To assemble the peppermint pieces, glue half of a red piece atop half of a white piece (use the crease line on each piece as a guide). Next glue half of a white piece atop half of the red piece, then half of a red piece atop half of the white piece, and so on until a round peppermint shape results.

Gift Of Writing

Special surprises often come in small packages, and this writing activity is no exception! Each student needs a white construction-paper copy of page 226, a pencil, markers or crayons, scissors, and a small gift bow. A student chooses a recipient for his gift; then, in Box One, he writes and illustrates a greeting to this person. Next he writes and illustrates a special message to the person in each of the three remaining boxes. When he is finished writing and illustrating, he cuts out his project along the bold lines. Then he folds Box Four inward along the thin line, Box Two inward along the thin line, and Box One inward along the thin line. To decorate his package, the student first draws a gift tag on the top surface. Then he unfolds the package, flips it over, and colors the paper to resemble gift wrap. Lastly he refolds the project and attaches the bow near the gift tag. His special gift is ready to deliver!

Snowflake Snippets

Most scientists agree that no two snowflakes are exactly the same. So it only makes sense that your students' snowflake snippets—brief student-written tales about snowflakes and the like—will be unique as well! To make a winter writing journal for each child, fold a 9" x 12" sheet of dark blue construction paper in half and staple a supply of writing paper inside. Have each child write "Snowflake Snippets" and her name on the front cover of her journal. On each of several days, provide a different snow-related journal-writing prompt. Follow up each writing session by inviting students to read aloud the snippets they wrote; then have each child cut a snowflake from a three-inch square of white or pastel paper. As students glue their snowflakes to their journal covers, praise the youngsters for the uniqueness of their writings. In just a few days, you'll have created a blizzard of writing interest!

Donna Figurski, Dumont, NJ

Snow-Related Prompts

Pretend you are a snowflake; then…

- write about the neatest place you have landed
- tell how it feels to be part of a blizzard
- describe the advantages of being part of a snow pal or snowball
- explain why you like being different from all the ` other snowflakes
- write about the loneliest day of your life
- write about the most famous person you have seen

Happy-Birthday Biography

Celebrate Martin Luther King, Jr.'s birthday with a biography project for beginners. Read aloud a picture book that tells about the boyhood, adult life, and dreams of Martin Luther King, Jr. To write a biography about this great man, a student folds a 9" x 12" sheet of blank paper in half three times. Keeping the fold at the top, she designs a cover for her biography. Then she unfolds her paper once and writes and illustrates a fact about Martin's boyhood. She then unfolds her paper again. On each half of the resulting blank paper, she writes and illustrates a fact about Martin's life as a young adult. Then she unfolds her paper one more time and writes about Dr. King's adult life. After the student illustrates her work, she refolds her paper. Her very first biography project is ready to share!

Completed Project

To:

From:

Fold like this:

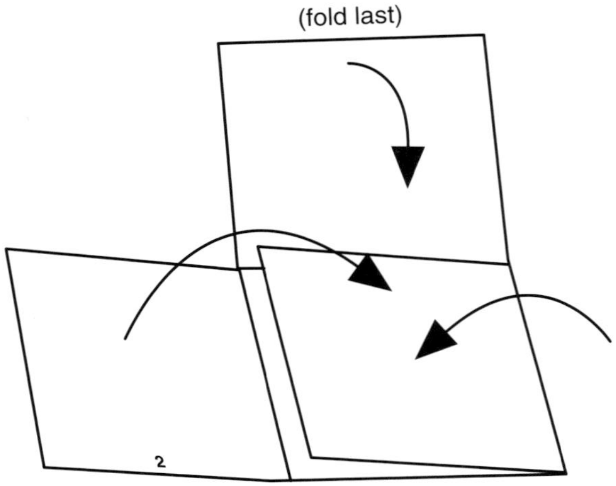

(fold last)

2

1

2

3

4

Note To Teacher: Use with "Gift Of Writing" on page 225.

A 100th-Day Celebration!

The 100th day of school is right around the corner and that means a celebration is in order! The following ideas have earned our subscribers' seal of approval, and we feel certain that you and your youngsters will enjoy them too. Have a ball celebrating this marvelous milestone!

100TH-DAY BREAKFAST

Plan to start off your 100th day with a kid-pleasing, tummy-approved activity! Give each student a personalized resealable plastic bag in which to bring to school 100 pieces of her favorite cereal. Ask that the bags be returned the day before your celebration. Then round up any extra cereal needed, plastic bowls and spoons, and milk. When students arrive on the 100th day, serve them their cereal with a smile. Now that's a tasty way to start the day!

Rebecca Taylor—Gr. 1
Phillis Wheatley School
Milwaukee, WI

ON A ROLL!

This partner game really adds up! Give each pair a die. To play, each student in turn rolls the die and makes a corresponding number of tally marks (in sets of five) on his math paper. The first partner to collect 100 tally marks wins the game. Roll 'em!

Kathy DiGrigoli—Gr. 1, Osbornville School, Brick, NJ

DRESSED TO THE 100s

As a family project, ask each student to decorate or create an item of clothing to be worn during your 100th-day celebration. What's the catch? The clothing item must have 100 objects drawn on it or attached to it. Suggest that students—with their parents' assistance—decorate items like T-shirts, hats, slippers, socks, and paper-bag vests, or fashion 100-piece jewelry items. Set aside time for students to model their 100th-day fashions for all to see. Be sure to invite parents to the viewing, too. Now that's 100th-day style!

Deborah Ross, Wayland Alexander School, Hartford, KY

227

100TH-DAY SONG

Celebrate the 100th day of school with this little ditty. It's the perfect way to commemorate a very special day!

100 Days Of School
(sung to the tune of "Jingle Bells")
Ready to celebrate?
It's the 100th day of school.
We've studied hard each day.
Learning is so cool!
We've made many friends
Here at [your school name].
What fun it is to say we've been at school 100 days!

100 days, 100 days,
100 days of school.
We've been in school 100 days.
We think that's really cool!

100 days, 100 days,
100 days of school.
We work and play every day.
We love to be in school!

adapted from an idea by Janice Jasmer—Grs. K–3
Leola Elementary School
Leola, SD

A PERFECT FIT

Creating these 100-item collections requires more than just counting! Gather a class supply of nonbreakable, lidded containers in a variety of sizes. Ask each child to choose a container, take it home, fill it with 100 identical objects, and return it to school on or before the 100th day. Challenge students to custom-fit their collections to their containers. For example 100 grains of rice fit nicely in a 35mm film container but not in a shoebox. On the day of the celebration, have each student share her 100-item collection. Encourage each child to explain how she decided what kind of item to collect. If desired, invite neighboring classrooms in to view the collections. Then send the collections home at the end of the day.

Deborah Ross, Wayland Alexander School, Hartford, KY

100 AUTOGRAPHS

Students will be buzzing about this extra-credit project! About a week before your 100th-day celebration, give each child a construction-paper booklet that contains several sheets of writing paper. Have each student personalize the front cover of his booklet and number the lines on the writing paper from 1 to 100. Challenge each student to gather 100 different autographs before the 100th day of school. Encourage students to gather signatures from schoolmates, teachers, classroom visitors, staff members, family members, and neighbors. Then set aside time during your 100th-day celebration for each child to tell his classmates about an autograph he gathered that he is especially proud of. If desired present each child who met the challenge with a special 100th-day award.

Dawn Hermann—Gr. 1, Rahn Elementary, Mt. Morris, IL

100 DOLLARS

This unique homework activity builds anticipation for a wealth of 100th-day fun! Design an oversized $100 bill for duplication, omitting Benjamin Franklin's picture. Duplicate a class supply of this bill on light green construction paper. A few days prior to your celebration, distribute the bills as a homework activity, and challenge each student to complete the bill by illustrating and naming the missing person. Ask students to return the bills on or before the 100th day of school. For a 100th-day activity, have each child write and illustrate a story about the day she spent $100.00. Tape each child's greenback to her story and display it for all to see. Now that's a profitable activity!

Kathy Graham—Gr. 1
Flossmoor, IL

POPCORN PREDICTIONS

Pop up a batch of predicting and graphing practice with this tasty idea! In advance and without your youngsters' knowledge, pop enough popcorn for a class snack. To introduce the activity, enlist your students' help in counting 100 popcorn kernels. Ask students to observe the kernels and predict if these kernels, when popped, would provide enough popcorn for a class snack. Then have each child write her name on a sticky note and indicate her prediction on a class graph. Evaluate the graph as a class; then pop the 100 kernels in an air popper. While the kernels are popping, lead the class in a discussion that results in your students understanding that 100 kernels would not feed the class. Next surprise the youngsters with the popped corn you prepared earlier! Yum!

Alice Arksey—Grs. 2–3
Northridge Public School
London, Ontario, Canada

MORE OR LESS

Estimation skills are in the bag with this 100-day activity! In advance sequentially number a class set of quart-sized, resealable plastic bags. In each bag place a collection of identical items that total either more or less than 100. Consider various-sized items such as pasta pieces, grains of rice, cotton balls, stickers, paper clips, and popcorn kernels. To begin the activity, have each student number her paper to correspond with the number of prepared bags. Give each child one sealed bag. The student studies the bag, estimates whether it contains more or less than 100 items, and writes her answer on her paper. Then, on your cue, she passes the bag to the next student along a predetermined route. When each student has recorded an estimate for every bag, check the activity. To do this, each child removes the items from the bag she holds, counts them, and records her total count on her paper. Then, beginning with the bag numbered 1, each student shares her count so all the children can check their papers.

Deborah Ross
Wayland Alexander School
Hartford, KY

229

FOR GOOD MEASURE

What better day to reinforce the difference between 100 inches and 100 centimeters, than the 100th day of school? Ask each student to bring to school (on the 100th day) an item that is 100 inches long and an item that is 100 centimeters long. Suggest that students measure items that can be brought to school easily, like lengths of string, yarn, lace, or paper. Set aside time for each student to share the items he measured; then have the students estimate which items within the classroom (school) probably measure either 100 centimeters or 100 inches. Students or student pairs can then use the items they measured to check their predictions.

Deborah Ross, Wayland Alexander School, Hartford, KY

100TH-DAY WEB SITE

You'll find a wealth of 100th-day activities at The 100th Day Of School Website—*http://users.aol.com/a100thday/index.html.* This site features ideas gathered from teachers across the country, a list of books to tie into your 100th-day festivities, links to other Web sites relating to the 100th day of school, and more. The Web site's creator is children's book author and illustrator Joan Holub. Hit this site today!

100 LETTERS

What can 100 letters teach you? Plenty, if you choose them carefully! For a unique 100th-day writing activity, challenge each child to use only 100 letters (or thereabouts) to write a paragraph that describes himself, a family member, or a pet. When the students have finished their 100-letter masterpieces, they'll be eager to share their informative paragraphs. They'll also have a much better idea of how to self-edit!

Rose E. Ferrigno—Gr. 1, Montowese School, North Haven, CT

A THREE-DIGIT SURPRISE

However you choose to complete this math activity, the end result is the same: 100! For younger students, randomly call the numbers found in the number box on this page. Instruct each youngster to color the matching numeral on her copy of a duplicated hundred chart. To increase the difficulty of this activity, provide an oral clue for each number like "Color the numeral that is one more than 33" or "Color the numeral that equals 40 plus 2." Or provide more advanced students with math problems that—when computed—equal the numbers shown in the number box. A student solves each problem and colors its answer on his hundred chart. There's that 100!

Cynthia Mason—Gr. 1
Clearwater R-1 Elementary School
Piedmont, MO

1	2	3	4	5	6	7	8	9	10
11	12	13	14	15	16	17	18	19	20
21	22	23	24	25	26	27	28	29	30
31	32	33	34	35	36	37	38	39	40
41	42	43	44	45	46	47	48	49	50
51	52	53	54	55	56	57	58	59	60
61	62	63	64	65	66	67	68	69	70
71	72	73	74	75	76	77	78	79	80
81	82	83	84	85	86	87	88	89	90
91	92	93	94	95	96	97	98	99	100

Number Box

22	30	40	50	60	70	80
24	32	42	52	62	72	
25	34	44	54	64	74	
26	36	46	56	66	75	
28	38	48	58	68	76	
29					78	
					79	

POP QUIZ

A 100th-day pop quiz? It's not as bad as it sounds! Ask each student to number her paper from 1 to 10. Then, for each number, announce a math problem (that equals 100). Each child solves the problem and writes her answer next to the corresponding numeral on her paper. At the conclusion of the quiz, reveal the answers—if necessary. This could very well be one quiz on which everyone scores a 100!

Alice Arksey—Grs. 2–3, Northridge Public School
London, Ontario, Canada

100TH-DAY CENTERS

It's easy to customize free-time centers for a 100th-day celebration! Combine the center ideas listed on this page with your own and you'll have plenty to celebrate. For easy management, number and list your center activities on a 100th-day contract. Then, for each student, staple a copy of this contract to the front of a construction-paper folder. Each time a youngster completes a 100th-day free-time center, he checks off that center on his contract and places his work (when appropriate) inside the folder. At the end of the day, reward each student who completed a predetermined number of free-time centers with a small prize.

Kathy Graham—Gr. 1, Flossmoor, IL

100TH-DAY CENTER IDEAS

- Write the year that you will turn 100 years old. Draw a picture of what you think you will look like then.
- Cut 100 words from a discarded magazine. Read each word as you glue it to a sheet of paper.
- Make a list of 100 words you know how to spell.
- Do 100 jumping jacks.
- Write a letter to a friend that contains exactly 100 words.
- Assemble a 100-piece jigsaw puzzle.
- Link 100 Unifix® cubes.
- Make a necklace using a length of yarn and 100 Cheerios®.
- Complete a dot-to-dot activity to 100.
- Write and illustrate a story that begins "I wish I had 100…"
- Flip a coin 100 times. Tally how many times you flip heads and tails.
- Roll a die 100 times. Graph how many times you roll each number.
- Use toothpicks and 100 minimarshmallows to create a sculpture.

Kathy Graham—Gr. 1
Alice Arksey—Grs. 2–3

100 DAYS TOGETHER

For a fun finale to your 100th-day activities, ask students to recall the different things they've learned, the friends they've made, and the fun they've had during the first 100 days of school. If desired list their ideas on the chalkboard. Then ask each child to write and illustrate a sentence or story that begins "My favorite thing about the first 100 days of school is…" Bind the students' completed work into a class book titled "Our 100 Days Together." Display this project in the class library for all to read.

Laura W. Burris—Grs. 1–4, Bellefonte Elementary, Bellefonte, PA

Hip! Hip! "Pooh-Ray"!

It's Pooh Day!

Looking for a *thoughtful* way to celebrate Pooh Day (January 18—the birthday of author A. A. Milne)? Then try this smackerel of cross-curricular activities. It's a Hundred-Acre original!

ideas contributed by Rebecca Brudwick

PHYSICAL EDUCATION

Morning Exercises

Even though Pooh is a bear of fluff and stuff, he does morning exercises—"Stoutness Exercises," that is! Have youngsters follow Pooh's fitness lead by stretching as high as they can, then bending over to touch their toes. After several stretches, ask volunteers to lead the class in additional stretching practice. For added fun, have students hum while they exercise, just like Pooh!

WRITING

Sticky Situations

Oh, bother! Pooh's hilarious honey habits get him into plenty of sticky situations. And since Pooh is a bear of very little brain, getting himself out of sticky situations is not always easy. Invite students to share their problem-solving skills with this writing activity. Post a list of sticky situations for students to write about. If desired, have each child make a Honey-Pot Journal in which to write his ideas.

MATH

Playing With Poohsticks

A favorite game among Pooh and his friends is Poohsticks—invented by Pooh of course. To play Pooh's game, each friend stands along the same side of a bridge and drops a marked stick into the water. Then the players hurry to the other side to see whose stick will be the first to float out from under the bridge! For this prediction game, students need Poohsticks of a different kind. To make her stick, a student illustrates Pooh's head on one side of a four-inch paper circle and Eeyore's tail on the other side. Then she glues her project to one end of a craft stick. To play the game, flip a coin ten times. Before each coin flip, ask students to display Pooh's head if they think the coin will land heads up, and Eeyore's tail if they think the coin will land tails up. If a child's prediction is accurate, she makes a tally mark on her math paper. After the tenth coin flip, have each child total her tally marks. A student who earns five or more marks is having a "Pooh-riffic" day!

Sticky Situations

- Pooh disguises himself as a black cloud to take honey from a beehive. Describe another creative way that Pooh can get honey from a hive.

- After a honey-eating binge, Pooh gets stuck in Rabbit's front door. To get out, he waits until he gets thinner. Describe other ways that Pooh could get unstuck.

- Pooh plans to give Eeyore a jar of honey for his birthday; then he eats all the honey in the jar himself! Describe how Pooh can turn an empty honey jar into a pleasing birthday present.

How To Make A Honey-Pot Journal

1. To make the front cover, personalize and cut out a yellow construction-paper copy of the honey pot on page 234.
2. To make the back cover, trace the front cover onto yellow construction paper and cut along the resulting outline.
3. Staple a supply of 6" x 7" writing paper between the journal covers.

232

Pooh And Pals

Lucky Pooh! He has a wide circle of friends! Remind students that to have many friends, you must be a good friend. For a fun cooperative-group activity, have small groups of students list qualities that make Pooh such a great pal. After a designated amount of time, compile these group lists into a class list; then add other friendship qualities that your students feel are important. For an added challenge, have students brainstorm the special qualities that make Owl, Piglet, Tigger, and Kanga each a good friend, too!

Pooh's Friendship Traits

- kind
- helpful
- modest (He doesn't brag.)
- considerate
- honest
- adventurous
- friendly
- gentle

A 100-Acre Map

Here's a fun way for students to brush up on their mapping skills and learn their way around the Hundred Acre Wood! To make a king-size map of the woods, refer first to the map at the beginning of *Winnie-the-Pooh*. Then, on a length of bulletin-board paper, draw the streams and label the specific sites (like "Bee Tree" and "Piglet's House") that are shown on the map. Next assign each map site to a small group of students. Ask each group to use a variety of materials—such as construction paper, scissors, glue, crayons, and markers—to decorate its site. Encourage students to use the map in *Winnie-the-Pooh* for inspiration. When the class map is completed, pose map-related questions for students to answer.

For Pooh Fans Only!

Find Pooh and all of his pals from Hundred Acre Wood at *http://welcome.to/pooh* on the World Wide Web. Hip! Hip! "Pooh-ray"!

Wobbly Spelling

Pooh admits that his spelling is Wobbly—a condition that causes letters to get in the wrong places. Pooh's pals are Wobbly spellers, too! Here's an activity that promotes your students' superb spelling skills! Post a list of Wobbly words and have a different student volunteer write the correct spelling for each word on the list. Then pair students and have each child write a friendly letter to his partner from Pooh's (or one of Pooh's friend's) point of view. Ask that each student use five or more Wobbly words in his writing. Next have each youngster exchange letters with his partner. Then have each partner use a colored pencil to circle the Wobbly words in his partner's letter and write the correct spelling of each circled word in the margin. Now that's an activity even the "wobbliest" speller will enjoy!

Wobbly Words	Real Words
hunny	honey
cnoke	knock
rnsr	answer
hipy	happy
plez	please
reqid	required
bthuthday	birthday
wol	owl

"Time-For-A-Little-Something"

A day to celebrate Pooh just wouldn't be complete without "a little smackerel of something." Make plans to serve milk, honey sandwiches, and Pooh Paw Cakes. If desired, serve these "Pooh-riffic" snacks when students begin to feel a little 11 o'clockish—Pooh's usual snacktime.

Pooh Paw Cakes

For one Pooh paw cake:
1 white cupcake
furry frosting*
1 round chocolate-flavored wafer cookie
5 chocolate chips

Directions:
1. Spread a layer of furry frosting on top of the cupcake.
2. Press the wafer cookie in the center of the cupcake.
3. Press the chocolate chips around the wafer to create a pawprint.

*To make furry frosting, stir a desired amount of coconut flakes into prepared lemon-flavored icing.

233

Presenting The PEANUT!

Celebrate National Peanut Month in March with this super sampling of integrated activities.

ideas contributed by Ann Flagg and Kimberly Taylor

Peanutty Facts

Spread the news about peanuts with these mouthwatering facts!

- Peanuts were first grown in South America at least 2,000 years ago.
- Peanuts are not nuts! They are vegetables that grow underground.
- A peanut is the seed of a peanut plant.
- As of 1998, the record for the largest peanut ever grown was four inches long!
- It takes about 810 peanuts to make an 18-ounce jar of peanut butter.
- A former U.S. president, Jimmy Carter, was a peanut farmer!
- During the Civil War, soldiers from the North tasted peanuts growing in the South and liked them. At the end of the war, they took peanuts home with them, and the demand for peanuts tripled!
- In the early 1900s, an Italian immigrant began selling clear bags of roasted, salted peanuts without their shells. The snack was so popular that soon Planters Peanuts Company was born!

CLAP! CLAP! CLAP!

SCIENCE

Thanks, George!

George Washington Carver was a creative Black American scientist who encouraged farmers to grow the peanut plant and convinced others of the peanut's great worth. He discovered more than 300 uses for the peanut plant. After teaching your class about Mr. Carver, cut out a large peanut shape from bulletin-board paper. Ask youngsters to name different ways peanuts are used, reminding them that every part of the peanut is useful. Write their ideas on the cutout. Supplement the list as needed to make sure that products generated from each part of the peanut are included (see the provided lists for less familiar uses). Next have each child choose a different product to label and illustrate on a half-sheet of drawing paper. For a peanutty display, label one peanut-shaped cutout for each part of the peanut plant. (If desired, label two cutouts for the peanut—"peanut [for eating]" and "peanut [not for eating].") Staple the cutouts along the bottom of a bulletin board titled "Peanut Possibilities." In turn, have each child tell the class which peanut part is used to make the product she has illustrated; then staple the student's project above the correct category.

shell
fire logs
cat litter
wallboard

skins
paper

peanut (for eating)
imitation cheese
margarine
salad dressing

stems and leaves
hay for animals
fertilizer

peanut (not for eating)
food for pigs
paints
soap
shampoo
face cream
shaving cream
lipstick
shoe polish

roots
soil enricher

MATH

Peanuts By The Pound

Believe it or not, the average person in the United States eats about ten pounds of peanuts per year! Share this fact with your students and then show them one pound of shelled peanuts in a clear container. Ask each child to estimate how many peanuts are in the container and have her write her estimate on a piece of scrap paper. Then count the peanuts under your youngsters' watchful eyes, sorting each ten peanuts into a paper muffin-tin liner. When the count is complete, have each student report the accuracy of her estimate to the class by clapping once for a low estimate, twice for a high estimate, and three times for an accurate estimate. Then multiply the official peanut count by ten to discover how many peanuts a person eats per year!

For a fun follow-up, group students and ask each group to create a list of the different ways that its members eat peanuts. If desired, give each group some peanuts to snack on as they work. Then compile the group lists into a class list. Students may find out that they're eating more peanuts than they thought!

Creative Concoctions

Set the stage for this recipe-writing activity by revealing that China is the largest producer of peanuts in the world, followed by India and the United States. Then rally your youngsters into writing recipes that could boost the popularity of peanuts. Ask each child to write and illustrate a recipe for an original peanut casserole, dessert, or other dish. Compile the students' work into a class cookbook titled "Peanuts, Anyone?" Encourage students to check out the cookbook and share the creative recipes with their families. Who knows? These newly released recipes just may force farmers to plant more peanuts!

Alyssa

Peanut Pizza Dessert

Ingredients:
giant sugar cookie
frosting
sliced bananas
roasted peanuts

Directions:
Frost the cookie. Put on the bananas. Sprinkle with lots of peanuts.

COOKING

Peanut-Butter Munchies

Investigating peanuts and peanut butter is sure to make students hungry! Here's a fun way to cure their peanut-butter munchies. For this high-protein activity, ask parent volunteers to donate some unusual fixin's for peanut-butter sandwiches like sliced fruits (bananas, strawberries) and vegetables (carrots, celery), lettuce, cinnamon, miniature marshmallows, raisins, dry cereal, chow mein noodles, and shredded coconut. Display these ingredients, along with plenty of sliced bread, peanut butter, paper towels, and plastic knives, at an adult-supervised center. Each child visits the center and makes a peanut-butter sandwich to which he adds one or more fixin's. As students munch on their sandwiches, share this incredible fact: The average child in the United States will have eaten 1,500 peanut-butter sandwiches by the time he or she graduates from high school.

SOCIAL STUDIES

From Plant To Peanut Butter

So how do peanuts end up as peanut butter? This booklet-making project gives students the inside scoop! First have each student complete a copy of page 237 by following the provided directions. Then have each child cut out the boxes along the bold lines and stack the resulting pages in sequential order. Next give each child a 4" x 6" rectangle of brown construction paper. Ask each student to center his stack of pages on the rectangle. Staple each child's project near the top of the stack; then have him carefully trim the brown paper into a peanut shape. To create the front cover of his booklet, have the student trace his peanut shape onto a second rectangle of brown construction paper and cut along the resulting outline. Staple the front cover in place, and the booklet is assembled. Invite students to add details to the front and back covers as desired.

The Peanut-Butter Story
as told by No-Nut Peanut and
Daniel

READING

A Splendid Spread Of Books

These teacher resources are packed full of pertinent peanut facts!

The Life And Times Of The Peanut
Written & Illustrated by Charles Micucci
Houghton Mifflin Company, 1997

Peanut Butter
Written by Arlene Erlbach
Illustrated by Jackie Urbanovic
Lerner Publications Company, 1995

George Washington Carver
Written by Margo McLoone
Includes photographs
Capstone Press, 1997

The Peanut Butter Cookbook For Kids
Written by Judy Ralph and Ray Gompf
Illustrated by Craig Terlson
Hyperion Books For Children, 1995

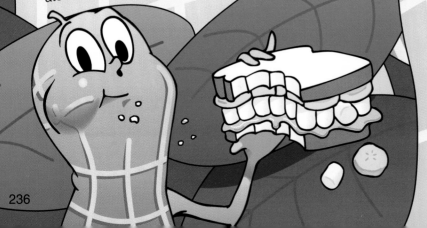

Directions:

Write your name on the line.

Read the sentences.

Number the boxes to show how peanuts become peanut butter.

Color the pictures.

The Peanut-Butter Story

as told by
No-Nut Peanut
and

_____
Name

There are peanuts growing under the ground.

The shelled peanuts are roasted in special ovens.

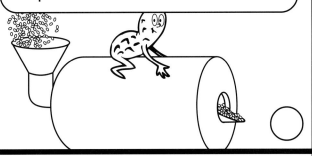

After lots and lots of mixing, the peanut butter is pumped into jars.

At a factory the peanuts are sorted by size. The smaller peanuts are shelled.

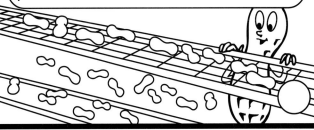

The roasted peanuts are crushed. Sugar, oil, and salt are mixed with them.

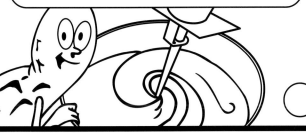

A farmer harvests the peanuts.

Note To Teacher: Use this page with "From Plant To Peanut Butter" on page 236.

'Tis The Season For...*Bunnies*

Hippity, hoppity! Celebrate the season with these carefully chosen "14-carrot" activities!
ideas contributed by Amy Barsanti—Gr. 2, Pines Elementary, Plymouth, NC

LANGUAGE ARTS

As Crunchy As A Carrot

Create an appetite for similes with this booklet-making project! On the chalkboard write "A bunny is _____ like a _____" and "A bunny is as _____ as a _____." Invite students to share a variety of similes by adding words to these sentences. Then give each child a copy of page 240 to complete. When the students are finished, instruct each child to stack her carrot-shaped cutouts so that the booklet cover is on top. Demonstrate how to join the cutouts by poking a brad through the black dots and ask each child to do the same. To make the top of the carrot, have each child cut a three-inch square of green paper into narrow strips and then glue one end of each strip to the back of her booklet. Too cute!

Bunny Business
by
Barry

CLASSROOM MANAGEMENT

Bunny Bucks

You can count on Bunny Bucks to keep your students hopping down a desirable bunny trail! Duplicate a colorful supply of the patterns on page 241 and cut them apart. Use the bucks to reward your students' good citizenship, tidiness, and outstanding work habits. Post a list of predetermined trade-in values for the bucks, and designate special days and times for redeeming them. If desired, have students personalize the bucks they earn. Then, when students redeem the bucks, void them and send them home so the youngsters can share their successes with their families.

SCIENCE

Bunny Homes

Promote critical-thinking skills with this bit of bunny business! Ask students to brainstorm similarities and differences between bunnies that live in captivity and ones that live in the wild. List the students' ideas in a Venn diagram like the one shown. Then have each student write and illustrate a story from a bunny's point of view that tells why the bunny prefers to live in captivity or in the wild. Bind the stories into a class book titled "Bunny Homes."

Bunnies
In The Wild — In Captivity
must find their food
have lots of enemies
are probably wild
are fluffy
hop
eat what people give them
are safe
may be tame

MATH

Carrot Estimates

Hop into estimation practice with this hands-on [activ]ity! For each student, wrap the wide end of a carro[t] [in] aluminum foil. Place paper plates, measuring cups, [a] large bowl, a few handheld graters, and the wrappe[d car]rots at an adult-supervised station. Have students vi[sit the] center in small groups. Each child estimates how mu[ch] grated carrot the unwrapped portion of his carrot will [make;] then he grates the carrot onto a paper plate. Next he [mea]sures the grated carrot to check his estimate and dep[osits it] in the large bowl. After each student has visited the [station,] use the grated carrots and the recipe below to make [a] salad for your busy bunnies to sample.

Carrot Salad
(makes 25–30 servings)
6 cups grated carrots
2 1/4 cups raisins
1 cup mayonnaise
Stir ingredients together in a large bow[l]

Bunny Tales

Keep your students' writing skills in tip-top shape with these student-made bunny journals. To make the journal cover, a student folds a 6" x 9" piece of brown or white construction paper in half to 4 1/2" x 6", trims away the bottom corners, and unfolds the paper. Next she staples a stack of 5 1/2" x 8 1/2" writing paper inside the cover and refolds the project. Lastly she cuts out ears and facial features from construction-paper scraps and glues them to the front cover of her journal as shown. Set aside time each day for students to write in their bunny journals. If desired, incorporate the following bunny-related prompts into your repertoire of writing activities:

- Write a tall tale about a bunny called Big Foot.
- Write a story about a bunny that can't hop.
- Describe three tricks you might teach a pet bunny.
- Writing from a bunny's point of view, tell how to find the juiciest carrot in a garden.

Hippity, Hoppity!

Here's a fun way to energize your cottontails and determine their favorite ways to hop! On the chalkboard write a student-generated list of hopping styles (like a right-foot hop, a left-foot hop, and a two-foot hop) and maneuvers (like hopping forward, backward, and in circles). Then take the students to an open area and have them try out the different hops under your direction. Challenge each child to choose a favorite hopping style and maneuver. When the youngsters are settled back in the classroom, have each one personalize two sticky notes. In turn, have each child attach both notes to the chalkboard—one beside his favorite hopping style and the other beside his favorite maneuver. Students are sure to enjoy interpreting the resulting graph and answering questions about it. Hop to it!

Characters Of Choice

This poster-making activity puts your youngsters' favorite bunny characters in the spotlight. Ask each child to illustrate his favorite bunny character on an eight-inch square of white paper and then glue his artwork near the top of a 12" x 18" sheet of drawing paper. Without revealing the corresponding book title, have him complete the following phrases about the bunny below its illustration: *lives…*, *likes…*, *hangs around with…* Lastly have each child draft a sentence that tells whom to contact if this bunny is found. Display the posters on a bulletin board titled "Missing Bunnies!" Students will be hopping to the library to solve these missing bunny mysteries! When a student is notified that his bunny character has been found, he makes a sign like the one shown and tapes it to his poster.

- lives with a family
- likes the juice of vegetables
- hangs around with a dog and a cat

If this bunny is found, please contact Mary.

This bunny was found in the book Bunnicula.

Bunny Books

Your youngsters will be all ears as you read aloud these bunny books!

Good Job, Oliver!
Written & Illustrated by Laurel Molk
Crown Publishers, Inc.; 1999

Rabbits & Raindrops
Written & Illustrated by Jim Arnosky
G. P. Putnam's Sons, 1997

Cottontail At Clover Crescent
Written by C. Drew Lamm
Illustrated by Allen Davis
Soundprints, 1995

Miss Penny And Mr. Grubbs
Written & Illustrated by Lisa Campbell Ernst
Aladdin Paperbacks, 1995

Order books on-line. www.themailbox.com

Name _____

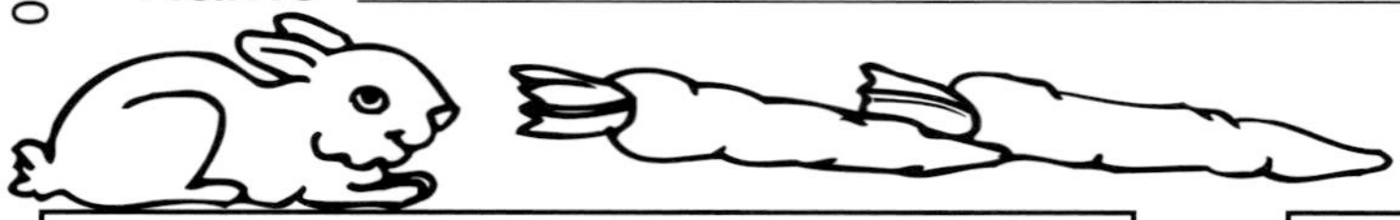

240

Bunny Business

Use orange to outline each carrot.

Cut out the carrots.

Fill in each blank.

Bunny Business
by _____

A bunny's nose is as _____
as a _____.

A bunny's foot is as _____
as a _____.

A bunny's tail is _____
like a _____.

A bunny is _____
like a _____.

A bunny's teeth are _____
like a _____.

Note To Teacher: Use with "As Crunchy As A Carrot" on page 238.

Play Ball!

A Winning Lineup For The End Of The Year

As the end of the school year draws near, keep your youngsters actively engaged in learning by bringing baseball into the classroom. With the following lineup of activities, you're sure to score a home run with your little sluggers. Batter up!

ideas by Cecelia Fister and Deborah L. Ross

A Winning Environment

Create a baseball atmosphere by having students arrange their desks in a semicircle to resemble stadium seating. Also display an assortment of baseball equipment around the classroom. Then, throughout the unit, assume the role of team manager. Dress casually—consider wearing a baseball hat and sneakers. Finally, remind students that with a team sport, such as baseball, the most important parts of the game are cooperation and good sportsmanship.

BASEBALL ALL-STAR

Name: Riley Boyle
Nickname: Slugger Boyle
Age: 7   Phone Number: 123-4567
Birthday: 1-8-92
Favorite food: pizza
Favorite hobby: playing video games
Winning play of the school year:
I have been at school every day this year.

Limited Edition Cards

Everyone knows that a baseball player's claim to fame is his baseball card—and that will be the case with your all-stars, too! Show students a few baseball cards, explaining that the cards give information such as a player's name, birthday, team, career highlights, and playing *statistics*—or how well he plays the game. Then give each student a copy of the open player card on page 247 and ask him to make a card about himself. To do this, the student trims a photo of himself and glues it inside the box. (If photos are not available, have students draw self-portraits.) Then he completes the information on the card.

Duplicate a class supply of each child's player card. Give each student a copy of his own card and each of his classmate's cards to cut out. Next give each child a resealable plastic bag. Suggest that he store his limited edition cards inside the bag to keep them in mint condition. See "Preseason Training" for different ways to use the cards.

242

Preseason Training

Shape up students for the playing season with the following review activities. Each student needs a class set of the baseball cards described in "Limited Edition Cards."

- **All-Star Alphabetizing:** Pair students and have each child select a designated number of baseball cards from his bag. Announce an alphabetizing method (by first name, last name, or nickname) and have each student alphabetize his cards. Then signal for each child to check his partner's work. Repeat the activity several times using a variety of cards and alphabetizing methods.

- **Three Cheers For Classification:** Challenge students to sort and classify their cards in a variety of ways. For example, by a player's age, favorite food, or favorite hobby.

- **Grand-Slam Graphing:** Draw a bar graph on the chalkboard. With students' input, select a subject from the baseball cards to graph. Label the graph accordingly. Next have each student tape her card in the appropriate column of the graph. After students have evaluated the resulting graph, have each child remove her card. Then repeat the activity with a different subject.

- **Preseason Hits:** Use this sequencing activity to reveal which student had the most hits during preseason training. For each baseball card, a student writes on her paper the player's name and the sum of the digits in his or her phone number. The player with the highest sum is the team's biggest preseason hitter!

- **World-Class Code:** Have players determine their uniform numbers with this addition activity. Post an alphabet code like the one shown. A student writes his player nickname on a sheet of paper and then he uses the code to assign a value to each letter. The sum of these values equals his uniform number.

World-Class Code

A–E = 5
F–J = 4
K–O = 3
P–T = 2
U–Z = 1

Planning The Season

With preseason training behind them, your youngsters will be ready to play ball! Use the activities on this page to create identities for a class team and several opposing teams, and to determine a playing schedule.

Creating A Team Identity

Before students collaborate on a team identity, invite them to bring from home memorabilia from other baseball teams. Set aside time for students to share the items they bring from home and tell about the teams they represent. Lead students to realize that the name of a major-league baseball team includes the city where the team is located, and that each team has a team color and a mascot. (For example, the Baltimore Orioles's mascot is the Oriole Bird.) Then, using your most successful strategy for making class decisions, help students select a team name, color, and mascot. Post this information on a chart and display it for everyone to see.

A Site To See!

If you have access to the Internet, be sure to visit the official major-league baseball Web site at http://www.majorleaguebaseball.com. This site features information about the current season as well as a link to each major-league baseball team's official Web site.

Pigsboro Piggies

Hometown: Pigsboro, NC
Mascot: Pig
Team Color: Orange

Wolftown Huff-'n'-Puffers

Hometown: Wolftown, PA
Mascot: Wolf
Team Color: Purple

Creating The Opponents

Every baseball team needs opponents and your class team is no exception! Decide how many game days you wish to schedule. (On each game day students participate in one or more baseball-related activities.) Then divide students into as many groups as there are game days and designate a recorder in each group. Give each recorder a sheet of paper, a pencil, and a United States map. To create the identity of an opposing team, a group chooses a city on the map. Then the group agrees upon a name, mascot, and color for the team. Ask each recorder to list this information on the provided paper. Next choose a spokesperson from each group to tell the class about the opponent his group created. Record this information on a chart like the one shown. Later use the charts to create a playing schedule. Post the schedule in a prominent classroom location. On each game day also post the opposing team's chart. No doubt students will be ready to step up to the plate on each game day!

Schedule For Pigsboro Piggies	
Opponent	Game Date
Wolftown Huff-'n'-Puffers	
Boston Beanstalk Giants	
Sherwood Forest Robins	
Nashville Neverland Bells	
Pittsburg Puppets	

Making Pennants For The Team

Students have completed preseason training, they're members of a class team, their team has opponents, and a playing schedule is posted. What's next? The making of team pennants, of course! Give each child a large pennant cutout to decorate in honor of her team. Suggest that she include the team's name and mascot in her design, and utilize the team color. Then promote team spirit by displaying the colorful pennants around the classroom. Also suggest that students wear the team color on game days. Hurrah for the team!

Pigsboro Piggies

Game Day Preparations

Prior to each game day, plan a lineup of baseball-related activities. Your plan might include reading aloud a picture book from "Major-League Literature" on page 246, several "Pregame Warm-Ups," and one or two "Grand Slams." Before your little sluggers arrive on game day, display the opposing team's information poster (from "Creating The Opponents" on page 243). Then, when appropriate, gather the team together and announce the lineup for the day. Not only will you cover the curriculum bases but you'll provide major-league fun, too!

Game Day Activities

Pick and choose from the activities below and on page 245 to create a lineup for each game day.

Pregame Warm-Ups

Each game day, limber up your players with a few brief activities that focus on the day's opponent. Conclude the workout with an inspirational pep talk and a team cheer.

- **Morning Stretches:** Lead students through several minutes of light stretching exercises as you discuss the day's opponent with them.
- **Where Oh Where?:** Have a student volunteer locate the opposing team's hometown on a map or globe. If desired, assist students in determining the mileage to that city or town.
- **Mapping A Route:** Ask students to determine the most efficient form of transportation for the opposing team to reach your city. Then help the students map a route the team can take to the game. Have students name the states and/or cities the team would travel through.

Grand Slams

Step out of the dugout and pitch one or two of these activities each game day.

The Pigsboro TIMES
Ms. Martin's class   June 7, 1999

Jake Siler Pitches a No-Hitter!

Jamie Kistler Hits 90!

Hall Of Fame

Tell students that they are being inducted into baseball's Hall of Fame! Ask each child to write a brief speech that tells about himself and his baseball career. Suggest that he include information like his playing position, the best play of his career, and the number of home runs he's hit to date. When the projects are finished, pair students and have the partners exchange papers. Then ask each student to introduce his partner. If desired, provide a microphone prop for the student speakers to use. Be sure to lead a round of applause for each inductee!

The Playbook

Challenge the class to make a book of playing strategies for next year's class. Have students brainstorm tips for how to learn and succeed in your classroom. List the students' responses on the chalkboard. Have each child select a different strategy from the board. Then give each child a white paper circle. Have him copy the sentence starter "You will always score a home run with [your name] when you…," and complete it with his strategy. Bind the students' work between two white construction-paper circles. Draw red stitching on the resulting front cover (to resemble a baseball) and add the title "The Playbook For _____ Grade." Plan to share this enlightening book with your new class in the fall.

Hot Off The Press!

Have each youngster write and illustrate a newspaper article describing a game in which she breaks a baseball record (by hitting the most home runs during the season, pitching the most strikes in a game, etc.). To publish the students' works, mount the projects on a series of newspaper pages. Decorate the front page of the resulting newspaper to show the title "The [team's hometown] Times," the date, and a class byline. Laminate the pages for durability; then place the publication in your class library. Extra! Extra! Read all about it!

All-Star Fan Clubs

Thrill the team by asking each child to make a king-size membership card for her personal fan club. Then thrill them again by letting the students sign their classmates' cards! To make her card, a student writes "Official Members Of [student's name] Fan Club" on a 7" x 11" sheet of tagboard and then decorates the membership card as desired. Next she turns her card over and writes her name on the back, near the top. To begin the signing, establish a route for students to follow that takes each child to every classmate's desk. Instruct each student to leave her card on her desk. Then, on your signal, have her move to her first stop along the route, taking a pencil or fine-tipped marker with her. Allow time for students to sign their names; then signal them to move to the next stop and sign their names. Continue in this manner until each student has signed every classmate's card and then returned to her desk. If desired, temporarily collect the cards so you can laminate them for durability. Then send the cards home with the students. What a positive way to end a great year!

Major-League Milestones

Help students showcase their achievements from the past school year on keepsake awards. On the chalkboard, write a list of sentence starters that prompt students to reflect on the past school year. Consider starters such as "The most difficult thing I learned…," "I feel proud that…," "I learned how to…," and "I am really good at…." To make an award, a child copies and completes each of four different sentence starters on a 1" x 7" paper strip, leaving a margin at each end of the strip. Next she writes "[student's name]'s Accomplishments" and the dates of the school year on a 4 1/2-inch white circle. She glues this circle atop a colorful and slightly larger construction-paper circle. Then she scallops the outer edges of the larger circle. To assemble her award, she glues one end of each strip to the back of the circle. Now that's a lasting reminder of a winning season!

Betsy's Accomplishments 1998–1999

Batter Up!

Invite students to take a swing at logic problems! To do this, have each child complete a copy of page 248. Or, if desired, lead the class through the activity. Then challenge each student to use her collection of baseball cards (from "Limited Edition Cards" on page 242) to create similar problems for her classmates to solve.

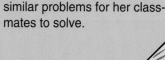

Pennant Pride

Have each all-star player highlight his winning plays of the school year on a personalized pennant! On the chalkboard, write a student-generated list of favorite events, activities, projects, and visitors from the past school year. To create a personalized pennant, a student writes "[student's name]'s Winning Plays Of The Season" on a large pennant cutout. Then he describes and illustrates his favorite memories, referring to the class list as needed. Exhibit the pennants in the hallway for passersby to admire.

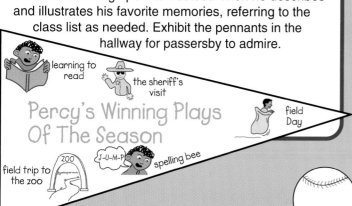

learning to read
the sheriff's visit
Percy's Winning Plays Of The Season
field Day
field trip to the zoo
J-U-M-P
spelling bee

Answer Key For "Batter Up!"

Game 1 Batting Order:
1. Lefty
2. Slugger
3. Slim
4. Flash

Game 2 Batting Order:
1. Flash
2. Slugger
3. Slim
4. Lefty

Game 3 Batting Order:
1. Flash
2. Slugger
3. Lefty
4. Slim

Game 4 Batting Order:
1. Slim
2. Lefty
3. Flash
4. Slugger

Clevell Harris

Winding Down The Playing Season

As the playing season draws to a close, create a game plan for summer *and* celebrate the winning efforts of your all-star players!

Summer Reading In A Nutshell

Rely on your most valuable reading resource, your students, to assist the team in fielding individual summer reading lists. Give each player a couple of days to choose a favorite book from the school year and write its title and author on a personalized paper strip. Collect these strips. When you have a class collection, give each child a red and white peanut bag and one or more sets of the peanut patterns on page 247. One at a time, display the book titles you've collected and ask the student who recommended the book to tell his teammates something about it. If a student thinks he wants to read the book, he copies the information on a peanut shape. When the presentations are finished, each player cuts out his programmed peanuts and places them inside his bag. Encourage students to take their bags home and dig into them throughout the summer!

Off-Season Training

Keep your players' minds in shape this summer with a list of student-approved activities. As a group, brainstorm a list of things to do during summer vacation. Write the students' suggestions on the chalkboard. Later type the list and duplicate it on colorful paper. Give each player a flyer of summertime activities to take home. Now that's a winning play that's sure to strike out summertime boredom.

An All-Star Celebration

As a grand finale, host a celebration to honor your little sluggers. Hold an autographing session during which players may ask teammates to sign their Limited Edition player cards from preseason training. Serve traditional baseball snacks like popcorn and peanuts, and distribute any awards you've prepared for the all-stars. Top off the festivities with a rousing rendition of "Take Me Out To The Ball Game."

Major-League Literature

Step up to the plate and hit a grand slam with this unbeatable collection of baseball-related literature. It's sure to help spread baseball fever throughout your class!

Picture Books

Moon Ball
Written by Jane Yolen
Illustrated by Greg Couch
Simon & Schuster Books For Young Readers, 1999

The Bat Boy & His Violin
Written by Gavin Curtis
Illustrated by E. B. Lewis
Simon & Schuster Books For Young Readers, 1998

The Baseball Counting Book
Written by Barbara McGrath
Illustrated by Brian Shaw
Charlesbridge Publishing, Inc.; 1999

Playing Right Field
Written by Willy Welch
Illustrated by Marc Simont
Scholastic Inc., 1995

Take Me Out To The Ballgame
Original Lyrics by Jack Norworth
Illustrated by Alec Gillman
Aladdin Paperbacks, 1999

Order books on-line. www.themailbox.com

Home Run: The Story Of Babe Ruth
Written by Robert Burleigh
Illustrated by Mike Wimmer
Harcourt Brace & Company, 1998

Lou Gehrig: The Luckiest Man
Written by David A. Adler
Illustrated by Terry Widener
Gulliver Books®, 1997

Resources For The Teacher

Game Day: Behind The Scenes At A Ballpark
Written by Robert Young
Photographed by Jerry Wachter
Carolrhoda Books, Inc.; 1998

The Young Baseball Player
Written by Ian Smyth
Includes photographs
Dorling Kindersley Publishing, Inc.; 1998

Take Me Out To The Bat And Ball Factory
Written by Peggy Thomson
Illustrated by Gloria Kamen
Albert Whitman & Company, 1998

BASEBALL ALL-STAR

Name: _____

Nickname: _____

Age: _____ Phone number: _____

Birthday: _____

Favorite food: _____

Favorite hobby: _____

Winning play of the school year:

_____
_____
_____
_____
_____

©1999 The Education Center, Inc.

BASEBALL ALL-STAR

Name: _____

Nickname: _____

Age: _____ Phone number: _____

Birthday: _____

Favorite food: _____

Favorite hobby: _____

Winning play of the school year:

_____
_____
_____
_____
_____

©1999 The Education Center, Inc.

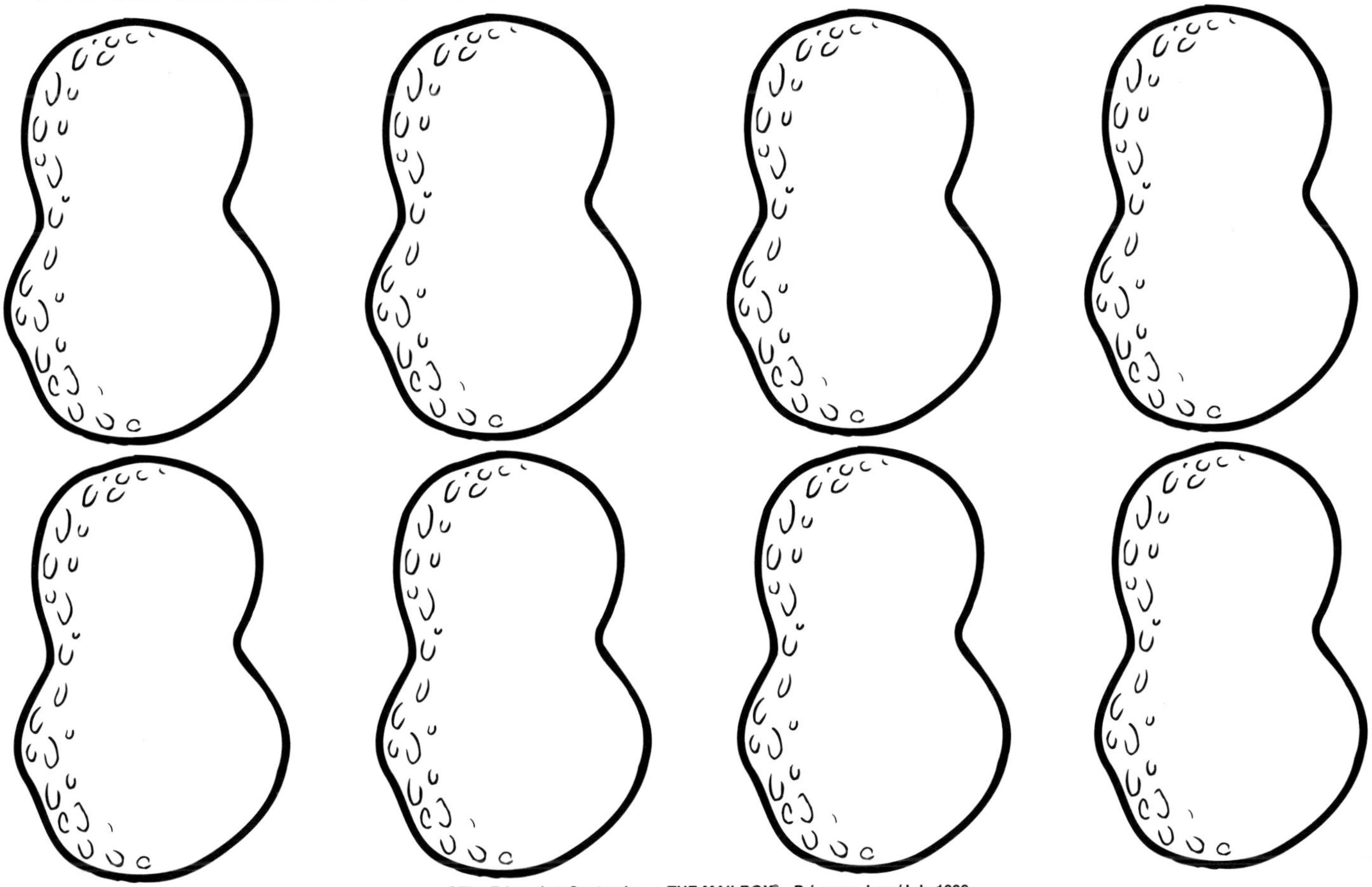

Note To Teacher: Use the player cards with "Limited Edition Cards" on page 242. Duplicate the peanut patterns on tan construction paper for use with "Summer Reading In A Nutshell" on page 246.

Batter Up!

Color and cut out the baseball cards.
Write the batting order for each game.
Use the clues.

Game 1:
- Flash bats right behind Slim.
- No one bats before Lefty.
- Slugger does not bat last.

Game 2:
- Slim is not the last batter.
- No one bats before Flash.
- Slugger bats between the first and the third batter.

Game 3:
- Everyone bats before Slim.
- Lefty bats right before Slim.
- Flash bats first.

Game 4:
- Flash bats between the second and the fourth batter.
- Slugger bats after Flash.
- Lefty is not the first batter.

Game 1 Batting Order:

1. _____

2. _____

3. _____

4. _____

Game 2 Batting Order:

1. _____

2. _____

3. _____

4. _____

Game 3 Batting Order:

1. _____

2. _____

3. _____

4. _____

Game 4 Batting Order:

1. _____

2. _____

3. _____

4. _____

Slim

Flash

Slugger

Lefty

On A Roll With Marbles!

Use this collection of cross-curricular ideas to give your end-of-the-year activities a creative spin!

ideas contributed by Stacie Stone Davis

Marble Chatter

Young and old have been playing marble games for thousands and thousands of years. To get the lowdown on the history of the game, different types of marbles and playing surfaces, marble lingo, and 101 playing options, investigate *Marbles: 101 Ways To Play* by Joanna Cole and Stephanie Calmenson (A Beech Tree Paperback Book, 1998). Clear, detailed instructions and clever illustrations make it the perfect choice for beginning *mibsters* (marble players) and there's a good chance that marble pros will want this book for *keepsies,* too!

Taking Aim

Keep your students' interest in reading alive and rolling with this motivational idea. On a carpet sample or in a carpeted area of the classroom, use masking or colored tape to make a gameboard of four graduated squares. Label the perimeter of each square as shown. Then give each child a copy of the reading record on page 254. Each time a student reads a book, he writes its title on his record sheet. After he tells you about the book, he shoots a marble onto the gameboard. The square in which his marble lands determines how many points he scores. Each week announce a different prize or privilege that 100 or more points earns. When a child redeems his record sheet, give him a new one. For easy management, designate a time each day when you or an adult volunteer will listen to book summaries and provide marbles for shooting. Roll on!

Sue Dwars, Griffith, IN

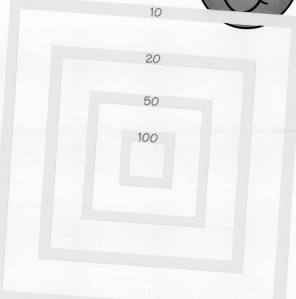

10
20
50
100

Marbles!

Students think this spelling review is simply "marble-ous" and you will too! To play this large-group game, have students sit in a circle, facing inward. Designate the first player of the game and announce a spelling word. This player says the first letter of the word. The player to his left says the second letter of the word, and so on. If a player miscalls a letter, he stands up. When this occurs, call the word again and restart the process with the next player in the circle. After a word is spelled, the next player in turn states the word. The following player declares "Marbles!" and stands up. Announce another spelling word and continue play as described. A player who is standing continues to play and may be seated once he supplies a correct letter. Your youngsters' spelling skills are sure to stay in fine form!

adapted from an idea by Wendy Chastain—Gr. 3
Woodrow Wilson Elementary School, Rapid City, SD

Marbles!

Memorable Math

Introduce this unique math review and you'll receive an enthusiastic response from your youngsters—even though they may think you've lost your marbles! Make a copy of " 'Marble-ous' Math" on page 252. Program each blank rectangle with several addition, subtraction, multiplication, and/or division problems for students to solve. Also program number five with the name of the school principal or a staff member and a corresponding location. (If desired, supply this person with a container of wrapped candies and ask him to present a candy to each child when she provides the correct answer to the corresponding problem.) Then duplicate a class supply of the page and give each child a copy to complete. Now that's a memorable math activity!

Mary C. Barron—Gr. 3, Morningside Elementary, Twin Falls, ID

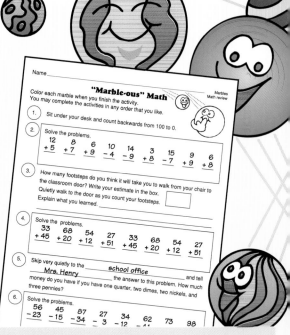

Name_____

"Marble-ous" Math

Marbles
Math review

Color each marble when you finish the activity.
You may complete the activities in any order that you like.

1. Sit under your desk and count backwards from 100 to 0.

2. Solve the problems.

12	8	6	10	14	3	15	9	6
+ 5	+ 7	+ 9	− 4	− 9	+ 8	− 7	+ 9	+ 8

3. How many footsteps do you think it will take you to walk from your chair to the classroom door? Write your estimate in the box. Quietly walk to the door as you count your footsteps. Explain what you learned.

4. Solve the problems.

33	68	54	27	33	68	54	27
+ 45	+ 20	+ 12	+ 51	+ 45	+ 20	+ 12	+ 51

5. Skip very quietly to the __Mrs. Henry__ __school office__ and tell the answer to this problem. How much money do you have if you have one quarter, two dimes, two nickels, and three pennies?

6. Solve the problems.

56	45	87	27	34	62	73	98
− 23	− 15	− 34	− 3	− 12			

Marbleized Masterpieces

Students will have a ball rendering masterpieces from rolling marbles. Partially fill each of four plastic cups with a different color of tempera paint. Place one marble and a plastic spoon in each cup. Lay a 12" x 18" sheet of construction paper in the inverted lid of a sturdy box (like one in which copy paper is delivered). Using the provided spoon, remove one marble from a cup and place it on the paper. Repeatedly tilt the box lid back and forth, causing the marble to leave trails of paint on the paper. Carefully return the marble to its paint cup. Repeat the procedure with the same marble. Or, to create contrasting trails, remove a marble from another paint cup and repeat the procedure. Continue in this manner until a desired effect is achieved. When the paint trails are dry, cut an abstract shape from the paper, glue the cutout to a contrasting color of construction paper, and then trim the paper as desired. Or trace a seven-inch tagboard circle onto the project twice and cut along the resulting outlines. Use the resulting journal covers with "A Mixed Bag" on this page.

A Mixed Bag

Add some zip and zing to your writing center with a mixed bag of marble-related writing prompts. Write several prompts like the one shown on individual cards. Place the prompts in a zippered bag. Store the bag, pencils, crayons, and a supply of circular writing paper at a center. A student chooses a marble and completes the writing activity on the provided paper. Or have each child make a writing journal in which to complete the activities. To make her journal, she staples a supply of circular writing paper between the covers she created in "Marbleized Masterpieces." Have each child personalize the first page of her writing journal and then complete the writing activities on the remaining pages. Either way, everyone's a winner at this writing center!

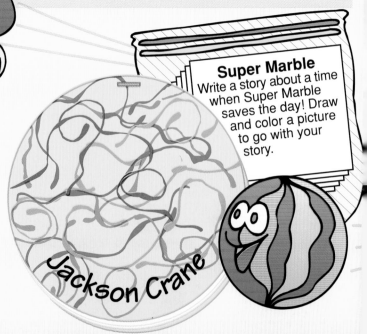

Super Marble
Write a story about a time when Super Marble saves the day! Draw and color a picture to go with your story.

Jackson Crane

On A Roll!

Watch students knuckle down for this end-of-the-year review! Duplicate two copies of the open gameboard on page 253. Program the open spaces on each gameboard with a different set of review challenges. Then duplicate each version of the gameboard for one-half of your students. Pair students and give each twosome one copy of each gameboard version, a coin, two white construction-paper circles about the size of marbles, and a large zippered bag. Each child colors one game marker and one gameboard. Then each pair chooses one gameboard and begins play. When the winner of this game is determined, the twosome plays a second game using its other gameboard. Each pair continues alternating play between its two gameboards until game time is over. Then have each pair store its gameboards, markers, and coin in the zippered bag. Place the bags at a center and invite students to play the games during free time with a variety of partners.

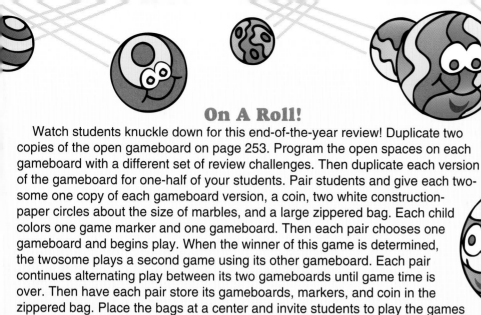

Pam Crane

I remember when Mr. Gulf talked to us about bats.

I remember when Chad brought his goat to school.

I remember when we painted snowflakes on the windows.

I remember when I won an award for coming to school every day!

I remember when Mrs. Davis read us Stone Fox.

I remember when Mr. Field sat on the roof of the school because we read so many books. He was so funny!

Marbles And Memories

For this activity, marbles hold a multitude of memories. Ask students to think about their favorite events, activities, and projects from the past school year. Then have them sit in a large circle on the floor. Give one child a marble. Ask him to describe a favorite memory for the class and then carefully roll the marble to a classmate. This child shares a memory and then rolls the marble to a different classmate. Continue the activity until every child has participated one or more times. Then have the students return to their desks as you distribute five-inch, white, construction-paper circles. Challenge each child to use his crayons or markers to write his favorite memories from the past year on his cutout in such a way that he designs a one-of-a-kind marble. Mount the marbles on a bulletin board titled "These Marbly Memories Are For Keepsies!"

Marble Contraptions

Creativity and problem-solving skills will be on a roll when students build marble contraptions! First have students observe as you build a simple marble track. To do this, fold a few strips of tagboard in half and tape the resulting chutes together. Elevate one end of the track to create a slope. Insert the other end of the track into a cardboard tube. At the opposite end of the tube place a domino and behind it a three-ounce paper cup. Explain to students that you hope to drop a marble onto the start of the track and have it end up inside the cup. Invite their predictions and then test the contraption you've built. Next ask students how to improve your contraption. Make adjustments based on their suggestions and retest the project.

When appropriate, invite students to build their own marble contraptions! Allow each child to work independently, with a partner, or with a group. Supply marbles, masking tape, and a supply of paper scraps, paper tubes, and craft sticks. Invite students to bring from home additional building supplies for their projects. Set aside time on each of several days for students to build and fine-tune their contraptions. Then, on a predetermined date, have students present their projects to the class. Let the good times roll!

"Marble-ous" Math

Color each marble when you finish the activity.
You may complete the activities in any order that you like.

1. Sit under your desk and count backwards from 100 to 0.

2. Solve the problems.

3. How many footsteps do you think it will take you to walk from your chair to the classroom door? Write your estimate in the box.
Quietly walk to the door as you count your footsteps.
Explain what you learned. _____

_____

4. Solve the problems.

5. Skip very quietly to the _____ and tell
_____ the answer to this problem. How much
money do you have if you have one quarter, two dimes, two nickels, and
three pennies?

6. Solve the problems.

Bonus Box: On the back of this paper write one reason why you liked (or did not like) this math activity.

©The Education Center, Inc. • THE MAILBOX® • Primary • June/July 1999

On A Roll!

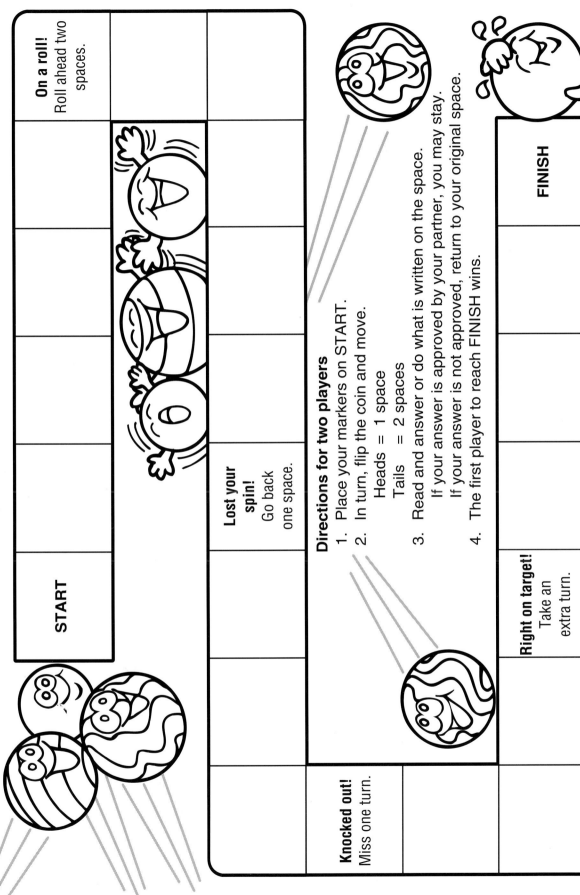

On a roll!
Roll ahead two spaces.

START

Lost your spin!
Go back one space.

Knocked out!
Miss one turn.

Right on target!
Take an extra turn.

FINISH

Directions for two players
1. Place your markers on START.
2. In turn, flip the coin and move.
   Heads = 1 space
   Tails = 2 spaces
3. Read and answer or do what is written on the space.
   If your answer is approved by your partner, you may stay.
   If your answer is not approved, return to your original space.
4. The first player to reach FINISH wins.

Note To Teacher: Use with "On A Roll!" on page 251.

Name _____

On A Roll With Reading!

Each time you read a book, complete a marble.
   Write the book title in the blank space.
   Write the points you score in the box.

You're On A Roll!

Simply "Marble-ous!"

You Aim To Please!

You're On A Roll!

Simply "Marble-ous!"

You Aim To Please!

Note To Teacher: Use the reading record with "Taking Aim" on page 249. Duplicate and present the awards to students as desired.

BUILDING CHARACTER

BUILDING CHARACTER
WITH...RESPECT!

Encourage respect among your students with this unique collection of learning activities. You'll be reinforcing positive behaviors and your youngsters will soon see respect as a valued trait in your classroom.

ideas by Darcy Brown

RESPECT

Respect is following the rules.

Respectful Reminders

Introduce the meaning of *respect* with these good-as-gold reminders. Begin by asking students to discuss the Golden Rule: *Treat others the way you would like to be treated.* Tell students that when they follow the Golden Rule, they are being respectful and considerate of others and themselves. Next have students name ways they show respect. Then have each youngster make a badge to remind himself (and others) of respectful behaviors. To make a badge, have each child write one way to show respect on a four-inch tagboard circle. Next have him use glue and gold glitter to decorate his badge. When the glue is dry, have the student tape a large safety pin to the back of his badge. Invite your youngsters to wear their badges as respectful reminders throughout your unit of study.

At home I listen to Mom and Dad.
At Home
At School
In Public

Who's Respectful?

Here's an ideal way to help students understand that showing respect is the first step towards practicing it. Tell your students they can show respect by using good manners. Then read aloud your favorite book about manners. One excellent choice is *Perfect Pigs* by Marc Brown and Stephen Krensky (Little, Brown And Company; 1983). The book's simple text and colorful pictures portray a wide variety of respectful behaviors. Next invite each student to make a flip booklet that shows how she uses good manners. To make a booklet, instruct each youngster to stack two 8 1/2" x 11" sheets of white paper and hold the pages vertically in front of her. Have her slide the top sheet upward approximately one inch. Next direct the youngster to fold the papers forward to create four graduated pages (see the illustration). Have her write the title "Who's Respectful? [Child's name] Is!" and her name on the cover. Then, on the pages, have the youngster write and illustrate how she exhibits good manners at home, at school, and in public. Your students will be flipping over respectful behaviors!

RESPECT

Portraits Of Respect

Promote student dignity and self-respect with one-of-a-kind portraits! Explain to your students that when they have a good attitude, make good decisions, and always do their best, they are showing self-respect. Challenge each youngster to name one way she shows self-respect. Then foster self-respect in your students when you invite them to make portraits of themselves. To make a portrait, have each youngster trace a large oval template on a 9" x 12" sheet of drawing paper. Then have her draw a portrait of herself inside the oval. Instruct her to cut out the oval and glue it to a 9" x 12" sheet of construction paper. Next have the student write about self-respect on a sheet of writing paper; then instruct her to attach her sentences to the bottom of her portrait. Have each youngster share her portrait and sentences with her classmates. Display the portraits around the room to remind your students that self-respect begins with them.

I am a good listener.
I follow the rules.

R E S P E C T

256

Respecting Differences

Convey to your students that respect means treating others the way they would want to be treated—regardless of their differences. To begin, have each youngster name something he likes. Then ask students if they all had the same response. Explain that sometimes people tend to like different things, yet they should all be treated with the same respect. Then ask students to name other ways they may be different from one another. (For instance, students may have different cultural backgrounds, abilities, and appearances.) Next have your students work together to create a mural that honors the differences among people. First have each student cut pictures from catalogs, magazines, and store circulars of different people participating in a variety of activities. Then have the students glue their pictures to a large sheet of bulletin-board paper. Mount the mural under the heading "We Respect Each Other's Differences." What a great way for students to learn to respect one another!

Pledge Of Respect

Wrap up your study of respect by having youngsters make a pledge to respect themselves and each other. Review the different aspects of respect. Copy the pledge shown onto white paper and duplicate one for each student. Read the pledge aloud as your class follows along. Then have students talk about what the pledge means. Next challenge each student to memorize the pledge. If desired, expand the value of respect by having youngsters recite the pledge as part of your morning routine.

Karyn McCroskey—Gr. 2
Pleasant Hope Elementary
Pleasant Hope, MO

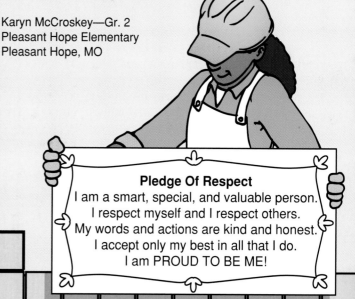

Pledge Of Respect
I am a smart, special, and valuable person.
I respect myself and I respect others.
My words and actions are kind and honest.
I accept only my best in all that I do.
I am PROUD TO BE ME!

RESPECT

Two Thumbs-Up!

Your youngsters will give two thumbs-up as they learn about respectful and disrespectful behaviors. As a review, have your students name respectful and disrespectful behaviors; then ask them to describe the possible outcomes of each one. Next read aloud a type of behavior. Have each student display two thumbs-up if the behavior is respectful or two thumbs-down if the behavior is disrespectful. Continue in the same manner until each student has an understanding of respectful and disrespectful behaviors. Extend the lesson by presenting each youngster with a "Thumbs-Up" reward (see illustration) when you observe him displaying a respectful behavior.

Josh
student's name
deserves a thumbs-up for helping Ashley finish her work.

Books About Respect

Foster respect in your students when you share these delightful stories.

How To Lose All Your Friends
Written & Illustrated by Nancy Carlson
Viking Penguin, 1997

Jamaica's Find
Written by Juanita Havill
Illustrated by Anne Sibley O'Brien
Houghton Mifflin Company, 1986

Make Someone Smile And 40 More Ways To Be A Peaceful Person
Written by Judy Lalli
Photographed by Douglas L. Mason-Fry
Free Spirit Publishing Inc., 1996

Mufaro's Beautiful Daughters
Written & Illustrated by John Steptoe
Lothrop, Lee & Shepherd Books; 1987

The Patchwork Quilt
Written by Valerie Flournoy
Illustrated by Jerry Pinkney
Dial Books For Young Readers, 1985

The Wednesday Surprise
Written by Eve Bunting
Illustrated by Donald Carrick
Houghton Mifflin Company, 1989

BUILDING CHARACTER
WITH...TRUSTWORTHINESS!

Dependable, responsible, and honorable. Reliable, faithful, and honest. Each of these behaviors contributes to trustworthiness. So what exactly is trustworthiness? Use these character-building activities to promote a better understanding of this very important virtue.

ideas contributed by Amy Erickson

Getting Started

Begin your investigation into trustworthiness by inviting students to name people—such as family members, friends, and community members—whom they trust and rely upon. Ask students to explain why they feel they can count on these people. On chart paper note key words and phrases from the students' explanations that describe trustworthy traits like "on time," "honest," and "cares about me." Lead students to understand that the trustworthy traits they admire in others are the same traits that will enable others to put their trust in them. Then invite students to describe ways in which they display the traits that are listed on the chart paper. Look who's trustworthy now!

First-Class Folks

Reinforce trustworthy behaviors by showcasing the folks your students count on the most! Ask each child to write the name of a person he depends on, and one or more sentences about this person, on a five-inch square of blank paper. Then have each student create a likeness of the person he has named and described. To do this the student cuts a seven-inch circle and a 3 1/2-inch circle from skin-toned paper. He adds facial features and hair to the larger circle using supplies such as crayons, markers, construction-paper scraps, yarn, and glue; then he cuts the smaller circle in half to make two semi-circular hands. To make a long-sleeved shirt or blouse, the student glues two 4 1/2" x 12" construction-paper strips to a 9" x 12" sheet. Next he glues the hand and head cutouts to the paper clothing. Lastly he glues his writing on the front of the clothing, then glues the hands to the writing as shown. Display the completed projects on a bulletin board titled "People We Can Count On!"

Mr. Bartlett

Mr. Bartlett works in the post office. I depend on him to deliver the mail.

258

Character Study

Children's literature is an excellent place to find examples of trustworthy and untrustworthy characters. Prepare a four-column chart like the one shown; then read aloud a story that includes at least one trustworthy and/or untrustworthy character (see "Trustworthy Titles" on page 259 for reading suggestions). Discuss the story with students; then enlist their help in completing the relevant information on the chart. Repeat this activity with as many different books as desired. Conclude each activity by challenging students to look for patterns in how problems originate and are resolved in the stories the class has critiqued thus far. You can depend on this ongoing activity to build a better understanding of trustworthiness!

Title	Trustworthy Characters	Untrustworthy Characters	Problem	Solution
Too Many Tomales	Mama	Maria	Maria and her cousins ate all the tomales.	Maria helpe her mom an aunt make mo
Strega Nona	Strega Nona	Big Anthony	Strega Nona	Anthony ate

Trusty Students

Bring your students' trustworthy behaviors into the limelight with this book-making project. To begin, ask youngsters to brainstorm ways that they demonstrate trustworthiness at school, such as faithfully completing classroom jobs, being honest, and coming to school prepared. List the students' ideas on the chalkboard. Then have each child write on precut paper the following sentence starter: "We can depend on [student's name] to…." Ask each child to complete the sentence about herself, then illustrate her work. Provide time for each child to proudly share her work; then compile the pages into a class book titled "The Trusty Students Of Room [number]." This special book will quickly become a class favorite!

We can depend on Dina to do her homework.

Homework

A Daily Dose

Each morning salute your students' trustworthiness with a version of this snappy song. To create additional verses, replace "trustworthy" with other desired adjectives like "dependable," "reliable," "responsible," and "honest." You can count on your students to be inspired *and* beaming with pride throughout the day.

You Can Depend On Us!
(sung to the tune of "For He's A Jolly Good Fellow")
Oh, we are <u>trustworthy</u> children.
Oh, we are <u>trustworthy</u> children.
Oh, we are <u>trustworthy</u> children,
And you can depend on us!

Top Ten Tips

Promote trustworthiness with a top ten list. Remind students that to gain the trust of others, they must be trustworthy at all times. Divide students into small groups and have each group brainstorm ten tips for building trustworthiness. Compile the lists and remove any duplications. Then, by student vote, determine the students' top ten tips. Copy the resulting list onto a length of white bulletin-board paper labeled "Top Ten Tips For Building Trustworthiness." Have students use colorful markers to autograph the outer edges of the resulting poster; then display the colorful reminder in a prominent classroom location.

Sam   Maria   Matthew

**Top Ten Tips
For
Building Trustworthiness**

1. Always tell the truth.
2. Be dependable.
3. Keep your word.
4. Follow directions.
5. Be honest.
6. Make good choices.
7. Never try to get away with anything.
8. Be respectful of others.
9. Believe in yourself!
10. Be consistent.

Marcella

Fiona

Jackson

Breyanna   Ben

TRUSTWORTHINESS

Book Buddies

What better way to reinforce trustworthy behavior than to have your students put it into practice? And a book-buddy program can do just that! Buddy up each of your students with a younger child in a colleague's class; then arrange for your students to read aloud to their buddies each week. Remind students that their younger buddies are counting on them to deliver fun reading experiences. Encourage them to be well prepared and to read with plenty of expression. After each visit, ask each child in your class to evaluate his buddy experience and to share one highlight from it with his classmates. Your class will quickly realize that the younger buddies look forward to the weekly visits and depend on their older buddies to be enthusiastic and well prepared. As your youngsters' recognition of their trustworthy behavior grows, so will their self-esteem!

Trustworthy Titles

You can count on these popular tales to strengthen your students' understanding of what is—and what is not—trustworthy behavior!

The Principal's New Clothes
Written by Stephanie Calmenson
Illustrated by Denise Brunkus
Scholastic Inc., 1991

Strega Nona
Retold & Illustrated by Tomie dePaola
Simon & Schuster Children's Division, 1997

Horton Hatches The Egg
Written & Illustrated by Dr. Seuss
Random House Books For Young Readers, 1966

Too Many Tamales
Written by Gary Soto
Illustrated by Ed Martinez
PaperStar Books, 1996

The Frog Princess
Written by Laura Cecil
Illustrated by Emma Chichester Clark
Greenwillow Books, 1995

The Frog Prince
Retold by Edith H. Tarcov
Illustrated by James Marshall
Scholastic Inc., 1993

BUILDING CHARACTER
WITH...GENEROSITY!

Lending a listening ear, giving a special present, and assisting someone in need—what do these acts of kindness have in common? They are all forms of generosity. Promote this unselfish quality with these thoughtful classroom activities!

ideas by Amy Erickson

Generosity Is…

Get to the heart of generosity! Display a large heart-shaped piece of bulletin-board paper that you have labeled "Generosity." Tell students that *generosity* means showing kindness without expecting anything in return. Explain that some people also define it as a big or kind heart. Ask youngsters to brainstorm examples of generosity as you record their ideas on the paper heart. Display the completed heart for all to see.

giving a Christmas present

sharing my lunch

Generosity

teaching my little sister how to ride a bike

sending a Hanukkah card to Grandma

clearing the table without being asked

More About Generosity

The booklet-making activity on page 268 will surely strengthen your youngsters' understanding of generosity. Write the following words on the chalkboard: *new, friend, pie,* and *card.* Read the words with students; then instruct each youngster to use these words to complete the sentences on his copy of page 268. Next have each student color each booklet page and cut it out along the thick lines, then stack and staple his pages in order. With this booklet of caring deeds, students will surely take the topic of generosity to heart!

The Reward Of Giving

Happiness comes from performing acts of kindness, as well as being the recipient of such acts. *Alejandro's Gift* by Richard E. Albert (Chronicle Books, 1996) provides an endearing example of this truth. Alejandro is a lonely desert farmer who selflessly works long and hard to provide a water supply for desert animals. When the animals use his gift of water, Alejandro realizes that he has received a gift too—happiness in knowing that he has helped others. Read aloud this heartwarming story; then lead your students in a discussion about how Alejandro felt before (and after) he made the water holes. Next share the factual information about desert animals found at the end of the book. Finally, using *Alejandro's Gift* as a model, have each student write and illustrate a story in which a desert animal gives a gift to Alejandro. Remind each student to include in his story how both Alejandro and the animal feel in the end.

GENEROSITY

Generosity Gems

Generosity doesn't necessarily involve store-bought presents. Try some of these selfless activities with students to show them that time, caring, and a helping hand are valued and priceless gifts too.

- Schedule regular class visits to a local nursing home. Have youngsters bring along some of their favorite books to enjoy with the residents.
- Spruce up the school office, entryway, or cafeteria with the students' seasonal artwork.
- Devote time to the upkeep of the school with a class project, such as washing windows or picking up litter from the school grounds.
- With their parents' permission, have youngsters bring to school canned food items for a donation to a local food bank.
- Establish a class buddy system to welcome and orient new students to your school.

Gift Book Of Wishes

Creating a thoughtful book of wishes is a great way for a youngster to show someone she cares! To make a booklet, a student begins with a stack of 6 1/2" x 4 1/2" drawing-paper rectangles that are stapled along one long side. On the first page she writes the poem shown. On each remaining page she draws and labels something she would like to give to a loved one, such as a week's vacation, a sporty new car, or a trip to see a relative. Next she glues a 7" x 10" tagboard rectangle onto a slightly larger piece of wrapping paper, being especially careful to apply glue close to the tagboard edges. When the glue is dry, she trims away the excess wrapping paper, folds the tagboard in half, and staples her pages inside the resulting cover. Finally, she uses a gift tag and ribbon to decorate the front of her booklet as desired. You can be sure that making, giving, *and* receiving this gift will be a rewarding experience!

Turn the page,
Just look and see.
Gifts I wish
For you from me.

To Mom
From Emily

a trip to see
Aunt Melissa

Giving Box

Wrap up each day by recognizing your students' generosity! Separately cover a shoebox and its lid with wrapping paper. In the center of the lid, carefully cut a slit approximately three inches long. Place the lid on the box, label the box as shown, and place it in an area easily accessible to students. When a student observes a classmate being generous, he writes a short note about his observation on a slip of paper and deposits it in the box. At the end of the day, read aloud the notes inside the box. Present each note to the recognized student; then return the box to its designated location. No doubt youngsters will treasure the complimentary gifts inside this unique package!

Giving Box

A Generous Helping Of Great Literature

From the youngsters about to enjoy a snack in *The Doorbell Rang,* to the proud and vain fish in *The Rainbow Fish,* the characters in these selections provide wonderful examples of generosity.

The Legend Of The Bluebonnet
Retold & Illustrated by Tomie dePaola
PaperStar, 1996

Mrs. Rose's Garden
Written & Illustrated by Elaine Greenstein
Simon & Schuster Books For Young Readers, 1996

The Doorbell Rang
Written & Illustrated by Pat Hutchins
Mulberry Books, 1989

Milo And The Magical Stones
Written & Illustrated by Marcus Pfister
North-South Books Inc., 1997

The Rainbow Fish
Written & Illustrated by Marcus Pfister
North-South Books Inc., 1992

The Giving Tree
Written & Illustrated by Shel Silverstein
Lectorum Publications, Inc.; 1996

BUILDING CHARACTER
WITH...COMPASSION!

True compassion comes straight from the heart—which makes February the perfect month to highlight this most important value. Use these engaging activities to foster an understanding of compassion and to promote its importance in everyday life.

ideas contributed by Candi Deal

What Is Compassion?

Begin your study of compassion with a quilt-making project. Explain that *compassion* means reaching out to help others simply because you care. Invite students to talk about times they have shown or received compassion. List the students' examples on the chalkboard. Then have each child make a quilt patch. First have each child trace a seven-inch tagboard square in the center of a nine-inch white construction-paper square. Ask each child to illustrate an example of compassion in the center square (a student may also write a descriptive caption) and create a colorful border design. Mount the completed quilt patches on a length of bulletin-board paper. Use a marker to draw stitches around each project; then attach a crepe-paper border to the outer edges of the quilt. This class project is sure to inspire and promote compassionate behaviors.

I carried my brother's books when he broke his leg.

COMPASSION

Compassionate Solutions

This thought-provoking activity encourages students to think compassionately. On individual index cards, describe situations that will prompt compassionate responses from your students. Place the cards facedown on a table. Ask a child to select a card and read it aloud. Invite youngsters to describe how this situation makes them feel and how they might show the compassion they are feeling. Then have another student select and read aloud a different card. Continue in this manner until all of the cards have been read and discussed. Next tell students that you would like to repeat the activity on another day. Invite them to submit written descriptions of situations that they would like the class to discuss. Provide blank index cards for this purpose. Your classroom will be teeming with compassionate solutions!

All of your friends are going to the movies. You want to go too. The boy next door, who is new to the town and doesn't have any friends, asks you to play with him. What do you do?

A neighbor has lost his cat. The neighbor walks with a cane. He is slowly walking down the street, calling to his cat. How do you feel? What can you do to show how you feel?

Full Of Good Cheer

Arnold Lobel's *Frog And Toad Are Friends* (HarperCollins Children's Books, 1970) is a wonderful source of compassionate behaviors. In the chapter "The Story," the two characters take turns caring for each other. Read the chapter aloud and ask students to describe the compassion that each character shows his friend. Next ask students to think of ways that they could cheer up a family member, neighbor, or friend who is feeling a bit under the weather. List their ideas on the chalkboard; then later copy the ideas onto a large teapot cutout titled "Compassion Is Our Cup Of Tea!" Showcase the cutout at a free-time center along with supplies for drawing pictures, writing stories, and designing notes and cards. Encourage students to visit the center when they're looking for ways to share their compassion with friends and family members.

Compassion Is Our Cup Of Tea!

Ways to make a person feel better:
- tell her a story
- write him a letter or note
- draw her a pretty picture
- hold her hand
- make him a card
- read to her
- fluff his pillow

Charting Feelings

Nurture compassion with a feelings chart. Create a chart like the one shown that lists a variety of emotions. Laminate the chart and mount it in an easily accessible classroom location. Place a wipe-off marker nearby. Each morning ask students to write their names below the emotions that best describe their current feelings. Suggest that the students refer to the chart to better understand how their class-mates (and teacher!) are feeling. Encourage students to share the compassionate feelings that the chart inspires. At the end of the day, wipe the chart clean to provide a fresh start for the following morning!

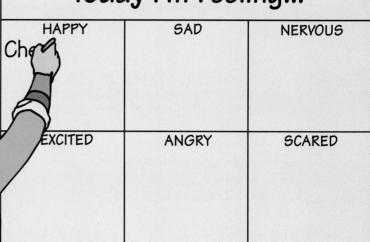

Today I'm Feeling...

HAPPY	SAD	NERVOUS
Che		
EXCITED	ANGRY	SCARED

COMPASSION

Reaching Out

Ask students if they believe someone can feel compassion for a person or animal that they do not know. Encourage plenty of discussion. Then lead students to understand that compassionate feelings have no boundaries. Further explain that there are special organizations like American Red Cross®, Salvation Army®, United Way®, and others that promote shar-ing compassion across the community. Plan for representa-tives from several of your local community-help organizations to visit the classroom and explain how they enlist the help of volunteers to foster compassion. As a follow-up, post a stu-dent-generated list of ways youngsters can share compassion within the community. Each month initiate a community-related compassion goal; then enlist students' help in organizing a plan of action for that month. Students will quickly realize that there is great joy in sharing compassion.

PLEASE DONATE CANNED GOODS FOR THOSE IN NEED

FOOD FOR FRIENDS

Tales Of Compassion

In addition to being delightful stories, these books provide noteworthy examples of compas-sionate behavior.

Mufaro's Beautiful Daughters
An African Tale
Written & Illustrated by John Steptoe
Lothrop, Lee & Shepard Books; 1987

The Talking Eggs
Written by Robert D. San Souci
Illustrated by Jerry Pinkney
Dial Books For Young Readers, 1989

The Paper Crane
Written & Illustrated by Molly Bang
Mulberry Books, 1987

Jamaica Tag-Along
Written by Juanita Havill
Illustrated by Anne Sibley O'Brien
Houghton Mifflin Company, 1990

The Bookshop Dog
Written & Illustrated by Cynthia Rylant
The Blue Sky Press, 1996

I Can Hear The Sun: A Modern Myth
Written & Illustrated by Patricia Polacco
Philomel Books, 1996

Alejandro's Gift
Written by Richard E. Albert
Illustrated by Sylvia Long
Chronicle Books, 1996

BUILDING CHARACTER
WITH...COOPERATION!

Teach your youngsters to become top-notch collaborators with this collection of cooperation-building activities.

ideas contributed by Cyndee Perdue Moore

Hear Ye, Hear Ye

Introduce youngsters to the concept of cooperation with this special activity. Ahead of time, obtain a bell and a feather pen, if possible, and copy the proclamation shown onto bulletin-board paper. Roll the paper to resemble a scroll. To introduce the concept of cooperation, stride to the front of the room, ringing the bell and attracting attention much like a town crier might do. Read the proclamation; then lead students in a discussion about cooperation and its connection to teamwork. Ask volunteers to share examples of teamwork and discuss its benefits. Brainstorm with students ways that shared effort makes the classroom a better place to be. Write these thoughts on the back of the scroll; then have each student sign the proclamation using the feather pen.

Time To Evaluate

Help youngsters become aware of their cooperative habits by having them occasionally follow up collaborative tasks, like those in this section, with self-assessments. Soon after a cooperative group activity, instruct each child to complete a copy of the form on page 269. Then collect the forms and tally the positive results on bulletin-board paper. For each question, ask students who were successful in that area to share their strategies. Encourage discussion about potential growth in each aspect mentioned on the form. Once students have had time to practice improving their cooperative actions, repeat the evaluations, tally the positive results, and have them note their growth in cooperation.

COOPERATION

Pep Rally

Do your youngsters respect other people's ideas? This activity inspires youngsters to cooperate by accepting the opinions of others—and cheering about them! Divide students into groups of four or five. Explain that each group's first collaborative task is to choose a team name. Have a recorder for each group note each suggestion. Encourage students to listen respectfully to one another as they discuss the suggestions and collaboratively narrow the choices to two. Then have each child cast her vote for her group's official name. Tally the votes.

When each team has a name, teach the cheer shown. Allow time for each group to choreograph and practice its cheer; then hold a pep rally and let each group perform. The results of this teamwork are double! Students will be in tune with listening respectfully, and you'll have groups formed for future collaborative activities. Hip, hip, hooray for teamwork!

We, the students of Room [number], proclaim to be
A+ Cooperators
and hereby pledge to

- listen to and respect other people's ideas
- do our share when working in a group
- let others do their share when working in a group

Ben   Jackson   Breyan
Cassie   Erin
Matthew James
Beth   Maggie

We are the [group name]; that's our name!
Co-op-er-a-tion is our game.
Teamwork! Teamwork! Oh, what fun!
We work together and get the job done!

Let's Write A Story

Challenge your young authors to listen respectfully and share the workload as they complete this fun writing assignment. Using teams formed in "Pep Rally," instruct each group to write a story that includes a giant (or another selected character). Challenge students to communicate with one another about characters, a setting, a plot, and an ending. Then instruct students to determine how to share the workload equally to write the story. After the stories are written, have each group cooperatively illustrate its story and share it with the class. What a great way to get your youngsters thinking, listening, speaking, and collaborating!

Laurie L. Reddinger—Grs. K–3
John E. Ford Elementary
Jacksonville, FL

discuss   support   listen

respect   teamwork   collaboration   share

share
to enjoy with others

Building Blocks Of Cooperation

Expand your youngsters' cooperation vocabularies with this fun and easy game that builds a word wall. Each day choose one or more words that relate to cooperation, such as *compromise*, *collaboration*, or *teamwork*. Draw a blank on the board for each letter in each word; then write each word's definition beneath the blanks. Explain to students that each time you see someone acting out the definition, you will let that student guess a letter to fill in a blank. When an entire word is revealed, have a student write it and its definition on a copy of the brick pattern on page 269. Post the brick cutout, a pair of brick mason bulletin-board characters, and the title. When your collection of cooperation words has really stacked up, continue the wall with words related to other attributes of character.

Planning A Playground

Give your groups a more involved challenge, emphasizing that sharing the workload and listening respectfully are at the heart of cooperation. Working with the teams formed in "Pep Rally," explain that each group will create a plan for a new school playground. After discussing various kinds of equipment students have seen or used, encourage members of each group to come to an agreement about the playground equipment to include in their plan. Then have the team members decide collaboratively how to work together, sharing responsibility, to create a map of the plan. As students work with art supplies, commend collaborative efforts. When each team has completed its work, have each group share its plan with the others. Teamwork makes for a job well done!

Books About Cooperation

Use these delightful books to help your youngsters understand how teamwork makes everything easier and more fun.

Franklin Plays The Game
Written by Paulette Bourgeois
Illustrated by Brenda Clark
Scholastic Inc., 1995

The Berenstain Bears And The Trouble With Friends
Written and Illustrated by Stan and Janice Berenstain
Random House, Inc.; 1987

The Turnip
Written by Harriet Ziefert
Illustrated by Laura Rader
Puffin Books, 1996

Whale Is Stuck
Written by Karen Hayles
Illustrated by Charles Fuge
Simon & Schuster Books For Young Readers, 1993

Let's Play As A Team!
Written and Illustrated by P. K. Hallinan
Ideals Children's Books, 1996

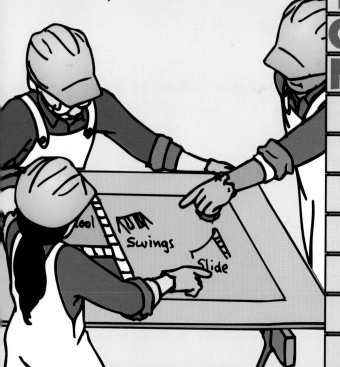

Swings

Slide

BUILDING CHARACTER
WITH...FAIRNESS!

Children learn at an early age that fairness is important. But daily questions of fairness are often complex. Use these ideas to help students begin to understand the complexities and benefits of fairness and the habits that promote it.

ideas contributed by Jill D. Hamilton

Building Fairness Awareness

Introduce the issue of fairness with a five-minute building contest. Divide students into small groups. Give each group a unique set of building supplies. For example, give one group marshmallows, one group drinking straws, one group marshmallows and drinking straws, one group clay, and one group clay and toothpicks. Then give each group five minutes to use its materials to build the tallest building it can. When time is up, congratulate the group with the tallest building. Invite students to comment on the contest. Investigate complaints that relate to fairness. Write "fair" on the chalkboard and ask students what this word means. After some discussion explain that fairness often involves having equal opportunity. Help students evaluate whether each group had the same opportunity to build a tall building. Then ask students to recommend a fair distribution of building supplies. Redistribute the supplies accordingly, repeat the contest, and help students evaluate the fairness of the second contest.

That's Not Fair! Or Is It?

Fairness is often disputed—especially among siblings. To delve deeper into the issue of fairness, read aloud *The Pain And The Great One* by Judy Blume (Yearling Books, 1985). In this humorous tale, the author first reveals an older sister's perceptions of inequity where her little brother, the Pain, is concerned. This is followed by the younger brother's perception of inequity where his older sister, the Great One, is concerned. Write two student-generated lists on the chalkboard. On one list write things the sister feels are unfair. On the other list write things the brother feels are unfair. Then challenge students to take on the role of the siblings' parents and explain why they perceive the listed actions to be fair. For example, the sister gets to feed the cat because she can safely operate the can opener, and the younger brother cannot. On the other hand, the brother gets help getting dressed each morning because he needs the help, and the older sister does not. Conclude the activity by confirming that fairness does not always mean having equal opportunities.

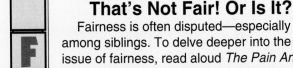

Fairness Rules In School

Students may not be aware of how they promote fairness each day. This student-created display highlights eight different ways that youngsters practice fairness at school and how each behavior benefits others. Divide students into eight groups. Ask the members in each group to talk about the different ways they practice fairness at school. Then have each group select one fairness habit to spotlight. Confirm that eight different habits have been chosen; then give each group crayons and a large sheet of construction paper that you've folded in half. Have one student in each group unfold the paper and write the habit chosen by his group on the upper half of the paper. Next challenge each group to think about the positive results of this habit. Encourage each group member to write a different positive result on the lower half of the unfolded paper. Collect the papers, refold them, and glue one letter cutout on the front of each project, spelling out the word "FAIRNESS." Mount the projects as shown. Routinely refer back to these different acts of fairness and the benefits of each whenever related fairness issues arise.

Rules
In School

be honest

You are helpful.

You are more fun to be around.

People trust you.

All Eyes On Fairness

School-related fairness issues are the focus of these eye-catching posters. To collect your youngsters' fairness concerns, provide a Fairness Awareness Box like the one shown, blank cards, and pencils. When a student has a fairness concern, he describes it on a blank card and drops the card in the box. Regularly remove the cards from the box and select specific concerns to spotlight on individual posters. To make a poster, write a concern on construction paper and then trim the paper into the shape of a speech balloon. Mount the speech balloon and eye and mouth cutouts (that you've fashioned from paper scraps) near the top of a large sheet of construction paper. Then display the poster and discuss the fairness issue with the class. When students understand the circumstances surrounding the concern, invite them to offer fair solutions (if needed) and state the benefits of being fair in this situation. Write on the poster the thoughts that students agree upon. Then display the completed poster in the classroom.

When a fairness concern is actually a case of unusual circumstances, have a complete discussion with students so they understand why the situation is being handled the way that it is. Encourage students to have a positive outlook, despite the fact that things seem unfair at first glance.

> I don't think it's fair that some people get to leave in the middle of math. I want to get out of doing math too!

Some kids leave class to see other teachers. They are getting the help they need. Many times these kids have extra homework to do to make up the work they missed.

This is fair because each person should get the help he needs.

FAIRNESS

Always think about how others will feel before you act.

Whenever you play a game, follow the same rules everyone else does.

Share the playground equipment.

Fairness Tip Of The Day

Make fairness a priority in your classroom by starting each day with a student-generated fairness tip. Ask students to brainstorm habits that promote fairness. List the students' ideas on the chalkboard along with a few of your own. Then have each student choose a different habit from the list to describe and illustrate on a large blank card. Collect the personalized cards. Each day, as a part of your calendar routine, post a different tip card. Ask the student who created the card to explain how this fairness tip can be applied throughout the day. By the time each card is posted, your youngsters will know oodles of ways to assure they're being fair to others.

The Role Of Honesty

Making trustworthy decisions is a key factor in practicing fairness. Highlight this concept by reading aloud *Tops & Bottoms* by Janet Stevens (Harcourt Brace & Company, 1995). In this trickster tale a very clever hare outwits a rich and lazy bear. But does the hare play fair? Read aloud the first two pages of the story—stopping where Hare and Mrs. Hare put their heads together to cook up a plan. On the chalkboard write the headings "Bear" and "Hare." Ask students to recall what they already know about these two characters. Write their ideas under the appropriate headings. Next challenge students to cook up a fair plan that will benefit both Bear and Hare. Write the students' plan on the chalkboard and then read aloud the remainder of the story. Finally have students evaluate the fairness and honesty of Hare's actions. For a fun finale, have each child pen a letter to Hare in which she includes pointers about being honest and fair.

Bear   Hare
lazy   clever
        hungry

What Is Generosity?

Name _____

Generosity is...

sharing your last piece of chocolate _____

1

and helping a _____
who is starting to cry.

2

Generosity is...

giving a gift that's all shiny and

_____

3

...taking a _____
to a friend with the flu.

4

Big, small, made, or store-bought—
all presents start
with a generous thought.

5

Cooperation Self-Evaluation

Read each sentence.
Color the face that shows how you did.

	Great	OK	Need Improvement

1. I listened to others.

2. I respected what others had to say.

3. I gave others a chance to talk.

4. I did my share of the work.

5. I let others do their share of the work.

_____
(student signature)

_____
(date)

©The Education Center, Inc. • THE MAILBOX® • Primary • April/May 1999

Use the pattern with "Building Blocks Of Cooperation" on page 265.

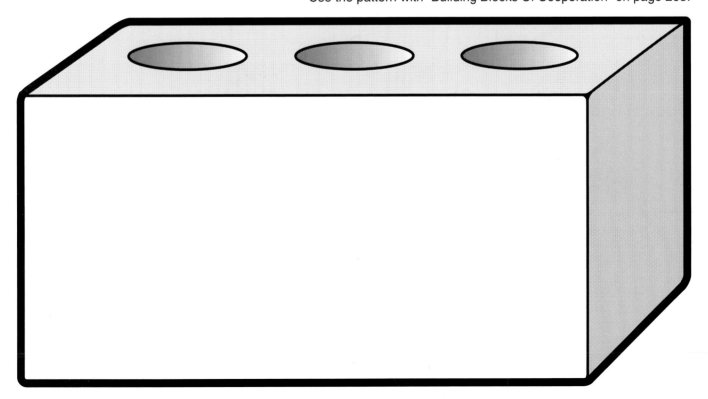

Patterns

Use with "Raining Cats And Frogs!" on page 280.

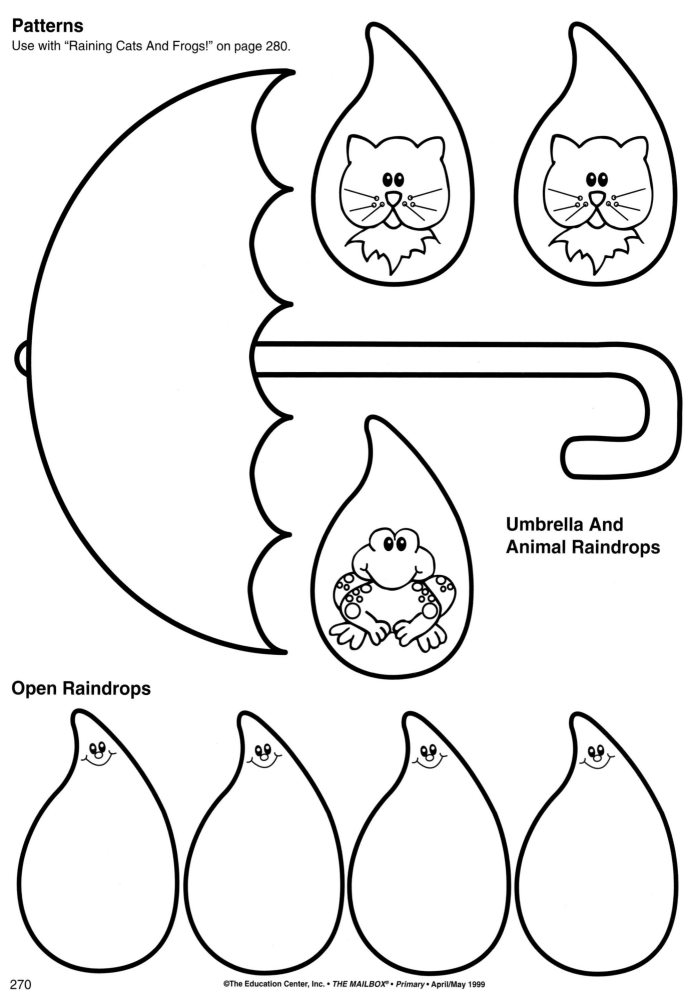

**Umbrella And
Animal Raindrops**

Open Raindrops

Reading Skills Roundup

Reading Skills Roundup

For Beginning Readers

Roll And Write

RIMES

With just a roll of a die, this small group activity gives word-family lessons a new twist! Each small group needs a die that you've programmed with different rimes like *-ot, -ip, -an, -ell, -ug,* and *-ap.* Each group member needs a piece of paper and a pencil. To play, one student in each group rolls the die and announces the rime. Then each group member writes on his paper a word that contains the rime. Next each child shares the word that he wrote with his group. Repeat this procedure until each group member has rolled the die. No doubt youngsters will be on a roll with this fun phonics activity!

Joy O'Gwen—Gr. 1, Oak Street School, Basking Ridge, NJ

not
bug
map
sip
dot

Classy Caps

There's no monkey business with this initial consonant idea! First read aloud *Caps For Sale* by Esphyr Slobodkina (Scholastic Inc., 1993). This timeless classic describes what happens when a peddler encounters a group of mischievous monkeys. At the conclusion of this delightful book, have students brainstorm words that begin with hard *c,* as in the word *cap.* Write the words on chart paper and add picture clues for student reference. Then have each youngster cut out a picture of an object that begins with hard *c* from a discarded magazine. Next ask him to cut out a simple cap pattern that you've duplicated on brightly colored construction paper and glue his magazine picture on it. Lastly use a marker to write the name of the item, as dictated by the student, on the cap cutout. For a "cap-tivating" display, mount a large paper tree trunk and staple the completed projects to its branches.

HARD C

To reinforce the rime *-ap,* instruct each student to write and illustrate an *-ap* word on a cap cutout. Direct each youngster to underline the rime on his cap. These completed caps can also be displayed in the manner previously described.

cake

cup

A Bag Of Short *A* Activities

SHORT A

A Bag Of Short A Activities

___ Collect five short *a* things in this bag.
___ Fold a piece of paper to make a fan.
___ Find Africa on a map.
___ Draw a map of your classroom.
___ Make a list of words that rhyme with cat.
___ Write 10 facts about bats and draw a bat.
___ Make a picture using stamps.
___ Write to a pen pal.
___ Name 10 short *a* places to visit.
___ Add 10 numbers.

Phonics skills are in the bag with this engaging idea! Schedule a "Short *A* Week" and celebrate it with a variety of short *a* activities. Program and duplicate a checklist like the one shown; then have each student glue a copy of the list onto a small paper bag. Each time a youngster completes an activity, he makes a check mark in the appropriate space on the list. Culminate this absolutely A-OK week with an appetizing short *a* snack such as apples or crackers with jam.

Linda Rabinowitz—General Studies Coordinator
Torah Day School Of Atlanta, Tucker, GA

Building Vocabulary On Sight

Build on the concept of a word wall with this ongoing castle-construction project. Every time you introduce a sight word, write the word on a construction-paper brick. Then staple the bricks on a bulletin board to build a castle shape. As your word collection grows, expand the castle by adding towers and turrets. Periodically review the sight-word collection and challenge students to "conquer the castle" by reading all of the words. To vary this project, focus on content-area vocabulary and create a related structure, such as a whale, space station, or dinosaur. Involve the class in deciding which structure or object to build. You can be sure that youngsters will be thrilled to see their work take shape!

Adapted from an idea by Rex Kingsbury—Gr. 1
Heart Of The Lakes Elementary School, Perham, MN

SIGHT WORDS

that	with	this	
to	down	each	at
them	him		how
out	like	time	see
when			you
can			will
up			then
that			wall

BLENDS

Sn
snow
snake
snail
snack
snapshot
By:
Miss Sn

Blend Day Celebration

Plan a special day to say "Bravo for blends!" Prior to the celebration choose a blend for each child; then make the child a nametag with a corresponding blend nickname, such as "Mr. Tr" or "Miss Pl." On the day of the event have youngsters wear their nametags. Encourage students to refer to each other by their new nicknames. Then, throughout Blend Day, conduct a variety of related activities. For example, ask each child to make a poster of several objects that begin with his blend; then have a Blend Show-And-Tell so that each youngster can share his poster. Or help each student write and illustrate a book that features his blend. A blend scavenger hunt and blend-related snacks—such as <u>cr</u>ackers, <u>sm</u>oothies, and <u>pr</u>etzels—are also great additions to the celebration. What a splendid way to reinforce blends!

Kay Wulf—Gr. 1, Cheney Elementary School, Cheney, KS

We're Rounding Up Great Reading Ideas!

Howdy, pardner! We could sure use your help in lassoing more rootin'-tootin' reading ideas for this department. Please follow the submission guidelines found on page 2 of *The Mailbox*® magazine under "How To Submit Ideas." We would love to hear your favorite strategies for the following:

- teaching phonics skills such as letter sounds, blends, digraphs, and word families
- using literature to reinforce beginning reading skills
- building sight- and high-frequency-word vocabularies

We're looking forward to hearing from you!

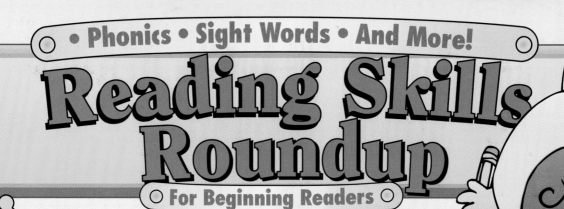

• Phonics • Sight Words • And More!

Reading Skills Roundup

For Beginning Readers

SHORT U

Pumpkin Patch Phonics

Short-vowel skills are sure to grow with this seasonal phonics activity! Read aloud your favorite pumpkin book or choose a title from the list shown. Follow up the story by asking students to brainstorm words that have the short *u* sound. List their responses on a large, pumpkin-shaped cutout for future reference. Then harvest a crop of short *u* sounds with this student-made booklet project.

To make a booklet, a student folds a 9" x 12" sheet of orange construction paper in half, traces (or draws) one-half of a pumpkin shape on the fold, and cuts along the resulting outline. Next she titles and personalizes the front cover of her resulting booklet. Then, using a copy of page 284, she colors and cuts out eight short *u* pictures and glues them inside her booklet. If desired, have each student store her remaining picture cards in a resealable plastic bag. On another day, feature apple books and have each child use eight of her remaining picture cards to create a short *a* apple-shaped booklet. No doubt these short-vowel projects will be the pick of the crop!

Kathleen Darby—Gr. 1
Community School, Cumberland, RI

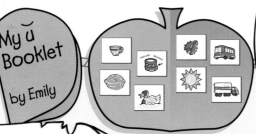

My ŭ Booklet
by Emily

A Harvest Of Pumpkin Books

It's A Fruit, It's A Vegetable, It's A Pumpkin
• Written by Allan Fowler & Includes photographs • Childrens Press®, Inc.; 1995

The Biggest Pumpkin Ever • Written by Steven Kroll & Illustrated by Jeni Bassett • Scholastic Inc., 1993

It's Pumpkin Time! • Written by Zoe Hall & Illustrated by Shari Halpern • Scholastic Inc., 1994

Apples And Pumpkins • Written by Anne Rockwell & Illustrated by Lizzy Rockwell • Aladdin Paperbacks, 1994

Pumpkin Pumpkin • Written & Illustrated by Jeanne Titherington • Mulberry Books, 1990

Word-Wall Chant

Find the word;
It is near.
Where's the word?
It's right here!

Say the word.
Clap the parts.
Tap the sounds.
What a start!

Time to spell.
Close each eye.
Do it now—
Don't be shy!

One more time,
Say the word
Loud and clear.
Now let's cheer!

Point and give a cheer.

Say the word.
Clap once for each syllable.
Tap once for each sound.

Spell the word aloud.

Say the word.

Give a cheer.

Word-Wall Chant

SIGHT WORDS

Looking for a motivating way to teach or reinforce sight words? Then try this catchy word-wall chant! Display the chant shown near your class word wall. Choose a student to point to a selected word on the word wall. Then lead the class in the chant, pausing for students to follow the provided directions. Next, if appropriate, have each child enter the word in a personal dictionary or practice writing it on scrap paper. Now that's a reading idea to cheer about!

adapted from an idea by Lynn L. Caruso—Gr. 1
Littlebrook Elementary, Princeton, NJ

Recommended Literature

Berenstains' A Book • Written & Illustrated by Stan & Jan Berenstain • Random House Books For Young Readers, 1997

Berenstains' B Book • Written & Illustrated by Stan & Jan Berenstain • Random House Books For Young Readers, 1971

There's An Ant In Anthony • Written & Illustrated by Bernard Most • Morrow Junior Books, 1992

Sheep In A Jeep • Written by Nancy Shaw & Illustrated by Margot Apple • Houghton Mifflin Company, 1997

Tally Time

Phonetic skills add up with great literature! For this listening activity, select a book that features a particular word family or letter sound (see "Recommended Literature"). Familiarize students with the chosen book by reading it aloud one or more times for listening pleasure. Then ask students to estimate how many times the selected sound appeared in the story. Read the book again and direct each child to make a tally mark on scrap paper every time she hears the sound. Then have each student count her tally marks and compare the total to her estimate. You can count on this idea to sharpen listening, math, and phonetic skills!

Christine Granda, Taft Elementary School, Joliet, IL

Short *I* Extravaganza

Students will flip over this innovative vowel study! Schedule a Short *I* Week and celebrate it with a variety of imaginative activities. Program and duplicate a checklist of 16 short *i* activities like the one shown. Each time a youngster completes an activity, he places a check mark in the appropriate space on the list. If desired, assign a point value to each activity. Reward each student who earns a specified number of points with a small prize, such as a sticker or an extra trip to the class computer or treasure box. Culminate this big week with a picnic of chicken-salad sandwiches, chips, pickles, and carrot sticks.

Linda Rabinowitz—General Studies Coordinator, Torah Day School Of Atlanta, Tucker, GA

Sixteen Short I Activities

____ 1. Make a rubbing of a nickel.
____ 2. Write five words that rhyme with pig.
____ 3. Play kick ball.
____ 4. Write the numerals 1–66.
____ 5. Cut six short *i* words from a newspaper and glue them onto pink paper.
____ 6. Write sixteen short *i* words.
____ 7. List six things that are big.
____ 8. Count how many windows are in your home.
____ 9. List six types of fish.
____ 10. Write a story about a trip you took.
____ 11. Write the names of two rivers.
____ 12. Skip for one minute.
____ 13. Read a book with a short *i* word in its title.
____ 14. List two cereals or snacks that have short *i* names.
____ 15. Bring an item to school for Short I Show-And-Tell.
____ 16. Highlight all of the short *i* words on this list.

WORD FAMILES & LETTER SOUNDS

SHORT I

Reading Skills Roundup

For Beginning Readers

BLENDS

Beanbag Blast

It's no toss-up—this fast-paced blend activity is a surefire winner! In advance, use a permanent marker to draw a nine-space grid on a solid-colored vinyl tablecloth. Program each section of the grid with a blend of your choice. Place the tablecloth on the classroom floor and seat children nearby. In turn, each student stands in front of the tablecloth and tosses a beanbag onto the grid. He then reads the blend in the space where the beanbag landed and names a word with this blend. After everyone has taken at least one turn, roll or fold the tablecloth for easy storage. Quick, simple, and engaging—this phonics activity is sure to please!

fr	sk	b
cl	tr	s
dr	sl	cr

VOWELS

Vowel Song

A, E, I, O, U, and sometimes *Y.*
A, E, I, O, U, and sometimes *Y.*
Oh, these are all the vowels.
Oh, these are all the vowels.
A, E, I, O, U, and sometimes *Y.*

Oh, you need a vowel in each and every word.
Oh, you need a vowel in each and every word.
Yes, the vowels are important!
Yes, the vowels are important!
So you need a vowel in each and every word!

Vowel Song

This teacher-tested vowel tune is guaranteed to be a hit! Copy the song shown onto colorful paper. Then point to each word as you sing the song with students to the tune of "She'll Be Comin' Round The Mountain." Don't be surprised if youngsters request an encore!

Julie Orton—Grs. K–1
Morton Avenue School
Dover Foxcroft, ME

SHORT E

A Tempting Menu

What's on the menu? Ten tempting short *e* activities! Program and duplicate a class supply of an activity menu like the one shown. Have each student take a menu home and complete a specified number of the listed activities. Each time a youngster completes an activity, she makes a check mark in the appropriate space on her menu. Present an award to each student who meets her goal and returns her menu within a designated time. Now that's made-to-order learning fun!

Linda Rabinowitz—General Studies Coordinator
Torah Day School Of Atlanta, Tucker, GA

Short E Menu

_____ Eat an egg.
_____ Investigate how long it takes an ice cube to melt.
_____ Make a list of red things.
_____ Eat some crackers and jelly.
_____ Draw a web. Add a spider and some insects.
_____ Make your bed.
_____ Write a list of words that rhyme with nest.
_____ Make a list of animals that would make good pets.
_____ Write a letter.
_____ Highlight the short *e* words on this list.

Shorty

A Family Affair

Keep phonics all in the family with this center activity! Each week select a different word family to reinforce, and make a tagboard tracer that represents the featured sound. (For example, cut out a stop sign for *-op*, a hat for *-at*, or a nest for *-est*.) Label the tracer with the corresponding word family; then place the tracer at a center along with construction paper and blank paper for making booklets, pencils, scissors, crayons, glue, and a stapler. For best results, display an assembled booklet at the center too. A student makes a blank booklet and decorates its front cover to reflect the word family of the week. Then, on each blank page, she writes and illustrates a sentence that includes one or more words from the featured word family.

Lisa Kelly—Gr. 1, Wood Creek Elementary, Farmington, MI

Heads Up!

Boost sight-word vocabularies with this memorable activity! Select several words to introduce and write each word on a separate index card. In turn, show and read each card to students. Then use tape or magnets to display the cards on the chalkboard. Next have each student rest his head on his desk and close his eyes. Quickly remove a word card and announce, "Heads up!" Have youngsters study the remaining word cards to determine which one is missing. If desired, ask the student who correctly names the missing word to use it in a sentence, define it, or name an antonym or synonym for it. Then return the card to its original place on the chalkboard. Repeat this activity until each word card has been removed at least once. For an added challenge, remove more than one card at a time.

Sandra Williams—Gr. 1, Oak Knoll School, Summit, NJ

Reading Rings

Students will flip over this word-family teaching tool! To make a reading ring, visually divide an index card in half and write a word family *(rime)* on the right side. Then cut several other index cards in half. On each of these cards, write a different initial consonant, blend, or digraph *(onset)*. Hole-punch the top left corner of each programmed card. Slide the cards onto a metal ring as shown. A student reads the word formed by the cards, then flips the top card to create a new word. What a nifty way to teach word families!

Kathy L. Kersul—Reading Specialist, K–5, Limerick Elementary, Royersford, PA

Reading Skills Roundup

SHORT O

A Pocketful Of Phonics

Each of these student-made folders provide a pocketful of short *o* practice! To make his short *o* folder, a youngster folds a 12" x 18" sheet of white construction paper in half. On the front of the folder he writes "What is in my pocket?" and draws and colors himself wearing clothing with a pocket. Then he opens his folder and writes "Lots of fun!" to the left. At the bottom right he glues a library pocket labeled "ŏ." Finally he places a checklist of short *o* activities (prepared by you) in the pocket. Ask each child to take his folder home and complete a specified number of activities by a predetermined date. Remind students to check off each task as they complete it. When the folders are returned, ask each child to illustrate his favorite short *o* activity inside his folder. After each child has shared his illustration with the class, celebrate a job well done with popcorn or hot chocolate!

Linda Rabinowitz—General Studies Coordinator, Torah Day School Of Atlanta, Tucker, GA

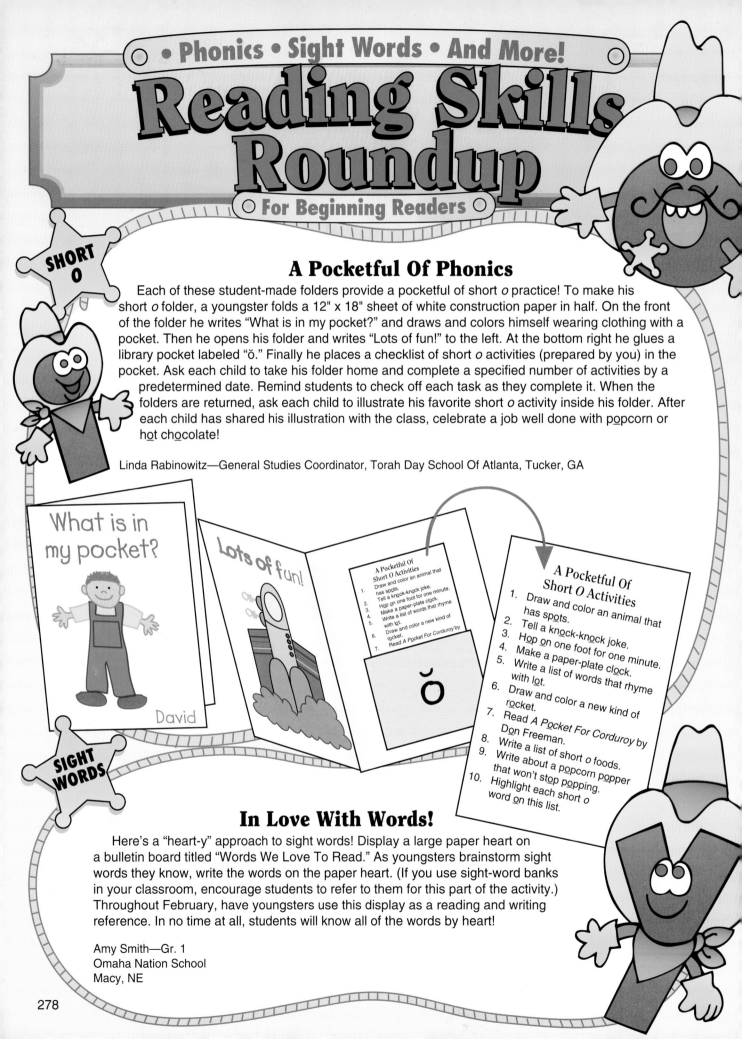

What is in my pocket?

David

Lots of fun!

A Pocketful Of Short O Activities
1. Draw and color an animal that has spots.
2. Tell a knock-knock joke.
3. Hop on one foot for one minute.
4. Make a paper-plate clock.
5. Write a list of words that rhyme with lot.
6. Draw and color a new kind of rocket.
7. Read *A Pocket For Corduroy* by Don Freeman.
8. Write a list of short *o* foods.
9. Write about a popcorn popper that won't stop popping.
10. Highlight each short *o* word on this list.

In Love With Words!

Here's a "heart-y" approach to sight words! Display a large paper heart on a bulletin board titled "Words We Love To Read." As youngsters brainstorm sight words they know, write the words on the paper heart. (If you use sight-word banks in your classroom, encourage students to refer to them for this part of the activity.) Throughout February, have youngsters use this display as a reading and writing reference. In no time at all, students will know all of the words by heart!

Amy Smith—Gr. 1
Omaha Nation School
Macy, NE

SIGHT WORDS

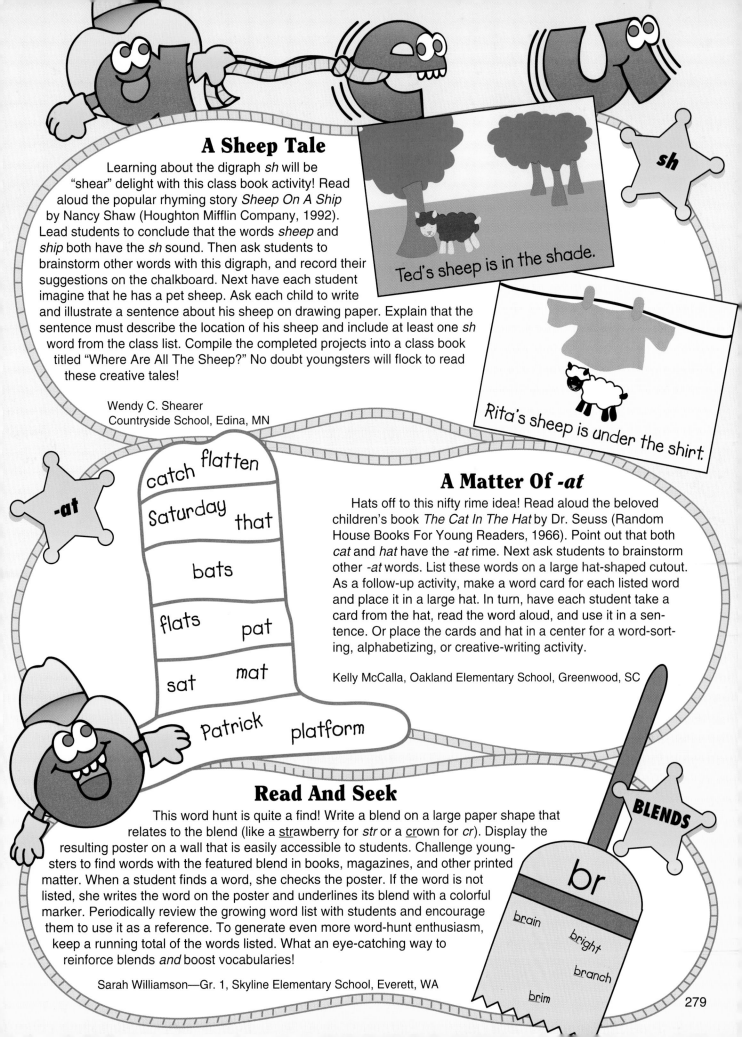

A Sheep Tale

Learning about the digraph *sh* will be "shear" delight with this class book activity! Read aloud the popular rhyming story *Sheep On A Ship* by Nancy Shaw (Houghton Mifflin Company, 1992). Lead students to conclude that the words *sheep* and *ship* both have the *sh* sound. Then ask students to brainstorm other words with this digraph, and record their suggestions on the chalkboard. Next have each student imagine that he has a pet sheep. Ask each child to write and illustrate a sentence about his sheep on drawing paper. Explain that the sentence must describe the location of his sheep and include at least one *sh* word from the class list. Compile the completed projects into a class book titled "Where Are All The Sheep?" No doubt youngsters will flock to read these creative tales!

Wendy C. Shearer
Countryside School, Edina, MN

Ted's sheep is in the shade.

Rita's sheep is under the shirt.

A Matter Of -*at*

Hats off to this nifty rime idea! Read aloud the beloved children's book *The Cat In The Hat* by Dr. Seuss (Random House Books For Young Readers, 1966). Point out that both *cat* and *hat* have the -*at* rime. Next ask students to brainstorm other -*at* words. List these words on a large hat-shaped cutout. As a follow-up activity, make a word card for each listed word and place it in a large hat. In turn, have each student take a card from the hat, read the word aloud, and use it in a sentence. Or place the cards and hat in a center for a word-sorting, alphabetizing, or creative-writing activity.

Kelly McCalla, Oakland Elementary School, Greenwood, SC

catch   flatten
Saturday   that
bats
flats   pat
sat   mat
Patrick   platform

Read And Seek

This word hunt is quite a find! Write a blend on a large paper shape that relates to the blend (like a <u>str</u>awberry for *str* or a <u>cr</u>own for *cr*). Display the resulting poster on a wall that is easily accessible to students. Challenge youngsters to find words with the featured blend in books, magazines, and other printed matter. When a student finds a word, she checks the poster. If the word is not listed, she writes the word on the poster and underlines its blend with a colorful marker. Periodically review the growing word list with students and encourage them to use it as a reference. To generate even more word-hunt enthusiasm, keep a running total of the words listed. What an eye-catching way to reinforce blends *and* boost vocabularies!

Sarah Williamson—Gr. 1, Skyline Elementary School, Everett, WA

br
brain
bright
branch
brim

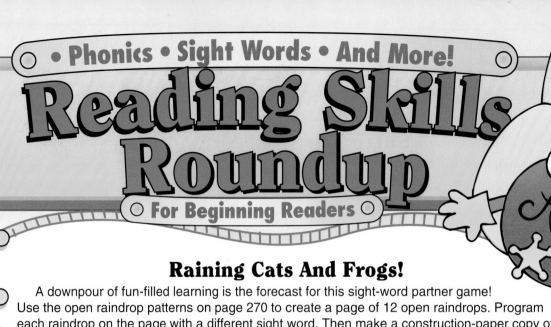

Raining Cats And Frogs!

A downpour of fun-filled learning is the forecast for this sight-word partner game! Use the open raindrop patterns on page 270 to create a page of 12 open raindrops. Program each raindrop on the page with a different sight word. Then make a construction-paper copy of both this page and the umbrella and animal raindrop patterns on page 270 for each student. Have each child cut out his patterns and store them in a resealable plastic bag.

To play the game, a pair of students stacks a set of 15 raindrops on an umbrella cutout. In turn, each student takes the top raindrop. If a sight word is drawn and the student reads it correctly (as verified by his partner), he earns one point. Then he places the raindrop in a discard pile. If the student reads the word incorrectly, he puts the raindrop on the bottom of the stack. If a student draws a frog, he adds ten points to his score before he discards the raindrop. A cat earns five points. Play continues until one player earns 25 points and is declared the winner. (Have students shuffle the discarded raindrops and restack them as needed.) After each student has played the game with several different partners, encourage all students to take their games home and teach their family members how to play.

Renee DiMartin—Resource Room/Consultant Teacher K–6
Center Street School
Oneonta, NY

On The Button!

Students' short *u* skills will be right on the button with this motivating idea! Create a list of short *u* activities similar to the one shown. Label each button with two, three, or four buttonholes to reflect the amount of time or skill involved in completing the task. Then give each child a copy of the list to take home. Ask him to complete as many tasks as possible by a designated date and to lightly color a button each time he completes its corresponding task. When the lists are returned, have each child tally the buttons he colored. Present each student whose total meets or exceeds your expectations with an inexpensive short *u* prize, such as a muffin, a tiny plastic bug, or a coupon to solve a puzzle during free time. There's no doubt that youngsters will have bunches of fun!

Linda Rabinowitz—General Studies Coordinator
Torah Day School Of Atlanta
Tucker, GA

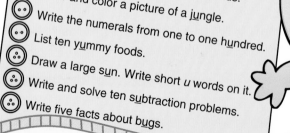

Short *U* Activities
- Run in place for one hundred seconds.
- Draw and color a picture of a jungle.
- Write the numerals from one to one hundred.
- List ten yummy foods.
- Draw a large sun. Write short *u* words on it.
- Write and solve ten subtraction problems.
- Write five facts about bugs.

Poetic Phonics

PHONICS IN CONTEXT

If you're looking for a fun way to reinforce phonics skills in context, try this "verse-atile" approach! Copy a desired poem onto a transparency (see "Poetry Resources") and use an overhead projector to exhibit it. Read the poem aloud several times with your students. Then challenge the class to look for particular phonics elements, such as blends, digraphs, rimes, or vowel sounds. Have student volunteers use overhead pens to circle the targeted phonics elements on the transparency. Then, under your students' guidance, copy the circled words onto chart paper, categorizing them as desired. Display the resulting list(s) for future use. The possibilities are endless when poetry and phonics are combined.

Beth Cordy—Gr. 3
Prospect School
Lake Mills, WI

Poetry Resources
A Pizza The Size Of The Sun by Jack Prelutsky (Greenwillow Books, 1996)
The Random House Book Of Poetry For Children selected by Jack Prelutsky
   (Random House Books For Young Readers, 1983)
Lunch Money And Other Poems About School by Carol Diggory Shields
   (Dutton Children's Books, 1995)

Order books on-line.
www.themailbox.com

Food For Thought

BLENDS & DIGRAPHS

Cook up a better understanding of blends and digraphs with these tasty phonics activities! To reinforce the meaning of *blend,* make a batch of trail mix. As students sample the yummy snack, point out that each ingredient can be tasted even though it is combined with other ingredients. Explain that a blend such as *cr* in *crispy* is similar because each letter keeps its own sound, even though it is combined with another letter. To reinforce the meaning of *digraph,* enlist your students' help in making and baking a giant chocolate chip cookie like the one shown (use the provided recipe if desired). When the students eat the snack, ask them if they can taste the different cookie ingredients, such as the flour, sugar, and egg. Lead students to conclude that instead of keeping their own flavors, these ingredients combine to create a new flavor. Use this tasty experience as a delicious analogy for consonant digraphs like *ch* in *chip*—where two consonants combine to create one new sound. Phonics never tasted so good!

Alice Ackley—Gr. 1
Our Lady Of Fatima School
Artesia, CA

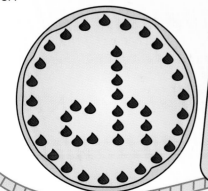

Jumbo Chocolate Chip Cookie
(makes approximately 24 servings)

1/2 cup packed brown sugar
1/4 cup sugar
1/2 cup margarine or butter, softened
1 teaspoon vanilla

1 egg
1 1/4 cups flour
1/2 teaspoon baking soda
1 small bag chocolate chips

Preheat oven to 350°. Mix sugars, margarine or butter, vanilla, and egg in large bowl. Stir in flour and baking soda. Spread dough on an ungreased 12-inch pizza pan. Use chocolate chips to create a border and the digraph *ch* as shown. Bake for 15 minutes or until lightly browned. When cool, cut into small pieces and serve.

SHORT I

Fish For Phonics

Promote teamwork and reinforce short *i* skills with this literature-based class project. Cut a jumbo fish shape from white bulletin-board paper and display it in an easily accessible area. Then read aloud *Swimmy* by Leo Lionni (Knopf Children's Paperbacks, 1992). This Caldecott Honor book shows the value of cooperation with simple text and unique collage illustrations. After discussing the book's message, brainstorm short *i* words with students and list the words on the chalkboard. Next give each youngster a red construction-paper fish cutout. Have him use a black marker or crayon to write a short *i* word on his cutout, referring to the list for ideas. Glue a small black fish cutout onto the jumbo fish for an eye. Then ask each student to glue his prepared cutout onto the fish display, using Lionni's illustration as a model. Count on this short *i* reference to be quite a catch!

Rita Burke and Cathy D'Amour—Gr. 1
St. Jane deChantal School
Bethesda, MD

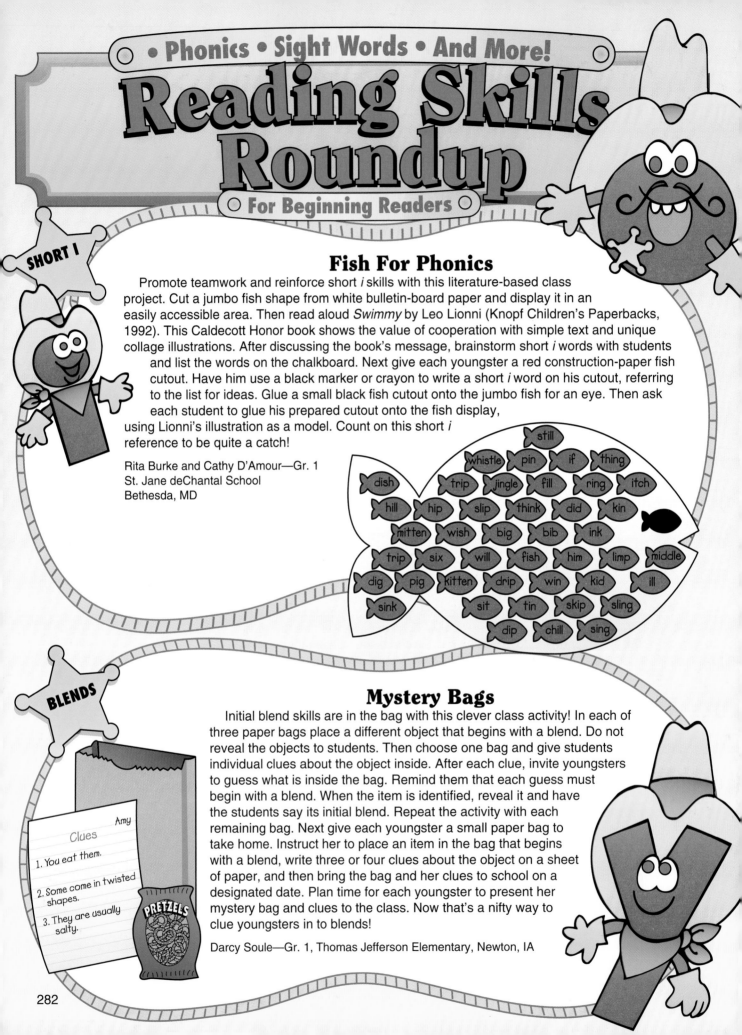

still, whistle, pin, if, thing, dish, trip, jingle, fill, ring, itch, hill, hip, slip, think, did, kin, mitten, wish, big, bib, ink, trip, six, will, fish, him, limp, middle, dig, pig, kitten, drip, win, kid, ill, sink, sit, tin, skip, sling, dip, chill, sing

BLENDS

Mystery Bags

Initial blend skills are in the bag with this clever class activity! In each of three paper bags place a different object that begins with a blend. Do not reveal the objects to students. Then choose one bag and give students individual clues about the object inside. After each clue, invite youngsters to guess what is inside the bag. Remind them that each guess must begin with a blend. When the item is identified, reveal it and have the students say its initial blend. Repeat the activity with each remaining bag. Next give each youngster a small paper bag to take home. Instruct her to place an item in the bag that begins with a blend, write three or four clues about the object on a sheet of paper, and then bring the bag and her clues to school on a designated date. Plan time for each youngster to present her mystery bag and clues to the class. Now that's a nifty way to clue youngsters in to blends!

Darcy Soule—Gr. 1, Thomas Jefferson Elementary, Newton, IA

Amy
Clues
1. You eat them.
2. Some come in twisted shapes.
3. They are usually salty.

PRETZELS

Left Or Right?

This class word-family game is right on! Prepare a word list that includes several -ight words. Instruct students to arrange their chairs in a large circle and then be seated. Tape a wrapped candy or a sticker (with its backing in place) under one chair. To begin play, read aloud a word from your list. If a student agrees that the word has the -ight word family (rime), he gives a thumbs-up. If he does not, he gives a thumbs-down. Reveal the correct response. If it is thumbs-up, students stand and move two chairs to the right. If it is thumbs-down, they stand and move one chair to the left. Continue in this manner until you have read the first half of the word list. Then momentarily stop the game and instruct each child to look under the chair in which he is seated. If he finds a prize taped there, he removes the prize and the chair, and becomes the word caller for the last half of the game. Before continuing the game, tape another prize to the bottom of one chair within the circle. With this lively game, students' word-family skills will move right along!

Sara Harris—Gr. 2, West View Elementary, Knoxville, TN

Word List

fight	sight
tight	might
side	find
light	lightbulb
boat	rise
bright	read
sky	twilight
fly	frighten
night	nighttime

All Aboard For Digraphs!

Choo-choo! It's full steam ahead with this partner digraph game! Give every student a resealable plastic bag and white construction-paper copies of pages 285 and 286. Have each child color and cut out the pattern and cards, and then store the resulting game pieces in his bag. To play, pair students. Ask one student in each pair to shuffle his playing cards and place them facedown on the playing surface. Then have each player place his train in front of him. In turn, each partner takes the top card from the stack and names the pictured item. If the word has *ch*, the student places the card behind his train. If it does not, he places the card in a discard pile. Play continues until all cards in the stack are played. The player who has the longest train is declared the winner. In the case of a tie, both students win! Encourage youngsters to play the game at school and at home for additional digraph practice. What a great way to keep students' digraph skills on track!

Sara Harris—Gr. 2

Digraph Express

Here's a center activity that provides trainloads of digraph practice! Make three construction-paper copies of the train pattern on page 285. Cut out the patterns and label one for each of the following digraphs: *ch, th,* and *sh.* Duplicate the picture cards (pages 285 and 286) on construction paper and cut them out. Program the back of each card with the corresponding digraph and then laminate the patterns and cards for durability, if desired. Store the cutouts in a large decorated envelope at a center. To use the center, a student places the train cutouts on a work surface. Then she shuffles the cards and places each card behind the appropriate train. To check each train's cargo, she turns over the picture cards and verifies that the digraphs match. No doubt this center will be one of your students' favorite destinations!

Adapted from an idea by Sara Harris

Short-Vowel Picture Cards
Use with "Pumpkin Patch Phonics" on page 274.

Digraph Picture Cards

Use with "All Aboard For Digraphs!" and "Digraph Express" on page 283.
If desired, have younger students put aside the branch, watch, and bench picture cards.

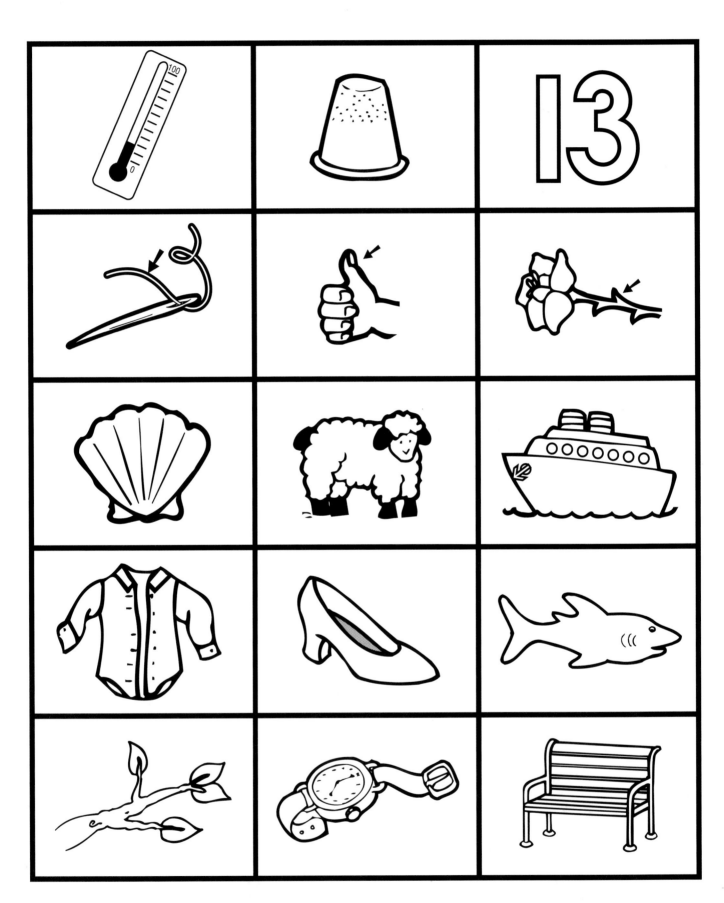

WRITE ON!

Write On!

Ideas And Tips For Teaching Students To Write!

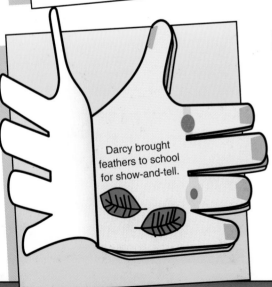

Yeah!

3
+3
6
2
2
4

1
+1
2

5
+5

I was so surprised when my brand-new pencil came to life! It danced on my desktop. Then it filled in all my math answers. But when I sneezed, it got still. I sneezed again and it did not move. I hope my pencil comes to life again very soon!

It was a long bumpy ride to Grandpa's house. The hot sun beat down on our red car. When we got there, Grandpa was sitting on the porch. There were six yellow chickens in the yard!

Darcy brought feathers to school for show-and-tell.

It's Alive!

Who can resist new school supplies? Your students won't be able to when you introduce this creative-writing activity! Ask students to name the new supplies they brought to school at the start of the year. List their responses on the chalkboard. Next challenge youngsters to imagine what school might be like if their supplies came to life. Then have each student select an item from the list, and write and illustrate a school-supply adventure story. Invite each youngster to read aloud her story after introducing its main character—the supply she wrote about. Now that's a writing activity that really comes to life!

Jennifer Smith, Espy Elementary School, Kenton, OH

Summer Memories

Make your first descriptive-writing activity of the school year a memorable one! To begin ask each student to illustrate a favorite summer memory on drawing paper. Have the student list several nouns that he pictured on another sheet of paper, then write several descriptive words beside each one. Next encourage each child to refer to his word list as he writes four descriptive sentences about his illustration. Now the fun begins! Collect the students' illustrations; then divide the youngsters into small groups. Redistribute the illustrations to the appropriate groups, but do not reveal which group member created each one. In turn have each student read the sentences he wrote to his group members as they try to pinpoint his illustration. After an illustration has been identified, encourage the group to share suggestions for making the corresponding sentences even more descriptive. Periodically repeat the activity with different topics to promote descriptive writing throughout the year.

adapted from an idea by Eleanor Anderson—Gr. 2, Shady Brook Elementary, Bedford, TX

Give Show-And-Tell A Hand!

Here's a handy way to incorporate writing into each child's weekly sharing opportunity. Each time a student brings an item from home to share, she traces a large hand shape onto paper and cuts it out. On the resulting cutout, she illustrates the item she plans to share, then copies and completes the sentence "[Student's name] brought _____ to school for show-and-tell." Invite students to add fingernails and jewelry to their cutouts, too. Collect a student's cutout either immediately before or after she shares. Each week bind the collected cutouts into a booklet that students can check out and share with their family members.

Kathryn Shanko—Gr. 1, Erieview Elementary School, Avon Lake, OH

Ideas And Tips For Teaching Students To Write!

Haunted Houses For Sale

Strengthen community ties and persuasive writing skills with this "spook-tacular" Halloween activity! To set the stage, read aloud and discuss several real-estate ads. Invite students to explain why some ads appeal to them more than others. Then have students brainstorm the kinds of things that ghosts, goblins, and other Halloween creatures might look for in a house. Instruct each youngster to use these ideas to write and illustrate an ad for a haunted house. Next invite a local realtor to speak to the class about his career. Allow time during his visit for your young writers to share their spine-tingling work. Then showcase the ads at a display titled "Haunted Houses For Sale."

JoAnne Condelli—Gr. 2 and Carol Masek—Teaching Assistant, Spruce Run Elementary School Nazareth, PA

Turkey Tales

Thanksgiving just wouldn't be complete without turkey and all of the fixings—or would it? Your students may decide it's time for a change of menu when you deliver this writing activity! Ask each child to describe—from a turkey's point of view—a perfect way to celebrate Thanksgiving. When the children are finished writing, have each student make a Colorful Turkey (see directions below) on which to display his work.

Making A Colorful Turkey

Materials Needed:

11" brown circle	white copy of page 292
nine 4" x 9" rectangles in assorted colors	crayons
9" x 12" sheet of orange paper	scissors
two 1 1/4" x 12" brown strips	glue

Directions:
1. Color and cut out the head and feet patterns on page 292.
2. Trim each rectangle to resemble a turkey feather.
3. Glue the turkey head to the brown-circle body; then glue the turkey feathers in place.
4. To make two wings, trace your hand on the orange paper twice and cut out the resulting outlines. Glue the wings to the body.
5. Accordion-fold each brown strip to make a turkey leg.
6. Glue a foot cutout to one end of each turkey leg; then glue the legs to the body.

Martha Kelley, Roanoke, VA

Picturesque Poetry

Focus on fall with this decorative poetry project. First have each student completely cover a 9" x 12" sheet of yellow construction paper with red, orange, and green sponge-painting. While the paintings are drying, ask children to brainstorm words and phrases that describe the fall season. Record their ideas on chart paper. Next have each student write "FALL" on a 5" x 8" sheet of white paper as shown and refer to the student-generated list to write an acrostic poem. Remind students that each line of their poems must start with the corresponding letter in "FALL." Then have each child glue his acrostic in the center of his sponge-painted paper. For an eye-catching seasonal display, mount the completed projects on a bulletin board titled "Poetry Paints A Pretty Picture." This combination of paint and poetry will receive rave reviews!

Amy Erickson—Gr. 1, Montello Elementary School, Lewiston, ME

The Land Of No Night

I turned my key. A door
opened. I walked into a new
world. It was day all the time.
No one ever went to bed!
Children played until they got
tired. It was very, very fun!

Ideas And Tips For Teaching Students To Write!

Keying In On Creativity

These colorful key cutouts may be just what students need to unlock their creativity! Give each child a two-foot length of yarn and a tagboard key that you have hole-punched near the top. Have each student use markers, crayons, and glitter pens to decorate his key. Then have him thread his yarn through the hole in his cutout and tie the yarn ends to create a necklace. Prior to creative-writing time, suggest that each child place his key around his neck, then guide the key through the air to unlock the door to his next writing adventure.

Ann Marie Stephens—Gr.1, George C. Round Elementary, Manassas, VA

Picture-Perfect Memories

We made cookies for our Valentine's
Day party. We measured the ingredients.
We mixed the ingredients. We rolled the
dough. Making cookies was lots of fun!

Here's a picture-perfect way to bring your students' paragraph-writing skills into focus. Capture a special activity or a holiday party on a roll of film. When the film is developed, discuss the details that can be seen in each snapshot. Next pair the students and give each twosome a photograph, writing paper, a 9" x 12" sheet of construction paper, glue (or tape), and scissors. Challenge each pair to write a paragraph about its photograph. The paragraph should include a topic sentence, three or more supporting details, and a concluding sentence. Then each student pair trims away the extra writing paper around its paragraph before mounting the photograph and paragraph on construction paper. Enlist your youngsters' help in sequencing the projects; then bind the pages into a class book of precious memoirs!

Lynn Brengle—Gr. 2, Wren Hollow School, Ballwin, MO

Very Healthy Caterpillars

apple bread milk carrot cheese fish

Paper Needed For Each Booklet
Writing paper: two 3" x 9" strips
Construction paper: 4 1/2" wide
  green: two 12-inch lengths
  white: 2" long, 4" long, 6" long,
      8" long, 10" long, 12" long

Reinforce good eating habits with this literature-based writing activity. Read aloud *The Very Hungry Caterpillar* by Eric Carle and lead students to conclude that the insect gets a stomachache because it is not eating healthful foods! Then have students write original versions of the story in which the caterpillar eats a well-balanced meal. To begin, a student stacks her white construction paper (see the paper list below) to create graduated layers; then she staples this paper between her green paper to create a step booklet. On the front cover, she writes her name and the title "The Very Healthy Caterpillar." Next she illustrates the caterpillar and a nutritious food on each booklet page, making sure the size of the caterpillar increases on each page. Then she labels and hole-punches each food item. On the back of the last page, she illustrates a gorgeous butterfly. To complete the project, the student writes a beginning and an ending for her story (on separate strips of writing paper) and glues the writing inside the front and back booklet covers. Spectacular!

Lisa Plackner—Gr. 2, Westside Elementary, River Falls, WI

My Mom Is Smart
I wanted to go to Ben's house. My mom said I could go if my room was clean. I promised my brother a quarter if he would put my clothes away. He even found the green sock I lost last week! My dog ate all the crumbs on the floor plus a plastic ring and a toothpick. I gave him a dog bone. At first my mom was very happy. Then she looked under the bed. I hope I get to go to Ben's next Saturday!

...lly Shari set sail for Sweden ...th six salami sandwiches and ...ven strawberry sodas.

o Mom

...ts of Love, ...odney

...ay 7, 1999

Mom, you are special to me because you make pancakes on Saturday morning!

Write On!

Ideas And Tips For Teaching Students To Write!

It's In The Bag!

Adding a touch of mystery to your next creative-writing lesson is sure to produce intriguing results. The day before the writing activity is to be completed, give each child a paper lunch bag to take home with instructions to return the bag the following school day with five small items inside. Tell students that the contents of their bags should remain a secret. For the writing activity, challenge each child to pen a story that incorporates the five items in her bag. Next have each student read her story aloud. At the end of each reading, invite the class to guess which five items from the story are in the writer's bag. When a correct guess is made, have the writer remove the item from her bag. If the five items are not guessed in five tries, the writer has outsleuthed her audience! Repeat this activity as often as desired. Clever writers and excellent listeners are sure to follow.

Maryann Chern Bannwart—Gr. 3, Antietam Elementary, Woodbrige, VA

Entertaining Tongue Twisters

What could be more fun for students than writing tongue twisters? How about writing tongue twisters about themselves? To set the stage for this activity, read aloud assorted tongue twisters from a book such as *Six Sick Sheep: 101 Tongue Twisters* by Joanna Cole and Stephanie Calmenson (Morrow Junior Books, 1993). Then challenge students to pen several personalized tongue twisters. Next ask each child to choose her favorite twister to copy and illustrate on provided paper. Invite students to share their silly sentences with the class. Then collect the projects and compile them into a book titled "Several Silly Students." This tongue twister collection will quickly become a class favorite!

Catherine V. Herber—Gr. 1, Washington Elementary, Raleigh, NC

A Gift From The Heart

Begin this special writing project a few weeks before Mother's Day and each child will have a loving gift for his mother or another loved one. For a two-week writing project, give each child ten 4" x 6" sheets of drawing paper inside a quart-size resealable plastic bag. For each of the next ten school days, have every child remove one blank booklet page from his zippered bag and then copy, complete, and illustrate a sentence like "_____, you are special to me because…" Ask students to store their completed pages in their plastic bags. When all ten pages are written, have each child select a sample of wallpaper from which to make his cover. Cut a 7" x 9" rectangle from the wallpaper sample, fold the cutout in half, and staple the student's pages inside. If desired, have each child use a permanent marker to personalize and date the front inside cover of his booklet. The recipients of these loving keepsakes are sure to be thrilled!

Jeannette Freeman—Gr. 3, Baldwin School Of Puerto Rico, Guaynabo, Puerto Rico

LIFESAVERS

LIFESAVERS...
management tips for teachers

Substitute Helper

Try this easy alternative to finding substitutes for classroom helpers. In addition to the regular classroom jobs, include a position for a substitute helper. If a helper is absent, the substitute takes her place for the day. Rotate the substitute helper throughout the year so that all students have a chance to sub.

Mary Beth Hornak—Gr. 2, St. Matthew School, Indianapolis, IN

Picture Perfect

Labeling classroom learning centers is easy with the help of inexpensive, clear acrylic picture frames. Write the title and directions for each learning activity on an index card; then slip each card into a different frame. Place the frames at the corresponding learning centers. When it's time to change an activity, simply slide the card out of the frame and replace it with a new set of directions. Your centers will be neat and organized, and students will easily see the directions for each activity.

Liz Kramer—Gr. 2, Boyden School, Walpole, MA

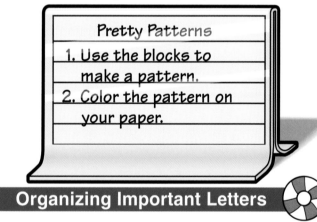

Organizing Important Letters

Locating important letters and handouts for parents is a breeze with this timesaving idea. Label one pocket folder for each of these topics: beginning of the school year, end of the school year, conferences, articles, report cards, invitations, permission slips, and miscellaneous. Hole-punch the folders and place them in a large, three-ring binder. Keep original copies of letters and handouts for parents in the folders. At the beginning of the month, browse through the folders and duplicate the items you need. Locating needed materials has never been easier!

Linh Tran—Gr. 1, Charles B. Wallace Elementary, York, PA

Awesome Art Mats

These awesome art mats make cleanup as easy as one, two, three! Have each student personalize and decorate an 18" x 24" sheet of construction paper. Laminate the paper mats and store them in an accessible area. Before your next art activity, pass out the mats and have students place them on top of their desks. When it is time for cleanup, simply wipe the mats with a damp paper towel or rinse them in the sink. What an easy way to keep desks clean!

Melinda Casida—Gr. 1, Crowly Elementary, Visalia, CA

Fantastic Folders

Help your youngsters organize their papers with this simple pocket-folder system. Have each student bring three pocket folders to school. Collect one of the folders and store it as a replacement. Have each student label and decorate one folder "Stay At School" and another folder "Take Home." Explain to your students that schoolwork for collection at the end of each day should be placed in their "Stay At School" folders. Papers that need to be taken home should be placed in their "Take Home" folders for review with a parent each night. (You may choose to include a parent sign-off sheet in each "Take Home" folder.) Parents and students will agree—this organized approach is fantastic!

Margie Siegel—Gr. 2, Wren Hollow Elementary School Ballwin, MO

294

LIFESAVERS...
management tips for teachers

Ask Three Before You Ask Me

Put a familiar phrase to good use as students take responsibility for their own learning. Post the phrase "Ask Three Before You Ask Me" in a prominent location as a reminder for students. Tell your youngsters that if they have a question, they should ask three other students before asking you. Before a child asks you a question, have him name the three students he's already asked. Students will create an atmosphere of cooperation, and you'll minimize the number of times you repeat directions!

Cheryl A. Wade—Gr. 2, Golden Springs Elementary, Oxford, AL

Colorful Student Roles

Pipe-cleaner bracelets are a colorful way to remind students of their assigned roles in cooperative groups. On a sheet of poster board, list each student role followed by a different color word. Post the resulting chart in a prominent classroom location and gather a supply of pipe cleaners in the colors you've listed. When you assign student roles within a cooperative group, give each child the appropriate color of pipe cleaner and have him fashion it into a bracelet to wear throughout the activity. These colorful reminders are sure to promote successful student interaction!

Deb Callan—Gr. 1, Bel Air Elementary School, Evans, GA

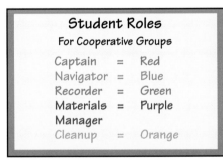

Student Roles		
For Cooperative Groups		
Captain	=	Red
Navigator	=	Blue
Recorder	=	Green
Materials Manager	=	Purple
Cleanup	=	Orange

Wonderful Wipes

This tip makes classroom cleanup a breeze! In a note to parents, request that each student bring a container of baby wipes to school. Leave one container in a location that is easily accessible to students and store the rest of the containers for later use. You and your students will discover that baby wipes are especially handy for cleaning desktops, tabletops, chalk ledges, overhead transparencies, and sticky hands. As an added bonus, you'll have the freshest-smelling room around!

Laura Peter—Gr. 3, Our Lady Of The Rosary, Cincinnati, OH

Blooming Books

Do you wish you had more space to display books in your classroom? A plastic planter box may be just what you need! Set a planter box on a countertop near a window or on the floor beneath your chalkboard ledge; then fill the box with books. If desired, post a sign titled "Blooming Books" nearby. There's a good chance that this new display will sprout a renewed interest in reading, too.

Angela T. Sawyer—Gr. 3, Burnett Elementary School Austell, GA

Behavior Incentive

Encourage positive student behavior with an easy-to-manage incentive. Think of an incentive in the form of a sentence, such as "An extra recess sure would be nice!" Then, on the chalkboard, draw a series of blanks to represent each word in the sentence—one blank per letter. Each time you observe students exhibiting a positive classroom behavior, write a letter in one blank. When all the blanks are filled and the incentive is revealed, reward the students accordingly. You can count on students trying to guess the class reward as they practice positive classroom behaviors!

Sandy Wiele—Gr. 2, Peoria Christian School, Peoria, IL

Pencil Sharpener Cover-Up

Here's an easy way to signal when students may sharpen their pencils. When you don't want students using the pencil sharpener, simply slip an empty, cube-shaped, decorative tissue box over it. Remove the decorative box to signal that pencils may be sharpened. Now that's a sharp idea!

Nancy Y. Karpyk—Gr. 2 Broadview Elementary Weirton, WV

LIFESAVERS...
management tips for teachers

Spotting Good Behavior

Help your youngsters stretch toward perfect hallway behavior with this fun-filled idea. Cut out a tall giraffe shape from yellow paper and 20 giraffe spots from brown paper. Add facial features and other desired details to the giraffe; then laminate the cutout and the spots. Display the giraffe in an accessible classroom area and store the spots nearby. Each time the class shows exceptional hallway behavior, have a student tape a spot on the giraffe. Reward the class with a special treat or privilege when all 20 spots are in place. What a gigantic way to encourage positive hallway behavior!

Leann Schwartz—Gr. 2, Ossian Elementary School, Ossian, IN

Center Management

If you have centers that are consistently overcrowded, try this center management chart. First determine how many students can occupy each center at one time. Label one library pocket per center. Then label one paper strip per center occupant. Glue the library pockets to a sheet of poster board and slip the strips in the corresponding pockets. To visit a center, a student takes a paper strip labeled with the name of the center. If no strips are available, he makes another center choice. When the student completes the center, he returns the strip. Eliminating center pileups has never been easier!

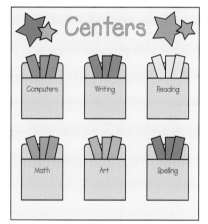

Jennifer P. Gann—Gr. 2
Seymour Primary School, Seymour, TN

Storing Strips

A check register box is the perfect container for storing sentence strips. The box is intended to store canceled checks; however, if you turn it lengthwise, the box is the ideal size for sentence-strip storage. Check your local office-supply store for these reasonably priced boxes. You'll be glad you did!

Heather Winkopp—Gr. 1, Indian Trace Elementary
Ft. Lauderdale, FL

Taking Papers Home

Save precious class time by sending home corrected student work once a week. Have each child personalize the front of a file folder. Laminate the folders for durability and tape a parent response sheet, like the one shown, inside each one. Once a week set aside a few minutes to distribute the folders and your students' corrected work.

Each child carries his papers home inside his folder. A parent removes and reviews the contents of the folder; then he or she dates, signs, and adds a comment to the response sheet. The following school day the student returns the empty folder. Each week you'll save time *and* communicate with parents!

Tomara Steadman—Gr. 1, St. Marks Elementary, Colwich, KS

Attendance At A Glance

Here's a quick and interactive way to take attendance! Display a poster-board chart, like the one shown, in an easily accessible location. Use a wipe-off marker to write a yes/no question on a laminated sentence strip; then mount the strip above the chart. Place a basket containing one personalized clothespin per student near the display. A student enters the room, reads the question (provide assistance as needed), and indicates her answer by clipping her clothespin on the appropriate side of the chart.

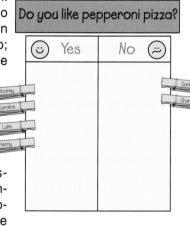

A quick glance in the basket reveals which students are absent. At the end of the day, return all clothespins to the basket and reprogram the sentence strip with another yes/no question. Now that's a wonderful way to start the day!

Karen M. Moser—Gr. 1, Wells Elementary, Plano, TX

LIFESAVERS...
management tips for teachers

Terrific Tickets

This idea is just the ticket for motivating students to complete their homework on time! Each morning give a raffle ticket to every student who completes her homework assignment. A student writes her name on the back of her ticket and drops it in a designated container. On Friday draw several tickets from the container, and award each selected student a special treat or privilege. Then discard the personalized tickets and repeat the procedure the following week.

Benita Kuhlman—Gr. 1
Avon Elementary
Avon, SD

"All Set? You Bet!"

Here's a quick way to find out which students are ready for the next task at hand. Simply ask, "All set?" and snap your fingers twice. The students who are ready respond, "You bet!" The others say, "Not yet." If necessary, wait a few moments; then repeat the question. This upbeat exchange prompts students to ready themselves in a timely manner, without making them feel anxious.

Maryann Chern Bannwart—Gr. 3
Antietam Elementary
Woodbridge, VA

Dice Mats

These easy-to-make mats muffle the sounds of rolling dice. To make the mats, cut one-foot squares from nonslip drawer lining. Store the resulting dice mats near your supply of dice. To use a mat, a student presses it flat against his playing surface. Roll 'em!

Marcia Hopkins—Gr. 1
James Ellis Elementary
Niles, MI

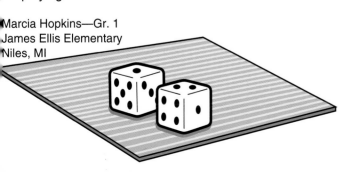

Borrow Until Tomorrow!

Avoid time-consuming delays caused by misplaced school supplies. Place a container of sharpened pencils, scissors, erasers, and glue sticks on your desk. As needed, students borrow items from the container and return them by the following school day. Also keep a stack of request forms near the container so students can alert their parents to their supply needs.

Kristi Gullett—Gr. 2, Peoria Christian School
Peoria, IL

"Class-y" Books

Here's a smart way to publish students' writing. Stock a view binder with clear sheet protectors. To make a class book, slip your students' writings into the sheet protectors; then slide a student-decorated cover into the binder's clear pocket. Display the publication in your class library for all to enjoy. In addition to being extremely durable, the class book can be used again and again by simply replacing the students' work.

Joan Hodges—Gr. 2, Lantern Lane Elementary
Houston, TX

Pairing Partners

Pair students and develop their vocabulary skills with this seasonal approach. Program a class set of seasonal cutouts with pairs of homonyms, antonyms, or synonyms. To assign partners, distribute the shapes and ask each child to find the classmate who holds the homonym (antonym, synonym) of his word. Once the students are paired, collect and store the cutouts. Your youngsters' vocabulary skills will quickly take shape!

Janice Keer—Grs. 1–2, Irvin Pertzsch School
Onalaska, WI

LIFESAVERS...
management tips for teachers

Manipulatives Coordinator

Save time by enlisting your students' help in organizing classroom manipulatives for quick and easy distribution. Every Monday assign a student to be the Manipulative Coordinator, or M.C., for the week. Each morning have the M.C. count and sort the manipulatives needed for that day. You can count on plenty of student interest in this official-sounding job.

Kim Lehmker—Grs. 1–3, Our Shepherd Lutheran School
Birmingham, MI

Foldaway Flannelboard

Open your door to this space-saving flannelboard! Cut a rectangle of felt that is the width of your classroom door-way and a desired length plus two inches. Fold and stitch a one-inch casing across the top and bottom of the felt. Then slip a spring-style curtain rod into each casing. Position the flannelboard in your doorway and it's ready to use. To store, simply release the curtain rods and roll up the project. This portable flannelboard also makes a terrific puppet theater!

Karen Smith—Grs. K–1
Pine Lane Elementary
    Homeschool
Pace, FL

Problem-Solving Solutions

The next time there's a classroom predicament to solve or a holiday party to plan, enlist your youngsters' problem-solving expertise. Post a brief note that requests your students' advice. In the note, ask that each student submit his ideas to you in the form of a friendly letter. With this simple idea, youngsters have an opportunity to polish their letter-writing skills, share their views, and contribute to classroom solutions!

Jan Keer—Grs. 1–2, Irving Pertzsch Elementary School
Onalaska, WI

298

Bulletin-Board Binder

Find your bulletin-board titles with ease! Stock a three-ring binder with top-loading, plastic page protectors. Place the letters of each bulletin-board title in a separate page protector and label the front of the protector with the title. Next year you'll have all your favorite bulletin-board titles right at your fingertips!

Robin Wright
New Franklin
    Elementary
    School
New Franklin, MO

The Earth Is In
Our Hands

Cluster Buster

Do your students cluster around your desk as they wait to consult with you? Try this! Ask youngsters to organize themselves as if they were standing in line at the checkout counter of a local store. Explain that this is how you would like for them to line up at your desk. The next time students begin to cluster, ask them to get in checkout formation. It works like a charm!

Deanna Whitford—Gr. 1, Holt Elementary, Holt, MO

Signing Out And In

This classroom checkout system is a time-saver and a teaching tool. Each morning post a daily sign-out sheet like the one shown. When a student needs to leave the classroom, she signs the sheet and records the time. Then when she returns to the classroom, she records the current time. You'll spend fewer minutes monitoring the classroom door and your students' time-telling skills are sure to improve. As an added bonus, you have documentation of the frequency in which students exit the classroom.

Sue Lorey
Arlington Heights, IL

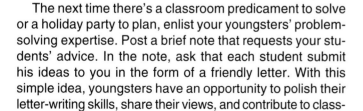

Name	Out	In
Katie	8:30	8:34
Ben	8:52	8:57
Caroline	9:15	9:21
Danielle	9:30	9:36
Nicholas	10:06	10:11

What's The Time?

OUR READERS WRITE

Our Readers Write

Tooth Taxi

To guarantee that a lost tooth arrives home from school safely, provide a Tooth Taxi for its transportation. Cut out a small picture of a tooth and label it "Tooth Taxi." Secure the picture to an empty film container with clear packaging tape. When a student loses a tooth, simply drop the tooth into the container and snap on the cap. The tooth will travel in style!

Dee Kaltenbach Riesen
Gr. 1
Tri County Elementary School
DeWitt, NE

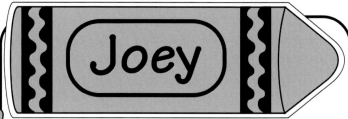

Colorful Nametags

Brighten up your class with these easy-to-make nametags. For each student, round one end of a 6" x 18" colored construction-paper rectangle to resemble a crayon tip. Use a black marker to personalize and decorate the nametag. Then laminate the tag for durability and tape it to the student's desktop. What a vivid way to deck out desks!

Gina Parisi—Grs. 1–6 Basic Skills
Brookdale School, Bloomfield, NJ

Weekly Bulletin

What's in the news? Students will be eager to answer this daily question! Monday through Thursday, conclude each day by asking volunteers to report the day's key events. Record the students' comments on a laminated chart and use the resulting classroom news for a spontaneous language-arts lesson. Before wiping the chart clean, record one student's comment on a weekly newsletter form like the one shown. On Friday add a personal note to the form; then duplicate the publication and send it home with students. Parents will be pleased to receive the news "hot off the press" and students will love making the headlines!

Linda Johnson—Gr. 1
Rockway School, Springfield, OH

Weekly News From First Grade
September 18, 1998

David C. said, "We did the mystery bag and ate what was inside!"

Rachel H. said, "We watched a movie about animals looking for their homes."

Andy B. said, "We talked about houses and made a neighborhood."

Evan D. said, "We used our Geoboards to make patterns and we read about mice."

Pins For Pennies

Here's a quick and inexpensive way to create appealing pins for student wear. To make a class set of back-to-school pins, adhere on poster board one back-to-school sticker for each student. Then laminate the poster board or cover it with clear Con-Tact® covering. Cut out the stickers and use craft or hot glue to attach a pin fastener to the back of each one. The unique welcome-to-school jewelry will make quite a fashion statement! Plan to create additional sticker pins to recognize student achievements, stimulate interest in topics of study, and celebrate student birthdays.

Ann Marie Stephens—Gr. 1
George C. Round Elementary School
Manassas, VA

Parent Pen Pals

Foster positive communication between parent and child with this noteworthy idea! At the beginning of the school year, ask parents to supply several self-addressed, stamped envelopes. Periodically have students write letters to their parents about their accomplishments and upcoming school events. Facilitate responses from parents by providing them with several postcards addressed to the school. Parents will appreciate being kept up-to-date, and students' writing skills will improve as well.

Karen Smith—Grs. K–1
Pine Lane Elementary Home School
Pace, FL

Reading On The Job

Set the stage for a fun-filled year of reading with this engaging bulletin-board idea! Before the school year begins, photograph several community workers reading. Mount the photos on a brightly colored bulletin board titled "Everybody Reads." As the school year progresses, invite a variety of guest readers to share their favorite books. Photograph each guest reading; then add his photo to the display. Not only will the display demonstrate the value of reading to your students, but it will also serve as a springboard for lessons about careers.

Carolyn Cantrell—Gr. 1
Wills Point Primary School
Wills Point, TX

Classy Clips

These student-made display clips are perfect for greeting classroom visitors and showcasing students' work. Provide each student with a head and shirt-shaped cutout made from poster board. Have each student create and label a likeness of himself using markers, crayons, construction paper, and glue. Laminate the cutouts for durability and hot-glue two clothespins to the back of each shirt. Hole-punch the top of each project and use monofilament to suspend it from the classroom ceiling. As students complete work they'd like to exhibit, clip it to their cutouts. What a wonderful way to showcase students' work during Open House and throughout the year!

Robin Pizzichil—Gr. 2
Evergreen Elementary School
Collegeville, PA

Blue-Ribbon Buses

Look who's in the driver's seat! For this back-to-school idea, duplicate on yellow construction paper a class supply of a bus pattern that has several windows. Instruct each student to glue a small photo of herself in the driver's seat, then provide information about herself in each window. Ask each student to cut out her bus and share her busload of information with the class before you post the projects around the room. Students will be ready to roll into a new school year with these clever introductions to their classmates.

Gina Parisi
Grs. 1–6
Basic Skills
Brookdale School
Bloomfield, NJ

Happy Birthday Book

Here's an inexpensive and creative way to celebrate a student's birthday. Have each classmate write a letter to the honored child on decorative paper. Bind the students' letters, a letter from you, and a title page between two poster-board covers. For added appeal wrap each poster-board cover in birthday paper and use curling ribbon to bind the project. Then lead the students in singing a familiar birthday tune and present the book of letters to the birthday child. Plan to recognize all your students' birthdays—even those that occur during the summer—with this letter-perfect idea.

Anita De La Torre—Gr. 2
Hutton Elementary, Chanute, KS

"VIB" Treasure Chests

Each week award a Very Important Buccaneer with a bounty of treasured compliments. Fold, staple, and decorate a sheet of 12" x 18" construction paper to make a treasure chest like the one shown. After the buccaneer of the week has been selected, give each of his classmates a duplicated pattern of a smiling coin. Ask each student to cut out the paper coin and label the back with a positive comment about the VIB of the week. Encourage students to write thoughtful messages and explain that they have until noon on Friday (or another designated day and time) to complete the coins. Verify that each child has signed his coin before collecting them in the treasure chest. Then add a personalized coin yourself and use a yellow sticky dot to seal the chest before you present the treasure to the VIB. No doubt he'll be pleased with his good fortune!

Ann Marie Stephens—Gr. 1
George C. Round Elementary School, Manassas, VA

Moon Munchies

These luscious lunar snacks teach youngsters about moon phases! To demonstrate a complete cycle of the moon, each student needs 2 1/2 refrigerated biscuits. A student uses one whole biscuit to represent a full moon and the half biscuit to represent a quarter moon. Then, using a knife and an inverted cup, the student cuts off a small sliver of the remaining biscuit to create gibbous and crescent moons. Bake the biscuits as directed and serve them with butter and jelly. After each student has finished eating his tasty treats, he'll have an example of a new moon—it's there, he just can't see it!

Jan McManus—Gr. 2
St. Clement School
St. Bernard, OH

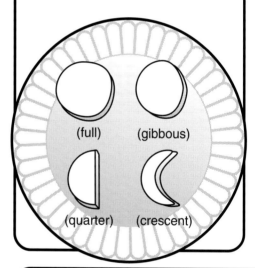

Seasonal Storage

Looking for a way to organize and store paint-center supplies? Then try this canny idea! Obtain one large empty food can for every month or season of the school year. To prepare each can, apply a base coat of rust-resistant paint in a seasonal color; then label and decorate the painted container as desired. Next apply a clear sealant to protect your artwork. Store your paint-center supplies in the appropriate container, and store the other containers for later use. Not only will students enjoy looking at each container, they'll be more likely to use it—and that means a tidier center area!

Jackye Bowen
Young American's Christian School
Conyers, GA

Bone-Chilling Stories

Send chills up your students' spines with this small-group writing activity! First have each group brainstorm spooky words and write them on a large bone-shaped cutout. Next ask each group to share five words from its cutout. Encourage the other groups to add these words to their collections if appropriate. Then have each group write a scary story that includes ten spooky words from its cutout. After each group has shared its work with the class, mount each story and its corresponding bone cutout on a bulletin board titled "Bone-Chilling Tales!"

Jill Hamilton—Gr. 1
Schoeneck Elementary
Stevens, PA

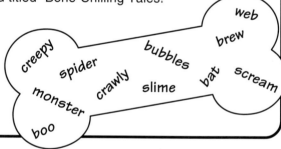

Chalkboard Clock

Here's a king-size manipulative clock that just keeps on ticking! Draw a large clock face on a magnetic chalkboard; then use magnetic tape to attach laminated hour and minute hands. The clock is perfect for any number of large-group, time-telling activities. And it makes a great partner center too. Taking turns, one student positions the clock hands and his partner writes the corresponding digital time on the chalkboard. To modify the clock for young learners, remove the manipulative minute hand and draw a stationary chalk one. Your youngsters' clock-reading skills will improve in no time!

Julie Reef—Gr. 2
South Adams Elementary, Berne, IN

Marvelous Manipulative Holders

Managing manipulatives will be a sweet success with these minia-ture containers! Collect a class supply of empty mini M&M's® snap-top containers. Then fill each container with a desired number of small manipulatives, such as dried beans, buttons, or corn kernels. With this handy storage idea, working with manipulatives will be a snap!

Yolanda Matthews, Huntsville, AL

Daily Finale

Youngsters love music, so why not end the day with this upbeat song? You'll provide closure to the day and rein-force the days of the week. Sing this little ditty to the tune of Beethoven's "Ode To Joy." Or, if you prefer, recite the lyrics as a rhyme.

Good-Bye Song
Our day is through.
Our jobs are done.
We did some work.
We had some fun.

We worked real hard.
We played with friends.
And on [day of the week]
We'll be back again.

Donna W. Harrison—Gr. 1, Bridgeton, NJ

Pillowcase Keepsake

A good-bye pillowcase will hold a lot of memories for a student who is moving away. Have each child use fabric crayons to draw a picture on precut paper. Insert heavy paper into a prewashed white pillowcase; then iron the completed pictures onto the pillowcase as directed on the crayon package. Next have each youngster use a fabric marker to sign his name near his artwork. Remove the paper from inside the pillow-case, and present the completed project to the departing student. Not only is this farewell gift a wonderful keep-sake, it's practical too!

Roberta Boyd—Gr. 2
Barnstead Elementary
Alton, NH

Lunch-Count Savvy

Put math on the menu with a daily problem-solving activity! Each morning have a different child tally the classroom lunch chart to de-termine how many children are ordering hot lunch. Then invite the rest of the class to guess the total number of hot-lunch orders. The child in charge responds to each guess by stating whether the guess is greater than or less than the hot-lunch order. For a greater chal-lenge, ask students to present each guess in a number sentence like "Six plus two equals eight hot-lunch orders for today." Students will surely eat up this daily math warm-up!

Jan Smith—Gr. 1, Foothill Elementary, Boulder, CO

Holiday Horn Of Plenty

These student-made snacks are a perfect Thanksgiving treat! To make a colorful horn of plenty, a child uses prepared icing to affix pieces of Trix® cereal inside a Bugles® corn snack. Make a few extra treats; then, as a class, present them to staff members and volunteers who assist you and your students. Now that's a tasty way to say "Thank you!"

Patt Hall—Gr. 1
Babson Park Elementary
Babson Park, FL

Cooks' Corner

With the help of a few eager parents and the use of your school's cafeteria, you can serve up plenty of positive cooking experiences! Meet with your school's caf-eteria staff to schedule days and times that your class may use an oven. Once your schedule is in place, enlist parent volunteers to gather needed cooking sup-plies and ingredients, and to set up a cooking area in the corner of your class-room. You will also need volunteers to assist you in your classroom on desig-nated cooking days. Once your program is in place, keep parent volunteers in-formed of the recipes you'd like students to make. If desired, keep a computer record of each recipe your students pre-pare throughout the year. Then, at the end of the year, publish a Cooks' Cor-ner cookbook for a Mother's Day, a Father's Day, or an end-of-the-year project.

Jan Coxon—Gr. 1
Harrisburg Academy, Wormleysburg, PA

Season's Greetings

Brighten up the holiday season with this personalized Christmas greeting! Have each student use a pencil to draw her self-portrait on a two-inch square of white paper. Then have her use a pen to trace over her drawing and write her name. Reduce the students' drawings on a copier. Next use a pen to draw a circle around each portrait. Cut out the circles and arrange the resulting ornaments on a Christmas tree outline. Add a greeting and then duplicate two copies per student.

Have each student decorate one greeting for a member of the school staff and one for her family.

Linda Kemp—Gr. 2
E. G. Ross Elementary
Albuquerque, NM

No-Mess Glitter

'Tis the season to use glitter! This year minimize the mess by purchasing glitter fabric paint in small, easy-to-use bottles. The bottles allow students more control over how much glitter they use and where the glitter goes. (Caution students to work carefully since glitter paint is permanent and will stain clothing and carpet.) Now students can add glittery touches to holiday projects in half the time and without the mess!

Andra Hulstine—Gr. 2
Mt. Carmel Elementary
Douglasville, GA

Multicultural Celebrations

Collaborate with co-workers to create a merry multicultural event! Ask each participating teacher to prepare 30 minutes of activities celebrating a different December holiday. Activities might include playing a dreidel game for Hanukkah, decorating and eating cookies for Christmas, and making necklaces from red-, black-, and green-tinted pasta for Kwanzaa. Encourage each teacher to read aloud a holiday-related literature selection, too. On the day of the event, each class rotates along a predetermined route to each multicultural celebration. What a festive way to culminate the holiday season!

Marsha Joyner—Gr. 3
Davis Elementary School
Marietta, GA

Pencil-Can Presents

Wrap up the holidays with this practical student gift idea. Collect a class supply of clean potato-chip cans with lids. Cover the cans with colorful Con-Tact® covering. Inside each can, put two pencils, a glue stick, and an eraser. Then add some stickers and a few individually wrapped candies before snapping on the lid. Your students will be excited over the contents of the cans, and they'll also have nifty storage containers that they can continue to use.

Mary Hemp—Gr. 3
Ness City Elementary School
Ness City, KS

Tasty Tuesdays

This monthly hands-on idea is a recipe for handwriting success! One Tuesday per month, display a recipe for a seasonal or theme-related snack. After the students have made and eaten the snack, have each child carefully copy the posted recipe on provided paper. Then have him illustrate and date his work. File the students' work in individual folders. At the end of the school year, have each child chronologically compile his recipes into a cookbook. The resulting keepsake will be filled with tasty memories and outstanding penmanship progress!

Leann Schwartz—Gr. 2, Ossian Elementary School, Ossian, IN

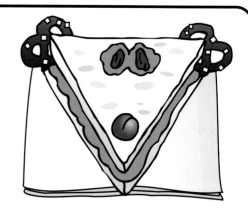

Doctor, Doctor, what do you do?

I take care of people who are sick.

That's how I help you!

Community Helper Booklet

Create a kid-pleasing class book about community helpers by modeling the book's text after *Brown Bear, Brown Bear, What Do You See?* by Bill Martin Jr. (Henry Holt And Company, Inc.; 1996). Ask each student to select an index card on which you've written the professional title of a community helper. Then post the following model for each student to use as he writes his page: "[Profession], [Profession], what do you do? I [job description]. That's how I help you!" Ask each child to illustrate his work; then compile the projects into a class book. Your budding authors will be eager to read this nonfiction selection again and again!

Kelly Finch—Gr. 1, Ford Elementary, Acworth, GA

Time For T.A.G.

How do you teach students to peer-edit properly? Try the T.A.G. approach. At the end of a writing session, pair students. Have each child carefully read what his partner has written. Then provide time for each child to do the following: Tell his partner what he likes about his writing; Ask his partner questions about his writing; Give his partner suggestions for improving his writing. In no time at all, your youngsters will be giving positive critiques of their classmates' writing, and their written work will prove it!

Kimberly Hofstetter
Oakland County School District
Bloomfield Hills, MI

Nifty Nouns

This little ditty, sung to the tune of "The Farmer In The Dell," helps students better understand the concept of nouns. Divide students into small groups and have each group create a version of the second verse. Lead the class in singing the first verse together; then cue each group (in turn) to sing for the class the verse it created.

Getting To Know A Noun
A person, place, or thing.
A person, place, or thing.
A noun is the name
Of a person, place, or thing.

[Person], [person], and [place].
A [thing], [thing], or tray.
Nouns are a lot of fun;
I use them every day!

Francine Calpin—Gr. 1
West Side Elementary, Johnstown, PA

Calendar-Time Cube

You'll receive rave reviews when you roll poetry and music into your daily calendar activities. To create a calendar-time cube, cover an empty cube-shaped box with colorful paper; then label the sides with the numerals 1 through 6. Each month display six numbered posters that each feature a holiday-related poem or song. Bring your daily calendar time to a close by selecting a child to roll the cube. Then lead the youngsters in reading the poem or singing the song that is rolled. By the end of the month, there's a good chance the featured poems and songs will be committed to memory!

Dana Huff—Substitute
  Teacher
Central Valley School District
Spokane, WA

Even Or Odd?

Unravel the mystery of even and odd numbers with this visual aid. Have each child use craft glue to attach an 8-inch length of jumbo rickrack to a 2 1/2" x 9" strip of tagboard. When the glue is dry, show the youngsters how to label the rickrack as shown. Tape each child's project to his desktop. Case solved!

Kim Myers—Gr. 2, Clearview Elementary, Martinsville, VA

Even
0 2 4 6 8 10 12 14 16 18 20
1 3 5 7 9 11 13 15 17 19
Odd

Taylor

Wow! 100%

1. The pig sat in the mud.
2. The dog ran fast.
3. That was a red fox.
4. Go get the duck.

Beautiful Border

Wallpaper border creates an eye-catching and versatile display area. Cut border from discarded wallpaper books; then trim it into 2" x 12" strips. Laminate one strip per student. Make a small slit in the middle of each strip and insert a jumbo paper clip. Use Velcro®, Sticky-Tac, or tape to secure the strips to a classroom wall. Ask each child to choose a sample of his best work to exhibit at the display. Then put the students in charge of periodically replacing their own work with more current samples.

Sharon L. Brannan—Gr. 2, Holly Hill Elementary, Holly Hill, FL

Literature Lists

Start the new year off with a bulletin board that motivates youngsters to read different types of literature. Create a display like the one shown that features the literature genres you plan to read with your students. Each time the class completes a book, discuss which genre the book represents. Then ask a student to write the title of the book on a card and post the card on the display in the correct literature category. Students will feel proud to have the number and types of books they've been reading posted for classroom visitors to see. And you can count on your students requesting that specific genres be read in an effort to keep the categories equal!

Dianne Neumann—Gr. 2, Frank C. Whiteley School, Hoffman Estates, IL

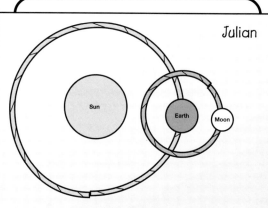

Julian

Earth orbits the Sun.
The Moon orbits the Earth.

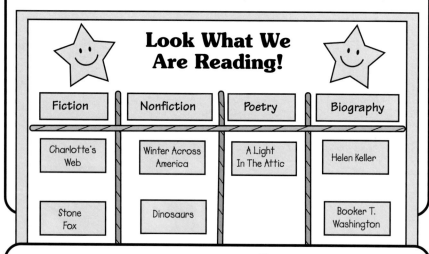

Look What We Are Reading!

Fiction	Nonfiction	Poetry	Biography
Charlotte's Web	Winter Across America	A Light In The Attic	Helen Keller
Stone Fox	Dinosaurs		Booker T. Washington

Out-Of-This-World Orbits

This hands-on activity helps students visualize the orbits of Earth and the Moon! Provide tagboard templates for the Sun (2 1/4" circle), Earth (1 1/2" circle), and the Moon (3/4" circle). A student traces each template onto colorful paper; then he labels and cuts out each shape. He glues the Sun cutout near the center of a 9" x 12" sheet of drawing paper. To show Earth's orbit, the student glues a 20-inch yarn length around the Sun; then he glues the Earth cutout atop the yarn. To show the Moon's orbit, he glues a 9-inch yarn length around Earth, and then he glues the Moon cutout on the yarn. At the bottom of the paper, he writes a brief caption that explains his work. With all the pieces in place, students are sure to have a better understanding of a very confusing concept!

Angela Vickers—Grs. K–5 EH
Orangewood Elementary
Lehigh Acres, FL

Paper-Scrap Spelling

If your students frequently ask you to spell words for them, try this! Display a basket of paper scraps (blank on one or both sides). When a student needs help spelling a word, he takes a piece of paper from the basket and writes how he thinks the word is spelled. Then he brings the spelling to you to be confirmed or corrected. This risk-free approach to spelling strengthens students' phonic skills and boosts their spelling confidence. And as an added bonus, you'll have more time to assist students in other areas.

Robyn Woolf—Grs. 1–2
Coolville Elementary
Coolville, OH

Sweet Symmetry

Get right to the heart of symmetry with this cookie-decorating activity! Plan for students to work at a center or in small groups. Each child frosts a heart-shaped cookie with prepared icing and uses a length of licorice to indicate a line of symmetry. Next he carefully positions small candies like red hots, conversation hearts, and mini chocolate chips on his cookie—making sure the shape remains symmetrical. These sweet treats are perfect for a Valentine's Day party. Now isn't that a scrumptious way to explore symmetry?

Amy Smith—Gr. 1
Omaha Nation School, Macy, NE

Three Cheers For You!

Your sentences are very well written!

Colorful Awards

If purchasing multicolored awards is not in your budget, here's a classy alternative! Place file folders containing class sets of duplicated awards, certificates, and bookmarks at a free-time center along with markers, crayons, colored pencils, and scissors. Invite early finishers to color and cut out the rewards, and return them to the appropriate files. You'll soon have a cache of colorful rewards to distribute!

Lisa Von Hatten—Gr. 3
St. Paul Elementary
   School
Highland, IL

Stamp Pad Solution

Does your stamp pad seem to dry out too quickly? It may be that the ink has sunk to the bottom of the pad. To alleviate this problem, store your stamp pad upside down. When you're ready to use it, the ink will be near the top of the pad, and you'll get the picture-perfect stamps you're hoping for!

Christen M. Reiner—Gr.2
Lavaland Elementary
   School
Albuquerque, NM

Seeking Simple Machines

Keep your youngsters' knowledge of simple machines in tip-top shape with a field trip to a local gym or fitness center. Arrange for a staff member to demonstrate different fitness equipment while the youngsters examine each apparatus for examples of simple machines. Your youngsters' thinking skills will be in high gear!

Patty Young—Gr. 1
Haymarket, VA

Too Hot!

Need a game for your Valentine's Day party? Try this heart-shaped version of Hot Potato! Seat students in a circle and hand one child an empty heart-shaped candy box. Start a recording of lively music, and repeatedly stop and start the music at unpredictable intervals. If a child is holding the candy box when the music stops, he moves out of the circle. If the candy box is dropped, everyone returns to the circle! Play continues until only one student remains or game time is over. Whether students are passing around a gold coin for St. Patrick's Day or a plastic egg for Easter, you can count on this game getting rave reviews!

Sara L. Warner—Gr. 2
Timberlake Christian School, Lynchburg, VA

Nifty Number Code

This spelling activity adds up to loads of fun! Clearly display a set of large alphabet letter cards. Then, for each alphabet letter, label a sticky note with a desired numeral and attach the note to the corresponding card. Students use the number values to find the sum of each spelling word. To modify the code, simply swap sticky notes between the cards. To increase the difficulty of the code, program a new set of sticky notes with higher numerals. The possibilities are endless—and each takes very little time! For an extension, invite each student to find the value of the name of his favorite pet, ice-cream flavor, book, or sports team!

Elaine Anderson—Gr. 2
Blairstown Elementary School, Blairstown, NJ

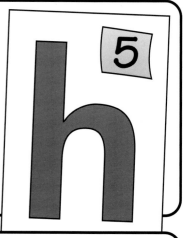

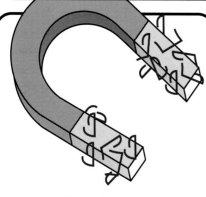

Staple Pull

Use this powerful suggestion to quickly remove staples from the classroom floor! Give a student a large magnet and ask him to use it to pick up the staples. Have the child deposit the staples he collects in the wastebasket. Now that's a cleanup job that's too much fun to be called work!

Dannie Davis—Gr. 3
Silver Creek Elementary, Azle, TX

Poetry With A Purpose

Promote added interest in poetry with this plan. Display two or three poems that relate to a current theme or topic of study. Try to choose poems of varying lengths and difficulty. Entice students to memorize the poems with the promise of a sticker or special privilege for each poem a student recites for you. Students will be so focused on memorizing the poems that they won't even notice that they're practicing their reading skills too! Introduce a new collection of poems each time you present a new theme or topic of study.

Sharon L. Brannan—Gr. 2
Holly Hill Elementary
Holly Hill, FL

Recess Coaches

Recess coaches offer solutions to common problems encountered on the playground. Who are the recess coaches? Your students! Assign each student a partner or coach. If a child needs help solving a problem during recess, he finds his coach and explains his predicament. The coach suggests three possible solutions. If the child tries one or more of the solutions and the result is unsatisfactory, he asks the teacher on duty for help. This approach nurtures problem-solving skills and encourages students to think, rather than react.

Julie Huff—Gr. 2
Rafé Shearer—Counselor
Filbert Street Elementary School
Mechanicsburg, PA

Orderly Ordinals

Stamp out confusion over ordinal numbers with this quick and easy activity. Use a rubber stamp and stamp pad to make a strip of ten stamped images for each student. Then give a series of oral instructions for students to follow that incorporate ordinal numbers. For example, "Color the fifth shamrock green," and "Draw a yellow circle around the ninth shamrock." You can count on this math activity being a class favorite!

Sister Helen Teresa—Gr. 1
Incarnation School
Trenton, NJ

Vocabulary Shuffle

This game for two or more players is great for ESL students. Cut out 20 small pictures of objects from discarded magazines and mount each picture on a blank card. Write "Oops!" on five additional cards. To play, one student shuffles the cards and stacks them facedown on the playing surface. In turn, each student draws a card. If the student says the corresponding English word, he keeps the card. If not, he returns the card to the bottom of the stack. If a student draws an "Oops!" card, he returns all his cards to the bottom of the stack. The winner is the student who has the most cards when game time is over.

Joanna Biello—Grs. K–5
Ferderbar Elementary, Langhorne, PA

R Is For Recycle

Celebrate Earth Day any day by having students make an alphabet booklet of earth-friendly tips. Cut out 26 eight-inch circles from white paper (booklet pages) and two from construction paper (booklet covers). Also cut out each letter of the alphabet from colorful paper. Have each student glue a letter cutout to a white circle and then on the circle write and illustrate an earth-friendly message that begins with her assigned letter. Enlist early finishers to complete leftover booklet pages and to decorate the booklet covers. Then alphabetize the pages and staple them between the covers. There you have it—a world of earth-saving information for your youngsters' reading pleasure!

Susie Kapaun—Gr. 2, Leawood Elementary, Littleton, CO

Motto Magic

Start each day on a positive note with this simple strategy. Write the motto shown on chart paper and post it in your classroom. Enthusiastically recite the motto with your students each morning to inspire them to work toward success every day.

Cynthia Schaffer—Gr. 1
Dunbar Primary School
Lufkin, TX

Our Motto
If I can believe it,
I can achieve it!
Because I am special,
I will be successful!

Pop-Up Book Reviews

Do you have a one-minute sand or kitchen timer? That's all you need to promote book sharing and assess student comprehension! Randomly select a student and give him one minute to pop up from his seat, tell the title of a book he has recently read, and describe what the book is about. When the last grain of sand has slipped to the bottom of the timer or the bell sounds, select another student to do a pop-up review. It's a great way to get youngsters thinking about the books they've read.

Candy Whelan—Gr. 3
Garlough Elementary
West St. Paul, MN

Bag It!

If your yarn always becomes a tangled mess, try this tip. Roll yarn into a ball. Diagonally snip one bottom corner from a resealable sandwich bag. Place the ball of yarn into the sandwich bag, pull the loose end of the yarn through the hole, and seal the bag. Voilà! You now have tangle-free yarn that's ready to use!

Jeanine Peterson—Gr. 2
Bainbridge Elementary School
Bainbridge, IN

Versatile Velcro®

Get hooked on this versatile way of displaying teaching charts and student work. Adhere the hook side of Velcro® strips to walls or chalkboard edges. Snip the loop side into pieces and attach them to clothespins. Clip prepared clothespins onto the items you wish to display and press the clothespins onto the mounted strips of Velcro®.

Connie Allen—Gr. 3
Immanuel Lutheran School
Manitowoc, WI

The Water Cycle

Pollination Stations

Create a springtime buzz about pollination. Cut out several large flower shapes and place them around your classroom. Using a hole puncher, punch a large supply of circles from yellow paper to represent pollen. Place the pollen in the center of one flower and place a small bucket of water nearby. Ask students to imagine that their fingers are the legs of bees. Then have each child in turn dip his fingers into the bucket of water, touch the pollen on the flower, and *fly* from flower to flower, stopping to touch the center of each one. As each child's fingers dry, pollen will drop onto the other flowers, much like what really happens when bees buzz from flower to flower.

Geoff Mihalenko—Gr. 1, Frank Defino Central School, Marlboro, NJ

Baby-Bootee Greetings

Is one of your students expecting a new baby brother or sister? Involve your class in a meaningful writing experience, while welcoming the new sibling into the world. Cut a class supply of baby-bootee shapes from lined paper. Then have each child write a welcome letter to the baby telling something wonderful about his or her big brother or sister. Make pink or blue baby-bootee covers and staple the letters between them. Everyone—including moms—will get a kick out of this letter-writing experience!

Anita DeLaTorre—Gr. 2, Hutton Elementary
Chanute, KS

Trayton Michael Smith
May 5, 1999

Dear Trayton,
It is fun to play with Virgil. I hope you are very happy in this world. I am.
From your friend,
Jenell

Fresh-As-Spring Writing Samples

Just in time for warm spring breezes, create a clothesline display for students to air their finest writing. Secure a length of string or cord beneath your chalkboard ledge and place a basket of spring-type clothespins nearby. If a student wishes to display a sample of his writing, he clips it to the clothesline using a couple of clothespins. To keep the display fresh, encourage students to routinely replace their own writing samples. Then invite students to hang out at the display and read what their classmates have written.

Deb Jacobson—Gr. 3
Wyndmere Elementary
Wyndmere, ND

Agree Or Growl

Get students excited about noun-verb agreement! Use a red marker to write ten singular and ten plural nouns on individual cards. On another 20 cards, use a blue marker to write ten singular and ten plural verbs. Give each child a card, passing out an equal number of noun and verb cards. Randomly ask noun-verb pairs of students to come to the front of the class and hold up their cards. If the noun and verb agree, the two students shake hands. If the noun and verb disagree, the two card holders face each other and give the most disagreeable growls they can muster! What an expressive way to practice noun-verb agreement!

Trish DePew—Gr. 2
Austin Elementary
Wichita Falls, TX

boys draws

Compliments To Keep

Accentuate the positive and boost student morale with this bookmaking project. Give each child a class list. Beside each name (including his own) have each student describe a positive trait of that person. Collect the papers and type the compliments about each child onto individual pages. Then duplicate the pages and compile them into books—one per student plus one for the class library. When you hand out the books, ask each child to read his personal page carefully and, if desired, highlight each comment that makes him feel especially proud. Although making these books does require an investment of time, youngsters will open them time and again for encouragement—confirming that the preparation time was well spent.

Cheryl Phillips—Gr. 3
Mt. Washington Elementary School
Baltimore, MD

Kevin Daniels

Kevin is kind, nice, and helpful.
Respectful.
Has great basketball skills.
He likes to make jokes and make people laugh.
A very comical person that will make you laugh.
You are very bold.
Kevin is too funny.
Kevin likes to read.
He plays nice.
Kevin is kind and helpful.
Kevin always works good.
He is a nice boy.
Kevin is always willing to show new people around the school.
He makes me laugh.
He is very kind.
I like your personality.
Kevin is a good artist.
Kevin likes to share his things.
Kevin is a sportsman.

Building "Math-letes"

Strengthen your students' ability to solve word problems with this daily exercise. Each morning feature a word problem on the chalkboard, occasionally listing multiple-choice answers. When the students arrive, have them read and complete the problem independently. This daily "math-ercise" will get your class in shape for a variety of word-problem challenges!

Beth Caraccio—Gr. 2
Ringgold, GA

Brag Line

Looking for a way to encourage helpfulness and positive attitudes during the final weeks of school? Create a brag line! Suspend a clothesline (heavy string or lightweight cord) in a convenient and safe classroom location. When you observe a student practicing praiseworthy behavior, write his name and a sentence that describes his action(s) on a colorful cutout. Clip the cutout to the clothesline with a clothespin. You'll soon have plenty to brag about!

Jennifer Murphy—Gr. 3
Bayview Academy
Riverside, RI

Thomas helped Maria pick up books.

Susan held the door open for Ms. Murphy

Classy Awards

Wouldn't you love to present several end-of-the-year awards to each child? You can when you enlist your youngsters' help! Write each student's name on five ribbon-shaped awards. Complete one award for each student; then distribute the remainder of the awards to your youngsters. Make sure that each child has four awards labeled with different names—none of which is her own. Ask each child to write a positive comment on each award about the named classmate. Then conduct an awards ceremony by having every child read aloud each compliment she wrote and award the ribbon to the corresponding classmate. Also present each award that you prepared. You'll boost self-esteem *and* end the school year on a positive note!

Susana C. Zinser—Grs. 1–6 EFL
Enrique de Osso
Guadalajara, Jalisco, Mexico

Sara is a good sport and a fair player

Counting Bag

Here's a year-end math activity that you can count on! Fold down the top of a paper lunch bag; then colorfully label the bag "Counting Bag." Program paper slips with a variety of directions for reviewing skip counting. Place these slips inside the bag. Once or twice a day ask a different student to pull a slip from the bag and follow the directions. Counting? It's in the bag!

Linnae Nicholas
Cuba Elementary School
Cuba, NY

Count by 5s. Start at 25. Stop at 75.

Counting Bag

Countdown To Summer Vacation

Stroll down memory lane as you count down the days to summer vacation! Have the students count off. Then have each child write his name and draw and color a king-size version of his numeral on a sheet of drawing paper. On the back of his paper, have him write about his favorite memory from the past school year. Display the numerals sequentially on a classroom wall. When there are as many days left of school as there are papers, have the owner of the highest numeral take down his paper and share his favorite memory of the year with the class. Continue this process until the last day of school, when the last paper will be read. 3–2–1! Hurrah for summer!

Julie Plowman—Gr. 3
Adair-Casey Elementary, Adair, IA

Diego

10

Reading Magic

Alakazam! Here's a fun way to review reading skills with a wave of a wand! Display your students' favorite songs and poems from the year around the room. Next make a pair of magic glasses by removing the lenses from an old pair of frames. Then create a magic wand by placing a decorative pencil eraser on the tip of a small wooden dowel. Invite a student to wear the glasses, wave the wand, and read aloud any song or poem on display. These simple props make reading a magically fun experience for any youngster. Gather a class collection of glasses and wands, and presto!—you'll have just the ticket for enthusiastic choral reading!

Cynthia Parello—Gr. 1
Hudson Maxim School
Hopatcong, NJ

Geography Lotto

Put your youngsters on top of the world with a game of Geography Lotto! Program 15 or more cards with geography-related review questions. Write the answer to each question on the chalkboard. Then give a blank lotto card and paper markers to each student. Allow time for each child to copy a different answer in each square of her card. To begin play, read aloud a question card. If the answer to the question is on a child's card, she covers it with a paper marker. The first student to cover all the answers on her card calls out, "I'm on top of the world!" After the youngster has verified her answers, have the rest of the students clear their game cards and prepare to play again.

Cheryl Sergi—Gr. 2, Greene Central School, Greene, NY

Edible Remainders

Introducing division with remainders has never been so yummy! In a letter to parents, invite students to bring a class snack to school for upcoming division lessons. Ask that the snack include one item per child plus a few extras. To begin the activity, give each child a paper plate or napkin. Display one collection of snacks and invite the students to count the number of treats with you. Next count the number of students and write the corresponding division problem on the chalkboard. Distribute the snacks one at a time until all children have the same amount and there are not enough left to give each child one more. Count aloud the number of remaining snacks. Then return to the original division problem and complete it by indicating a remainder. Lastly, draw names from a bowl to see which students get to eat the remainder snacks! Over the next several days repeat the activity with provided snacks. Division with remainders will become deliciously clear!

Laurie Albanos—Gr. 3
Powers Ferry Elementary School
Marietta, GA

Cornered!

Get a corner on skill review with this kid-pleasing plan! To review nouns and verbs, post a sign for each part of speech in a different corner of the classroom. Give each child a card that you've programmed with either a noun or a verb. Then, on your signal, have students read their cards and then move to the appropriate corners of the classroom. Ask each resulting group to form a circle and determine if every student in the group holds a correct card. When the groups are ready, ask the members of each group to announce their words as you collect the corresponding cards. For a fun math review, label each of four corners with a range of answers like "0 to 19," "20 to 34," and so on. Then have each child solve a provided math problem on scrap paper and proceed to the appropriate corner. There are endless possibilities for skill review right around the corner!

Julie Wise—Gr. 3
Norman A. Trimmer School, York, PA

Special Delivery

This first-class idea encourages students to read and write over the summer. For each student, place a colorful bookmark and a self-addressed, stamped postcard in an envelope. Label each envelope "Keep Reading And Writing!" On the last day of school, distribute the envelopes. Urge students to read during the summer and invite them to write to you, too. Promise to send a reply to each child who writes. Stock up on stationery—students will surely respond to your invitation!

Julie Bulver—Gr. 1
Rice School
Des Moines, IA

Keep Reading And Writing!

Monthly Math Review

On the last day of each month, use your classroom calendar for a spontaneous math review. Gather students around the calendar and then pose a series of math problems that equal the dates (numerals) on the calendar. For example, "How many inches are in one foot?" or "What is the sum of 9 + 9?" The student who gives the correct answer removes the corresponding cutout from the calendar. Or turn the tables and ask students to pose problems for you to answer! Either way, you've created a fun math review and taken down the calendar, too!

Joan Costello—Gr. 1
McGinn Elementary School
Scotch Plains, NJ

Morning Math Review

Looking for a fun way to review math skills from the past year? Begin each day with a game of math tic-tac-toe! Before students arrive, draw a tic-tac-toe grid on the chalkboard and program each of the nine spaces with a different math problem. Have each student solve the problems on a sheet of paper or in her math journal. When the students have finished solving the problems, designate an X and an O team; then flip a coin to determine which team goes first. In turn, a player from each team chooses an unanswered problem to solve. If the answer is correct, the player draws her team's symbol in the corresponding space on the chalkboard as the rest of the students check their answers. The first team to earn three in a row is declared the winner. When the game is over, ask volunteers to solve any unanswered problems. Now that's a math review with plenty of student appeal!

Rebecca Brudwick—Gr.1
Hoover Elementary School
North Mankato, MN

Ellis Island Day

Enrich your youngsters' knowledge of our country's rich heritage by planning an Ellis Island Day. Explain that over the years millions of people have left their homelands to live in our great country and that many of these people first touched American soil at Ellis Island. Discuss with students the benefits of living in a country that has numerous cultures and traditions. Explain that on Ellis Island Day you would like each child to role-play an immigrant coming to America in the early 1900s. Ask each youngster to decide from which country she is coming and then make a passport for her trip. On Ellis Island Day, encourage each student to dress as an immigrant. Then, acting as a government official, carefully examine each child's passport. Also invite the school nurse to give each child a simple physical (an eye and ear exam). When all students have been accepted into this great country, explain that not all immigrants were as fortunate. Then celebrate your students' patriotism by distributing small U.S. flags and serving cookies and punch. What a patriotic way to celebrate citizenship!

Jennifer Smith
Espy Elementary
Kenton, OH

It Was A Banner Year!

Banners and self-esteem will be flying high with this last-day activity! Using large, traceable letters or a computer program, write each child's name on a large sheet of paper to create a banner. Encourage your youngsters to decorate their banners; then instruct them to circulate about the room, autographing and writing positive notes on their classmates' banners. Students will treasure these mementos and go home feeling special!

Diane Vogel—Gr. 3
W. B. Redding School
Lizella, GA

Remember When...

This end-of-the-year project creates a class book of memories that students and parents will treasure for years to come. Invite students to share their fondest memories from the past year. List their responses on the chalkboard, starting each one with "Remember when." When you have several ideas listed, have each child copy one memory from the list on provided paper, write a few sentences about it, and render a black-and-white illustration of it. Make a class supply of each student's completed page. Then collate and bind the pages so that each child has a book of his own. Invite your youngsters to take the books home and color them. No doubt this class book will receive rave reviews!

Remember when we made a class cookbook? We each brought a recipe from home. Then we copied the recipe and drew a picture of what it made. My mom loves this cookbook!

Ruth Heller—Gr. 3
P.S.156, Laurelton, NY

Answer Key

Page 164

New Dinosaur Names	Dinosaur Descriptions
Ankylobrachiodromeus	two foot runner
Tetrastegosaurus	four foot runner
Megatyrannosaurus	crooked arm runner
Allocerattops	giant speedy lizard
Bipoddromeus	four roofed lizard
Tridontosaurus	two arm ruler
Segnobarysaurus	giant ruler lizard
Tetrapoddromeus	slow heavy lizard
Bibrachiotyranno	three tooth lizard
Megavelocisaurus	different horn face

Index

319